AF540652

GLOBAL NETWORKING

GLOBAL NETWORKING

Architecture • Protocols • Optical Networks • Multimedia Networks • High-Speed Networks • Wireless/Mobile Networks : Routing • Security • Applications

Edited by

Dr. S. NAKKIRAN

Former Principal, Sree Saraswathi Thyagaraja College,
Pollachi, Tamilnadu

and

S. RAMAKRISHNAN

Former Head, Department of Computer Science,
Sree Saraswathi Thyagaraja College,
Pollachi, Tamilnadu

and

T. DEIWANAYAKAM

Lecturer, Department of Computer Science,
Sree Saraswathi Thyagaraja College,
Pollachi, Tamilnadu

Foreword by

Lion. M.A. VIJAYAMOGHAN

Secretary, Sree Saraswathi Thyagaraja College,
Pollachi, Tamilnadu

from

DEEP & DEEP PUBLICATIONS PVT. LTD.

F-159, Rajouri Garden, New Delhi - 110 027

GLOBAL NETWORKING

ISBN 81-7629-735-6

Printed in India at MAYUR ENTERPRISES,
WZ Plot No. 3, Gujjar Market, Tihar Village, New Delhi - 110 018.

NuTech Books are Published by DEEP & DEEP PUBLICATIONS PVT. LTD.,
F-159, Rajouri Garden, New Delhi - 110 027 • Phone : 25435369, 25440916
E-mail : deep98@del3.vsnl.net.in • ddpbooks@yahoo.co.in
Showroom :
2/13, Ansari Road, Daryaganj, New Delhi - 110 002 • Telefax : 23245122

Contents

Part IV

HIGHSPEED NETWORKS

Part V

WIRELESS/MOBILE COMPUTING

Part VI

NETWORK ROUTING

PART VII

NETWORK SECURITY : THREADS AND SOLUTIONS

Part VIII

NETWORK APPLICATIONS

Foreword

World is a Web and Networking is an excellent connecting tool. If Internet is a Window, the ability to look at the world through the Internet will depend upon the speed and accuracy with which one can handle the Computer. Networking plays a crucial role in this context. Thanks to AICTE, New Delhi for sponsoring the National Seminar on "Recent Trends in Global Networking" and this publication is compilation of papers presented in the above seminar held on 14th February 2004.

On behalf of the Management, Principal, Staff and Students of Sree Saraswathi Thyagaraja College, I express my sincere gratitude to AICTE, Deep & Deep Publications Pvt. Ltd., New Delhi, Paper Presenters and Organizers for the excellent job done.

LION. M.A. VIJAYAMOGHAN
Secretary
Sree Saraswathi Thyagaraja College
Pollachi

Preface

We are living in an era in which the other side of the world is, literally, at our fingertips! Business and Enterprise have dissolved International boundaries and 'anytime-anywhere' access to information is the order of the day. All this is possible because of global connectivity or what is better known as Networking. The subject of Computer Networking is enormously complex, involving many concepts and technologies that can woven together in an interactive manner. The proliferating use of the Internet and the emerging technology of network computers and mobile devices have spurred a scientific approach to network management that includes academic research.

The book is divided into eight parts. The Part I deals with the Network Architecture and the newly emerged Communication Protocols. Part II reviews Optical Networking with a slant on its advantages. Part III provide a brief survey of fundamental principles involved in Multimedia Networks and latest development in its use. Part IV presents a comprehensive study on High-Speed Networks. Part V incorporates many changes that have occurred in the Wireless/Mobile Technology. Part VI covers the major approaches to Routing and its advantages. In this age of universal electronic connectivity: proper measures can be taken to evade viruses, hackers, electronic eavesdropping and electronic fraud. Part VII deals with the advancements in the Network Security area. Part VIII covers the Application of Networks and how the introduction of new developments may be organized and managed.

"The better things in life are the little things that you do for others;" our endeavour stands incomplete without dedicating our gratitude to the people who have contributed a lot towards the successful completion of this book. We express our deep sense of gratitude and sincere thanks to the authors who contributed their articles in the National Seminar on "Recent Trends in Global Networking."

We express our heartfelt thanks to Lion. T. Sethupati, Chairman, Rtn. S. Venkkatesh, Vice Chairman, Lion M.A. Vijayamoghan, Secretary and Mr. M. Settu, Director of our college for providing us all the facilities and encouragement. We would like to thank all the staff members of Computer Science Department, of our college for their timely help throughout the work. Finally, we thank Deep & Deep Publications (P) Ltd., New Delhi for bringing out this book.

Pollachi

Dr. S. NAKKIRAN
S. RAMAKRISHNAN
T. DEIWANAYAKAM

List of Contributors

1. **S. Siva Suthan, S. Kamala Nathan, M.Y. Abul Kashim**, Final BCA Students, E.G.S.P. Arts & Science College, Nagapattinam.
2. **S. Sujatha, Saju Mathew**, Lecturers, G.R.D. College, Coimbatore.
3. **S. Devaraju, P. Ramesh, R. Alaguraja**, Lecturers, Sree Saraswathi Thyagaraja College, Pollachi.
4. **Anuradha Vinod Kumar**, Lecturer, Sree Saraswathi Thyagaraja College, Pollachi.
5. **S. Annadurai,** HOD, **T. Purusothaman**, Lecturer, **P. Reji**, Student, Government College of Technology, Coimbatore.
6. **C. Lakshmi Bharathi,** Lecturer, **B. Murali**, HOD, PSG College of Arts & Science, Coimbatore.
7. **Ajitha Krishnan**, Lecturer, St. Joseph College of Arts & Science, Cuddalore.
8. **D. Kannan, S.C. Punitha, Annabelle Joseph**, Lecturers, SNMV College of Arts & Science, Coimbatore.
9. **S. Celine, B. Sudha**, Lecturers, Marudhar Kesari Jain College for Women, Vellore.
10. **V. Ganesh, K. Nirmal Kumar**, Lecturers, Tamilnadu College of Engg., Coimbatore.
11. **S. Ashok Kumar**, Lecturer, Park's College, Thiruppur.
12. **P. Bavitra Maharishi, C. Selvi**, Lecturers, Fatima College, Madurai.
13. **C.M. Karkuvel Raajan, V. Neelavannan, G. Srinath**, IV M.Sc. (SS) Students, Sree Saraswathi Thyagaraja College, Pollachi.
14. **P. Radha**, HOD, **N. Sudha Bhuvaneswari**, Lecturers, G.R.D. College of Science, Coimbatore.
15. **K.S. Maharasan, G. Ravi, J. Lennin,** Lecturers, Thiagaraja School of Management, Madurai.
16. **G.S. Kausalya, N.C. Geetha, S. Sampath**, Lecturers, PKR College for Women, Gobichettipalayam.
17. **S. Poorna Chandrika**, Lecturer, **K.A. Neethu**, IInd Year BCA Student, Sree Saraswathi Thyagaraja College, Pollachi.
18. **I. Rajeshwari**, Lecturer, Rani Anna Government College for Women, Tirunelveli.

19. **Arumugam Rathinavelu, Annadurai Gowri Shankar**, Lecturers, Dr. Mahalingam College of Engg. & Technology, Pollachi.
20. **S. Anitha, K. Sangeetha, R. Sumangali**, Lecturers, Gobi Arts & Science, Gobichettipalayam.
21. **S. Anantha Krishnan**, Lecturer, Park's College, Thiruppur.
22. **S. Anitha, P. Narendran, K. Sangeetha, R. Sumangali**, Lecturers, Gobi Arts & Science, Gobichettipalayam.
23. **S. Vimala, N. Kavitha**, Lecturer, Sree Saraswathi Thyagaraja College, Pollachi.
24. **T. Amudha, S. Rohini**, Lecturers, G.R.D. College of Science, Coimbatore.
25. **Mangaraj Sahoo**, Lecturer, **B. Majhi**, Asst. Prof., NIT, Rourkela.
26. **G. Sudharsan**, IV BE (ECE) Student, Vellore Institute of Technology, Vellore.
27. **S. Ramesh, R. Aravind Babu**, IV M.Sc. (SS) Students, Sree Saraswathi Thyagaraja College, Pollachi.
28. **V.K. Karunamoorthy**, Lecturer, Bannari Amman Institute of Technology, Sathyamangalam.
29. **N. Radhika, R. Rathinapriya**, Lecturers, Amirtha Viswa Vidhyapeetham, Ettimadai, Coimbatore.
30. **S. Arumugam**, Dean, Anna University, G.C.T. Campus, Coimbatore.
31. **T. Santha, S. Umamaheswari**, Lecturers, G.R.D. College, Coimbatore.
32. **R.S.D. Wahida Banu, G. Varaprasad**, Ph.D. Scholar, Govt. College of Engg., Salem.
33. **V.S. Dhenesh, K.K. Suresh Kumar, P. Ramesh, N. Senthilkumaran**, Lecturers, Kongu Arts & Science College, Erode.
34. **A. Agilandeeswary, S. Narmatha,** IV M.Sc. (SS) Students, Sree Saraswathi Thyagaraja College, Pollachi.
35. **R. Vijayalakshmi,** HOD, **S. Sampath Kumar**, Lecturers, PKR College for Women, Gobichettipalayam.
36. **S. Kavitha, K. Tamil Selvi, M. Rathamani and E. Nirmala Rajeswari**, Lecturers, SNMV College of Arts & Science, Coimbatore.
37. **K.R. Vallimaan, V. Roopa**, Lecturers, Sengamalthayar Education Trust, Mannar, Gudi.
38. **P. Felcy Judith, S. Rajeswari**, Lecturers, Trichy Engineering College, Trichy.
39. **V. Kalaichelvi,** IInd ME, Student, **R.M. Chandrasekaran**, Lecturers, Annamalai University, Chithambaram.
40. **K. Duraiswamy**, Principal, K.S.R. College of Technology, Tiruchengodu.
41. **R. Uma Rani**, Lecturer, Sri Sarada College for Women, Salem.
42. **A. Kannammal**, Lecturer, Coimbatore Institute of Technology, Coimbatore.
43. **N. Ch. S.N. Iyengar**, Lecturer, Vellore Institute of Technology, Vellore.
44. **S. Ramakrishnan, T. Deiwanayakam**, Lecturers, Sree Saraswathi Thyagaraja College, Pollachi.

45. **N.R. Wankhade, P.D. Patil**, Lecturers, K.K. Wagh College of Engg., Nashik.
46. **Prof. S.H. Patil**, HOD, Bharathi Vidhyapeeth, Pune.
47. **S. Anandhi, Arul Vendhan**, Lecturers, D.J. Academy for Managerial Excellence, Coimbatore.
48. **K. Gomathi, S. Punithadevi, S. Vidya**, Lecturers, Sree Saraswathi Thyagaraja College, Pollachi.
49. **Antony Selvadoss Thanamani**, Senior Grade Lecturer, NGM College, Pollachi, **D. Saravana Prakash, P. Jayakumar**, Lecturers, Sree Saraswathi Thyagaraja College, Pollachi.
50. **S. Sumathy, N. Narayana Moorthy**, Lecturers, Vellore Institute of Technology, Vellore.
51. **R. Manoharan, V. Ashok**, Lecturers, **S. Sivanandam**, Programmer, Sree Saraswathi Thyagaraja College, Pollachi.

PART I

Network Protocols and Architecture

Network Protocols and Architecture

S. Siva Suthan, S. Kamala Nathan and
M.Y. Abul Kashim

Introduction

"The world is biggest one, we cannot access all over world" in this life once, yet now we can access any of world in one mouse click. The Internet can achieve it. To construct the network we must know the big concepts of network. This paper illustrates the basic concepts of network and its protocols and architecture.

Protocols

Definition : Protocol is a set of rules for ultra transmission for similar processes. Without protocols the transmission of data cannot achieve successively.

Protocols are the formal rules and conventions for the exchange of information between computers.

In general the protocols are defining the format of data in which the messages are to be send and it also describes how the messages address the specific communication protocols.

Layering

The individual layers of network architecture are realized with *service* and *protocol* definitions. In OSI architectural terms, the implementation of layer, *n* is an *n*-entity. The calling layer above an *n*-entity is an (*n*+1)-entity and is the *n*-service user. The layer below layer *n*, from which the *n*-entity requests services, is an (*n*–1)-entity. An *n*-service, according to the OSI reference model, is a "capability of the *n*-layer and the layers beneath it, which is provided to (*n*+1)-entities at the boundary between the *n*-layer and the (*n*+1)-layer."

The syntax and semantics of protocol interfaces, however, are rigidly standardized; these define the rules used in communication among *n*-entities.

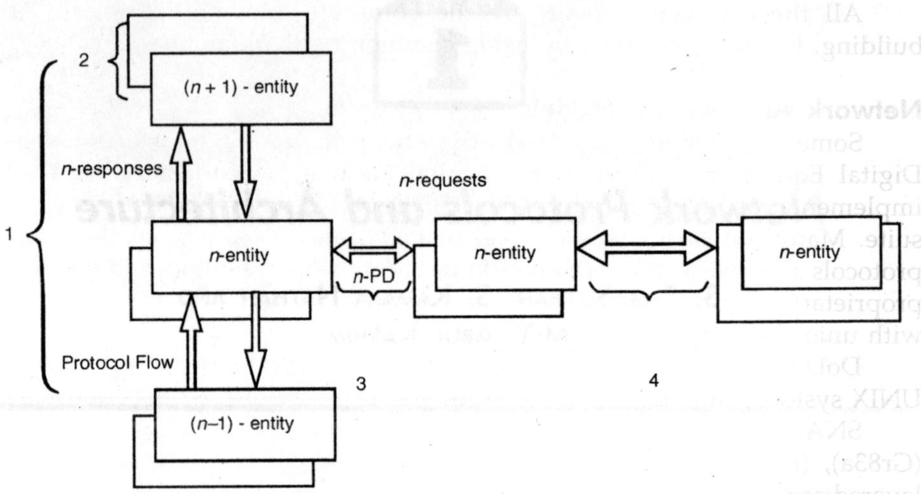

Fig. 1.1
OSI Service Flow and Protocol Flow

1. Service Flow
2. *n*–service user
3. (*n*–1)-responses
4. (*n*–1)-requests

Protocol Data Units

The combination of protocol control information and user data is a *protocol data unit* (PDU). PDU syntax and semantics are thoroughly specified by OSI protocol standards. PDUs may be qualified by the layer name (e.g., *network protocol data unit or* NPDU).

When an *n*-entity sends *n*-interface-data to an (*n*–1)-entity, that data forms an (*n*–1)-service-data-unit (SDU). SDUs are usually qualified by the service being used, such as *transport service data unit* (TSDU) for the transport service.

There need not be a one-to-one correspondence between *n*–SDUs and the (*n*–1) PDUs used to transfer them, or between n-connections and the (*n*–1)-connections over which PDUs flow. An (*n*–1)-connection may support more than one *n*-connection; placing multiple *n*-connections onto an (*n*–1)-

connection is called *multiplexing,* and its reverse is called *demultiplexing*. The converse of multiplexing is *splitting,* where multiple (*n*-1) connections support a single *n*-connection; the reverse of splitting is *recombining. Blocking* and *deblocking* refer to the combination of multiple *n*-SDUs into a single *n*-PDU, and recovering the SDUs.

Network Architecture

All the connection made by the complete and similar model of building. It can be achieved by using common network architecture.

Network Architecture Models

Some of the models are IBM's Systems Network Architecture (SNA), Digital Equipment Corporation's Digital Network Architecture (and its implementation, DECnet), and the U.S. Department of Defense protocol suite. Many industry observers feel that OSI and SNA will be the main protocols in general use as networking becomes increasingly widespread; proprietary protocols will be seen more in special applications, such as those with unique performance requirements.

DoD protocols are widely used in the United States, especially in the UNIX systems community, and are popular in academic institutions .

SNA is IBM's proprietary architecture for networking (Cy79), (Gr83), (Gr83a), (Ho83), (Ja83), (Ma83), (We83) and (Sy87). SNA, like OSI, is a layered architecture, but its layers have different functions. SNA emphasizes a *master-slave approach,* rather than the *peer-to-peer approach* of OSI.

Open System Interconnection Model

In 1978 the International Standard Organization proposed a model for Network communication called OSI Reference Model. Open System Interconnection refers to the exchange of information among devices like computers and some processes. The OSI Model is not a standard, it defines the tasks of network.

The OSI model has seven layers. The principles that were applied to arrive at the seven layers are as follows :

- ➢ A layer should be created where a different level of abstraction is needed.
- ➢ Each layer should perform a well-defined function.
- ➢ The function of each layer should be chosen with an eye towards defining internationally standardized protocols.
- ➢ The layer boundaries should be chosen to minimize the information flow across the interfaces.
- ➢ The number of layers should be large enough. It should be noted that the OSI model itself is not network architecture. It just tells what each layer should do. The functions of each layer are described in the following sections starting at the bottom.

The Physical Layer

- The physical layer is concerned with transmitting raw bits over a communication channel.
- The design issues have to do with making sure that when one side sends a 1 bit, it is received by the other side as a 1 bit, not as a 0 bit.
- The design issues here largely deal with mechanical, electrical, and procedural interfaces, and the physical transmission medium that lies below the physical layer.

The Data Link Layer

- The main task of the data link layer is to take a raw transmission facility and transform it into a line that appears free of transmission errors to the network layer.
- It accomplishes this task by having the sender break the input data up into data frames (typically a few hundred bytes), transmit the frames sequentially, and process the acknowledgement frames sent back by the receiver.
- Since the physical layer merely accepts and transmits a stream of bits without any regard to meaning or structure, it is up to the data link layer to create and recognize frame boundaries.
- This can be accomplished by the attaching special bit patterns to the beginning and end of the frame, which are called the header and trailer respectively.
- A noise burst on the line can destroy a frame completely. In this case, the data link layer software on the source machine must retransmit the frame.
- However, multiple transmissions of the same frame introduce the possibility of duplicate frames.
- A duplicate frame could be sent, for example, if the acknowledgement frame from the receiver back to the sender was destroyed.
- It is up to this layer to solve the problems caused by damaged, lost, and duplicate frames.
- Another issue that arises in the data link layer (and most of the higher layers as well) is how to keep a fast transmitter from drowning a slow receiver in data. Some traffic regulation mechanisms must be employed to let the transmitter know how much buffer space the receiver has at that moment.
- Frequently, this flow regulation and the error handling are integrated for convenience.

The Protocols which are used in a Data Link Layer :

Address Resolution Protocol/Reverse Address (ARP/RARP)

TCP/IP uses the Address Resolution Protocol (ARP) and the Reverse

Address Resolution Protocol (RARP) to initialize the use of Internet addressing on an Ethernet or other network that uses its own media access control (MAC). ARP allows a host to communicate with other hosts when only the Internet address of its neighbours is known. Before using IP, the host sends a broadcast ARP request containing the Internet address of the desired destination system.

The Network Layer

- The network layer is concerned with controlling the operation of the network. A key design issue is determining how packets or frames are routed from source to destination.
- Routes could be based on static tables that are wired into the network and rarely changed. They could also be highly dynamic, being determined anew for each packet, to reflect the current network load.
- If too many packets are present in the network at the same time, it is forming bottlenecks. The control of such congestion belongs to the network layer.
- There is often some accounting function built into the network layer.
- At the very least the software must count how many packets or characters or bits are sent by each customer, to produce billing information.
- When a packet crosses a national border, with different rates each side, the accounting can become complicated.
- When a packet has to travel from one network to another to get to its destination, many problems can arise.
- The addressing used by the second network may be different from the first one.
- The second one may not accept the packet at all because it is too large.
- The protocols may differ, and so on. It is up to the network layer to overcome all these problems to allow heterogeneous networks to be interconnected.

The Protocols which are used in Network Layer :

The Dynamic Host Configuration Protocol (DHCP)

It provides Internet hosts with configuration parameters. DHCP is an extension of BOOTP. DHCP consists of two components : a protocol for delivering host-specific configuration parameters from a DHCP server to a host and a mechanism for allocation of network addresses to hosts. The Dynamic Host Configuration Protocol (DHCP) provides Internet hosts with configuration parameters.

Distance Vector Multicast Routing Protocol (DVMRP)

Distance Vector Multicast Routing Protocol (DVMRP) is an Internet routing protocol that provides an efficient mechanism for connectionless datagram delivery to a group of hosts across an internet work. It is a distributed protocol that dynamically generates IP multicast delivery trees using a technique called Reverse Path Multicasting.

DVMRP is developed based upon RIP and it routes and forwards datagrams to a particular destination. The purpose of DVMRP is to keep track of the return paths to the source of multicast datagrams. To make the explanation of DVMRP more consistent with RIP, the term destination is used instead of the more proper term source, however, datagrams are not forwarded to these destinations, but rather, originate from them.

Internet Control Message Protocol (ICMP/ICMPv6)

ICMP messages generally contain information about routing difficulties with IP datagrams or simple exchanges such as time-stamp or echo transactions.

Internet Protocol version 6 (IPv6)

IP version 6 (IPv6) is a new version of the Internet Protocol based on IPv4, IPv4 and IPv6 are demultiplexed at the media layer. For example, IPv6 packets are carried over Ethernet with the content type 86DD (hexadecimal) instead of IPv4's 0800.

IPv6 increases the IP address size from 32 bits to 128 bits, to support more levels of addressing hierarchy. A new type of address called an any cast address is also defined, to send a packet to any one of a group of nodes.

Improved support for extensions and options—IPv6 options are placed in separate headers that are located between the IPv6 header and the transport layer header. Changes in the way IP header options are encoded allow more efficient forwarding, less stringent limits on the length of options, and greater flexibility for introducing new options in the future. The extension headers are : Hop-by-Hop Option, Routing (Type 0), Fragment, Destination Option, Authentication, and Encapsulation Payload.

Routing Information Protocol (RIP2)

RIP2 (Routing Information Protocol) is used by Berkeley 4BSD (Berkeley Software Distribution) UNIX systems to exchange routing information.

RIP2 is an extension of the Routing Information Protocol (RIP) intended to expand the amount of useful information carried in the RIP2 messages and to add a measure of security.

Routing Information Protocol for IPv6 (RIP for IPv6)

RIP for IPv6 is a routing protocol for the IPv6 Internet. It is based on protocols and algorithms used extensively in the IPv4 Internet.

Resource ReSerVation setup Protocol (RSVP)

RSVP is a Resource ReSerVation setup Protocol designed for an integrated services Internet. It is used by a host on behalf of an application data stream to request a specific quality of service from the network for particular data streams or flows. It is also used by routers to deliver QoS (Quality of Service) control requests to all nodes.

The Transport Layer

- The basic function of the transport layer is to accept the data from the session layer, split it up into smaller units, if need be, pass these to the network layer, and ensure that the pieces all arrive correctly at the other end.
- The transport layer determines what type of service to provide the session layer, and ultimately, to the users of the network.
- The most popular type of transport connection is an error-free point-to-point channel that delivers messages in the order they were sent.
- However, other possible kinds of transport service are, transport of isolated messages with no guarantee about the order of delivery, and determined when the connection is established.
- The transport layer is a true source-to-destination or end-to-end layer. In other words, a program on the source machine carries on a conversation with a similar program on the destination machine, using the message headers and control messages. In the lower layers, the protocols are between each machine and Its Immediate neighbours, and not by the ultimate source and destination machines, which may be separated by several other machines.
- In the transport layer, the transport header must contain the address of the destination machine. In addition to this, the transport layer must take care of establishing and deleting connections across the network.
- There must also be a mechanism to regulate the flow of Information, so that a fast host cannot overrun a slow one.

Mobile IP Protocol

The Mobile IP protocol enables nodes to move from one IP subnet to another. Each mobile node is always identified by its home address, regardless of its current point of attachment to the Internet. While situated away from its home, a mobile node is also associated with a care-of address, which provides information about its current point of attachment to the Internet. The home agent sends datagrams destined for the mobile node through a tunnel to the care-of address. After arriving at the end of the tunnel, each datagram is then delivered to the mobile node. It can be used for mobility across both homogeneous and heterogeneous media.

The IP packet consists of the IP source and destination addresses, followed by the UDP source and destination ports, followed by the Mobile

IP fields. Mobile IP packets can be either registration request or registration reply.

Reliable UDP (RUDP)

The Reliable UDP protocol is a simple packet-based transport protocol. A reliable transport protocol is needed to transport telephony signaling across IP networks. This should provide architecture for a variety of signaling protocols needing transport over IP. RUDP is designed to allow characteristics of each connection to be individually configured so that a number of protocols with different transport requirement can be implemented simultaneously not on the same platform. It is layered on the UDP/IP protocols and provides reliable in-order delivery for virtual connections.

User Datagram Protocol (UDP)

The User Datagram Protocol (UDP), provides a simple, but unreliable message service for transaction-oriented services. Each UDP header carries both a source port identifier and destination port identifier, allowing high-level protocols to target specific applications and services among hosts.

Van Jacobson Compressed TCP

Van Jacobson is a compressed TCP protocol, which thereby improves the TCP/IP performance over low speed (300 to 19,200 bps) serial links.

The Session Layer

- The session layer allows users on different machines to establish sessions between them.
- A session allows ordinary data transport as does the transport layer, but it also provides some enhanced services.
- One of the services of the session layer is to manage dialogue control. Sessions can allow traffic to go in both the directions at the same time, or in only one direction at a time.
- A related session service is token management. To manage, the session layer provides tokens that can be exchanged. Only the side holding the token may perform the critical operation.
- Another session service is synchronization. Consider the problems that might occur when trying to do a two-hour file transfer between two machines on a network, and the network crashed.
- After each transfer was aborted, the whole transfer would have to start all over again, and would probably fail again when the network next crashed.
- To eliminate this problem, the session layer provides a way to insert checkpoints into the data stream, so that after a crash, only the data after the last checkpoint have to be transferred.

The Protocols which are used in Session Layer.

Diameter

The Diameter base protocol provides an Authentication, Authorization and Accounting (AAA) framework for applications such as network access or IP mobility. Diameter also works in both local AAA and roaming situations. Diameter runs over reliable transport mechanisms.

Domain Name Service (DNS)

The Domain Name Service (DNS) protocol searches for resources using a database distributed among different name servers.

The Internet Security Association and Key Management Protocol (ISAKMP) define a framework for security association management and cryptographic key establishment for the Internet. It combines the security concepts of authentication, key management, and security associations to establish the required security for government, commercial, and private communications on the Internet.

Small Computer Systems Interface (iSCSI)

The iSCSI (Small Computer Systems Interface) protocol is a mapping of the SCSI remote procedure invocation model over the TCP protocol. SCSI commands are carried by iSCSI requests and SCSI responses and status are carried by iSCSI responses.

Lightweight Directory Access Protocol (LDAP)

The LDAP (Lightweight Directory Access Protocol) provides access to X.500 directories without using the DAP (Directory Access Protocol). It is used for simple management applications and browser applications that provide simple read/write interactive access to the X.500 directory and should complement the DAP.

Main Features

- Protocol elements are carried directly over TCP or any other transport layer protocol.
- Protocol data elements are encoded in ordinary strings.
- Lightweight BER encoding is used to encode all protocol elements.

The Presentation Layer

The presentation layer is concerned with the syntax and sometimes of the information transmitted.

A typical example of a presentation service is encoding data in a standard agreed upon way. Different computers have different codes for representing character strings (e.g., ASCII and EBCDIC), integers (e.g., one's complement and two's complement), and so on. In order to make it possible for computers with different representations to communicate, the data structures to be exchanged can be defined in an abstract way, along with a standard encoding to be used on the wire. The presentation layer is also concerned with other aspects of information representation. For example, data compression can be used here to reduce the number of bits that have to be transmitted and cryptography is frequently required for privacy and authentication.

The Application Layer

The application layer contains a variety of protocols that are commonly needed. For example, there are hundreds of incompatible terminals types in the world.

To handle each terminal type, a piece of software must be written to map the functions of the network virtual terminal onto the real terminal. For example, when the editor moves the virtual terminal's cursor to the upper left-hand corner of the screen, this software must issue the proper command sequence to the real terminal to get its cursor there too. All the virtual terminal software is in the application layer.

Another application layer function is file transfer. Different file systems have different file naming conventions, different ways of representing text lines, and so on. Transferring a file between two different systems requires handling these and other incompatibilities.

Finger User Information Protocol

The Finger user information protocol is a simple protocol which provides an interface to a remote user information program. It is a protocol for the exchange of user information based on the Transmission Control Protocol, using TCP port 79 decimal (117 octal). The local host opens a TCP connection to a remote host on the Finger port. An RUIP becomes available on the remote end of the connection to process the request. The local host sends the RUIP a one line query based upon the Finger query specification, and waits for the RUIP to respond. The RUIP receives and processes the query, returns an answer, then initiates the close of the connection. The local host receives the answer and the close signal, then proceeds closing its end of the connection.

Hypertext Transfer Protocol (HTTP)

The Hypertext Transfer Protocol (HTTP) is an application-level protocol with the lightness and speed necessary for distributed, collaborative, hypermedia information systems. Messages are passed in a format similar to that used by Internet Mail and the Multipurpose Internet Mail Extensions (MIME).

Simple Network Management Protocol (SNMP)

The Internet community developed SNMP to allow diverse network objects to participate in global network management architecture. Network managing systems can poll network entities implementing SNMP for information relevant to a particular network management implementation.

Network management systems learn of problems by receiving traps or change notices from network devices implementing SNMP.

TCP/IP Terminal Emulation Protocol (TELNET)

TELNET is the terminal emulation protocol of TCP/IP. Modern TELNET is a versatile terminal emulation due to the many options that have evolved over the past twenty years. Options give TELNET the ability to transfer binary data, support byte macros, emulate graphics terminals, and convey information to support centralized terminal management.

TELNET uses the TCP transport protocol to achieve a virtual connection between server and client. In a typical implementation, the TELNET client sends single keystrokes, while the TELNET server can send one or more lines of characters in response. Where the Echo option is in use, the TELNET server echoes all keystrokes back to the TELNET client.

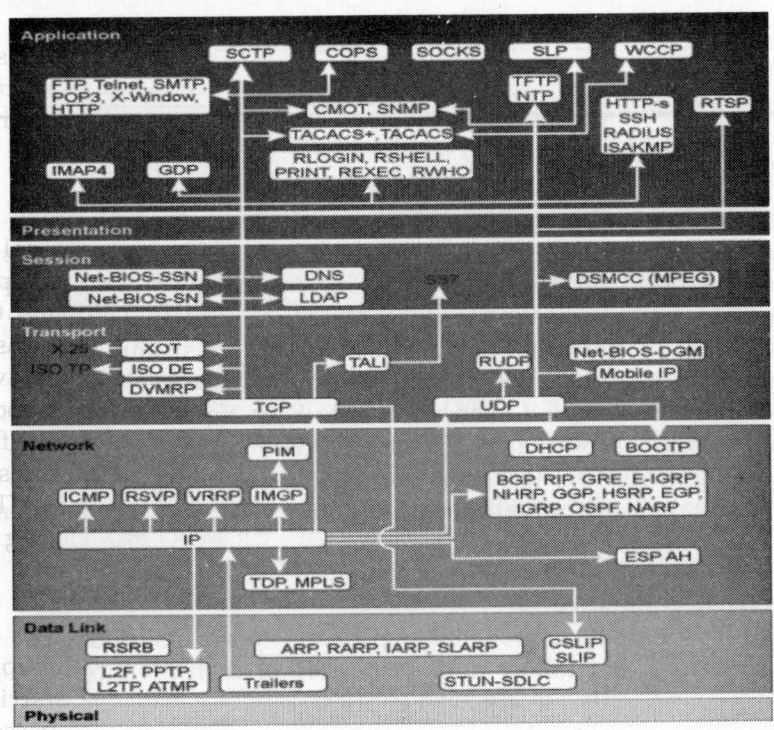

Fig. 1.2

OSI Model Seven Layers and its Protocols

Conclusion

We conclude that, there are so many protocols, which were developed by different corporation. By using those, we can provide an effective communication to all kinds of users including novice users.

System Network Architecture (SNA)

S. Sujatha and Saju Mathew

Introduction

Networking today consists of essentially two separate architectures that branch, more or less, from a common origin. Before contemporary networks existed, IBM's System Network Architecture (SNA) ruled the networking landscape, so it often is referred to as traditional or legacy SNA. With the rise of personal computers, workstations, and client/server computing, the need for a peer-based networking strategy was addressed by IBM with the creation of Advanced Peer-to-Peer Networking (APPN) and Advanced Program-to-Program Computing (APPC).

Although many of the legacy technologies associated with mainframe-based SNA have been brought into APPN-based networks, real differences exist.

IBM SNA Architecture

IBM SNA model components map closely to the OSI reference model. The descriptions that follow outline the role of each SNA component in providing connectivity among SNA entities.

- *Data Link Control (DLC)*—Defines several protocols, including the Synchronous Data Link Control (SDLC) protocol for hierarchical communication, and the Token Ring Network communication protocol for LAN communication between peers.
- *Path Control*—Performs many OSI network layer functions, including routing and data gram segmentation and reassembly (SAR).

- *Transmission Control*—Provides a reliable end-to-end connection service, as well as encrypting and decrypting services.
- *Data Flow Control*—Manages request and response processing, determines whose turn it is to communicate, groups messages, and interrupts data flow on request.
- *Presentation Services*—Specifies data-transformation algorithms that translate data from one format to another, coordinate resource sharing, and synchronize transaction operations.
- *Transaction Services*—Provides application services in the form of programs that implement distributed processing or management services.

SNA Physical Entities

Traditional SNA physical entities assume one of the following four forms : hosts, communication controllers, establishment controllers, and terminals. Hosts in SNA control all or part of a network and typically provide computation, program execution, database access, directory services, and network management. (An example of a host device within a traditional SNA environment is an S/370 mainframe.) Communication controllers manage the physical network and control communication links. In particular, communication controllers—also called front-end processors (FEPs)—are relied upon to route data through a traditional SNA network.

Establishment controllers are commonly called cluster controllers. These devices control input and output operations of attached devices, such as terminals. Terminals also referred to as workstations, provide the user interface to the network.

Figure 2.1 illustrates each of these physical entities in the context of a generalized SNA network diagram.

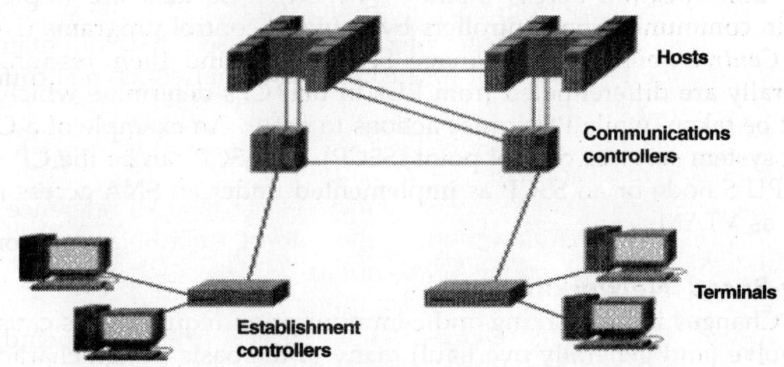

FIG. 2.1
SNA Physical Entities can Assume one of four Forms

In addition to the basic suite of media types, IBM added support for several other widely implemented media, including IEEE 802.3/Ethernet,

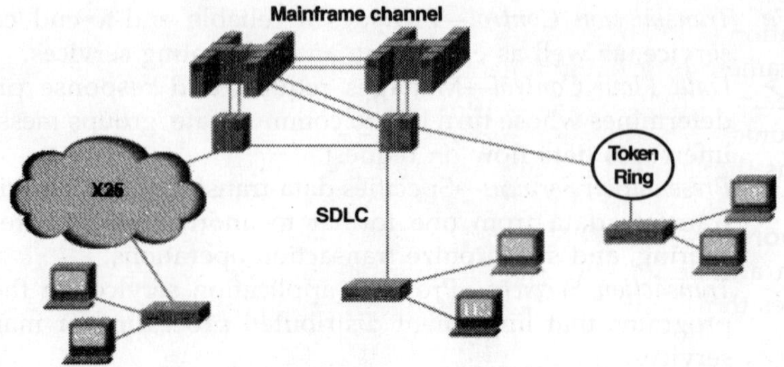

FIG. 2.2
SNA has Evolved to Support a Variety of Media

Fiber Distributed Data Interface (FDDI), and Frame Relay. Figure 2.2 illustrates how the various media generally fit into an SNA network.

Network Addressable Units

SNA defines three essential network addressable units (NAUs) : logical units, physical units, and control points. Each plays an important role in establishing connections between systems in an SNA network.

Logical Units (LUs) function as end-user access ports into an SNA network. LUs provide users with access to network resources, and they manage the transmission of information between end-users.

Physical Units (PUs) are used to monitor and control attached network links and other network resources associated with a particular node. PUs are implemented on hosts by SNA access methods, such as the virtual telecommunication access method (VTAM). PUs also are implemented within communication controllers by network control programs (NCPs).

Control Points (CPs) manage SNA nodes and their resources. CPs generally are differentiated from PUs in that CPs determine which actions must be taken, while PUs cause actions to occur. An example of a CP is the SNA system services control point (SSCP). An SSCP can be the CP residing in a PU 5 node or an SSCP as implemented under an SNA access method, such as VTAM.

Peer-Based Networking

Changes in networking and communication requirements caused IBM to evolve (and generally overhaul) many of the basic design characteristics of SNA. The emergence of peer-based networking entities (such as routers) resulted in a number of significant changes in SNA. Internetworking among SNA peers hinges on several IBM-developed networking components.

Advanced Peer-to-Peer Networking (APPN)

Advanced Peer-to-Peer Networking (APPN) represents IBM's second-generation SNA. In creating APPN, IBM moved SNA from a hierarchical, mainframe-centric environment to a peer-based networking environment. At the heart of APPN is an IBM architecture that supports peer-based communications, directory services, and routing between two or more APPC systems that are not directly attached.

Components of APPN

In addition to the APPN environment, peer-based SNA networking specifies three additional key networking concepts :

- Logical Units (LUs)
- Advanced Program-to-Program Computing (APPC)
- Node type 2.1.

Types of APPN Nodes

Under APPN, peer-based communication occurs among several well-defined node types. These nodes can be broken down into three basic types : low-entry nodes (LENs), end nodes (ENs), and network nodes (NNs).

The *Low-Entry Network (LEN)* node is a pre-APPN era peer-to-peer node. A LEN node participates in APPN networking by taking advantage of services provided by an adjacent network node (NN).

An *End Node (EN)* contains a subset of full APPN support. An end node accesses the network through an adjacent NN and uses the routing services of the same adjacent NN.

A *Network Node (NN)* contains full APPN functionality. The CP in an NN manages the resources of the NN, as well as the attached ENs and LEN nodes. In addition, the CP in an NN establishes CP-to-CP sessions with adjacent ENs and NNs, and maintains the network topology and directory databases created and updated by gathering information dynamically from adjacent NNs and ENs.

Figure 2.3 illustrates where each of these peer types might be found in a generalized APPN environment.

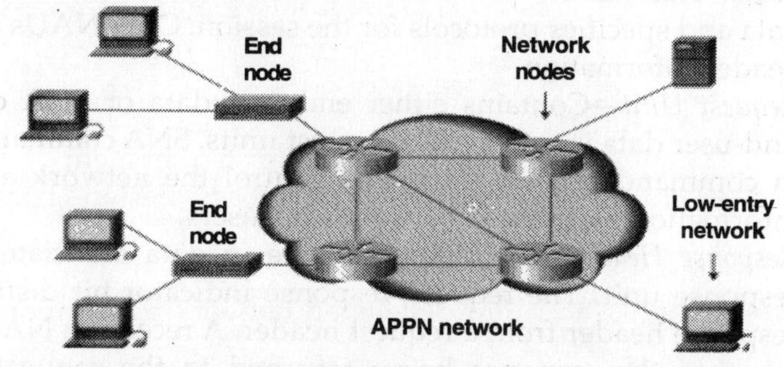

FIG. 2.3
APPN Supports Several Well-Defined Node Types

Services of APPN

Basic APPN services fall into four general categories : configuration, directors, topology, and routing and session services—

- APPN Configuration Services,
- APPN Directory Services,
- APPN Topology and Routing Services, and
- APPN Session Services.

Basic Information Unit (BIU) Format

SNA NAUs employ basic information units (BIUs) to exchange requests and responses. Figure 2.4 illustrate the BIU format.

BIU Fields

The following field descriptions summarize the content of the BIU, as illustrated in Figure 2.4.

Size in bytes

3	Variable
Request header	Request unit

Size in bytes

3	1 to 7
Response header	Response unit

FIG. 2.4
A Basic Information Unit (BIU) can be either a Request or a Response

- *Request Header*—Identifies the type of data in the associated request units. This header provides information about the format of the data and specifies protocols for the session. Only NAUs use request header information.
- *Request Unit*—Contains either end-user data or SNA commands. End-user data is sent in data request units. SNA commands are sent in command request units that control the network and contain information exchanged between end-users.
- *Response Header*—Identifies the type of data associated with the response unit. The request/response indicator bit distinguishes a response header from a request header. A receiving NAU indicates whether the response being returned to the request sender is positive or negative by setting the response type indicator (RTI) bit in the response header.

➤ *Response Unit*—Contains information about the request indicating either a positive or negative response. Positive responses to command requests usually contain a 1- to 3-byte response unit that identifies the command request. Positive responses to data requests contain response headers but no response unit.

Negative response units are 4 to 7 bytes long and always are returned with a negative response. A receiving NAU returns a negative response to the requesting NAU under one of three conditions :

➤ Sender violates SNA protocol,
➤ Receiver does not understand the transmission, and
➤ Unusual condition, such as a path failure, occurs.

Path Information Unit (PIU) Format

The Path Information Unit (PIU) is an SNA message unit formed by path control elements by adding a transmission header to a BIU. Figure 2.5 illustrates the PIU format.

Size in bytes

Variable	3	Variable
Transmission header	Request header	Request unit

Size in bytes

Variable	3	1 to 7
Transmission header	Response header	Response unit

FIG. 2.5
The Path Information Unit (PIU)

PIU Fields

The following field descriptions summarize the content of the PIU, as illustrated in Figure 2.5.

➤ *Transmission Header*—Routes message units through the network. This header contains routing information for traditional SNA subarea networking. Transmission header formats are differentiated by the Format Identification (FID) type. Path control uses the FID types to route data among SNA nodes.

In general, the transmission header is used to route data between adjacent sub-area nodes when both the sub-area nodes support explicit and virtual route protocols.

- *Request Header*—Identifies the type of data in the associated request units. This header provides information about the format of the data and specifies protocols for the session. Only NAUs use request header information.
- *Request Unit*—Contains either end-user data or SNA commands. End-user data is sent in data request units. SNA commands are sent in command request units that control the network and contain information exchanged between end-users.
- *Response Header*—Identifies the type of data associated with a response unit. The request/response indicator bit distinguishes a response header from a request header. A receiving NAU indicates whether the response being returned to the request sender is positive or negative by setting the RTI bit in the response header.
- *Response Unit*—Contains information about the request indicating either a positive or a negative response. Positive responses to command requests usually contain a 1- to 3-byte response unit that identifies the command request. Positive responses to data requests contain response headers but no response unit.

Negative response units are 4 to 7 bytes long and always are returned with a negative response. A receiving NAU returns a negative response to the requesting NAU under one of three conditions : The sender violates SNA protocol, a receiver does not understand the transmission, or an unusual condition, such as a path failure, occurs.

Conclusion

IBM's SNA was one of the first networking protocols. Although it is now considered a legacy networking protocol, it is still widely deployed. SNA was designed around the host-to-terminal communication model that IBM's mainframes use.

IBM expanded the SNA protocol to support peer-to-peer networking. This expansion was deemed Advanced Peer-to-Peer Networking (APPN) and Advanced Program-to-Program Communication (APPC).

Packet Voice Protocols

S. Devaraju, P. Ramesh and R. Alaguraja

Introduction

VoIP supplies many unique capabilities to the carriers and customers who depend on IP or other packet-based networks. The most important benefits include the following :

- *Cost Savings* : By moving voice traffic to IP networks, companies can reduce or eliminate the toll charges associated with transporting calls over the public switched telephone network (PSTN). Service providers and end-users can also conserve bandwidth by investing in additional capacity only when it is needed. This is made possible by the distributed nature of VoIP and by reduced operations costs as companies combine voice and data traffic onto one network.
- *Open Standards and Multivendor Interoperability* : By adopting open standards, both businesses and service providers can purchase equipment from multiple vendors and eliminate their dependency on proprietary solutions.
- *Integrated Voice and Data Networks* : By making voice "just another IP application," companies can build truly integrated networks for voice and data. These integrated networks not only provide the quality and reliability of today's PSTN, but they also enable companies to quickly and flexibly take advantage of new opportunities within the changing world of communications.

As the packet telephony networks grew and interconnection dependencies emerged, it became clear that the industry needed standard

VoIP protocols. Several groups took up the challenge, resulting in independent standards, each with its own unique characteristics. In particular, network equipment suppliers and their customers were left to sort out the similarities and differences between four different signaling and call-control protocols for VoIP :

- H.323.
- Media Gateway Control Protocol (MGCP).
- Session Initiation Protocol (SIP).
- H.248/Media Gateway Control (MEGACO).

H.323

H.323 was originally created to provide a mechanism for transporting multimedia applications over local-area networks (LANs). Although H.323 is still used by numerous vendors for videoconferencing applications, it has rapidly evolved to address the growing needs of VoIP networks. Because of its early availability and these advancements, H.323 is currently the most widely used VoIP signaling and call-control protocol, with international and domestic carriers relying on it to handle billions of minutes of use each year.

H.323 is considered an "umbrella protocol" because it defines all aspects of call transmission, from call establishment to capabilities exchange to network resource availability. H.323 defines Registration, Admission, and Status (RAS) protocol for call routing, H.225 protocols for call set-up, and H.245 protocols for capabilities exchange.

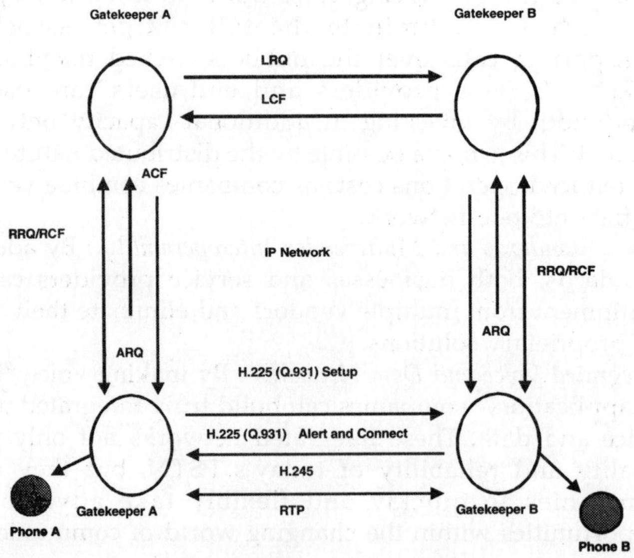

FIG. 3.1
H.323 Networks

H.323 is based on the Integrated Services Digital Network (ISDN) Q.931 protocol, which allows it to easily interoperate with legacy voice networks such as the PSTN or Signaling System 7 (SS7). As a protocol used in a distributed architecture, H.323 allows companies to build large-scale networks that are scalable, resilient, and redundant. It provides mechanisms for interconnecting with other VoIP networks and supports network intelligence on either the endpoints or the gatekeepers.

Making Sense of the VoIP Standards

VoIP comprises many standards and protocols. Basic terminology must be understood in order to comprehend the applications and usage of VoIP. The following definitions serve as a useful starting point (the protocols are listed in alphabetical order) :

- *H.248* is an ITU Recommendation that defines "Gateway Control Protocol." H.248 is the result of a joint collaboration between the ITU and the IETF. It is also referred to as IETF RFC 2885 (MEGACO), which defines a centralized architecture for creating multimedia applications, including VoIP. In many ways, H.248 builds on and extends MGCP.
- *H.323* is an ITU Recommendation that defines "packet-based multimedia communication systems." In other words, H.323 defines a distributed architecture for creating multimedia applications, including VoIP.
- *IETF* refers to the Internet Engineering Task Force, a community of engineers that seeks to determine how the Internet and Internet protocols work, as well as to define the prominent standards.
- *ITU* is the International Telecommunication Union, an international organization within the United Nations System where governments and the private sector coordinate global telecom networks and services.
- *MEGACO*, also known as IETF RFC 2885 and ITU Recommendation H.248, defines a centralized architecture for creating multimedia applications, including VoIP.
- *MGCP*, also known as IETF RFC 2705, defines a centralized architecture for creating multimedia applications, including VoIP.
- *Real-Time Transport Protocol (RTP)*, also known as IETF RFC 1889, defines a transport protocol for real-time applications. Specifically, RTP provides the transport to carry the audio/media portion of VoIP communication. RTP is used by all the VoIP signaling protocols.
- *SIP*, also known as IETF RFC 2543, defines a distributed architecture for creating multimedia applications, including VoIP.

MGCP/H.248/MEGACO

MGCP and H.248/MEGACO were designed to provide an architecture where call control and services could be centrally added to a VoIP network. In that sense, an architecture using these protocols closely resembles the existing PSTN architecture and services.

MGCP and H.248/MEGACO define most aspects of signaling using a model called packages. These packages define commonly used functionality, such as PSTN signaling, line-side device connectivity, and features such as transfer and hold. In addition, session definition protocol (SDP) is used to convey capability exchange.

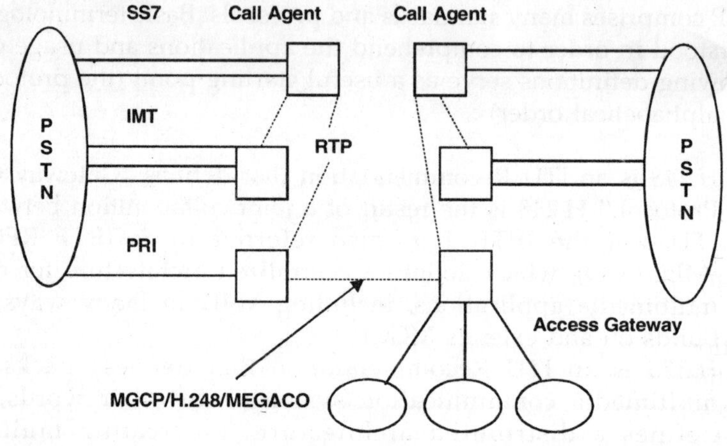

FIG. 3.2
MGCP/H.248/MEGACO Networks

In a centralized architecture, MGCP and H.248/MEGACO allow companies to build large-scale networks that are scalable, resilient, and redundant. It provides mechanisms for interconnecting with other VoIP networks and for adding intelligence and features to the call agent.

SIP

SIP was designed as a multimedia protocol that could take advantage of the architecture and messages found in popular Internet applications. By using a distributed architecture—with universal resource locators (URLs) for naming and text-based messaging—SIP attempts to take advantage of the Internet model for building VoIP networks and applications. In addition to VoIP, SIP is used for videoconferencing and instant messaging.

As a protocol, SIP only defines how sessions are to be set-up and torn down. It utilizes other IETF protocols to define other aspects of VoIP and multimedia sessions, such as SDP for capabilities exchange, URLs for addressing, Domain Name Systems (DNSs) for service location, and Telephony Routing Over IP (TRIP) for call routing.

Although the IETF has made great progress defining extensions that

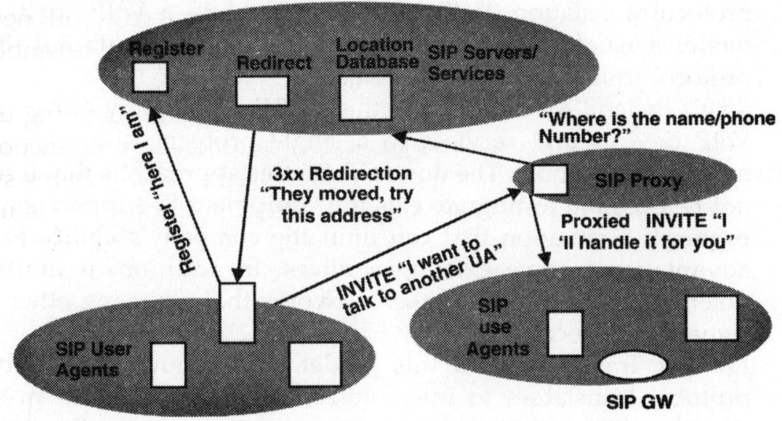

FIG. 3.3
SIP Networks

allow SIP to work with legacy voice networks, the primary motivation behind the protocol is to create an environment that supports next-generation communication models that utilize the Internet and Internet applications.

As a protocol used in a distributed architecture, SIP allows companies to build large-scale networks that are scalable, resilient, and redundant. It provides mechanisms for interconnecting with other VoIP networks and for adding intelligence and new features on either the endpoints or the SIP proxy or redirect servers.

Interconnecting VoIP Protocols

VoIP networks continue to be deployed at a rapid pace, and VoIP vendors and service providers continue to add new functionality. Because vendor support for each protocol differs and companies have varying business requirements, it is very likely that VoIP networks will continue to be made up of multiple protocols.

Having various protocols gives customers the flexibility that they need to connect services from multiple carriers. Using standards, even multiple standards, still simplifies deployment of multivendor end-points and increases options for network management and provisioning.

As companies expand their networks, they are faced with choices about how to interconnect segments using differing VoIP protocols. These choices often fall into one of three categories :

- *Translation through Time Division Multiplexing (TDM)* : In this model, a company uses either TDM equipment or VoIP gateways to translate from one protocol domain to another. The benefits of this model are that it can be used today. The downside is that it introduces latency into the VoIP network and involves yet another protocol translation (VoIP no. 1 <—> TDM <—> VoIP no. 2). This model is usually considered as a short-term solution until IP–based protocol translators are available.

- *Single Protocol Architecture* : In this model, a company moves all its VoIP devices and services to a single protocol, simplifying the network as a whole. The downside to this approach is that it might not be possible to migrate existing equipment to support the new protocol, a situation that can limit the company's ability to take advantage of some existing services. In addition, it limits the potential connectivity to other networks that are using other VoIP signaling protocols.
- *Protocol Translation* : In this model, a company uses IP–based protocol translators to interconnect two or more VoIP protocol domains. IP translators allow a company to retain the flexibility of using multiple VoIP protocols, do not introduce the delay problems that additional TDM interconnections do, and do not require a wholesale replacement or swap of existing equipment.

The downside to this approach is that there is no standard for protocol translation, so not all VoIP protocol translators are exactly the same. Although the IETF has attempted to define a model for translating H.323 to SIP, it involves more than just building a protocol-translation box.

TABLE 3.1
Details of VoIP Products

	H.323	*SIP*	*MGCP/H.248/MEGACO*
Standards Body	ITU	IETF	MGCP/MEGACO—IETF; H.248—ITU
Architecture	Distributed	Distributed	Centralized
Current Version	H.323v4	RFC2543-bis07	MGCP 1.0, Megaco, H.248
Call control	Gatekeeper	Proxy/Redirect Server	Call agent/media gateway controller
End-points	Gateway, terminal	User agent	Media gateway
Signaling Transport	Transmission Control Protocol (TCP) or User Datagram Protocol (UDP)	TCP or UDP	MGCP—UDP; Megaco/H.248—both
Multimedia capable	Yes	Yes	Yes
DTMF–relay transport	H.245 (signaling) or RFC 2833 (media)	RFC 2833 (media) or INFO (signaling)	Signaling or RFC 2833 (media)
Fax–relay transport	T.38	T.38	T.38
Supplemental services	Provided by end-points or call control	Provided by end-points or call control	Provided by call agent

As shown in Table 3.1, although protocols are somewhat similar, they do have differences.

Vendors of protocol translators need in-depth knowledge of all the protocols being used in the VoIP network, and they must be aware of how various VoIP components utilize different aspects of the protocol.

For example, H.323 and SIP can send dual-tone multi-frequency (DTMF) digits in either the signaling path or the media path (via RTP). But H.323 mandates only that the H.245 signaling path be used, and SIP does not specify how DTMF should be carried. This means that SIP devices could be sending DTMF in the media path (RFC 2833), and H.323 devices could be sending DTMF in the signaling path (H.245). If the VoIP protocol translator cannot properly recognize both the signaling path and the media path, then it might not function properly.

Conclusion

Just as companies choose various protocols for their data networks, they will choose various protocols for their VoIP requirements, depending on the business and technical requirements at hand. Although the variety in VoIP protocols has caused some confusion in the marketplace, it is precisely this protocol flexibility that makes VoIP-based voice systems so much more useful than legacy voice systems. Companies should choose vendors based on three very important requirements :

- Customers need vendors that are committed to supporting open standards within their products and are actively developing voice strategies that consider interoperability with all VoIP protocols. Without this commitment, VoIP systems are in danger of becoming as proprietary as legacy voice systems.
- Customers need products that support multiple protocols. This way, if a company finds that it needs to migrate its systems or add products that support a different protocol, it will not be required to perform upgrades to the network.
- Customers need voice solutions with end-to-end support for all VoIP protocols, meaning vendors must provide solutions that work in both single-protocol and multi-protocol environments.

By working with vendors that can provide this VoIP flexibility, companies can focus on building scalable and reliable networks that support the requirements of next generation networks.

Policy Based Network Architecture

Anuradha Vinod Kumar

Introduction

In business decision more and more effect the entire network infra architecture to manage the business, the network must be reliable. The network must be predictable. To accomplish this, end-to-end strategy must be established to correlate the business with the overall network actions. The policy-based network architecture document details some of the goals and procedures involved in developing the system. Allots policy-based network system delivers a comprehensive architecture that allows the merging of high-level application resources policy information with network wide policy actions.

Each day companies strive to correlate business decision to things that actually happen on their network.

- Selecting which users have access to which network resource.
- Prioritizing which applications are critical to company operations.
- Delivering the tired bandwidth and differentiated service to each customer according to their need.
- Managing the voice video data demands on corporate LAN, WAN links.
- Managing the overall flow of traffic through internal and external networks.

All these actions share common requirement by applying corporate business policies to specific network actions including bandwidth management, fire walling, caching, routing, and VPN equipment. Today, the network manager are network service provide must manage policies for all of the devices by managing wide array of users applications and resources to determine the policies and configuring each piece of equipment.

What is a need of comprehensive; policy-based system that will allow the network manager to define in sufficient and organized fashion, corporate policies that automatically effect change on specific equipment. The end result is that the end to end to end network performance will meet the general expectation of corporate, commerce or service provider environment.

Goals of the Policy Based Network Architecture

The goals of the policy-based network architecture outlined in this document, include the creation of standards based the system that addresses both the enforcement of policies. Specifically the system will perform various functions including.

Policy Administration

Creating a disturbed hierarchical system to coordinate and manage policies between policy management devices, directories and various policy enforcement devices using standards based architecture approach.

Interface to Directory Database

Provides access to higher level, user and application level, and policy information via data stored in common directory depositories. This high database information can then translated into policy enforcement actions.

QoS Gateways

Providing end to end policy enforcement and management via standards based signals protocols including differentiated services, TOSLS, RSVP, MPLS & 802.1P.

Bandwidth Broker

Providing bandwidth brokerage service allowing an automatic system for multiple domains to negotiate service level guarantees.

Centralized Monitoring and Accounting

Providing centralized policy based account and remote monitoring.

Basic Models For Policies

In a standard policy based network policy consists two components :

1. A set of condition under which policy applies. This might include parameters such as user name, address, protocols and application type.
2. A set of actions that applies a consequence of satisfying (or not satisfying) the condition including Bandwidth guarantees, access

controls service load balancing, cache indirection's and intelligent routing.

These conditions and actions consist of series of active and passive components of network. As a simple model this would include a policy manager which is the central policy administration and directory depository points policy enforcer which consists of remote active management component that make up local policy decision enforcement point throughout the local WAN.

Policy Enforcer

It can be a simple router that makes policy decisions that based on the field in a particular "tagged" packet. The policy enforcer may be a piece of equipment that locally consolidates and analyzes traffic flows and network conditions in order to perform complex actions such as :

- ➢ Traffic conditions and shaping,
- ➢ policy,
- ➢ tagging/signal provisioning server,
- ➢ resource control.

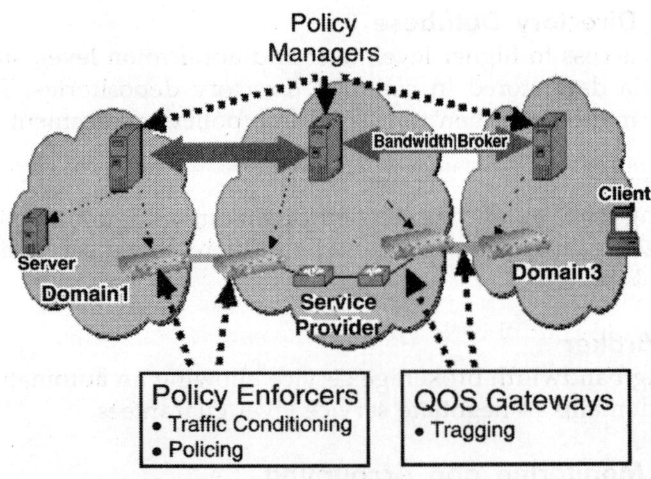

FIG. 4.1
Policy Enforcer

The Policy Enforcer is placed at the edge of specific domains. It communicates with the Policy Manager to understand overall network policies and then performs various enforcement functions including traffic shaping/conditioning policy and signal provisioning. The Policy Managers will communicate with each other for purposes of coordinating service level agreements and brokering bandwidth between the different domains.

Policy Management

The policy management functions are responsible for coordinating

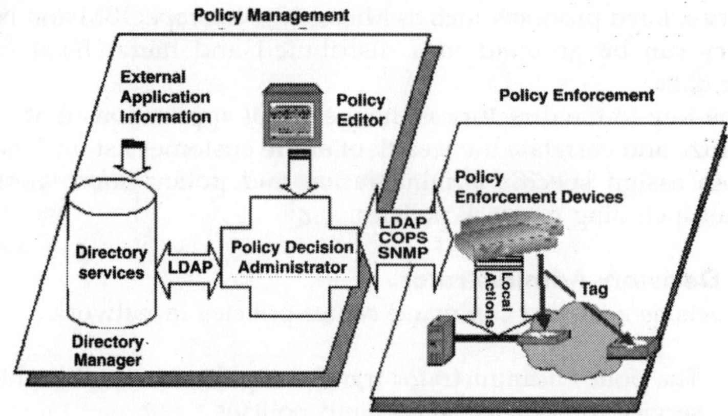

FIG. 4.2
Policy Management Functions

The Policy Management functions are responsible for coordinating user input with other external and internal policy information into concise network terminology. This information is then relayed to the Policy Enforcement equipment for possible network actions.

administrator input width other external and internal policy information and translating this information into concise network terminology.

Policy manager functionality can be distributed and hierarchical in structure representing various physical and logical domains. Policy manager consists of various logical pieces that can each run on separate levels or combined into a single system including the policy editor, interface to directory database and the policy decision administrator.

Policy Editor

The policy editor provides the network manager with capabilities to centrally configure rule-based policies that take high level concepts and translate them to control of services within the network infrastructure. The policy editor can be accessed directly by the network managers for the input via a java web interface or can be a part of centralized management structure provided by system management products such as HP open view or Tivoli.

The editor will in general, store information on LDAP basically database directory. Communication with the directory can be through the policy administrator or through third party applications. The policy administrator will have added capabilities for translating generic policy information stored in directory to actual policy rules.

Interface to Directory Database Server

The directory database server provides the central repository for policy information. In general the directory database resides on a directory server as a third party LDAP-based application provided via companies delivering directory-related products such as Microsoft, Netscape, IBM and Novell. The directory can be grouped in a distributed and hierarchical fashion for sharing data.

The Key to the directory is the wealth of applications that allows user to organize and correlate the wealth of entire customer list into the directory and then assign specific administration and policy information on each customer including network policies.

Policy Decision Administrator

It acts as a central command center policies in network.

- The policy administrator translates policies stored in the directory service to network station and policies.
- It discovers and identifies all policies manageable enforcement devices in the domain.
- It responses to request from policy enforcement devices for specific policy information. In the case of nodes that have local decision capababilities, it will act as a high level administrator of policies.
- It relays information to policies enable network devices using standard-based protocols such as LDAP & COPS. This information in general is derived from information stored in the directory server.
- It interfaces to policy editors allowing network manager to define specific network wide policies and actions.
- It acts as a distributed collector of monitoring and connecting information.
- It provides added capabilities for coordinating discovery and management of specific policy enforcement device. It tracks changes to the directory server and relays the information to the policy enforcer to its domain.

The policy decision administrator is software based and can run simultaneously on the directory server or as a separate entity that communicate with the directory via LDAP.

Decision Administration Architecture

It acts s a central command center for policies in the network. The decision administrator of various layers that provide policy management functions that interface to various components including the directory enforcement devices and management user interface. The layers are :

1. Data Abstraction Layer.
2. Devise Abstraction Layer.

QoS Gateway Functionality

Policy enforcement can come out by performing specific services at the

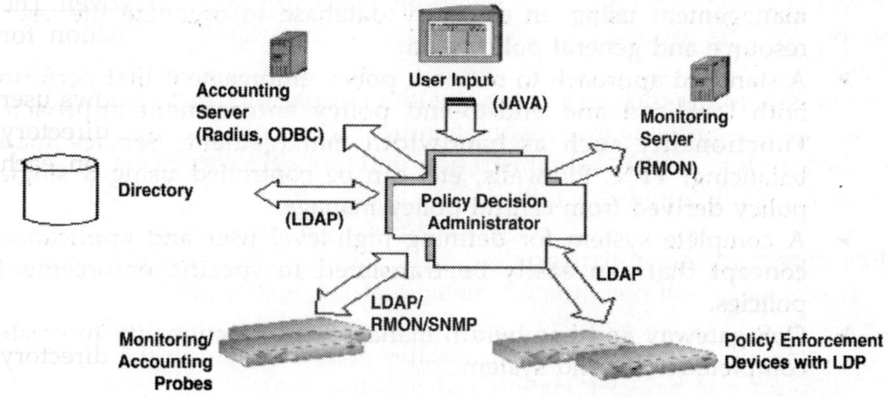

FIG. 4.3

Decision Administration Architecture

The Policy Decision Administrator performs many functions including creating policies based on static information in the directory and other databases as well as transient information based on the status of the network. This information is then relayed to various policy enforcement devices for specific network actions.

policy enforcer. Alternatively simple policy devices such as a router, can take policy enforcement decisions based on informations that is relayed through the network by various standards based on signaling protocols.

1. End-to-End Signaling mechanism;
   a. RSVP
   b. Differentiated service
2. LAN based Signaling mechanism;
   a. 802.1 P/Q
   b. MPLS

A policy enforcer can act as a QoS gateway.

Bandwidth Broker Functionality

It allows various domains to automatically negotiate policies. An ISP for example can dynamically negotiate different service with a given customer. Alternatively a server provider could charge different rate for bandwidth depending on the demand.

The bandwidth broker provides the maximum performance of the domain and the number of other guarantees that have been granted.

Conclusion

The policy based network architecture system includes in intelligent approach that combines :

- ➢ Centralized distributed and hierarchal approach to network policy management using an directory database to organize the user, resource and general policy data.

- A standard approach to network policy enforcement that perform both localized and end-to-end policy enforcement approach. Functionality such as bandwidth management, Service load balancing, VPN, Firewalls, etc. can be controlled using a single policy derived from central policy manager.
- A complete system for defining high-level user and application concept that can easily be translated to specific enforcement policies.
- QoS gateway and bandwidth management functionality to create complete end-to-end system.

This policy based system presents an overall business tool that allow corporations to organize business concepts with specific network policies.

References

Books

1. "How Network works", Frank J. Defler & Les freed.
2. "The Network technical guide", from Micro house Technical series.

Web References

1. www.dse.doc.ic.ac.uk
2. www.ansa.co.uk
3. www.sun.com/policy.pdf
4. www.allot.com

Key Management in Group Communications

S. ANNADURAI, T. PURUSOTHAMAN AND P. REJI

Introduction

The concept of Key management has been under discussion for over two decades now. For any *Group Key Management Protocol* (GKMP) the basic requirements are : Scalability, Independence, Practicality, Security and Interoperability.

The basic issues, which we are to consider in Group Key Management, are :

- Providing member identification and authentication.
- Access control.
- Generation, Distribution and Installation of key material :
  - New Multicast Group Initiation.
  - Re-keying issues.

In this paper we will be reviewing the different techniques of Key Management in Group Communication by categorizing them into three major classes :

- Centralized Protocols.
- Decentralized Protocols.
- Distributed Protocols.

The protocols are arranged chronologically and each one of them is described in brief. A comparative study of the advantages, problems and limitations of each is also done.

Centralized Schemes

The protocols used here require minimizing the requirements of both group members and KDC in order to increase the scalability of the system.

GKMP [1997—Harney and Muckenhirn]

The group creates a Group Key Packet (GKP) that contains a Group Key Encryption Key (GKEK) and a Group Traffic Encryption Key (GTEK). When re-keying is needed the KDC generates a new GKP and encrypts it with the current GKEK.

Benefits : (1) virtually invisible to operator, (2) only group members have the key, (3) sender or receiver-oriented operation.

Limitations : There is no solution for keeping the *forward secrecy* when a user leaves the group. We would have to recreate the entire group.

One-way Function Tree [1998—McGrew and Sherman]

Here a node's KEK is generated rather than just attributed. The KEKs held by a node's children are *blinded* using a one-way function and then mixed together using a mixing function. The result of this mixing function is the KEK held by the node. Ancestors of a node are those nodes in the path from its parent node to the root.

- Canetti *et. al.* in 1999 proposed an extended version of this scheme known as the One-Way Function Chain Tree. This scheme uses a pseudo-random-generator to generate the new KEKs rather than a one-way function and it is applied only on users removal.
- Rafaeli *et. al.* in 2001 presented a variation of this scheme called the efficient hierarchical binary tree (EHBT) protocol.

Benefits : This scheme reduces the size of the re-keying message. For a balanced tree, each member stores only $log_2 n+1$ keys.

Limitations : In the case of One-Way Function Chain Trees we need to double the size of the input increasing the overhead of the algorithm.

Logical Key Hierarchy (LKH) [1999-2000—Wong and Wallner et. al.]

A KDC maintains a tree of keys. The nodes of the tree hold key encryption keys. Each leaf holds a KEK associated with one member. Each member receives and maintains a copy of the KEK associated with its leaf and the KEKs corresponding to each node in the path from its parent leaf to the root. The root holds the group key. When a member leaves a group, its parent node's KEK and all KEKs held by nodes in the path to the root are compromised and changed.

Walvogel in 1999 proposed LKH+ where, instead of generating fresh keys and sending them to members already in the group, all keys affected

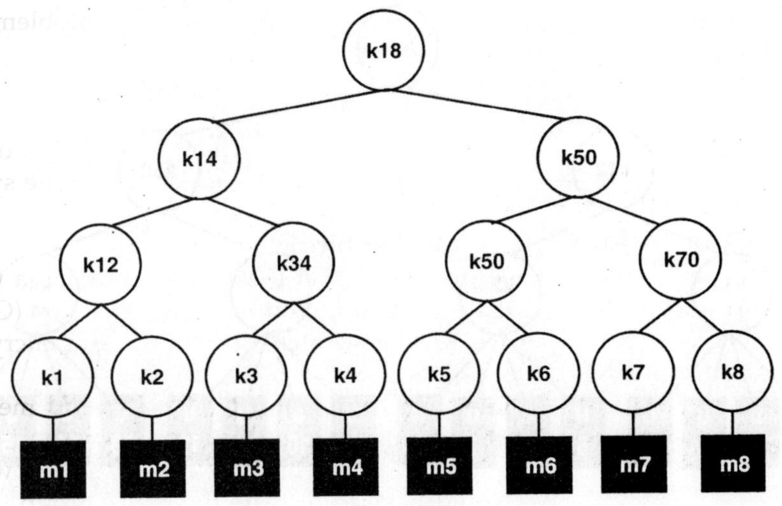

Fig. 5.1
LKH Tree Structure

by the membership changes are passed through a *one-way function*.

Benefits : Re-keying is done efficiently during membership changes. In LKH+, every member can calculate the new keys locally.

Limitations : A large database has to be maintained regarding the key-member-node association. The KDC has to store a large number of keys.

Boolean Minimization [1999—L. Chang, R. Engel, D. Kandlur, D. Pendarakis and D. Saha]

This scheme uses a virtual key hierarchy based scheme. There are 2 log N auxiliary keys and one group key. When a member leaves the group, the group key along with the auxiliary keys held by the member is changed. A new group key is generated by the group controller and is encrypted with the keys that are complementary to the keys held by the departing member. This scheme has a tree structure similar to the LKH tree.

Benefits : The number of keys to be stored and maintained is very less. This scheme can handle bulk membership changes and is more scalable than LKH.

Limitations : The major problem faced here is the *Collusion* problem.

Hierarchical a-ary Tree with Clustering [1999—Canetti et. al.]

This improved version proposed the clustering of members around single leaves of a *a-ary* tree. Dividing the group with *n* members into clusters of size *m* and assigning a cluster to a unique leaf node, we have *n/m* clusters. (See Figure 5.2).

All members in a cluster share the same cluster KEK. Every member of the cluster is also assigned a unique key *ki* , which is shared only with the

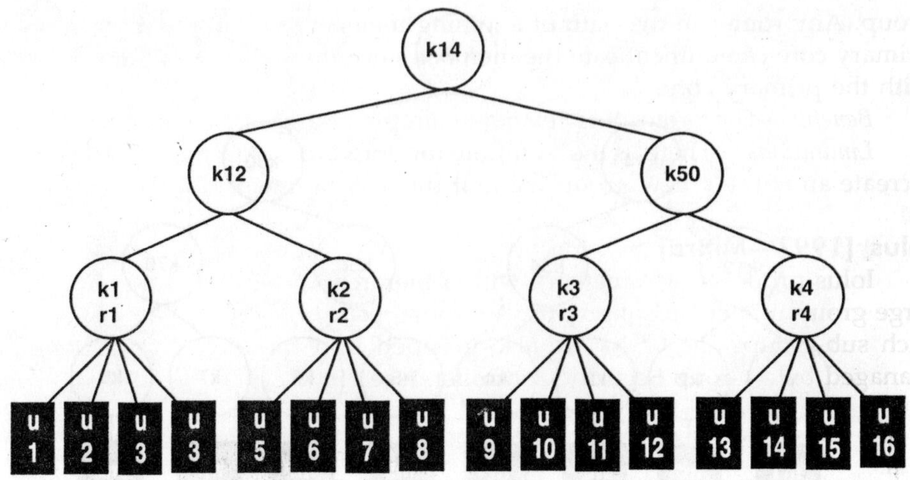

FIG. 5.2
A-ary Tree with Degree 2 and Cluster 4

KDC. The KDC uses a random seed *r* as an index for a pseudorandom function *fr* to generate the key *ki* for member *i* (*ki* = *fr* (*i*)).

Benefits : The number of users is virtually invisible as further clustering is done.

Limitations : The number of keys held by the KDC is more.

Centralized Flat Table [1999—Waldvogel et. al.]

The table has one entry for the Traffic Encryption Key (TEK) and 2*w* more entries for KEKs, where *w* is the number of bits in the member *id*. There are two keys available for each bit in the member *id*, one associated with each possible value of the bit. A member knows only the key associated with the state of its bit. In total, each member holds *w*+1 keys. When a member leaves the group, all keys known by it are changed and the KDC sends out a re-key message.

Benefits : In this scheme, every remaining member can update its old KEKs without gaining further knowledge about the KEKs other members had.

Limitations : This scheme is subjected to collusion problems.

Decentralized Schemes

In the decentralized sub-group approach, the large group is split into small sub-groups. Different controllers are used to manage each sub-group, minimizing the problem of concentrating the work on a single place.

Scalable Multicast Key Distribution [1996—Ballardic]

This technique proposes a scheme to use the trees built by the Core Based Tree (CBT) multicast routing protocol to deliver keys to a multicast group. Any router in the path of a joining member from its location to the primary core can authenticate the member since the router is authenticated with the primary core.

Benefits : The protocol is relatively simple and easy to understand.

Limitations : There is no solution for forward secrecy other than to recreate an entirely new group without the leaving members.

Iolus [1997—Mittra]

Iolus proposes a framework with a hierarchy of agents that splits the large group into small subgroups. A Group Security Agent (GSA) manages each sub-group. The GSAs are also grouped in a top-level group that is managed by a Group Security Controller. (see Fig. 5.3)

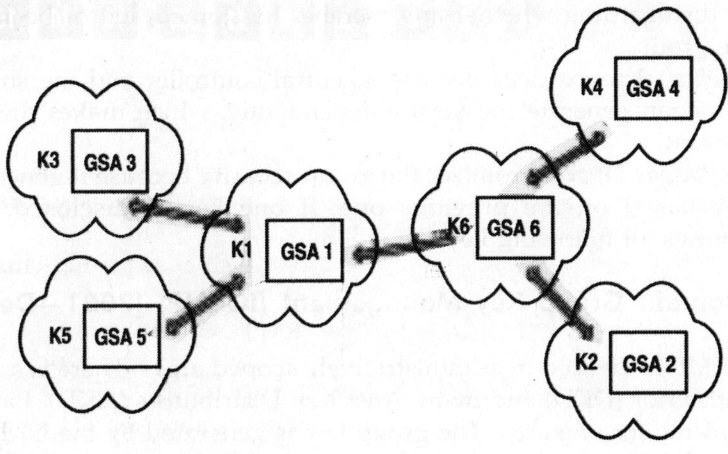

FIG. 5.3
Iolus Architecture

Iolus uses independent keys for each subgroup and the absence of a general group key means membership changes in a subgroup are treated locally.

Benefits : Changes that affect a subgroup are not reflected in other subgroups. The absence of a central controller contributes to the fault-tolerance of the system. If a subgroup controller (namely GSA) fails, only its subgroup is affected.

Limitations : It has the drawback of affecting the data path. There is a need for translating the data that goes from one sub-group, and thereby one key, to another.

MARKS [1999—Briscoe]

In this scheme the technique suggests slicing the time-length to be protected into small portions of time and using a different key for encrypting each slice. The encryption keys are leaves in a binary hash tree that is generated from a single seed. The internal nodes of the tree are also called seeds. A blinding function, such as MD5, is used on the seed to create the tree.

Benefits : Users willing to access the group communication receive only those seeds needed to generate the keys required.

Limitations : This system cannot be used in situations when a membership change requires change of the group key, since the keys are changed as a function of the time.

Kronos [2000—Setia et. al.]

It is an approach driven by periodic re-keys rather than membership changes, which means a new group key is generated after a certain period of time, disregarding whether any member has joined, left or been ejected from the group.

Benefits : Kronos does not use a central controller and the sub-group controllers can generate the keys independently, which makes the system fault-tolerant.

Limitations : It compromises the group security because it generates the new key based on the previous one. If one key is disclosed, then it compromises all following keys.

Intra-Domain Group Key Management (IGKMP) [2001—DeCleene et. al.]

IGKMP is divided in administratively scoped areas. There is a Domain Key Distributor (DKD) and many Area Key Distributors (AKD). Each AKD is responsible for one area. The group key is generated by the DKD and is propagated to the members through the AKDs. The key managers (DKD and AKD) are placed in a multicast group, named All-KD-group (see Figure 5.4).

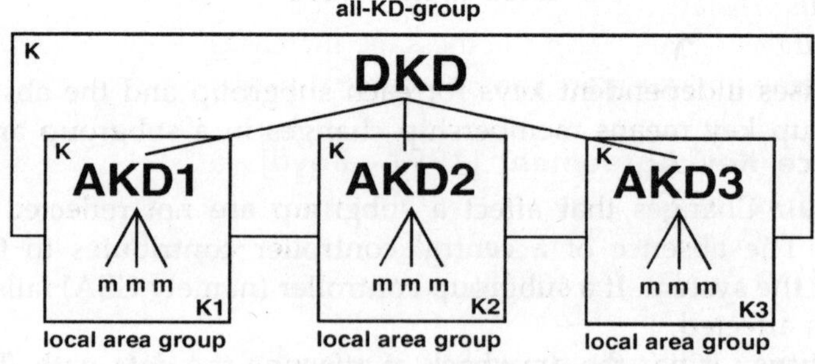

FIG. 5.4
IGKMP Elements

Benefits : Data packets do not need to be translated when passing from one area to another. In addition, the DKD does not need to keep track of all group members; it only has to keep track of the AKDs.

Limitations : If an AKD is unavailable no members in that area are able to access the group communication, since they will not be able to access AKDs from other areas.

Hydra [2002—Rafaeli and Hutchison]

In Hydra, the large group is divided into smaller sub-groups, and a server called the Hydra Server (HS) controls each sub-group. If a membership change takes place at HS*i* , and a new key must be generated, it can generate the new group key and send this key to the other HS*j* involved in that session.

In order to have the group key distributed to all HSs, a *synchronized group key distribution protocol* (SGKDP) is employed. The SGKDP protocol ensures that only a single valid HS is generating the new group key at every given time.

Benefits : The case when one or more HSs become unavailable will not cause a problem for the remaining HSs.

Limitations : Extra overhead is required for synchronization activities.

Distributed Schemes

The distributed key management approach is characterized by having no group controller. The group key can be either generated in a contributory fashion, where all members contribute their own share to computation of the group key, or generated by one member.

Group Diffie-Hellman Key Exchange [1996—Steiner et. al.]

The normal DH protocol is used for two parties to agree on a common key. In this protocol, instead of two entities, the group may have n members. The group agrees on a pair of primes and starts calculating in a distributive fashion the intermediate values.

Benefits : A large group can be managed together.

Limitations : The size of the message increases as the sequence reaches the last members and more intermediate values are necessary.

Conference Key Agreement [1997—Boyd]

The group key is generated with a combining function :

$$K = f(N1, h(N2), \ldots, h(Nn))$$

where, f is the combining function, h is a one-way function, n is the group size, Ni is the contribution from group member i. The protocol specifies that $n - 1$ member broadcast their contributions (Ni) in the clear. The group leader, encrypts its contribution ($N1$) with the public key of each $n - 1$ group member and broadcasts it. All group members who had their public key used to encrypt $N1$ can decrypt it and generate the group key.

Benefits : The number of keys is less.

Limitations : We have to choose complex algorithms for mathematical evaluations.

Octopus Protocol [1998—Becker and Willie]

This protocol is also based on DH key exchange protocol. In Octopus, the large group (composed by n members) is split into four sub-groups (n=4 members each). Each sub-group agrees internally on an intermediary DH value and then the sub-groups exchange their intermediary values. All group members can then calculate the group key. The leader member in each sub-group is responsible for collecting contributions from all its sub-group members and calculating the intermediary DH value.

Distributed Flat Table [1999—Waldovogel et. al.]

This approach proposes the use the flat table in a distributed (DFT) fashion with no Group Controller. In this scheme, no member knows all the keys at any time. Each member knows only the KEKs that it is entitled to. A joining member is obliged to contact a group of members to get all the keys needed. Since many members could be changing the same key at the same time, there could be serious delays in synchronizing the keys.

Conclusion

In this paper, we reviewed several proposals, placing them into three main classes : centralized protocols, which try to minimize the requirements of KDC and group members; decentralized architectures, which divide large group into smaller sub-groups in order to make the management more scalable; and finally, the distributed key management protocols, which gives all members the same responsibilities. Every class has its particularities, presenting different features, requirements and goals.

While centralized key management schemes are easy to implement, they tend to impose an overhead on a single entity. Protocols based on hierarchical sub-grouping are relatively harder to implement and raise other issues, such as interfering with the data path or imposing security hazards on the group. Distributed key management, by design, is simply not scalable. Additionally, the best solution for a particular application may not be best for another, hence it is important to understand fully the requirements of the application before selecting a security solution. Primarily, the usage of security mechanism for secure group communication should be made transparent to the user and it should also work well with other protocols.

References

S. Rafaeli, D. Hutchison. A Survey of Key Management for Secure Group Communication. ACM Computing Surveys, September 2003.

S. Banerjee, B. Bhattacharjee. Scalable Secure Group Communication Over IP Multicast. IEEE Journal on Selected Areas in Communication, Vol 20. October 2002.

M.J. Moyer, J.R. Rao, P. Rohatgi. A Survey of Security Issues in Multicast Communications. IEEE Network, Dec. 1999.

T. Hardjono, B. Cain. Secure and Scalable Inter Domain Group Key Management for N-to-N Multicast. Bay Networks, 1999.

W. Trappe, J. Song, R. Poovendran, K.J.R. Liu. Key Management and Distribution for Secure Multimedia Multicast. IEEE Transactions on Multimedia, Dec. 2003.

P. Judge, M. Ammar. Gothic : A group Access Control Architecture for Secure Multicast and Anycast. Networking and Telecommunications Group, 2002.

PART II

Optical Networking

Trends in Optical Networking

C. Lakshmi Bharathi, B. Murali

Introduction

Networking is an integral part of modern day life in a wide range of applications. The continuous expansion of the application possibilities has been made possible with continuous research and development in the transmission media. Commonly used transmission media are the Unshielded Twisted Pair Cable (UTP), Coaxial Cable and the Optical Fibre Cable.

The relative benefits of one transmission media over the other are usually decided based on factors such as the Transmission Rate, Distances, Cost and Ease of Installation and Resistance to Environmental Conditions. Of the available transmission media, Optical fiber has distinct advantages over the others because it has extremely large bandwidth. For example, in the case of single mode fiber, there is 25 THz of bandwidth that can be exploited by wavelength division multiplexing (WDM). With forecasts of

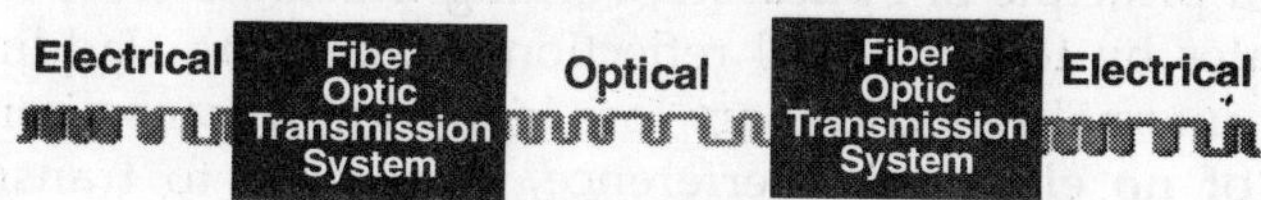

Fig. 6.1
Fiber Optic Transmission

Internet traffic doubling every nine months, optical fiber is the appropriate transmission medium to carry the bulk of future network traffic.

However, much more than transmission is required in a network. Network architecture may have a profound impact on the ability to efficiently and economically harness the transmission capacity of optical fiber. The emergence of optical technologies for transmission, switching, and signal processing has created new opportunities for application to future networks. The present paper looks at a few possibilities of how new optical networking technologies might be applied to meet the challenges of future high-speed networks.

Optical Networking Basics

Optical Networking is the mode of networking using optical fiber as the transmission media. The optical fiber transmission media is designed to transmit digital signals in the form of pulses of light.

The optical fiber construction generally consists of the following :

- CORE—made of glass.
- CLADDING—made of glass.
- Plastic coating.

The Fiber Optic Cable contains one or many fibers, each of them wrapped with a plastic tube and an external coating.

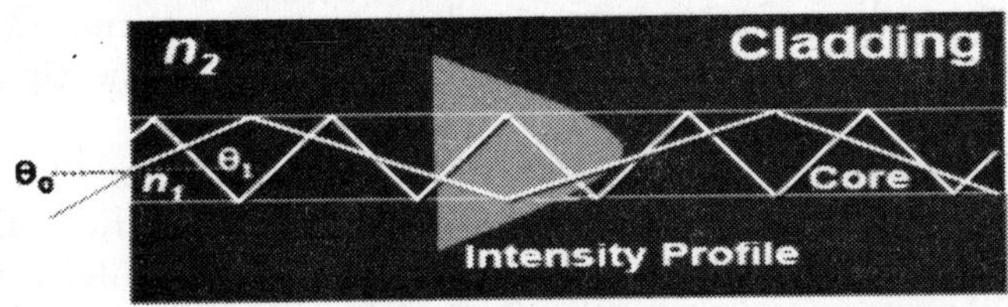

FIG. 6.2
Fiber Optic Cable

The main principle of optical networking transmission is the fact that light propagates by total internal reflections at the core cladding surface. Because total internal reflections are loss less, optical transmission derives the benefits of no electrical interference, possibility to transmit longer distances, send more information, and being more efficient than the other media.

Requirements of Future Networks

An important attribute of future networks is the support of high bandwidth communication at reasonable cost. To meet the exponentially increasing traffic demands, future networks must be scalable in terms of bandwidth, number of users, volume of messages, and message size.

Though future networks will certainly be supporting voice, video, and text traffic, it is likely that they must also support new types of communication. For example, new types of computer-to-computer communication may emerge and even dominate network resources.

Future networks will have service requirements other than bandwidth requirements. They should support multicast as well as unicast communication. They may be required to be flexible so that they can carry communication using diverse signal formats. Provision of security and reliability are of paramount importance. Finally, universal connectivity is a key requirement for future networks. To achieve this, distributed ownership of network resources will likely be important. A framework where resources such as bandwidth can be freely traded may be crucial for addressing the scaling problems associated with universal connectivity.

Optical Technologies : Emerging and Desired

In the following are some of the emerging as well as desired optical technologies, although the list is certainly not exhaustive.

Micro-Electro-Mechanical Systems (MEMS) : MEMS technology has begun to see application in large-scale cross-connects for switching light paths in WDM-based circuit switched networks. Other applications of MEMS should be explored. As an example, MEMS might be applied to create wavelength agile switches for integrated WDM cross connects.

Wavelength Converters : The ability to change the carrier wavelength of a signal may be a critical function in future network architectures. For example, wavelength conversion mitigates centralized wavelength management and is key to distributed control. Relevant performance characteristics may include power efficiency, signal distortion, and wavelength agility.

Variable Wavelength Switching : In large-scale networks it may be advantageous to dynamically translate or switch variable width bands of wavelengths.

Optical Memory : Current network architectures use packet buffering to resolve contention, implemented with electronics. It is natural to consider what network architectures may be possible if practical optical memories can be developed. Although we should not presuppose that optical packet switching will predominate in future networks, it is important to consider how best to use optical memory should it become available.

Emerging Transport Systems : Advances in ultra-long haul and short-reach transmission systems may have a large impact on future network architectures. For example, in the case of ultra-long haul, optimizing efficient long distance transmission could constrain the characteristics of network elements in the signal path, causing some architecture to be preferable over others. In the case of short-reach, its low cost over moderate distances makes it an attractive technology to integrate into a network towards achieving universal connectivity. It may lead to network configurations that are quite different from today's networks.

Signal Monitoring : A critical problem in the provision of transparent light paths is verification of signal integrity. The problem arises because of the requirement of transparency. New technology is needed to provide a means for transparent monitoring of optical signals at low cost, perhaps without the need for electro-optic conversion. Coherent Communications. Most optical transmissions in use today are based on intensity modulation. Coherent optical transmission techniques may hold the key to further improvements in the operational transmission capacity of optical fibers.

Architectural Issues

The network architect is faced with the challenge of designing networks that take full advantage of optical technologies to support current and future network applications. A network should be designed to efficiently transport communication traffic, efficient in minimizing delay, cost, traffic loss, and idle bandwidth. This brings up a number of questions. When are packet, light path, and burst switching appropriate, and are there cases that need another switching paradigm? Will we really need optical packet or burst switching technologies, or can well thought out traffic control achieve most of the performance gains? What should be the granularity and dimensions for switching, and where and how should traffic be aggregated and groomed? What are the key parameters of dynamic behaviour of the traffic and service requirements of the network applications, and how can they be used for efficient network design? In particular, how can we measure and use the time scales of dynamic behaviour? How should large bandwidth delay products of network links be dealt with? What kinds of optical layer functions are needed to realize multicast communication, or are any special functions needed at all? Will network architectures change dramatically if long haul bandwidth becomes cheap and in ample supply? Can CDMA have a role in optical networks such as to support distributed and asynchronous traffic transport? How can networks be made robust with respect to device parameter variations? Of course, a viable network is designed according to other objectives as well.

Supporting secure communications will be a required feature for many network applications, and so it will be of interest to find novel ways that optical technologies can support this. An issue is whether security means that the optical layer becomes simpler or more complicated, and where should the intelligence be placed. Future networks should be also reliable and survivable, and careful study should determine what functions should be done in the optical layer.

Another feature of optical networks that has functional advantages but presents design challenges is transparency. An advantage is the flexibility to support diverse communication signal formats, but management may be more difficult. For example, in a transparent network, routing signals should be done in the context of analog signal degradation.

Network management is an important aspect of network architecture that should be considered carefully at the outset. It is important to determine how signals should be monitored, evaluated, and used, and if necessary, to identify the development of new measuring devices and tools.

Seamless integration with networks based upon other technologies should be addressed. In particular, due to their importance in future networks, the integration between optical and broadband wireless networks should be studied. For example, it may be possible to transport signals in their native analog signal format for certain high bandwidth signal processing applications. Possible applications include exploitation of path diversity in wireless communications, and large scale distributed antenna networks for remote sensing.

Finally, although internetworking with legacy networks should not be ignored, such considerations should not inhibit the pursuit of radically different and innovative architectural approaches. Indeed, the role of NSF should be to spawn research initiatives that are more forward looking than undertaken by commercial enterprises, focusing on high risk, high potential impact research.

Optical Networking

AJITHA KRISHNAN

Introduction

Optical networking provides the "big pipes" that enterprises need for business resilience, storage, and multimedia.

Optical networking uses optical fiber very thin glass or plastic "wire" to carry data, voice, or video signals from one place to another. Those signals travel as pulses of infrared light, which are created by a Light-Emitting Diode (LED) or a laser at one end of the fiber. Because of this, optical networks can carry many forms of information simultaneously. For example, Internet Protocol (IP) data, ESCON (computer storage) traffic, and telephone calls can coexist on an optical network.

A Fiber-Optic Wire

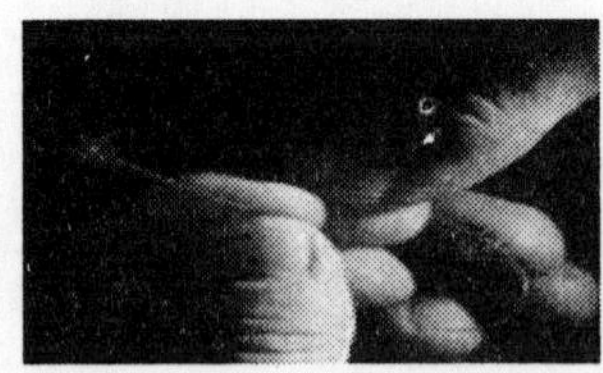

FIG. 7.1
Photo Courtesy : Corning

As networks face increasing bandwidth demand and diminishing fiber availability, network providers are moving towards a crucial milestone in network evolution : the optical network.

Modern optical networks can simultaneously carry up to 32 channels of information in a single optical fiber in a metropolitan or regional environment—and as many as 160 channels from city to city in a long-haul environment—with each channel using a different wavelength of infrared light. Devices called *multiplexers* can pump multiple data streams into a single optical channel using time-division multiplexing. Putting multiple services in a single optical fiber is sometimes called "aggregating services" or "packing" a channel. Each channel, or wavelength, can contain different types of data.

History of Optical Networks

The first digital networks were asynchronous networks in which each network element's internal clock source timed its transmitted signal. As optical-fiber deployment increased, no standards existed to mandate how network elements should format the optical signal. Synchronous Optical Network (SONET) standardized line rates, coding schemes, bit-rate hierarchies, operations and maintenance functionality. Optical networks began with Wavelength Division Multiplexing (WDM), which arose to provide additional capacity on existing fibers. Unlike SONET, rather than using a defined bit-rate and frame structure as its basic building block, the optical network will be based on wavelengths.

Types of Optical Networks

There are four main types of optical networks. Optical link networks consist of optical links with all electronic switches and routers. This means that the optical fibers are used only as a means of travel between the electronic switching devices. In broadcast and select networks data is transmitted on all the links in the network and transmitters and/or receivers are tuned to the wavelength that they are to be transmitting and/or receiving. Wavelength routed networks include optical switches that perform some of the switching responsibility of the network. If the network is a multihop network then it will include electrical switches as well as optical ones. Singlehop wavelength routed networks use only optical switching components The last type of network is the optical burst-switching network. This type of network combines the concepts contained in packet switching and circuit switching. Of all the network types discussed the only one that is prominent in current networks is the optical link network. Wavelength routed networks are currently being paid the most attention by industry.

Benefits of Optical Networks

Fiber Capacity

Providers needed more capacity between two sites. Hence more Time Division Multiplexed (TDM) signals on the same fiber are placed. WDM provided many virtual fibers on a single physical fiber. By transmitting each signal at a different frequency, network providers could send many signals.

Restoration Capability

For a WDM system with many channels on a single fiber, a fiber cut would initiate multiple failures, causing many independent systems to fail. By performing restoration in the optical layer rather than the electrical layer, optical networks can perform protection switching faster and more economically.

Reduced Cost

In systems using only WDM, each location that demultiplexes signals will need an electrical network element for each channel, even if no traffic is dropping at that site. By implementing an optical network, only those wavelengths that add or drop traffic at a site need corresponding electrical nodes which provides tremendous cost savings.

Wavelength Services

By maximizing capacity available on a fiber, service providers can improve revenue by selling wavelengths, regardless of the data rate required.

Enabling Technologies

The cornerstone of an optical network is the advanced optical technologies that perform the necessary all-optical functions.

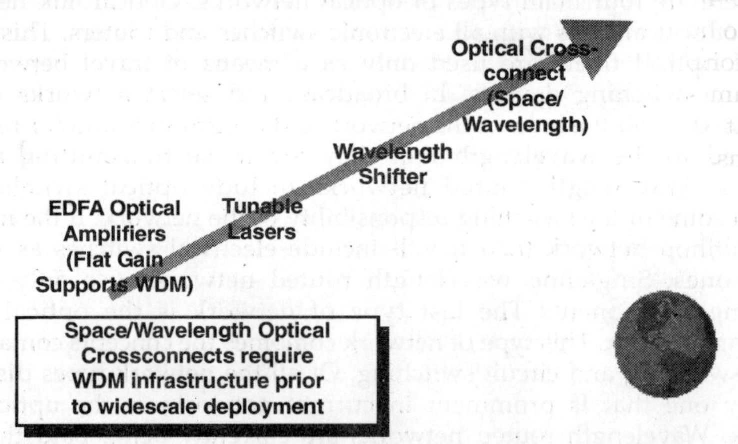

FIG. 7.2
WDM Infrastructures

Early Technologies

1. Broadband WDM

The first incarnation of WDM was broadband WDM. In 1994, by using fused biconic tapered couplers, two signals could be combined on the same fiber. Because of limitations in the technology, the signal frequencies had to be widely separated, and systems typically used 1,310-nm and 1,550-nm signals, providing 5 Gbps on one fiber. Although the performance did not compare to today's technologies, the couplers provided twice the bandwidth out of the same fiber, which was a large cost savings compared to installing new fiber.

2. Optical Amplifiers

The second basic technology, and perhaps the most fundamental to today's optical networks, was the erbium-doped optical amplifier. By doping a small strand of fiber with a rare earth metal, such as erbium, optical signals could be amplified without converting the signal back to an electrical state.

Current Technologies

1. Dense Wavelength Division Multiplexing (DWDM)

As optical filters and laser technology improved, the ability to combine more than two signal wavelengths on a fiber became a reality. Dense wavelength division multiplexing (DWDM) combines multiple signals on the same fiber, ranging up to 40 or 80 channels. By implementing DWDM systems and optical amplifiers, networks can provide a variety of bit rates (i.e., OC–48 or OC–192), and a multitude of channels over a single fiber.

Two basic types of DWDM are implemented today : unidirectional and bidirectional DWDM. In a unidirectional system, all the wavelengths travel in the same direction on the fiber, while in a bidirectional system the signals are split into separate bands, with both bands traveling in different directions.

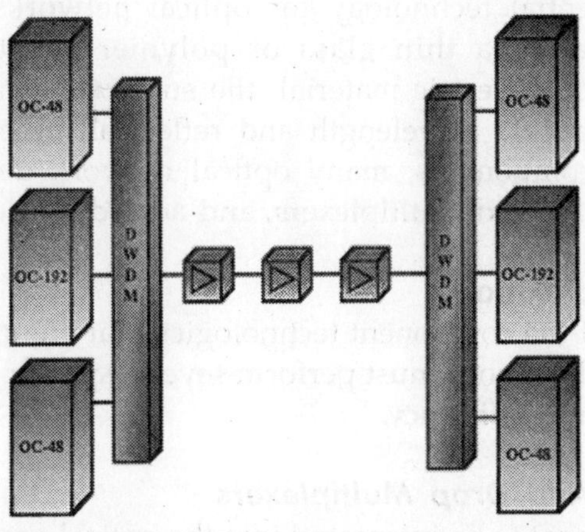

FIG. 7.3
DWDM Systems and Optical Amplifiers

2. *Optical Amplifiers*

The performance of optical amplifiers has improved significantly with current amplifiers providing significantly lower noise and flatter gain which is essential to DWDM systems. The total power of amplifiers also has steadily increased, with amplifiers approaching +20 dBm outputs, which is many orders of magnitude more powerful than the first amplifiers.

3. *Narrowband Lasers*

Advanced lasers with narrow bandwidths provide the narrow wavelength source that is the individual channel in optical networks.

These laser sources emit a highly coherent signal that has an extremely narrow bandwidth. Depending on the system used, the laser may be part of the DWDM system or embedded in the SONET network element. When the precision laser is embedded in the SONET network element, the system is called an embedded system. When the precision laser is part of the WDM equipment in a module called a transponder, it is considered an open system because any low-cost laser transmitter on the SONET network element can be used as input.

4. *Fiber Bragg Gratings*

A fiber Bragg grating is a small section of fiber that has been modified to create periodic changes in the index of refraction. Depending on the space between the changes, a certain frequency of light, the Bragg resonance wavelength is reflected back, while all other wavelengths pass through. The wavelength-specific properties of the grating make fiber Bragg gratings useful in implementing optical add/drop multiplexers.

5. *Thin Film Substrates*

Another essential technology for optical networks is the thin film substrate. By coating a thin glass or polymer substrate with a thin interference film of dielectric material, the substrate can be made to pass through only a specific wavelength and reflect all others. By integrating several of these components, many optical network devices are created, including multiplexers, demultiplexers, and add/drop devices.

Component Applications

Regardless of the component technologies that are implemented in the system, the optical network must perform several specific functions in order to achieve maximum efficiency.

1. *Wavelength Add/Drop Multiplexers*

The first element to be integrated into the optical network is the optical multiplexer. The multiplexer combines multiple wavelengths onto a single fiber, which allows all the signals to be routed along the same fiber.

2. *Wavelength Switches*

A wavelength switch provides functionality similar to an electrical switch by routing an incoming wavelength to a variety of physical output ports.

3. *Wavelength Converters*

The final element in optical networks is the wavelength converter, which converts an incoming signal's wavelength to a different outgoing wavelength, entirely in the optical domain.

Design and Planning

Span Designs

Planners must design optical networks so that signals traveling on the fiber between one network element site and another, called a span, maintain their quality. Many factors must be taken into account, including the Optical Signal-to-Noise Ratio (OSNR), chromatic dispersion, and a myriad of non-linear effects introduced by the interaction of the fiber with the optical signal. The challenge of designing optical networks increases with the introduction of optical cross-connects and add/drop multiplexers, which could dynamically change a signal path to travel across a different physical route.

Wavelength Routing Plans

The basic element in the optical network is the wavelength. As many wavelengths of signals are transported across the network, it becomes important to manage and switch each one individually. One of the benefits of optical networks is that they allow the network architecture to be different for each wavelength. For example, one wavelength may be established in the network to be part of a ring configuration, while another wavelength, using the same physical network, can be provisioned as a point-to-point system.

The flexibility of provisioning the network one wavelength at a time has led to two definitions of end-to-end services : Wavelength Paths (WPs) and Virtual Wavelength Paths (VWPs).

Wavelength Path

Using a WP, a signal enters and exits the optical layer at the same wavelength, without ever changing to a different wavelength throughout the network. Essentially a wavelength is dedicated to connect the two endpoints.

Virtual Wavelength Path

Although a WP is simple to implement, it can impose some limitations on the bandwidth available in the network and the cost of implementing it. In VWP a signal path can travel on different wavelengths throughout the network. By avoiding a dedicated wavelength for an end-to-end connection, the network can reuse and optimize wavelengths to provide the greatest amount of capacity.

Network Evolutions

On the one hand, access networks require a transparent optical network that is bit-rate and format independent. This would provide flexibility and allow connection to the network directly with Asynchronous Transfer Mode (ATM), Transmission Control Protocol/Internet Protocol (TCP/IP), SONET, or any other signal format without additional equipment costs.

Unfortunately, this transparent model for the access network falls completely apart when applied to metropolitan or long-haul networks. As the distances increase, carriers need to maximize the capacity to reduce costs, and allow any signal data rate onto the network would greatly increase costs. The solution for this dilemma is the optical gateway, which will integrate with existing optical-network elements.

Dense Wavelength Division Multiplexing

Fiber-congested, point-to-point segments of long-distance networks were one of the first applications for WDM terminals. Today, 16-channel dense WDM terminals are widely deployed to enhance the bandwidth capacity of the long-haul network backbone.

Optical Add/Drop Multiplexers (OADM)

The OADM systems have the capacity of up to 40 optical wavelengths. Most important, OADM technology introduces asynchronous transponders that extend the life of older lightwave systems by accepting its bandwidth directly into the optical layer, converting its frequency to an acceptable standard, and providing protection and restoration.

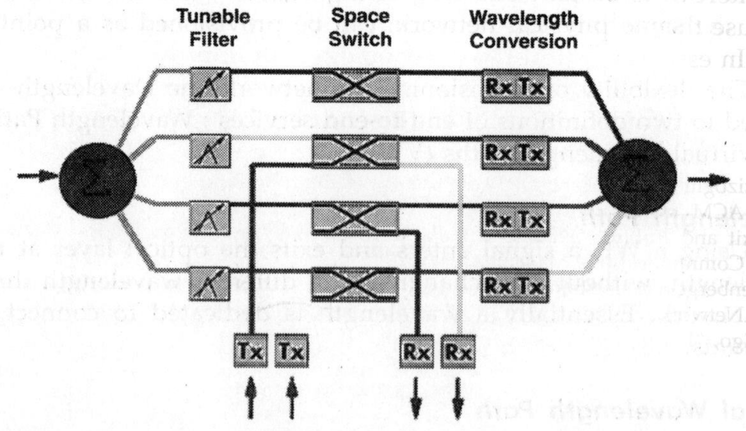

FIG. 7.4
Optical Add/Drop Multiplexers (OADM)

Optical Gateways

In order to access the optical network efficiently and maximize bandwidth capacity and transport-protocol transparency, the optical gateway becomes a critical network element. As a variety of bit rates and signal formats, ranging from asynchronous legacy networks to 10 Gbps SONET systems, a common transport structure must groom and provision traffic entering the optical layer. The emerging basic format for high-speed transparent transport is ATM, and optical gateways will allow a mix of standard SONET and ATM services. In the Real World the province of Alberta, Canada, is linking 422 communities with a combination of optical and wireless networks known as Alberta SuperNet.

It is high-speed access for schools, hospitals, libraries, and government offices to use. The province chose optical networking because it needed a service that had ample bandwidth and that could change as the needs of the province change. Using multiservices SONET equipment, they can support high-speed Internet access as well as voice traffic.

The Future of Optical Networks

Continued advancements in optical technology promise continued change as the optical network evolves to the ultimate goal of end-to-end wavelength services. Medical centers are looking at optical networking to expand the capabilities of *telemedicine*.

The impact of the new optical layer in the telecommunications network can be measured in two ways economic impact and carriers' ability to offer new services. Optical-layer technology will increase network capacity, allowing network providers to transport more than 40 times the traffic on the same fiber infrastructure. Consumers will have access to new high-bandwidth services. Services that today are considered prohibitively expensive, such videoconferencing to the desktop (or home), electronic commerce, and high-speed video imaging, will become commonplace because they will be technologically and economically feasible.

In essence, optical-layer technology will improve the way we live.

References

M. Azizoglu and A. Mokhtar, "Adaptive Wavelength Routing in All-Optical Networks," IEE/ ACM Transactions Networking, Vol. 6, No. 2, April 1998.

S. Dixit and P. Lin, "Advances in Packet Switching/Routing in Optical Networks," IEEE Communications Magazine, Feb. 2001.

F. Effenberger, H. Ichibangase, and H. Yamashita, "Advances in Broadband Passive Optical Networking Technologies," IEEE Communications Magazine, Dec. 2001.

V. Frigo, "Local Access Optical Networks," IEEE Network, Nov./Dec. 1996

Synchronous Optical Networking

D. Kannan, S.C. Punitha and Annabelle Joseph

Introduction

In the year 2002, there has been a significant shift in the optical networking industry. While Ethernet is trying to replace SONET/SDH in the carrier networks, SONET itself is changing to better meet the new demands of data traffic.

Optical networks are high-capacity telecommunication networks based on optical technologies and components that provide routing, grooming and restoration at the wavelength level as well as wavelength-based services.

The diminishing fiber availability and increasing bandwidth demand has made network providers to move towards optical networks.

Optical networks based on the emergence of the optical layer in the transport networks provide higher capacity and reduced costs for new applications such as : Internet, Video and multimedia interaction and Advanced digital services

Many factors are driving the need for optical networks : restoration capability, reduced cost and wavelength services.

Benefits and History of Optical Networks

In the early 1980s, a revolution in telecommunication networks began that was spawned by the use of a relatively unassuming technology, fiber-optic cable. Since then, the tremendous cost savings and increased network quality has led to many advances in the technologies required for optical networks, the benefits of which are only beginning to be realized.

History

Telecommunication networks have evolved during a century-long history of technological advances and social changes. The networks that once provided basic telephone service through a friendly local operator are now transmitting the equivalent of thousands of encyclopaedias per second. Throughout this history, the digital network has evolved in three fundamental stages : asynchronous, synchronous, and optical.

Asynchronous

The first digital networks were asynchronous networks. In asynchronous networks, each network element's internal clock source timed its transmitted signal. Because each clock had a certain amount of variation, signals arriving and transmitting could have a large variation in timing, which often resulted in bit errors.

More importantly, as optical-fiber deployment increased, no standards existed to mandate how network elements should format the optical signal. A myriad of proprietary methods appeared, making it difficult for network providers to interconnect equipment from different vendors.

Synchronous

The need for optical standards led to the creation of the Synchronous Optical Network (SONET). SONET standardized line rates, coding schemes, bit-rate hierarchies, and operations and maintenance functionality. SONET also defined the types of network elements required, network architectures that vendors could implement, and the functionality that each node must perform. Network providers could now use different vendor's optical equipment with the confidence of at least basic interoperability.

Optical

The one aspect of SONET that has allowed it to survive during a time of tremendous changes in network capacity needs is its scalability. Based on its open-ended growth plan for higher bit rates, theoretically no upper limit exists for SONET bit rates. However, as higher bit rates are used, physical limitations in the laser sources and optical fiber begin to make the practice of endlessly increasing the bit rate on each signal an impractical solution. Additionally, connection to the networks through access rings has also had increased requirements. Customers are demanding more services and options and are carrying more and different types of data traffic. To provide full end-to-end connectivity, a new paradigm was needed to meet all the high-capacity and varied needs. Optical networks provide the required bandwidth and flexibility to enable end-to-end wavelength services (see Figure 8.1).

Optical networks began with Wavelength Division Multiplexing (WDM), which arose to provide additional capacity on existing fibers. Like SONET, defined network elements and architectures provide the basis of the optical network. However, unlike SONET, rather than using a defined bit-rate and frame structure as its basic building block, the optical network will be based on wavelengths. The components of the optical network will be

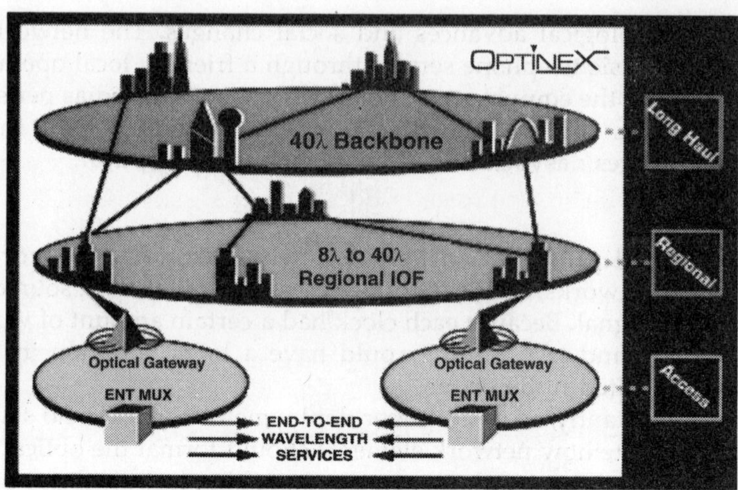

FIG. 8.1
End-to-End Wavelength Services

defined according to how the wavelengths are transmitted, groomed, or implemented in the network. Viewing the network from a layered approach, the optical network requires the addition of an optical layer. To help define network functionality, networks are divided into several different physical or virtual layers. The first layer, the services layer, is where the services—such as data traffic—enter the telecommunication network. The next layer, SONET, provides restoration, performance monitoring, and provisioning that is transparent to the first layer.

Emerging with the optical network is a third layer, the optical layer. Standards bodies are still defining the optical layer, but it will eventually provide the same functionality as the SONET layer, while operating entirely in the optical domain. The optical network also has the additional requirement of carrying varied types of high bit-rate non-SONET optical signals that bypass the SONET layer altogether. Just as the SONET layer is transparent to the services layer, the optical layer will ideally be transparent to the SONET layer, providing restoration, performance monitoring, and provisioning of individual wavelengths instead of electrical SONET signals.

Need for Optical Networks

Many factors are driving the need for optical networks. A few of the most important reasons for migrating to the optical layer are described in this module.

Fiber Capacity

The first implementation of what has emerged as the optical network began on routes that were fiber limited. Providers needed more capacity between two sites, but higher bit rates or fiber were not available. The only options in these situations were to install more fiber, which is an expensive and labour-intensive chore, or place more Time Division Multiplexed (TDM) signals on the same fiber. WDM provided many virtual fibers on a single physical fiber. By transmitting each signal at a different frequency, network providers could send many signals on one fiber just as though they were each traveling on their own fiber.

Restoration Capability

As network planners use more network elements to increase fiber capacity, a fiber cut can have massive implications. In current electrical architectures, each network element performs its own restoration. For a WDM system with many channels on a single fiber, a fiber cut would initiate multiple failures, causing many independent systems to fail. By performing restoration in the optical layer rather than the electrical layer, optical networks can perform protection switching faster and more economically. Additionally, the optical layer can provide restoration in networks that currently do not have a protection scheme. By implementing optical networks, providers can add restoration capabilities to embedded asynchronous systems without first upgrading to an electrical-protection scheme.

Reduced Cost

In systems using only WDM, each location that demultiplexes signals will need an electrical network element for each channel, even if no traffic is dropping at that site. By implementing an optical network, only those wavelengths that add or drop traffic at a site need corresponding electrical nodes. Other channels can simply pass through optically, which provides tremendous cost savings in equipment and network management. In addition, performing space and wavelength routing of traffic avoids the high cost of electronic cross-connects, and network management is simplified.

Wavelength Services

One of the great revenue-producing aspects of optical networks is the ability to resell bandwidth rather than fiber. By maximizing capacity available on a fiber, service providers can improve revenue by selling wavelengths, regardless of the data rate required. To customers, this service provides the same bandwidth as a dedicated fiber.

Technologies on the Horizon

Key functions have been identified as requirements for the emerging optical network (see Figure 8.2). As component technologies advance, each of the functions required, such as tunable filters, space switches, and wavelength converters, will become more cost effective and practical.

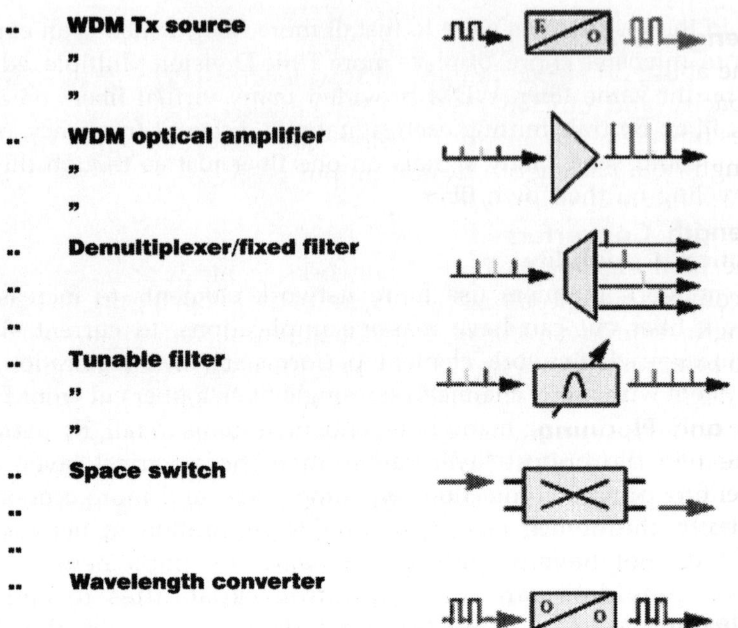

FIG. 8.2
Key Functional Blocks for WDM Transport Systems

One of the most promising technologies for optical networks is the Semiconductor Optical Amplifier (SOA). By integrating the amplifier functionality into the semiconductor material, the same basic component can perform many different applications. SOAs can provide integrated functionality of internal switching and routing functions that are required for a feature-rich network. Space switches, wavelength converters, and wavelength selectors all can be made from SOAs, which will lead to large cost reductions and improved performance in future optical-network equipment.

Component Applications

Regardless of the component technologies that are implemented in the system, the optical network must perform several specific functions in order to achieve maximum efficiency.

Wavelength Add/Drop Multiplexers

The first element to be integrated into the optical network is the optical multiplexer. The multiplexer combines multiple wavelengths onto a single fiber, which allows all the signals to be routed along the same fiber. The initial application for multiplexers has been to increase capacity on existing fiber routes without adding more fiber, but they will serve as entry points to the optical layer in many more aspects, including add/drop multiplexers and optical cross-connects.

Wavelength Switches

The ability to switch individual wavelengths is crucial to maximizing the capacity and efficiency of optical networks. A wavelength switch provides functionality similar to an electrical switch by routing an incoming wavelength to a variety of physical output ports.

Wavelength Converters

The final element in optical networks is the wavelength converter, which converts an incoming signal's wavelength to a different outgoing wavelength, entirely in the optical domain. This will allow the network traffic to be groomed to optimize for traffic patterns or network architecture.

Design and Planning

One of the largest challenges facing network planners who are implementing optical networks is the task of designing and planning the optical layer. Only when providers begin to plan the optical network do some of the more intricate and difficult issues arise.

Span Designs

Ideally, the optical network will provide end-to-end services entirely in the optical domain, without ever converting signals into electrical format. Unfortunately, for at least a decade, it is probable that technology will not progress to the point that it is possible to transmit signals for long distances without electrical regeneration. Even as optical regenerators become commercially viable, network spans will still need to be designed to maintain signal quality throughout the entire signal path.

Planners must design optical networks so that signals traveling on the fiber between one network element site and another, called a span, maintain their quality. Many factors must be taken into account, including the Optical Signal-to-Noise Ratio (OSNR), chromatic dispersion, and a myriad of non-linear effects introduced by the interaction of the fiber with the optical signal. The challenge of designing optical networks increases with the introduction of optical cross-connects and add/drop multiplexers, which could dynamically change a signal path to travel across a different physical route.

Wavelength Routing Plans

The basic element in the optical network is the wavelength. As many wavelengths of signals are transported across the network, it becomes important to manage and switch each one individually. One of the benefits of optical networks is that they allow the network architecture to be different for each wavelength. For example, one wavelength may be established in the network to be part of a ring configuration, while another wavelength, using the same physical network, can be provisioned as a point-to-point system. The flexibility of provisioning the network one wavelength at a time has led to two definitions of end-to-end services : Wavelength Paths (WPs) and Virtual Wavelength Paths (VWPs).

Wavelength Path

The simplest implementation of a wavelength service in the optical network is a WP. Using a WP, a signal enters and exits the optical layer at the same wavelength, without ever changing to a different wavelength throughout the network. Essentially a wavelength is dedicated to connect the two endpoints.

Virtual Wavelength Path

Although a WP is simple to implement, it can impose some limitations on the bandwidth available in the network and the cost of implementing it. One method by which to overcome this limitation is to use a VWP, in which a signal path can travel on different wavelengths throughout the network. By avoiding a dedicated wavelength for an end-to-end connection, the network can reuse and optimize wavelengths to provide the greatest amount of capacity.

Network Evolutions

As the optical network evolves, network planners must understand a dilemma in best utilizing the optical network. On the one hand, access networks require a transparent optical network that is bit-rate and format independent. This would provide flexibility and allow connection to the network directly with Asynchronous Transfer Mode (ATM), Transmission Control Protocol/Internet Protocol (TCP/IP), SONET, or any other signal format without additional equipment costs. It also would allow wavelengths be added and dropped completely optically without affecting the original signal format.

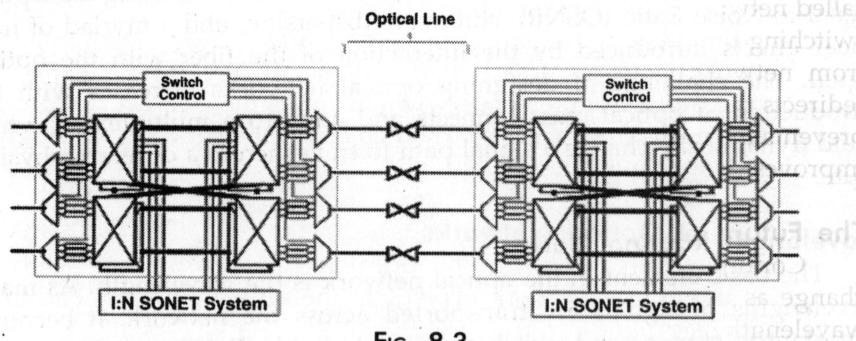

FIG. 8.3
SONET

Optical Bidirectional Line Switched Rings

Optical-ring architectures utilize reconfigurable OADMs; the ring architecture is a familiar scheme to the telecommunications industry and now applied to the optical domain. The optical ring uses the same principles as the fiber ring to provide protection against equipment and network failures (see Figure 8.4).

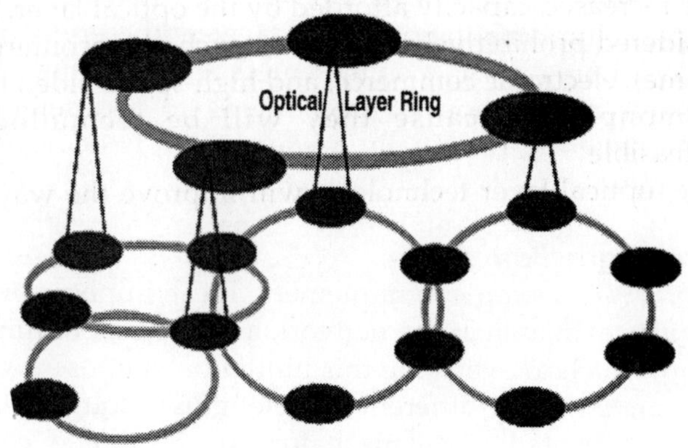

FIG. 8.4
Optical Rings

Network elements have intelligent software that senses a module failure or break in its fiber connection and automatically routes traffic in the opposite direction around the fiber ring. This architecture allows service providers to guarantee that customers' connection will not go out of service. However, the network elements now support multiple optical wavelengths as opposed to multiple DS–3 circuits. In the case of a fiber break, the optical network will automatically re-route up to 40 optical signals in less than 50 milli-seconds.

Because optical rings are most cost effective over large networks, the switching time is critical. One technology planned for implementation is called network protection equipment (NPE), which significantly reduces the switching time required in large optical networks. Instead of routing traffic from network elements adjacent to a fiber cut, the OBLSR using NPE redirects the traffic from the node where it enters the ring. This re-direction prevents the traffic from being backhauled across the network, which greatly improves overall switching time.

The Future of Optical Networks

Continued advancements in optical technology promise continued change as the optical network evolves to the ultimate goal of end-to-end wavelength services.

The impact of the new optical layer in the telecommunications network is astounding. It can be measured in two ways—economic impact and carriers' ability to offer new services. Optical-layer technology will increase network capacity, allowing network providers to transport more than 40 times the traffic on the same fiber infrastructure. That will ultimately lead to lower prices, and competition in the local exchange (as a result of the Telecommunications Reform Act of 1996) will ensure that bandwidth becomes more affordable.

Consumers will have access to new high-bandwidth services made possible by the increased capacity afforded by the optical layer. Services that today are considered prohibitively expensive, such videoconferencing to the desktop (or home), electronic commerce, and high-speed video imaging, will become commonplace because they will be technologically and economically feasible.

In essence, optical-layer technology will improve the way we live.

Survivability of Optical Networking

S. CELINE AND B. SUDHA

Introduction

Optical networks are high capacity telecommunication networks based on optical technologies. Also with the components that provide routing, filtering and restoration at the wavelength level.

Optical cables are thinner than a human hair and are made of glass. It reaches across the globe, transporting data in the form of light waves.

Overview

An attempt is made on the study of the evolution of the optical network, various elements required to construct optical network, ample application, switching techniques used and a tool for the survivability for the same.

Evolution of Optical Network

The telecommunication network evolved in three fundamental stages. They are :

- Asynchronous
- Synchronous
- Optical

Asynchronous Network

In asynchronous networks, there is a variation in electrical signals arriving, transmitting and coding scheme, because each network element's transmission speed is clocked, which often results in high bit-rate errors, and also difficult to monitor.

Synchronous Optical Network (SONET)

In SONET, a standard schemes for electrical signal handling, coding are followed, which leads to less bit-rate errors. It is easy to operate and monitor.

Optical Network

Optical networks began with Wavelength Division Multiplexing (WDM), which provides additional capacity on existing fibers. According to the wavelengths transmission, filtering and implement the network components are defined. The optical network layers and its functions are shown in Figure 9.1.

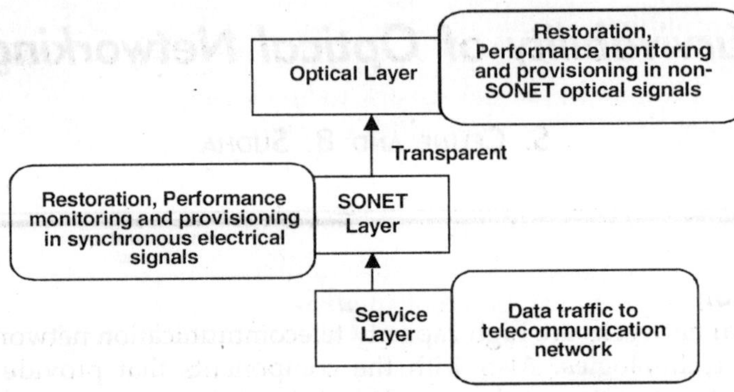

FIG. 9.1
Optical Network Layers and its Functions

Optical Network Enabling Technologies

Optical technologies continue to advance by ingenious technique and implementation to improve the performance and capabilities of the optical network. Development stages of Optical network technologies are shown in Figure 9.2.

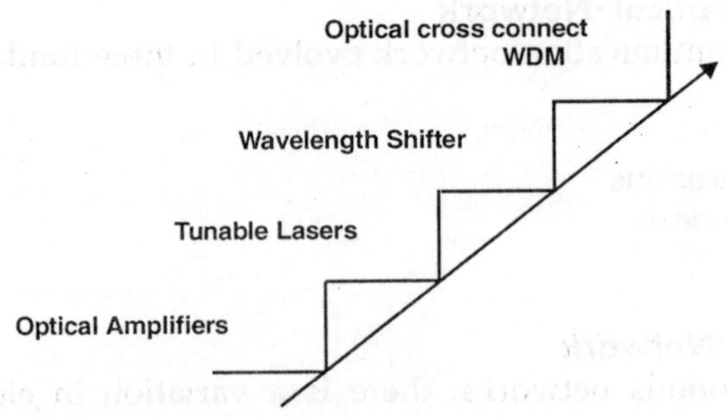

FIG. 9.2
Milestones in the Development of Optical Network Technologies

Early Optical Technologies

There were two technologies to increase capacity and reduce cost in the existing networks.

- ➢ Broadband WDM
- ➢ Optical Amplifiers

Broadband WDM

The broadband WDM uses fused biconic tapered couplers, combining two signals, to provide twice the bandwidth, out of the same fiber, but signal frequencies has to be widely separated.

Optical Amplifiers

Optical networks uses the erbium-doped optical amplifiers, which doesn't convert the optical signal back to an electrical signal. As a result, it reduces cost over electrical regenerator especially in long-haul networks. But it is unable to transmit varieties of bit rates.

Current Optical Technologies

Current optical network uses devices that are much more efficient and precise than the previous. Some of them are

- ➢ Dense WDM
- ➢ Optical Add/Drop Multiplexers
- ➢ Bragg grating tool

Dense Wavelength Division Multiplexing (DWDM)

By using DWDM the optical amplifiers allows combination of many wavelengths across a single fiber, which provides a variety of bit rates and multitude of channels over a single fiber. Its performance is also optical.

Optical Add/Drop Multiplexer

Add/Drop Multiplexers are used to insert and extract tributary streams without disturbing tributary streams that are in transit.

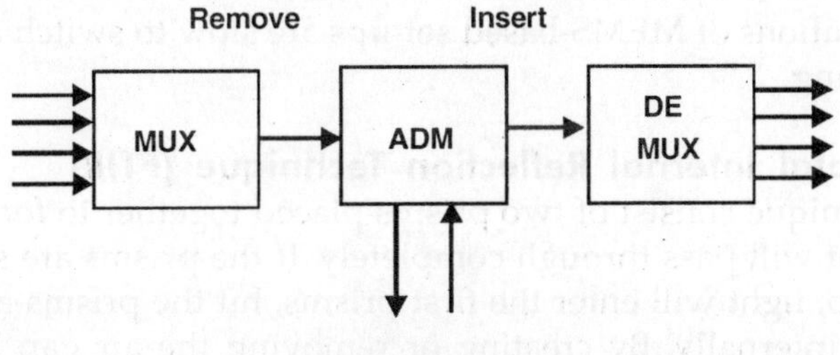

Fig. 9.3
Add/Drop Multiplexers

SONET Add/Drop Multiplexers are where data enter, leave or are routed through the network. They are usually arranged in a ring configuration as shown in Figure 9.4. Data can enter through an IP router, ATM switch, Digital Cross-Connect System (DCS), or from another SONET ring.

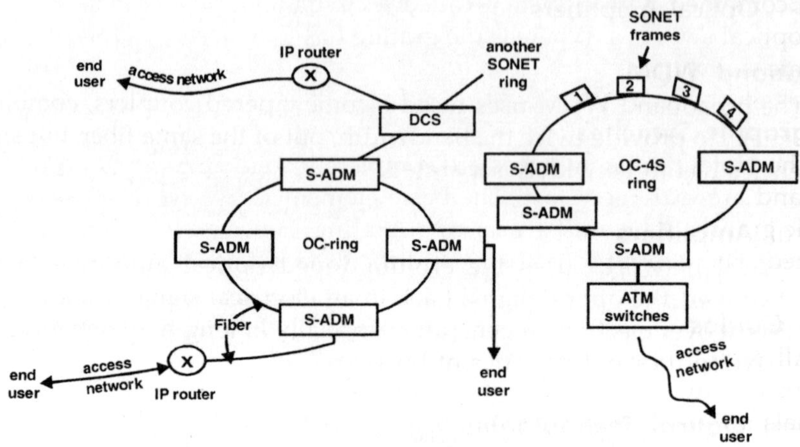

FIG. 9.4
Ring Configuration of Add/Drop Multiplexer

Bragg-grating

Bragg-grating tool is developed to aid in dispersion, compensation and signal filtering, which are mainly used in implementing add/drop multiplexers.

Optical Switching : The Technology Inside

Optical switching technology is still under development and some early implementations have only recently become available some of them are . . .

Micro Electro-Mechanical Systems (MEMS)

It uses tiny mirrors built onto a chip to physically reflect light to other directions, which is used in the telecom space.

The limitations of MEMS-based set-ups are slow to switch and far from packet switching.

Frustrated Total Internal Reflection Technique (FTIR)

This technique consist of two prisms placed together to form a cube. In this form, light will pass through completely. If the prisms are separated by a small air gap, light will enter the first prisms, hit the prisms-air boundary and reflected internally. By creating or removing the air gap between the two prisms, we have a switch element. This can be cascaded to provide more switching ports.

The latency involved in this technique is about 25 ms.

Gratings and Circulators

By applying a specific wavelength of laser to a conventional fiber, it's possible to change the properties of the fiber core to act as a grating. When this is combined with a system called a circulator, it is possible to built a static optical switches. Whereas the grating has to be changed physically for dynamic switching.

Holographic Switches

The Holographic Switches are completely solid state, with no moving parts and are extremely fast. The basic element is a piece of glass with l-specific grating, which uses a series of grating, hence all wavelength can be switched. The downside is that it is difficult to design.

Wave Guides

All optical fibers are wave guides, using total internal reflection from a control point guide the light within the core. Thermal or electrical materials are used as refractive index. In which thermo-optic wave guide switches are slow when compared with electro-optic wave guide switches.

Optical Space Switching

Optical switches are created by Arrayed Waveguide Gratings (AWGS) elements which are more efficient when combining discriminating prisms with tunable lasers. AWGs are solid-state and switching speed depends on the reflection of input laser.

An arrayed waveguide grating multiplexer made using waveguides etched on silica on silicon. Light from the input waveguides are spread out by the input coupler into the arrayed waveguides, and then coupled back to the output waveguides. Each waveguide in the middle section has a different path length. The wavelength of the light signal determines the interface between the signals coming out of the arrayed waveguides in the output couplers, and determines the output port that the exits on. This is shown in Figure 9.5.

This switching technique is pretty faster than the previous.

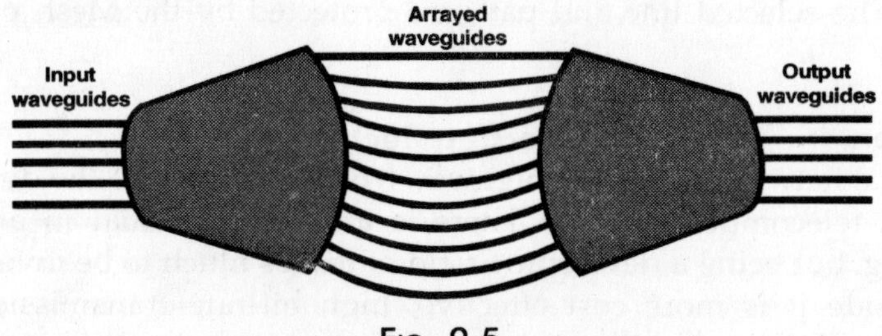

FIG. 9.5
Arrayed Waveguides

Benefits of Optical Network

- A high speed transmission of data in long-haul network.
- Optical networks are cost effective to replace the existing network.
- Lower noise in the network path hence more gain in data transmission.
- Power of optical network is increased by using Optical-Optical-Optical (O-O-O) process which saves time and is cheaper than the ethernet switches.
- With the restoration scheme a loss can be removed. And it allows better wavelength utilization.
- Network Management System (NMS) for optical networks are highly intelligent and provides better troubleshooting. It can also help to establish and monitor new end-to-end wavelength services to maximize their bandwidth.
- Optical networks have emerged as an attractive alternative to traditional copper wire or wireless networks.
- The optical networking is superior than the traditional telecom network in terms of capacity. It is the only way to support the data networks of the future.
- The future of data transmission seems to be moving from copper wire networks to optical networks, hence optical network one day become national backbone.

Applications

The survivability techniques can be broadly divided into pre-designed protection and dynamic restoration schemes. In which pre-design has four protection methods. They are :

- Automatic Protection Switching (APS),
- Dual Homing,
- Self-Healing Ring (SHR), and
- Mesh Protection.

APS provides protection for all kinds of networks. SHR is divided into uni-directional and bi-directional rings, which is used to select the line and the path. The selected line and path are protected by the Mesh protection techniques

Conclusion

Optical network is a super highway when compared to the dirt road of traditional telecommunications. There is a lot of potential in all optical networking, but being a developing field, it leaves much to be invented. On the plus side it is more cost effective, high bit-rate transmission, good restoration schemes, intelligent network management schemes and easy maintainability. In 1987, Charles kao, "the father of fiber optics" dreamt one

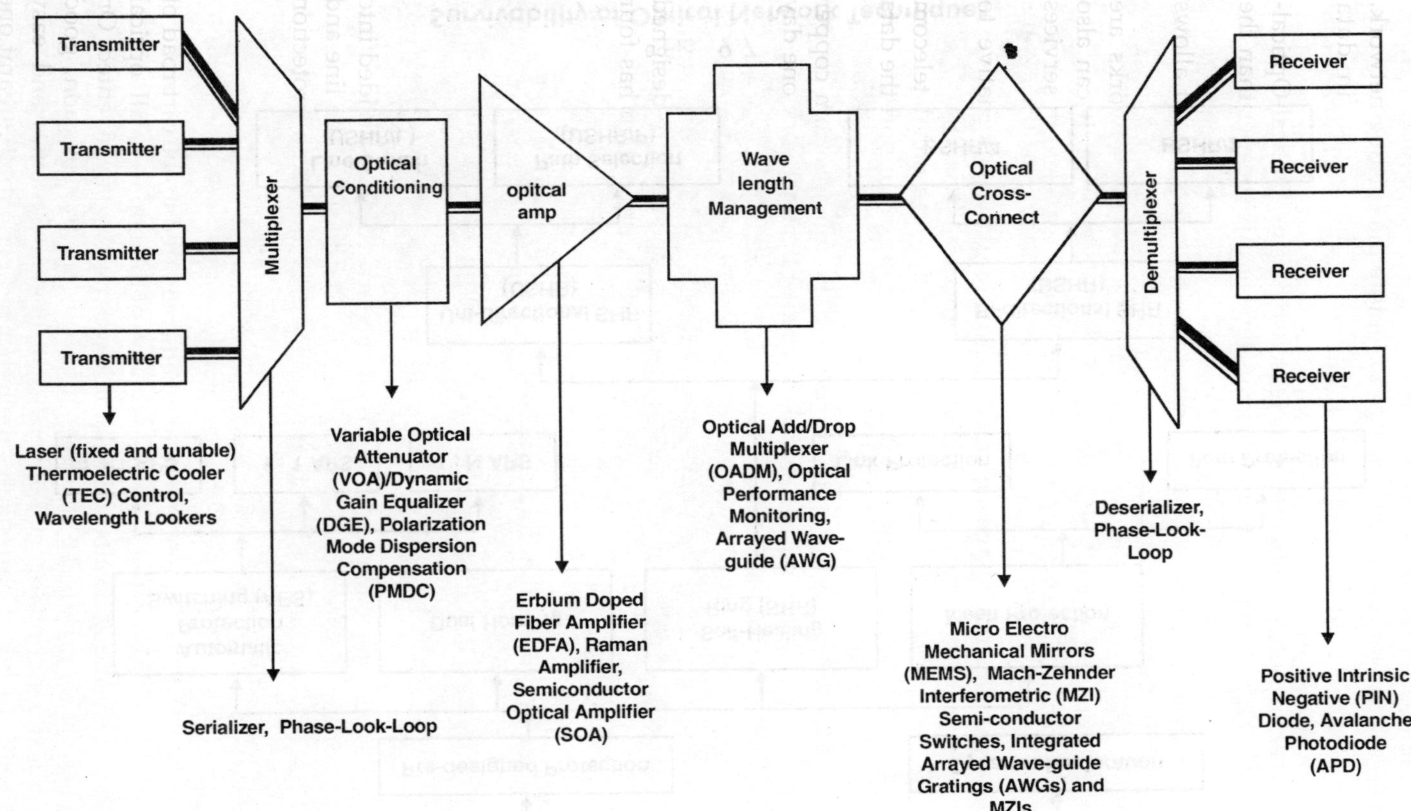

FIG. 9.6

Techniques for Survivability of Optical Network

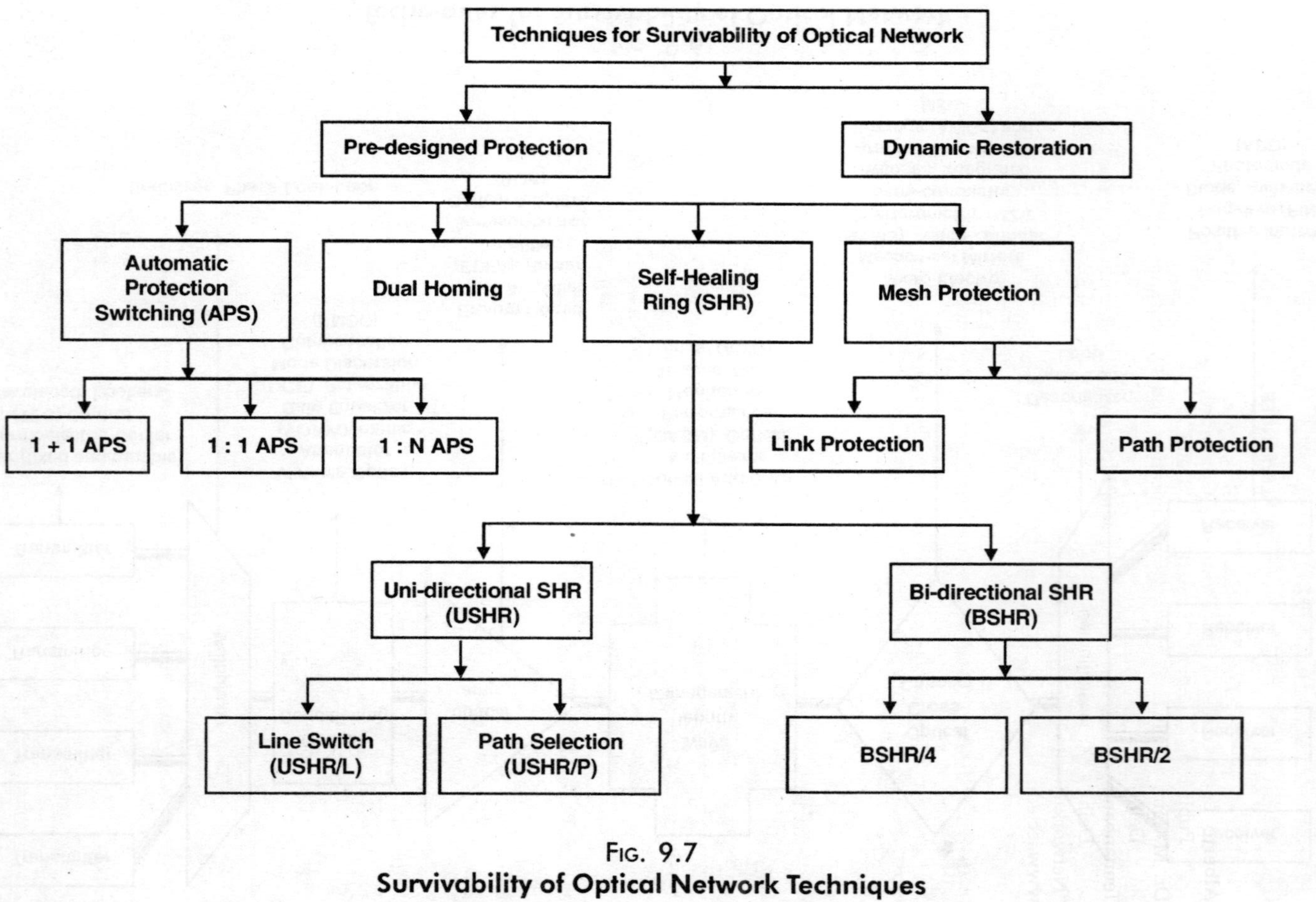

Fig. 9.7
Survivability of Optical Network Techniques

terabit-per-second transmission speed, which can be achieved through optical networking.

References

Alberto Leon-Garcia, Indra Widjaja; "Communication Networks;" Tata McGraw-Hill Publishing Company Limited; New Delhi.

Dr. M. Jain, Satish Jain; "Data Communication and Networking;" BPB Publications; New Delhi.

Tennanbaum; "Computer Networks"; Tata McGraw-Hill Publishing Company Limited; New Delhi.

"Network Computing;" Magazines.

www.iec.edu

CHAPTER

10

Asynchronous Transfer Mode (ATM) and Passive Optical Networks (PONs)

V. GANESH AND K. NIRMAL KUMAR

Definition

The Operator and customer benefits and technological development of optical distribution networks with Asynchronous Transfer Mode Passive Optical Networks (ATM PONs). ATM–PON infrastructure is widely cited by telecommunication carriers and equipment vendors as potentially the most effective broadband access platform for provisioning advanced multimedia services as well as legacy services such as tier 1 (T1). Since 1995, an influential group of worldwide carriers and equipment vendors has been developing requirement specifications for a full-service access network with ATM PON as the core technology.

Overview

The deployment of fiber-optic technology to homes and businesses is poised to change the way telecommunications services—primarily voice, data, and video services—will be delivered to the twenty-first century information-based economy. Interest is high among business and residential consumers for advanced, broadband services such as fast Internet access, electronic commerce, video on demand, digital broadcasting, teleconferencing, and telemedicine, among others. However, the lack of available bandwidth to deliver these services effectively to the last mile of homes and businesses has stifled development of new multimedia applications.

An optical distribution network with ATM PON as the core technology promises benefits to end users as well as carriers and service providers. When optical network access is achieved in scale, businesses and consumers will realize opportunities for advanced services at relatively low costs. Because of cost savings inherent with the ATM–PON platform, telecommunication carriers and service providers will realize efficiencies in provisioning future applications and upgrading bandwidth to satisfy customers' demands.

The Case for Fiber-Optic Access

Fiber-optic technology, offering virtually unlimited bandwidth potential, is widely considered to be the ultimate solution to deliver broadband access to the last mile. Today's narrowband telecommunication networks are characterized by low speed, service-provisioning delays, and unreliable quality of service. This limits the ability of a consumer to enjoy the experience at home or the ability of workers to be efficient in their jobs. The last mile is the network space between the carrier's Central Office (CO) and the subscriber location. This is where bottlenecks occur to slow the delivery of services. The subscriber's increasing bandwidth demands are often unpredictable and challenging for telecommunication carriers. Not only must carriers satisfy today's bandwidth demands by leveraging the limits of existing infrastructure, they also must plan for future subscriber needs.

A new network infrastructure that allows more bandwidth, quick provisioning of services, and guaranteed Quality of Service (QoS) in a cost-effective and efficient manner is now required. Today's access network, the portion of a public switched network that connects CO equipment to individual subscribers, is characterized by predominantly twisted-pair copper wiring.

Fiber-optic technology, through local access network architectures such as Fiber-To-The-Home/Building (FTTH/B), Fiber-To-The-Cabinet (FTTCab), and Fiber-To-The-Curb (FTTC) offers a mechanism to enable sufficient network bandwidth for the delivery of new services and applications. ATM-PON technology can be included in all these architectures, as shown in Figure 10.1.

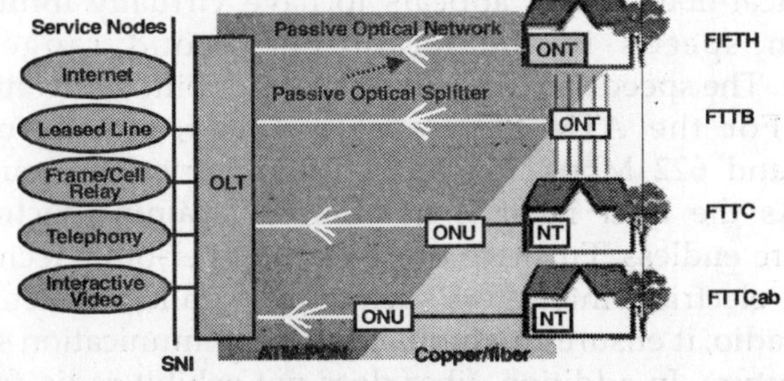

FIG. 10.1
ATM-PON Architecture

In general, the optical section of a local access network can either be a point-to-point, ring, or passive point-to-multipoint architecture. This tutorial focuses on the passive point-to-multipoint architecture (PON). The main component of the PON is an optical splitter device that, depending on which direction the light is traveling, splits the incoming light and distributes it to multiple fibers or combines it onto one fiber.

The PON, when included in FTTH/B architecture, runs an optical fiber from a CO to an optical splitter and on into the subscriber's home or building. The optical splitter may be located in the CO, outside plant, or in a building.

FTTCab architecture runs an optical fiber from the CO to an optical splitter and then on to the neighbourhood cabinet, where the signal is converted to feed the subscriber over a twisted copper pair. Typically, the neighbourhood cabinet is about 3 kft from the subscriber's home or business.

FTTC architecture runs an optical fiber from the CO to an optical splitter and then on to a small curb-located cabinet, which is near (typically within 500 ft) to the subscriber. It is then converted to twisted copper pair.

The PON can be common to all of these architectures. However, it is only in the FTTH/B configurations that all active electronics are eliminated from the outside plant. The FTTCab and FTTC architectures require active outside-plant electronics in a neighbourhood cabinet or curb. This tutorial will focus on FTTH/B architectures.

When fiber is used in a passive point-to-multipoint (PON) fashion, the ability to eliminate outside plant network electronics is realized, and the need for excessive signal processing and coding is eliminated. The PON, when deployed in an FTTH/B architecture, eliminates outside plant components and relies instead on the system endpoints for active electronics. These endpoints are comprised of the CO–based optical line terminal (OLT) on one end and, on the other, the optical network termination (ONT) at the subscriber premises. Fiber-optic networks are simple, more reliable, and less costly to maintain than copper-based systems. As these components are ordered in volume for potentially millions of fiber-based access lines, the costs of deploying technologies such as FTTH, FTTB/C, and FTT/Cab become economically viable.

One optical-fiber strand appears to have virtually limitless capacity. Transmission speeds in the terabit-per-second range have been demonstrated. The speeds are limited by the endpoint electronics, not by the fiber itself. For the ATM-PON system today, speeds of 155 Mbps symmetrical and 622 Mbps/155 Mbps asymmetrical are currently being developed. As the fiber itself is not the constraining factor, the future possibilities are endless. Furthermore, because fiber-optic technology is not influenced by electrical interferers such as cross-talk between copper pairs or AM band radio, it ensures high-quality telecommunication services in the present and future. In addition, fiber does not exhibit radio frequency (RF) emissions that can interfere with other electronics and is regulated by the Federal Communications Commission (FCC).

While copper-based transport technologies remain ubiquitous, the long-term industry belief holds that it is inevitable that fiber will replace copper throughout the access infrastructure. Because copper infrastructure is embedded in communications systems, this transformation to optical transport is expected to occur over many years. Over time, new builds ("Greenfield") will be all fiber-based, and existing builds will be rehabilitated by replacing copper with fiber or by overlaying new fiber on the existing copper infrastructure. Electronic equipment, as well, must be replaced with optical equipment.

How ATM PONs Work

Recent technological advances and economies of scale have drawn increasing interest to optical-distribution networks with ATM PON. A functional overview of ATM–PON architecture is presented in Figure 10.2.

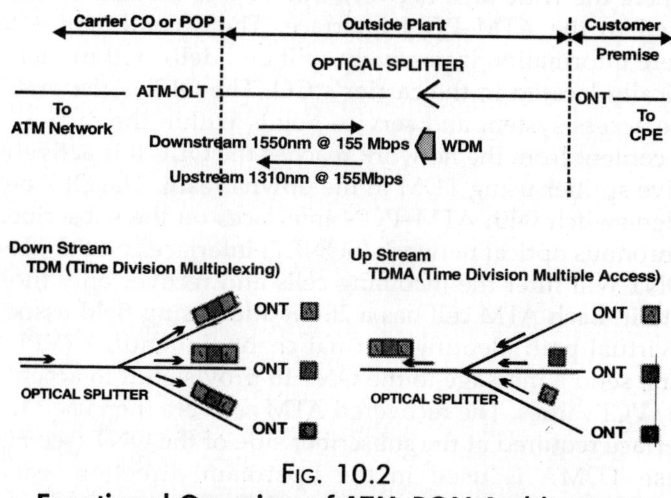

Fig. 10.2

Functional Overview of ATM–PON Architecture

Figure 10.2 shows the ONT placed at the customer premises, which suggests FTTH/B architecture. The carrier's demarcation point would be the subscriber side of the ONT, typically in the form of a T1, Ethernet, Integrated Services Digital Network (ISDN), Plain Old Telephone Service (POTS), etc.

For FTTCab and FTTC architecture, an optical network unit (ONU), rather than an optical network termination (ONT), is used. It is placed in the outside plant and must be temperature-hardened and properly enclosed. The final drop to the network termination (NT) at the customer premises may be copper or fiber. The carrier demarcation point is the subscriber side of the NT in the form of a T1, Ethernet, ISDN, POTS, and etc.

Access to bandwidth on the PON may be obtained by several methods, including time division multiple access (TDMA), wave division multiple access (WDMA), code division multiple access (CDMA), and sub-carrier multiple access (SCMA). TDMA in the upstream and TDM in the downstream were chosen by the Full-Service Access Network (FSAN) group and submitted to the International Telecommunications Union (ITU) for standardization, based on their simplicity and cost-effectiveness.

As shown in Figure 10.2, the network components supporting ATM PON consist of OLT, ONT, and a passive optical splitter. One fiber is passively split up to 64 times between multiple ONTs that share the capacity of one fiber. Passive splitting requires special actions for privacy and security, and a TDMA protocol is necessary in the upstream direction. The use of the optical splitter in the PON architecture allows users to share bandwidth, thus dividing the attendant costs. Costs are further reduced by a decrease in the number of opto-electronic devices needed at the OLT; one interface may be shared among many ONTs.

The ATM–PON system uses double-star architecture. The first star is at the OLT, where the wide-area network interface to services is logically split and switched to the ATM–PON interface. The second star occurs at the splitter where information is passively split and delivered to each ONT. The OLT is typically located in the carrier's CO. The OLT is the interface point between the access system and service points within the carrier's network. When data content from the network reaches the OLT, it is actively switched to the passive splitter using TDM in the downstream. The OLT behaves like an ATM edge switch with ATM–PON interfaces on the subscriber side and ATM–synchronous optical network (SONET) interfaces on the network side.

The ONT will filter the incoming cells and recover only those that are addressed to it. Each ATM cell has a 28-bit addressing field associated with it called a virtual path identifier/virtual channel identifier (VPI/VCI). The OLT will first send a message to the ONT to provision it to accept cells with certain VPI/VCI values. The recovered ATM cells are then used to create the service interface required at the subscriber side of the ONT (see Figure 10.2).

Because TDMA is used in the upstream direction, each ONT is synchronized in time with every other ONT. The process by which this happens is called ranging the ONTs. Basically, the OLT must determine how far away in distance each ONT is so they can be assigned an optimal time slot in which to transmit without interfering with other ONTs. The OLT will then send grant messages via the physical layer operation, administration, and maintenance (PLOAM) cells to provision the TDMA slots that are assigned to that ONT. The ONT will then adapt the service interface to ATM and send it to the PON using the TDMA protocol.

Ethernet and T1s are two examples of what can be transported over the ATM–PON. As ATM–PON is service-independent, all legacy services and future services can be readily transported.

The basic frame format between the OLT and ONT for the symmetrical 155 Mbps rate is shown in Figure 10.3.

The asymmetrical version of 622 Mbps/155 Mbps downstream/upstream is similar but beyond the scope of this document.

As can be seen in Figure 10.3 the downstream payload capacity is

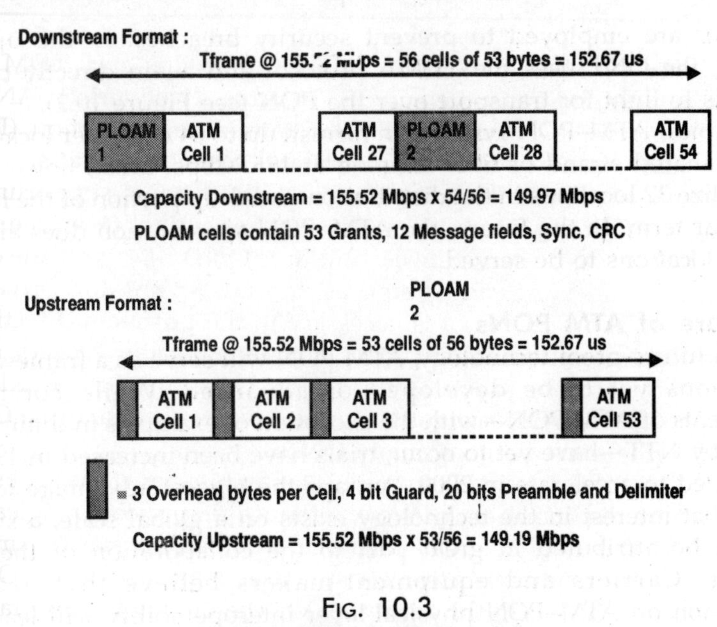

FIG. 10.3
ATM–PON Frame Formats

reduced to 149.97 Mbps because of the PLOAM cells. These cells are responsible for allocating bandwidth (via Grant cells), synchronization, error control, security, ranging, and maintenance.

In the upstream direction the capacity is reduced to 149.19 Mbps because there are 3 overhead bytes per ATM cell. In addition to the three overhead bytes per cell there are PLOAM cells in the upstream direction, the rate of which is defined by the OLT for each ONT, depending on the required functionality. The minimum PLOAM rate in the upstream direction is one PLOAM every 100 ms. This equates to approximately one PLOAM every 655 frames, which is negligible. Although the maximum PLOAM rate is undefined, it is also expected to be negligible. The 3 overhead bytes contain a minimum of 4 bits of guard time to provide enough distance in time to prevent collisions with cells from other ONTs. This field length is actually programmable by the OLT. The preamble field is used to acquire bit synchronization and amplitude recovery. The Delimiter field is used to indicate the start of an incoming cell.

Given that a single fiber is used for both the upstream and downstream paths, two wavelengths of light are used—1550 nm for the downstream and 1310 nm for the upstream. Although one wavelength can also be used, two provide better optical isolation between the laser transmitters and receivers and eliminate the need for expensive beam-splitting devices. Instead, low-cost planar light circuits (PLCs) can be used, which enable low-cost manufacturing techniques to be employed, somewhat similar to the production of silicon chips. ATM cells are directly converted to light and sent to the PON. Because of the broadcast nature of the PON, encryption techniques are employed to prevent security breaches. In the upstream direction, the ONT uses the TDMA protocol and again directly converts ATM cells to light for transport over the PON (see Figure 10.2).

A typical ATM–PON system can furnish up to 64 customer locations on a single, shared strand of fiber running at 155 Mbps. Most, however, will likely utilize 32 locations in the distribution and drop portion of the network in the near term. In the future, the ATM–PON specification does allow for up to 64 locations to be served.

The Future of ATM PONs

As a future-proof technology, ATM PON will serve as a framework for applications yet to be developed or advanced. While commercial deployments of ATM PON—with the exception of examples in limited areas in Japan by NTT—have yet to occur, trials have been increased in 1999 and are expected to accelerate in 2000. Perhaps the biggest advantage for ATM PON is that interest in the technology exists on a global scale, a situation that may be attributed in great part to the collaboration of the FSAN Initiative. Carriers and equipment-makers believe that extensive collaboration on ATM–PON physical-layer interoperability will lead to an increase in the production volume of silicon chipsets that can be created to the global specification. Interoperability among the technology's management layers will depend on alliances among strategic vendors. Settling on the core framework, however, is what will propel the technology forward.

Carriers and service providers are expected to focus initially on business uses through FTTB, as real revenue streams typically originate in these areas. As production accelerates, operators will increasingly look to the mass residential market. Through the Internet age, small- and medium-sized businesses have been characterized as being on the down slope of technology. However, ATM PON, with its cost savings and flexibility, is capable of bringing more of these businesses on-line quickly.

Future applications aimed at FTTH scenarios include asymmetric broadband services (such as digital broadcast, video on demand, distance learning, and fast Internet), symmetric broadband services (such as telecommunication services and teleconferencing opportunities), and narrowband telephone services (such as the Public Switched Telephone Network [PSTN] and Integrated Services Digital Network [ISDN]).

CHAPTER

11

Multiple Wavelength Data Transmission in Optical Networks through Wavelength Division Multiplexing and Dense Wavelength Division Multiplexing

S. Ashok Kumar

Introduction

The first thing to realize is that pushing light through glass is not at all like driving electricity through a wire. Networks based on electronics are very different from networks based on Fiber Optics. But why we bother with Multiple Wavelengths of light? Why not to use Multiple Wavelengths on single fiber? Why not to use a single wavelength and make it go faster and faster? Because there are lots of limitations on Single Wavelength Optical Networks and hence we need WDM and DWDM.

SONET/SDH [Synchronous Optical Network/Synchronous Digital Hierarchy] is the most common representation of optical network technique. It is based on Single Wavelength operation and hence if an optical network use Multiple Wavelength with WDM and DWDM the future of SONET/SDH looks awful!

Wavelength Division Multiplexing (WDM) uses wavelength spaced about 4 nanometer (nm) to 10 nm. Dense Wavelength Multiplexing (DWDM) uses wavelength spaced about 1 nm or less to 0.1 nm. It seems there is very little difference between WDM and DWDM and one can say both technologies are same. But that's not true since, in practice, close spacing of wavelength in DWDM makes a huge difference!!

Wavelengths

Wavelengths are so important in optical networks. Since this paper is a detailed study on multiple wavelength. Let us get some idea about wavelengths. In 1970s the best wavelength for optical networks was between the ranges from 800 nanometer to 900 nanometers (nm). It was called as the first window or 1970 window.

Later in 1980s the range of wavelength used was between 1,310 nm. This was called as the second window or 1980 window. This was the stage where the standard SONET/SDH got into higher stages of development

Today the wavelength ranges from 1,510 nm to 1,600 nm. This was called as the third window or 1990 window. This range is used in all modern Wavelength Division Multiplexing and Dense Wavelength Division Multiplexing. But in this range the light sources are so expensive

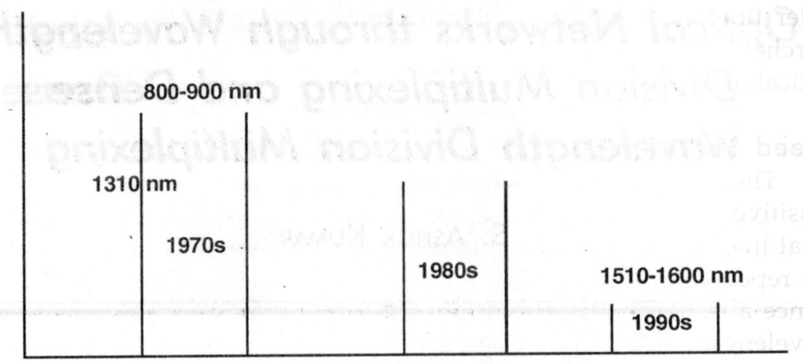

FIG. 11.1
Wavelength Ranges

SONET/SDH

The turning point in the history of optical networks was the development of Synchronous Optical Network (SONET) and Synchronous Digital Hierarchy (SDH) which made clear data transmission paths at higher speed. SONET/SDH was hold by many channels mainly for its support towards voice.

SDH is an international standard that defines a hierarchical set of transmission rates and transmission formats for optical fiber systems. Its transmission rate starts at 155.52 Mbps. SONET is a North American standard. It is used by the equipment vendors and service provides at or above the basic optical transmission rate of 51.84 Mbps. SONET/SDH transmission speeds from 10 Gbps to 40 Gbps.

The one main issue with SONET/SDH is it was a single wavelength technology. A second laser could not be added at different wavelength because SONET/SDH was designed to operate at 1,310 nm only. Due to the single wavelength technology and since new optical networks are using WDM and DWDM, SONET/SDH is in the state of crisis today.

Single Wavelength Limitations

Expensive New Fiber Runs

When the fiber optic link reaches the upper limit for bit transmission, there is no other way to increase the capacity on the link. The only way is to add new fiber. But how expensive is to run new facilities to handle new fiber installation? Few years ago U.S. Telephony Service suggested costs about 70,000 US $ per mile. There is also a need of purchase of new transmitters and receivers. Everything costs money—a lot of money.

If WDM and DWDM are used a lot of expense of running new fiber goes away. In many cases it is possible to use same fibers but is not always possible. Even if new fiber is needed, the new fiber can replace or add to the older fiber without the need to running new tools. But it is necessary to purchase and install new multi-wavelength transmitters, receivers and optical amplifiers.

Speed Specific Repeaters

The main problem with the digital repeaters is that they are code sensitive and timing sensitive, i.e., to reshape a pulse a repeater must know what line is used in representing 0's and 1's. Similarly to retime the signal, the repeater must know the bit rate of the line to receive the bit interval. Hence a digital repeater will not function on a fiber optic link if multiple wavelengths exist. Multi-wavelength repeaters can be used, but these are experimental devices at present.

When WDM and DWDM are in use there is a need to use optical amplifiers instead of digital repeaters. This is not only an equipment cost but a labour demanding process also.

Small Serial Bit Intervals

As the speed of bps of a serial link increases, the bit time or bit interval of each bit will reduce proportionately. On the links bits are grouped and represented as single baud, or change in line signaling condition. In optical networking, most modulation is done by varying the intensity of the light above or below the threshold of the receiver. This is called intensity modulation.

Hence transmitters and receivers must be able to generate and detect bits one after the other within 1 micro second or the link will drop bits and produce bit errors. Hence the only way to increase bit rates on links limited by timing variation effects (jitter) is to add WDM or DWDM Jitter causing a lost bit

Optical Components for WDM and DWDM

WDM devices and links involve two-channel multiplexing. These used

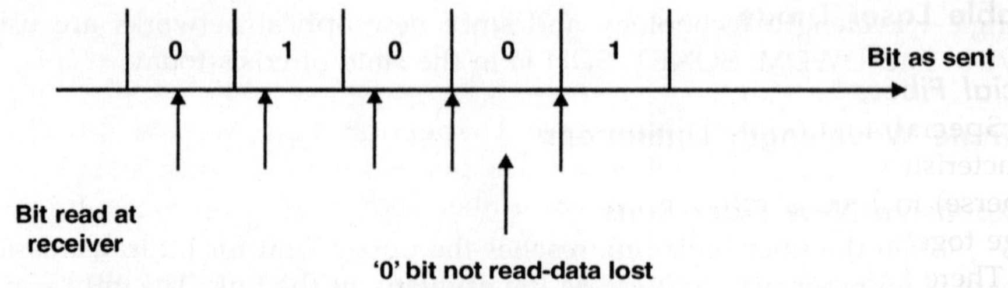

FIG. 11.2
Serial Bit Interval

1,310 and 1,550 nm laser operating regions for short span applications or two widely spaced channels in the 1,550 nm region (1,538 and 1,558 nm) for long span applications.

WDM can be unidirectional or bidirectional. A bidirectional WDM device will pass a number of multiplexed frequencies in both directions on one fiber. But a unidirectional WDM device multiplexes a number of different frequencies for transmission in one direction on one fiber.

The major difference between WDM systems and DWDM systems is that in DWDM the wavelengths used are packed within 1 nm or even 0.1 nm of each other or about ten to one hundred times denser than in WDM. So it would seem that there is very little difference between WDM and DWDM. But this is not really true.

The close spacing of wavelengths in DWDM system makes a big difference. Everything is magnified in DWDM so that even small effects in WDM become crippling in DWDM unless steps are taken to compensate for these impairments. In order to overcome the limitations of single wavelength systems and to move towards the multiple wavelengths the following 4 components are needed.

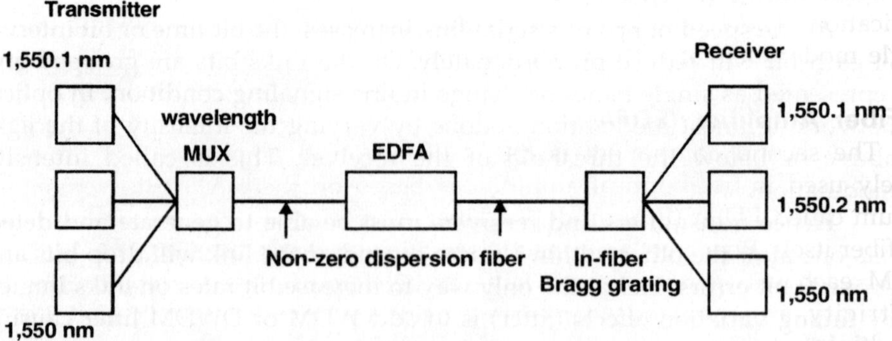

FIG. 11.3
Components of DWDM

Tunable Laser Diode

Special Fibers

Special Fibers with Non-Zero Dispersion and No Water Peak characteristics is the first requirement. The pulse of light becomes spread out (disperse) in time as it travels down a fiber and all the pulses eventually merge together. This is called as dispersion.

There is usually a "water peak" at around 1,400 nm caused by water ions that are always present in the fiber. In 1998, Lucent announced a new fiber called "All Wave" that had almost no water peak at all.

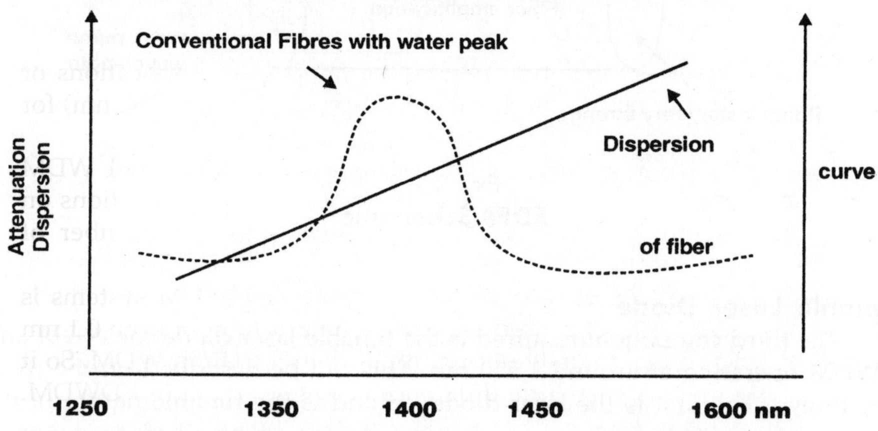

FIG. 11.4
Special Fibers with Non-Zero Dispersion and No Water Peak

Fibers without a water peak allow operation of transmitters in the 1,400 nm range, where dispersion is lower that is in the normal WDM and DWDM range around 1,500 nm. Non-water peak fibers almost completely eliminate the water ions that were an unavoidable by-product of fiber optic cable fabrication. There new fiber retains the dispersion characteristics of the single mode fibers at 1,310 and 1,550 nm.

In-Fiber Amplifier (EDFA)

The second component is the in-fiber optical amplifiers. The most widely used in-fiber optical amplifier is based on the rare earth element erbium called EDFA (Erbium-doped Fiber Amplifier). EDFAs are built into the fiber itself. Repeaters are tuned to specific wavelength and bit rate. With WDM each wavelength would have to be demultiplexed, converted to electricity, regenerated, converted back to optical signals and be remultiplexed. In-fiber amplifiers make WDM technically feasible.

The principle of EDFA is a relatively high powered laser source at 980 nm is mixed with the arriving input signal on a special section of erbium-doped fiber, typically about 10 meters of fiber coiled to reduce the form factor of the device. This is called the pump signal. The erbium ions present in the EFA fiber section are excited to a higher energy state by the pump laser.

When photons form the input signal in the range of about 1,530 to 1,620 nm strike the excited erbium ions some of the ions energy is transferred to the signal. The photons have the same phase and direction as the incoming photons, so the input signal is amplified.

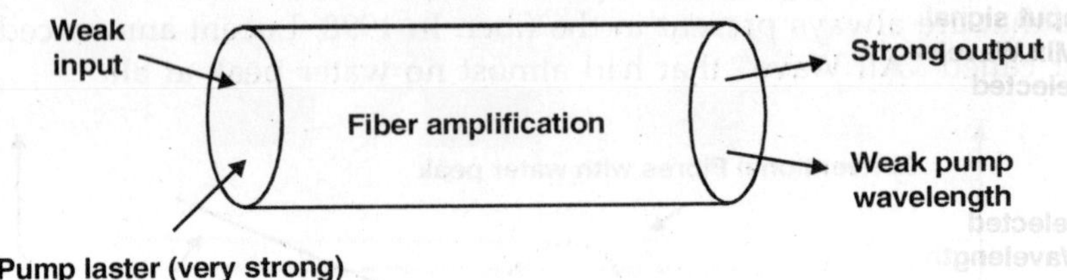

FIG. 11.5
EDFA Schematic

Tunable Laser Diode

The third component required is the tunable laser diode for WDM and DWDM operating at around 1,550 nm. This can be described on the three key things. The first is the laser diode, second is the tunable nature of the laser, which enables the same physical device to be used to generate different wavelengths of light and finally the third one is operation at around 1,550 nm

Laser diode is a semiconductor device mounted on a simple computer card assembly. Lasers can be turned on and off very quickly and produce higher power than LED's. Laser light which emerges highly parallel from the device can inject 50-80% of its power onto a fiber.

Laser diodes are used as transmitters of light; they would be useless without reliable optical receivers or detectors. The optical receiver is based on the photoconductor. It is a semiconductor material with a voltage applied across it by means of electrical contacts. Any arriving photon is absorbed by the semiconductor material and an electron and 'hole' pair is created. Electron has a negative charge and the hole left has a positive charge. The pair move through the applied filed to the metal contacts. So the amount of electrical resistance through the device depends on the number of photons received per unit time. The photodiode converts light directly to electric current.

In-Fiber Bragg Grating

The fourth and final component for optical networks is the in-fiber Bragg grating for WDM and DWDM system. The In-Fiber Bragg Grating (FBG) is simple, inexpensive and highly reliable. The FBG is just a short of ordinary single mode fiber that can be fixed using beams of UV radiation.

When fixed with the fight spacing the FBG will reflect (select) one wavelength back in the direction the light entered the fiber and pass the other (non-selected) wavelengths through the fiber unchanged. But there will be some small attenuation effect in other wavelengths.

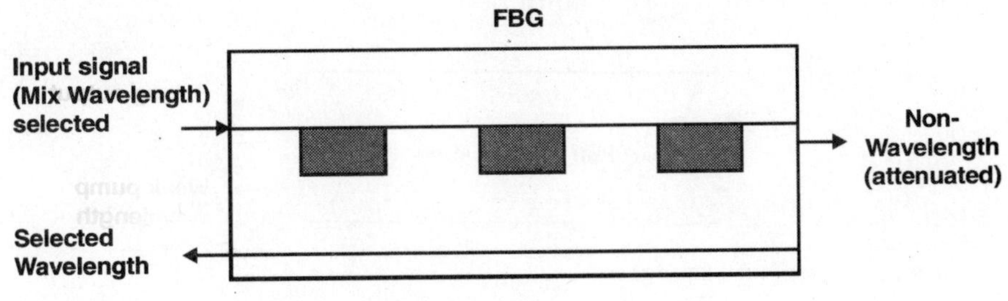

FIG. 11.6
In-Fiber Bragg Grating

The only problem with FBG has been some sensitivity to temperature variations and stretching of the fiber section with the grating. FBG not only used as filters in WDM and DWDM but also to control dispersion in 1,550 nm band and to stabilize the output of a laser tunable.

Conclusion

Thus in optical networking, with WDM and DWDM technology data transmission looks clear, fast and accurate. Only with proper transmitter, fiber optic cable and receiver can fiber optic link function. These concepts thus formed the foundations for the idea of multiple wavelengths of light in same fiber to produce WDM and DWDM.

PART III

Multimedia Networks

Multimedia Networks

P. Bavitra Maharishi and C. Selvi

Introduction

During the past few years, we have all witnessed a phenomenal growth in the deployment and use of the Internet by businesses and individuals. The networks gets wider and wider with more complex architecture and protocols. The end-to-end network bandwidth has had to grow, and the basic data networks have had to evolve into "multimedia networks" to enable new capabilities. New types of media such as voice, video, and 3D (in addition to the traditional text and graphics) are now part of the networks.

As a result, new demands have been placed on the scalability, fidelity, quality of service and the overall real-time behaviour of the content and the multimedia networks. Many compression schemes are used to reduce the bandwidth-hungry and processing-intensive multimedia applications. Using the Multimedia Networks we are going to Communicating beyond the sky. In today's world, computer has become a magical wand that does all magical works. And adding the flavor is the term Multimedia. Multimedia comprises of one or more media types like Text, Images, Audio and Video. It is used for designing both serious and entertainment works.

"One day doctors with voice-enabled mobile medical imaging systems will operate under the most adverse conditions."

"Virtual business meetings will also be commonplace with web-based conference calls that combine spreadsheets and streaming video."

"Family and friends will be able to participate in reunions and celebrations regardless of time and space boundaries."

"There will be no teachers in the schools and colleges, only the computers will rule."

Applications are designed using this multimedia. Applications involving text and images comprise blocks of digital data. Texts are represented by binary digits called bits. Likewise a digitized image comprises a two-dimensional block of picture elements also represented by bits. In applications involving audio and video, the signals vary continuously with time as the amplitude of those signals varies. This type of signals is known as analog signals. In applications that involve just a single type of media, the basic form of representation of the particular media type is often used. Similarly, in applications that involve either text and images or audio and video their basic form is often used, since the two media type in these applications have the same form of representation. However in applications that involve the different media types integrated together in some way it becomes necessary to represent all four media types in a digital form. In the case of text and images, this is their standard form of representation. For audio and video however, their basic forms of representations are analog signals, this must be converted into a corresponding digital form before they can be integrated with the two other media types. And this conversion is included in the network!

The main strength of multimedia technology is complex graphics and video images in computerized multimedia programs. But the bandwidth consumption of these applications is very huge. So automatically we go for various techniques to reduce the size of the application, which results in various compression algorithms. It is also called as Coding and Decoding. There are number of compression algorithms for each and every multimedia components. Compression technique is very useful in transmitting multimedia applications over N/Ws.

- To reduce the volume of an information-text, fax, images, and
- To reduce the bandwidth-speech, audio, video

Basically there are Two Types of Compression Schemes

1. *Lossy Compression*

In which some of the finer details are sacrificed. So the decoded application will not be the same as that of the original application. But the bandwidth consumption is reduced greatly also the transmitting rate is faster.

2. *Lossless Compression*

Lossless compression involves with compressing data which, when decompressed, will be an exact replica of the original data. This is the case when binary data such as executables, documents, etc. are compressed. They need to be exactly reproduced when decompressed. On the other hand, images (and music too) need not be reproduced 'exactly'. An approximation of the original image is enough for most purposes, as long as the error between the original and the compressed image is tolerable.

Now let us see the N/Ws in which the Multimedia applications are transmitted.

The N/Ws are basically classified into five main categories :

- Telephone n/w
- Data n/w
- Broadcast television n/w
- Integrated services digital n/w
- Broadband multiservice n/w

Telephone N/W

They were designed to provide a basic switched telephone service called "Plain Old Telephone Service" or POTS. When we want to connect one or more interconnected telephones, PBX (Private Branch Exchange) is used. International calls are routed to and switched by International Gateway Exchanges (IGEs). Modems are used to convert the analog signals to digitals and *vice versa.*

Data N/W

Data N/W operates in packet mode. Packet contains data, header field, and destination address. It is mainly used to transfer electronic mails and files. Here, there are two types of Data N/Ws.

- X.25—Which restrict low bit rate data application.
- Internet—Collection of interconnected N/W.

Broadcast Television N/W

It supports the diffusion of analog signal television and radio. A cable is integrated into STB for smaller area, whereas a satellite is used for wide area. Low bit rate channel is used to connect the subscriber to a PSTN. High bit rate channel is used to connect the subscriber to the Internet.

Integrated Services Digital Networks (ISDN)

It supports both analog and digital communication. These allow users either to have two different telephone calls and a data call simultaneously or two different calls. This ISDN N/W provides two separate communication channel over these circuits. It can be used independently or combined 128 kbps channel. But it can support only a maximum bit rate of 2 Mbps - 30*64 kbps. The main drawback here is, it will not support video signals.

Broadband Multiservice N/W

It supports wide range of multimedia communication applications. This technology associated with the digitization of a video signal. This

N/W support multiple services. All the different media types associated with a particular multimedia application are first converted in the source equipment into a digital form. These are then integrated together and the resulting binary stream is divided into multiple fixed size packet. This information stream provides a much more flexible way of both transmitting and switching.

Multimedia Applications

- Interpersonal communication—Video, Game, Email.
- Interactive applications over the internet—Information retrieval.
- Entertainment application—Audio/Video.
- Interactive applications over the Internet—WWW

CHAPTER

13

Concepts in Multimedia Networks

C.M. KARKUVEL RAAJAN, V. NEELAVANAN AND G. SRINATH

Introduction

Today Networks and Multimedia are the two buzzwords over the computer world. Multimedia can be said as visual images such as text, images, motion pictures, animations, etc. Network is the medium for sharing datum. In the past, only textual data are passed through networks. But today we have a great necessity of transferring audio and video files through network. Here we are going to know about multimedia, networks, and how multimedia is implemented over networks.

Today multimedia can be transferred over networks. This paper explains about multimedia, user interface, multimedia compression standards, transmission media, networks, and multimedia over networks. To transfer a multimedia over network, we need Human/Computer interface.

A multimedia file cannot be transferred without compression, because it takes larger time to transfer larger file. We need a transmission media to transfer that file to destination. Normally fibre optic cables are mostly used for effective communication. Various network protocols are to be followed while transferring, the destination should also have a interface supporting multimedia.

Super highway is driving towards us in the fast lane, but no one can quite say from which direction. Trials of video on demand are continuing but roll out of services have been delayed. We are told that home services on the highway will have to be kept simple for us to take in, and will be affordable. In education multimedia learning packages have been mounted on file-servers, use of the World Wide Web is widespread, and some video conferencing is being used. So networking of computer-based multimedia is possible. However, network delivery of multimedia is not new, the broadcast television system has been available since the 1950's. The difference now is that the information, which has previously been presented on radio, TV, or in books, is now being presented or can be accessed by computer networks. Or looking at this development in another way computer technology has almost caught up with the broadcasters. Multimedia producers are also looking for a wider market and lecturers are excited both by the new learning environments offered and possible efficiency gains.

Networked Multimedia Applications

Multimedia can roughly be defined as a technology that enables humans to use computers capable of processing textual data, audio and video, still pictures, and animation. Applications range over entertainment, education, information provision, design e.g. CAD/CAM, co-operative working such as video conferencing, application sharing, remote working and virtual reality experiences.

User Requirements for Multimedia

Human-Computer Interface

With the development of High Definition TV and beyond, it is likely that there will be a continual increase in the demands placed on computer-based multimedia systems. Multimedia applications like any other application, appliance or tool, benefit from being easy to use, with minimal training or self-learning. The need for a well designed human-computer interface, which may be screen or audio-based is well accepted.

Access, Delivery, Scheduling

Television channels can be changed at the touch of a button. On demand access times to computer information need to be below one second to be usable in real time. Alternatively the delivery of information at a later time is acceptable if it can be scheduled, as in a TV broadcast schedule, or a first class postal letter. Scheduling the delivery of multimedia information has not been widely implemented. Scheduling can have advantages for users over on demand delivery.

Interactivity

Interactivity, meaning the ability to participate in a video or audio process on a computer, by changing its behaviour or appending comments has become very important in multimedia. Some of this popularity stems from the perception of computer games as being enjoyable because they are interactive, and some from work done in education which shows that some types of learning becomes easier, and is retained more permanently if the learner participates in some way with the learning material.

Issues for Users

Characteristics of Multimedia

Multimedia can be as simple as a few images with some accompanying text to a multimedia presentation using video clips, sound, images animation and text. Multimedia files to use a lot of data when in a digital format. Video is the most demanding. Audio is less demanding but still requires 1.3 MByte for a 1-minute clip. Still images require use more data proportional to their size. Synchronization of sound and video is important.

Compression

Compression algorithms and techniques are critical to the viability of multimedia networking. Uncompressed digital television requires about 140 Mbps. Since few users have this sort of network access compression is the only hope for the widespread deployment of digital video and multimedia. Compression techniques depend on algorithms implemented in software or hardware.

Inter-Operability

The inter-operability of platform hardwatre, networks and applications and multimedia formats is a major issue for multimedia users.

Compression Standards

Uncompressed PAL video as a digital signal needs 140 to 270 Mbps, while uncompressed digital HDTV needs 1.2 Gbps. A digitised colour picture at 35 mm film resolution needs about 80 Mbyte. One minute of 8 bit sound sampled at 22 kHz needs 1.3 Mbyte. Compression must be done to a standard to enable decoding. However, there are many compression methods. Microsoft Video for Windows, Quicktime are proprietary examples. A standard called JPEG is used for still colour images. For video conferencing a standard called H.261 which is part of the H.320 standards family is used. Further video standards are MPEG-1 and MPEG-2 which gives a higher quality picture to MPEG-1, but at a higher data rate. MPEG is likely to be important for video on demand.

JPEG Compression

The JPEG (Joint Picture Experts Group) [ISO10] is the first international digital compression standard for multi-level continuous tone still, black and white or colour images. It typically compresses images to 1/10 or 1/50 of their original size.

MPEG Compression

The MPEG (Motion Picture Experts Group) [ISO11] has so far defined two compression algorithms : MPEG-1 and MPEG-2. A common misconception is that MPEG-2 is a replacement for MPEG-1. Each algorithms has been specifically targeted at different bit rates. MPEG-2 runs at higher bit rates than MPEG-1.

Transmission Media

Copper Conductors

Copper conductors twisted together are the basis of the telephone network. As used in the analogue telephone network, with modems turning digital data into analogue tones, the data rate is limited to around 28 kbps.

Coaxial Cable

Coaxial cable is still an effective medium to deliver multimedia. Cable TV networks use coaxial cable. One video conferencing provider has taken advantage of the potential additional bit rate available over coaxial cable and designed a proprietary video conferencing system for use over a LAN (C-Phone).

Optical Fiber

Optical fiber transmission has been a strong enabling factor in the creation of a high capacity digital network on which networked multimedia applications will depend.

Radio Systems

Radio systems are likely to impact on multimedia in two ways. Firstly, radio technology operating at microwave frequencies is available to provide wireless local area networks. Use of this technology for delivery of real time multimedia material should be treated carefully, because radio links are susceptible to fading, interference, random delays, etc.

Service Providers

Public Telecommunication Operators (PTO)

Services such as Kilostream and Megastream from BT are already extensively use to connect networks. There are synchronous channels and can carry data, voice, and compressed video.

Cable TV Providers

Cable TV networks are being installed in many areas of the UK. Many of these have an optical fiber backbone, and hence have the potential of carry other traffic then television distribution.

LAN Network Technologies

Ethernet at 10 Mbps

There is a vast installed base (about 40 million Ethernet nodes) of 10 Mbps Ethernet and 4 or 16 Mbps Token Ring Local Area Networks (LANs) using coaxial cable or twisted copper wire. Most new LANs used twisted copper wire cable. Ethernet uses a contention method to enable workstations attached to the same cable to share the data bandwidth on the cable.

Fast Ethernet

The IEEE has set out the aims of the 100 Mbps Ethernet LAN standard [Rame93] as follows :

- Line Rate of 100 Mbps.
- 100 metre distances permissible to the Ethernet Hub.
- Category 3 to 5 twisted pair operation.
- Equivalent error rates to 10 Mbps.
- Compliance with electromagnetic compatibility standards.
- Simultaneous support of 10 Mbps and 100 Mbps.
- Use of RJ-45 connector.

FDDI

The Fiber Distributed Data Interface (FDDI) [Minoli93] was the only standards-based technology operating at 100 Mbps for some time.

ISO-Ethernet

Architecturally, ISO-Ethernet, also known as IEEE 802.9 [Minoli94] is a multiplexing of four separate channels of information : a 10 Mbps packet channel (P) with the IEE 802.3 CSMA/CD media access protocol, 6.144 Mbps of isochronous information organized in 96 B channels of 64 kbps each, one 64 kbps D-channel for signaling, and a 96 kbps M-channel for maintenance.

Proprietary LANs

To enable video conferencing over existing LAN cabling some vendors have adopted proprietary solutions which replace the existing network hardware, but retain the cable infrastructure.

WAN Network Services

Frame Relay

Frame relay is a connection-oriented service operating at n x 64 kbps or 2.048 Mbps. It has evolved from X.25 packet switching and aims to reduce network delays, protocol overheads and equipment cost.

SMDS

The Switched Multi-megabit Data Service (SMDS) [King93] is a new switched broadband data service. One of the first users of the service in the UK have been SuperJANET sites. SMDS provides a switched connectionless data service at speeds of 34 Mbps (at present) for connection of LANs.

Integrated Services Digital Network (ISDN)

In the real world the delivery of multimedia requires a widespread network capable of delivering at high data rates. The current implementation of ISDN in the narrow band form is the best access and delivery medium available. ISDN is seen by many in the industry as the ramp through which multimedia networking will gain acceptance. The installed base of ISDN is growing rapidly (30,000 line per month in Germany). ISDN is able to provide connections throughout the world. In Europe the Euro-ISDN agreements between operators is valuable.

Multimedia and Internet Protocols

Existing Internet Protocols

The Internet is a more of phenomena than a network, but is important when discussing multimedia because a popular Internet Application, the World Wide Web is capable of accessing and displaying multimedia formats such as pictures, audio and video. The current Internet has thrived and grown due to the existence of TCP implementations for a wide variety of classes of host computers.

New Internet Protocols

A successor to the current version of TCP/IP Version 4 is being discussed. While some of motivation behind this is due to the need to increase the address space available, the opportunity is also being taken to review the need to increase the performance of Internet protocols, for multimedia applications.

Multimedia Programming Interfaces

- Design Issues
- Multimedia Communication Models
- First Implementations

Networked Multimedia Application Design

Real Time Multimedia Applications

- Desk Top Conferencing
- Video Conferencing or Videophone products
- Video Mail
- Image Viewing

Non-Real Time Multimedia Applications

- File Transfer
- World Wide Web
- Multimedia Mail

Networking Costs

The cost of broadband circuits such as SMDS and ATM are an

unknown quantity. Most of these systems are still at the trial stage. However, the cost of sending information over a WAN is likely to remain high.

Conclusion

Network Evolution in the Short Term

While TV networks have existed for sometime, data networks are only just beginning to approach their capabilities. Distribution of multimedia in the same way that TV is distributed is simply not possible on existing data networks.

Future Networks

The very different environments of wide area networks and local area network have led the development of computer communications. Wide-area networking is high cost, low speed, high error rate and large delay. The design of the switch was dictated by the need to manage and allocate the bandwidth effectively.

References

1. www.agocg.ac.uk
2. www.techonline.com
3. www.qosboxcs.virginia.edu
4. www.ctr.columbia.edu

Multimedia Networking

P. Radha and N. Sudha Bhuvaneswari

Introduction

The buzzword Multimedia Networking started late in 1994 with a heavy investment on cost and time. Trials of video on demand are continuing but roll out of services have been delayed. In education multimedia learning packages have been mounted on file-servers, use of the World Wide Web is widespread, and some video conferencing is being used.

So networking of computer-based multimedia is possible though network delivery of multimedia through the broadcast television system has been available since the 1950's. The difference now is that the information that has previously been presented on radio, TV, or in books, is now being presented or can be accessed by computer networks. This paper briefly explains the various technical requirements, architectures and user expectations for Multimedia Networking.

Networked Multimedia Applications

Multimedia can roughly be defined as a technology that enables humans to use computers capable of processing textual data, audio and video, still pictures, and animation. Applications range over entertainment, education, and information provision, design, e.g. CAD/CAM, co-operative working such as video conferencing, application sharing, remote working and virtual reality experiences.

Multimedia applications for computers have been developed for single computing platforms such as the PC, Apple Mac and games machines. Widening of access to multimedia sources and potential markets in multimedia, video and information are commercial driving force for networking multimedia. The reality of networking multimedia is the characteristics of multimedia that make heavy demands on storage and transmission systems.

User Requirements for Multimedia

The users do expect quite a lot from this Multimedia networking that includes :

1. Human-Computer Interface
2. Access, Delivery, Scheduling and Recording time
3. Interactivity
4. Educational Requirements and Cost

Technical Requirements for Multimedia Networks

Compression

Compression algorithms and techniques are critical to the viability of multimedia networking. Compression techniques depend on algorithms implemented in software or hardware.

Storage

Multimedia requires high capacity storage systems. But over and above the continuous improvement in storage capacity of magnetic and optical devices multimedia raises issues relating to the format in which audio, video and data should be stored.

Bandwidth

Multimedia applications, particularly those using video and images demand large bandwidth. However, bandwidth for the foreseeable future will be limited. The limitations arise from the cost of installing optical fiber transmission, terminal equipment complexity and speed, tariffing regimes, switching speeds, and increasing number of users sharing equipment and networks. Consequently users and applications need to formulate their demands so that bandwidth is used appropriately and efficiently.

Quality of Service

The availability of multimedia resources places new demands on the service that a network must provide. The most important of these are the bit error rate, the packet or cell loss, delay and delay variation.

Platform Support

Multimedia also makes new demands on the workstations used to reproduce audio and video. Processor speeds operating system, displays, storage medium and network interfaces and application must all be capable of handling multimedia. The Multimedia PC specification defines a 33 MHz 386SX processor with 4 Mbytes of RAM, a VGA graphics card, a sound card, a large hard disc and standard peripherals as being the minimum level of machine needed. There is no ideal platform for multimedia.

Inter-operability

The inter-operability of platform hardware, networks and applications and multimedia formats is a major issue for multimedia users. Providing networking standards are implemented on each platform, inter-operability between different platforms can be achieved. It is more difficult to enable applications to use different networks, and to integrate multimedia applications in a modular fashion. Recently bodies like the Interactive Multimedia Association (IMA) and the Multimedia Communications Forum (MMCF) [MCF] have been formed to develop technical solutions to multimedia inter-operability.

Compression Standards

JPEG Compression

The JPEG (Joint Picture Experts Group) [ISO10] is the first international digital compression standard for multi-level continuous tone still, black and white or colour images. It typically compresses images to 1/10 or 1/50 of their original size. It is based on use of a discrete cosine transform and requires same level of processing to compress and decompress an image.

MPEG Compression

The MPEG (Motion Picture Experts Group) [ISO11] has so far defined two compression algorithms—MPEG-1 and MPEG-2. A common misconception is that MPEG-2 is a replacement for MPEG-1. Each algorithm has been specifically targeted at different bit rates. MPEG-2 runs at higher bit rates than MPEG-1. MPEG-1 chips on the market provide about a 200 : 1 compression to yield VHS quality video at 1.2 to 1.5 Mbps.

Multimedia and Internet Protocols

Existing Internet Protocols

The system of connected networks, which comprise the Internet, has also been used to carry live audio and video. Extensions to the TCP/IP protocols currently used have been proposed as Real Time Protocols (RTP). Broadcast of audio and video has taken place on the Multicast Backbone (MBONE), by allocating higher priority to audio and video information from within routers.

The MBONE is being developed as a technology for low cost multimedia. Multicasting within MBONE enables multiple destinations to share the same information without replication. Audio and video on the MBONE must still compete with other traffic on parts of the network. This limits the quality of both the voice and video obtainable. Special purpose transport protocols have been developed that includes protocols such as

UDP (user datagram protocol), RDP (reliable datagram protocol), NVP (network voice protocol), PVP (packet video protocol) and XTP (Xpress Transfer Protocol). Voice can be multicast over XTP/FDDI. By using XTP rate control, full-motion, full-screen compressed video is delivered at a constant 1.2 Mbps, over switched-hub Ethernet to work stations. This network delivers at least 10 simultaneous video streams. To support multimedia features will be needed such as policy-based routing, flows, resource reservation, type-of-service and quality-of-service.

Multimedia Programming Interfaces

Design Issues

There are conflicting realities to consider when designing a common multimedia architecture :

- ➢ It is desirable to have a single architecture or protocol stack for multimedia and networks.
- ➢ In practice there will always be more than one protocol stack.
- ➢ Even within a single successful architecture forces of evolution will lead to periods of multiple protocols.

Designers of common multimedia architecture face three problems : At what level in the protocol stack should common interfaces be provided? Should the network level be the common point, able to handle many different requirements, or should a common transport layer be able to request the service of many networks? Secondly, any common architecture will have to recognize the existence and be able to operate with other architecture sets. Thirdly, each architecture will have to share resources at some point in the chain of memory, processing, network requests, and transport of packets on the network.

Achieving inter-operability and resource sharing is difficult. Attempts to achieve inter-operability and resource sharing may bring the multiple architectures into some level of harmonization, even if it is just to simplify the problems of inter-operability and sharing. Together with the normal process of evolution, there may then be lead to changes in one of the architectures, as well as the other suites. Thus, the need for new technologies leads to a natural process of diversion. The process of harmonization leads to conversion.

The Internet community have decided that there should be single next generation Internet (IPng) protocol and are developing methods to ease the transition from IPv4 to IPng. The intention is to promote different approaches at the applications layer and let the users' market decide which one is best for their needs. The Internet community have therefore staked a claim to the network layer, and it will be up to multimedia users and developers to decide if a similar common layer or architecture below multimedia applications is of benefit to users and achievable.

Multimedia Communication Models

The Multimedia Communications Forum (MMCF) is developing a reference model for multimedia architecture to allow easy application development for independent software producers. The first result of this work will be Transport Services Interface, which will be a type of multimedia WinSocket specification, able to negotiate bandwidth, delay, priority and other quality of service parameters required by multimedia. AT&T, Intel, Motorola, National Semiconductor, and Seimens are some of the companies involved. The MMCF work is intended to complement the work of the Interactive Multimedia Association that has initiated a compatibility project to develop solutions to multimedia cross platform compatibility issues.

The objectives of the MMCF Architecture Reference Model are to provide :

- End to end networked multimedia communication solutions independent of applications and transport technologies.
- Extensible Application Programming Interfaces and protocol infrastructure to support end to end multi-vendor inter-operability.
- Support horizontal and vertical integration of applications.
- Support distributed networking and computing architecture.
- Easy application development for independent software developers.

The MMCF have developed a concept of Middleware as part of the Multimedia Architecture Reference Model. Middleware is a suite of applications, functions and programming interfaces that reside above the transport level in the OSI stack, but below the application level. The interface from the Middleware domain to the application and transport levels will be via application programming interfaces (APIs). The intention is that through the use of these application programming interfaces and middleware 'software' that flexible, inter-operable multimedia communication applications can be built.

Networked Multimedia Application Design

Real Time Multimedia Applications

A number of real time applications are available for use over networks based on computers, which are capable of using audio or video. The two networks over which applications have been developed to date include ISDN, Local Area Networks, and Local Area Networks connected over high speed ATM or SMDS connections.

Desk Top Conferencing

Desk Top Conferencing is a means of working with a remote user on their computer running the same application. A voice conversation between the two users can be held at the same time.

Video Conferencing and Products

VidiMac for the Apple Mac based on the Planet ISDN card, which uses motion JPEG techniques. IBM, Fujitsu, and Olivetti have video conferencing products based on the BT VC8000 PC card. The IBM product is called Screen Call, the Fujitsu is called Team Vision, and the Olivetti is called PCC. All three use the services of the VC8000 card in different ways.

Video Mail

Video mail can be delivered via X.400 mail, or Internet mail with MIME extensions for file attachments. Obviously transmission times can be longer. An appropriate viewer (hardware or software) is then needed to replay the mail.

Image Viewing

An image database is considered to be a useful application for attachment to existing databases, or for stand-alone use. Products have been design for both general use and access via ISDN. Most products are designed not as stand-alone image viewers but as part of an information system or kiosk for tourism or specialist applications.

Information Kiosks

Information kiosks are starting to appear with multimedia features. Information kiosks have commercial applications in tourism, government information and education. Extensive multimedia material can be held on local hard discs and updated at regular intervals, manually or via a network connection such as ISDN.

Distance Learning

Distance learning applications can held on a network file server. They can then be accessed from the local LAN or by ISDN. The response of a distance learning application running over ISDN instead of a local LAN will depend on its design and the amount of visual material.

Non-Real Time Multimedia Applications

A number of non-real time multimedia applications are available for use over networks that can support audio or video.

Future Networks

The very different environments of wide area networks and local area network have led the development of computer communications. Wide-area networking is high cost, low speed, high error rate, and has huge delay. Both conventional circuit switching and packet switching are difficult to implement at higher data rates. In most current designs for local area networks, where bandwidth is not expensive, simplified addressing and switching has been employed at the expense of the effective use of the bandwidth.

Application	*ISDN*	*LAN's*
File Transfer	Various standards	Internet or OSI standards
Information Services with Multimedia Contents	Proprietary or via WWW or WWW technology	Any N/W information system
Multimedia Mail	Based on H.320 video conferencing	X.400 and MIME electronic mail with video content
Image databases	Proprietary systems	File Server access
Information Kiosks	Proprietary systems	

FIG. 14.1
Application Standards

Fiber optics has made high-speed information transmission possible. The problem is how to distribute or switch this information when the intelligence needed to make switching decisions is operating in comparatively low speed electronics. For optical switching to be possible the switch must use very simple switching logic, require very little storage and operate on packets of a significant size. For circuit switching to be efficient at high speeds, it must provide very fast circuit set-up and teardown to support the busty nature of most computer communication. In the future, the host may see the network as a message-passing system, or as memory. At the same time, the network may use classic packets, wavelength division, or space division switching. Future network protocols will need to provide a secure connection independent of the networks for applications to use. The implementation of Quality of Service requests flowing in one direction from application to network is a partial solution. It would be more useful if a two-way dialogue could be established between applications and the network(s) in a dynamic fashion. Implicit in managing this request is the presence of a more controlled allocation of resources. When data calls are mixed with new services such as video streams unless these are separately recognized and controlled, there is little reason to believe that effective service can be delivered unless the network is very lightly loaded.

As networks get faster, bottlenecks move into the host. Network adapters have a crucial role to play with speed. The future network adapter may be viewed as a memory interconnects, tying the memory in one host to another. The integration of the network adapter into the operating system with the transport level will be implemented largely, if not entirely, in the network adapter, would provide the host with reliable memory-to-memory transfer at memory speeds with a minimum of interrupt processing, bus overhead and packet processing.

Networked Multimedia—An Overview

K.S. Maharasan, G. Ravi and J. Lenin

Introduction

Business organizations has benefited a lot from Client/Server Computing domain of Information Technology. Client/server computing has enhanced users' productivity, revolutionized computer networking, and restructured the computer industry.

Networked Multimedia is another new technology, that will have a greater impact on business computing. Networked multimedia computer applications will significantly affect users and network managers and have a tremendous impact on computing and network infrastructures.

Multimedia networking applications such as video-conferencing, distance learning, kiosks, multimedia books, multimedia mail, and simulations can add significant value to today's businesses. Adding these applications to the existing data network is a cost-effective way of obtaining these benefits.

This paper discusses the basics of multimedia, user requirements, application design issues and network infrastructure requirements for multimedia networks.

Computer Network

Collection of two or more computers and other peripherals, using a medium with an intention of sharing resources and information by following some protocols.

Multimedia

Multimedia is the combined use of several media, such as text, graphics, movies, slides, music, and lighting, especially for the purpose of education or entertainment.

Networked Multimedia

Networked multimedia is to build the multimedia on network and distributed systems, so different users on different machines can share image, sound, video, voice and many other features and to communicate with each under these tools.

Need for Networked Multimedia

With networked multimedia, people can share the multimedia resource and communicate, work collaboratively, so they may produce more effective results and save more time and money. In the recent past, multimedia has emerged as a powerful tool used to support applications such as training, business presentations, and marketing kiosks. However, since most of these applications were stand-alone (which means, of course, expensive), to attract the mainstream user—the business user—they need to be more effective and affordable. Therefore, making move to networked or distributed multimedia becomes an inevitable trend today. Users on different machines at various locations can share multimedia data.

Multimedia—Application Tools

Multimedia requires the following application tools : authoring tools, graphic tools, animation tools, audio tools and video tools. Application services are also required; they are common user access services, object management facilities and data conversion services.

The Multimedia Industry

The multimedia industry consists of four tiers as shown in Figure 15.1.

- The top tier consists of the multimedia content providers. Ex. : The news industry, the television industry, and the entertainment industry. Recently companies that are producing multimedia CD-ROMs have started using networks as a vehicle for delivering their content to a larger set of consumers.
- The second tier constitutes the multimedia application developers. Applications include distance learning, desktop videoconferencing, workgroup collaboration, multimedia kiosks, entertainment, and imaging.
- The third tier consists of the multimedia platform builders. Some of them are Silicon Graphics, Sun, Intel and Apple. Apart from the multimedia capabilities available in the stand-alone machines, there is a growing demand for access to multimedia applications across a network.
- The fourth multimedia industry tier is the network infrastructure. There are two very different networking environments that will use

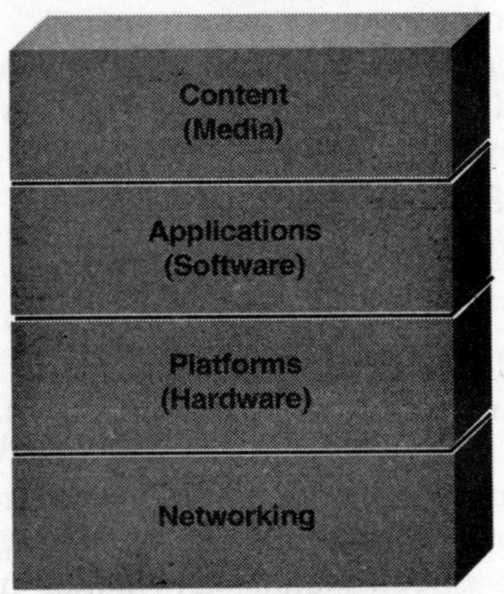

FIG. 15.1
Multimedia Industry Structure

multimedia applications : today's business networks and the emerging public networks. Networking of multimedia will initially occur in businesses over the private networking infrastructure followed by public networks such as the Internet for home, education, business, and entertainment.

User Requirements and Issues

Human-Computer Interface : A well designed human-computer interface, which may be screen or audio based is well accepted. The interface should be user-friendly in nature.

Access, Delivery, Scheduling and Recording

On demand access times to computer information need to be below one second to be usable in real time. Alternatively the delivery of information at a later time is acceptable if it can be scheduled, as in a TV broadcast schedule. Multimedia broadcasts can be recorded for future reference.

Interactivity

Interactivity, meaning the ability to participate in a video or audio process on a computer, by changing its behaviour or appending comments has become very important in multimedia.

The level of interactivity should be similar to the interaction existing in a school exercise book, or a laboratory experiment. Network plays a prominent role in providing interactivity, and for some applications the sense of interactivity is aided by the ability to deliver a moving picture, or a sound very quickly, so that a sense of two-way human participation can be generated. Real time video conferencing is an example.

Network Requirements

A network must provide bandwidth, consistent quality of service, and multipoint packet delivery to support multimedia applications. Compression algorithms and techniques are critical to the viability of multimedia networking. Compression should be done without any data loss.

Quality of Service

The availability of multimedia resources places new demands on the service that a network must provide. The most important of these are the bit error rate, the packet or cell loss, delay and delay variation. Network resources need to be committed to multimedia data streams to accommodate the peak bit rate and mean bit rate of the data stream.

Platform Support : Multimedia also makes new demands on the workstations used to reproduce audio and video. Processor speeds, operating systems, displays, storage medium and network interfaces and application must all be capable of handling multimedia. Plug-in cards will solve the problem of multimedia requirements to some extent. But Multimedia enabled motherboards is the best solution.

Design Issues

Designers of common multimedia architecture face three problems :

1. Place for the Interface in the protocol stack.
2. Inter-operability between the architecture models provided by various vendors.
3. Resource sharing in the networked environment.

Real Time Multimedia Applications

A number of real time applications are available for use over networks based on computers, which are capable using audio or video. The two networks over which applications have been developed include ISDN, Local Area Networks, and Local Area Networks connected over high speed ATM or SMDS connections.

Desk Top Conferencing

Desk Top Conferencing is a means of working with a remote user on their computer running the same application. Typically a drawing or spreadsheet will be transmitted via the ISDN line. A voice conversation between the two users can be held at the same time. Within desktop conferencing remote control of a computer is possible. Since these applications must reproduce the screen of a PC on another, the speed of the connection between the two computers is important.

Video Conferencing

Until recently the only implementations of video over the telephone network have been poor quality videophones or very expensive video conferencing for executives.

Video Mail

Video mail can be delivered via X.400 mail, or Internet mail with MIME extensions for file attachments. Obviously transmission times can be longer. An appropriate viewer (hardware or software) is then needed to replay the mail.

Image Viewing

An image database is considered to be a useful application for attachment to existing databases, or for stand-alone use. Products have been design for both general use and access via ISDN. Most products are designed not as stand-alone image viewers but as part of an information system or kiosk for tourism or specialist applications.

Information Kiosks

Information kiosks are starting to appear with multimedia features. Information kiosks have commercial applications in tourism, government information and education. Extensive multimedia material can be held on local hard discs and updated at regular intervals, manually or via a network connection such as ISDN.

Distance Learning

Distance learning applications can be stored on a network file server and accessed from the local LAN or by ISDN. The response of a distance learning application running over ISDN instead of a local LAN will depend on its design and the amount of visual material. Transfer of audio material will also take time and require a remote workstation set-up for audio playback.

Non-Real Time Multimedia Applications

A number of non-real time multimedia applications are available for use over networks which can support audio or video. Some of them are :

- File Transfer Protocols, and
- Multimedia Mail.

Design of Networked Multimedia Applications

A file transfer, as electronic mail, or in real time, can transfer multimedia depending upon the situations.

A file transfer can be initiated manually or automatically at any time. If done in advance of the anticipated time of use of the application, quite large files can be transferred. Electronic mail systems are increasingly multimedia aware. Both X.400 and the Internet MIME standards can deliver audio, images, pictures and video. The recipient of the mail will of course need to have software integrated into the mail system, which can recognise these data types and play them. Electronic mail can take longer to deliver than a file transfer, but the advantage is, it can be used at any time in the absence of the participants.

A real time multimedia connection is the most demanding multimedia access mode. File transfer and electronic mail do not require a sophisticated, high capacity network. But real time multimedia demands the correct information at the right time. Users expecting real time pictures or sound are intolerant of delays in reception.

Conclusion

Multimedia networking applications such as video-conferencing, distance learning, kiosks, multimedia books, multimedia mail, and simulations can add significant value to today's businesses. Adding these applications to the existing data network is a cost-effective way of obtaining these benefits.

The characteristics of multimedia make heavy demands on storage and transmission systems. Data compression can be used to reduce the demands of multimedia, particularly of video and audio on these systems, but usually at the expense of some loss in the detail compared with the source and at extra cost.

The ways in which users or participants in multimedia sessions access multimedia or connect with others have important consequences for the storage and transmission systems. The cost of transmitting multimedia information will determine the pace of development of networked multimedia applications.

The availability of standards for multimedia networking, particularly for inter-working between applications, the development of networked applications, and inter-working between networks are essential to reduce the complexity and level of skill required in using multimedia.

Reference

1. John, Louis Molina, Multimedia Production, Planning and Delivery.

CHAPTER

16

Multimedia Networks—Traffic Characterization Concepts for VBR Video

G.S. Kausalya, N.C. Geetha and S. Sampath

Introduction

A network that offers deterministic, i.e., worst-case, quality-of-service (QoS) guarantees to variable-bit-rate (VBR) video must provide a resource reservation mechanism that allocates bandwidth, buffer space, and other resources for each video stream. Such a resource reservation scheme must be carefully designed, otherwise network resources are wasted. A key component for the design of a resource reservation scheme is the traffic characterization method that specifies the traffic arrivals on a video stream. The traffic characterization should accurately describe the actual arrivals so that a large number of streams can be supported; but it must also map directly into efficient traffic policing mechanisms that monitor arrivals on each stream. In this study, we present a fast and accurate traffic characterization method for stored VBR video in networks with a deterministic service. We use this approximation to obtain a traffic characterization that can be efficiently policed by a small number of leaky buckets.

With the advent of integrated-services packet switching networks, it has become feasible to design multimedia networks that can transmit compressed variable-bit-rate (VBR) video in real time. Since video has strict quality-of-service (QoS) requirements, a multimedia network must maintain a resource reservation scheme that can allocate network resources for each video stream. In this paper we consider resource reservation schemes for QoS networks with a deterministic service, that is, a service that can provide worst-case delay guarantees to all packets on a video stream. Since over-allocating resources to a stream results in low network utilization, a resource reservation scheme must be carefully designed. The amount of resources to be reserved for a video stream is largely dependent on the traffic characterization method used to describe the traffic on a video stream. For a deterministic service we require a deterministic traffic characterization method that gives an upper bound on the traffic. The selection of particular traffic characterization method must trade-off between the following design goals :

1. *Accuracy* : The traffic characterization method should describe the actual traffic on a stream as accurately as possible. A pessimistic characterization will overestimate the resource requirements of a stream, resulting in poor network utilization. Recently, several traffic characterization methods for VBR video have been proposed that can express the complex timely correlations of VBR video sequences.
2. *Simplicity* : Traffic policing mechanisms which ensure that all traffic submitted to the network conforms to its traffic characterization must be able to operate at the speed of the transmission links. Therefore, the traffic characterization method must be simple enough so that fast traffic policing algorithms can be designed.
3. *Speed* : The effort to compute a traffic characterization for a video stream must be reasonably small. While traffic characterization for stored video can be computed off-line, networks that offer dynamic renegotiation of traffic parameters require availability of fast traffic characterization algorithms.

Possibly, the single most important approach to traffic characterization of VBR video is derived from the so-called leaky bucket which describes traffic in terms of rate and burstiness parameters. With leaky bucket traffic characterizations, the worst-case traffic on a stream is given in terms of piecewise-linear functions. Since each leaky bucket can be implemented with a single counter and a single timer, the traffic-policing algorithm for a single leaky bucket satisfies the demand for simplicity.

In this paper, a leaky bucket is equivalent to the Generic Cell Rate Algorithm (GCRA). Up to a dozen leaky buckets were needed to accurately characterize an MPEG-I video stream. Since practical considerations limit the number of available leaky buckets to a small value, e.g., the limit is two for ATM streams, methods are needed that yield an accurate VBR traffic characterization, yet, with only a small number of leaky buckets. In this study, we will show that concave piecewise-linear functions can be used for traffic characterization of VBR video traffic while satisfying all the goals of accuracy, simplicity, and speed.

We present an algorithm that takes as input a VBR video sequence and generates the parameters for a specified number of leaky buckets. Using empirical examples, we will demonstrate that three leaky buckets are sufficient to produce traffic characterizations leading to utilizations within 91% of the best possible characterization. The computation time necessary to generate a traffic characterization for a feature length movie is less than a second, thus, satisfying the demand for a fast characterization method.

This paper is based on an observation of a characteristic of MPEG video traces. Studying 'best-possible' time-invariant bounds, so-called empirical envelopes, of several 30-minute MPEG traces, it is found that the first few hundred data points of the empirical envelope can provide a traffic characterization that has almost the same accuracy as the entire envelope with 40,000 points. In other words for the purposes of deterministic traffic characterization, complete information on a video trace is retained in very few parameters.

The traffic characterization method in this paper will be evaluated against existing methods that have applied leaky buckets for VBR video characterizations. Note, however, that most methods select the traffic parameters according to network resource availability. Also, most studies use only a single leaky bucket. In the choice of the traffic parameters depends on the relative availability of unallocated bandwidth and buffer space. There are two heuristic algorithms that select leaky bucket parameters to approximate an "ideal" probabilistic traffic characterization, the so-called time-quantile function. The heuristic algorithms take an approach to traffic characterization that is similar to ours, in that they first determine a function that describes the traffic on a stream and then choose parameters based on this function. Finally, we want to point to studies that have explored the benefits of reducing the burstiness of VBR video traffic by either (1) shaping the traffic by spacing packets before submitting them to the network, or (2) sending packets early with respect to their playback time at the receiving application via workahead smoothing. These techniques involve modification of the traffic that is submitted to the network by buffering at the sender, receiver, or a combination of both. While shaping and smoothing techniques have been shown to increase the achievable network utilization, these methods are orthogonal to the traffic characterization problem. Note that even after traffic is shaped or smoothed, a characterization method must be available to determine an accurate and policable characterization for the traffic submitted to the network.

Sub-additive Traffic Characterizations

Let A denote the actual traffic on a stream, where A[t; t + t] denotes the traffic arrivals in time interval [t; t + t]. Then, a worst-case characterization of the traffic A is given by a characterization function A* which provides an upper bound on A. A characterization function A* should satisfy two important properties, namely, time-invariance and sub-additivity a function A* provides a time-invariant bound for A if for all times t > = 0 and t > = 0 the following holds :

A[t; t + t] < = A*

Fundamental Limits and Trade-offs of Providing Deterministic Guarantees to VBR Video Traffic.

Future packet-switching integrated services networks must support applications with diverse traffic characteristics and performance requirements. Of the many traffic classes in integrated services networks, delay-sensitive Variable Bit Rate (VBR) video traffic poses a unique challenge. Since the required service is delay-sensitive, the network must support a resource reservation scheme [3] that allocates network resources for each VBR video stream. However, the burstiness of VBR video traffic makes it difficult to determine the amount of resources required. On one hand, if resources are reserved according to the average rates of the VBR video sources, unacceptable delays or packet losses may result when the sources are transmitting near their peak rates. On the other hand, if resource reservations are based on sources' peak rates, the network may be under-utilized most of the time. In this study, we investigate utilization limits achievable in packet-switching networks with deterministic service guarantees to delay-sensitive VBR video traffic. A deterministic service ensures that no packets are dropped or delayed beyond their guaranteed delay bound. Such a service requires admission control tests to determine if the network has sufficient resources to support a new connection without degrading the service of existing connections. The tests for a new connection are based on a characterization of the expected traffic for the new connection. If accepting or admitting the new connection may result in violations of service guarantees for any existing connection, the connection is not established. For admitted connections, the network performs traffic policing, that is, it ensures that the admitted connections adhere to the traffic characterization given to the network for the admission control tests. If a connection's traffic is policed by the network, the traffic in excess of its specified characterization may not be permitted to enter the network. A key challenge of incorporating VBR video traffic into networks with service guarantees lies in the difficulty of finding an appropriate traffic characterization that captures the dynamics of the source. While such stochastic models of a source have the advantage that they may be used to potentially achieve higher network utilization via statistical multiplexing, they have several important disadvantages. First, it is difficult to implement a policing mechanism that enforces a stochastic traffic characterization. Moreover, most stochastic models for characterizing video traffic are either not powerful enough to capture the burstiness and the timely correlations of a video source, or they are too complex for practical implementation. Finally, since stochastic approaches to VBR traffic characterization provide only statistical guarantees, they cannot be applied to deterministic network services. For such reasons, in this work we consider only deterministic traffic models that characterize VBR traffic in terms of a worst-case description. It is a common belief that such a worst-case approach necessitates allocation of network resources according to sources' peak rates, necessarily leading to low network utilization for bursty traffic. However, several recent works show that this conventional wisdom is not correct and that peak-rate allocation is not required even for providing deterministic service.

This paper analyzes the fundamental limits in providing deterministic performance guarantees to VBR video. Such a study has become feasible with a set of recently developed tight, i.e., necessary and sufficient, admission control tests for networks that employ Earliest Deadline-First and Static Priority scheduling disciplines. We present an optimal characterization of VBR video traffic for a deterministic service using what we term empirical envelopes. Empirical envelopes represent the most accurate, time-invariant, deterministic characterization of a traffic source. Using this optimal characterization, together with Earliest-Deadline-First packet scheduling and the exact admission control tests, we provide insights into the highest achievable utilization for VBR video sources. For example, a realistic traffic characterization must be easily policable by the network. Furthermore, the traffic characterization should be concise so that the traffic of each source can be described with a small number of parameters. The impact of selecting easily policable and concise traffic characterizations on the utilization limits of the deterministic service. Also there are impacts of selecting simpler packet schedulers, such as Static Priority and First-Come-First-Served, on the achievable network utilization. In multimedia networks, the important concepts are : network components necessary to offer a service with deterministic delay bounds and a method to generate an optimal traffic characterization, the empirical envelope, for VBR video sources, an algorithm to approximate the empirical envelope by an easily policable deterministic traffic model, traces of MPEG-encoded VBR video traffic to empirically evaluate the limits of the deterministic approach as well as the above mentioned trade-offs.

Components of a Deterministic Network Service

For a network to provide deterministic performance guarantees on throughput, delay, delay-jitter, and loss, it must be able to tightly control certain resources. Admission control tests and policing mechanisms are effective means to control the number of connections as well as the traffic from each connection; they thus determine the degree to which network resources are utilized. Both admission control tests and policing mechanisms are influenced by three components : (1) the traffic model used for the characterization of the worst-case traffic from a connection, (2) the scheduling discipline at the network multiplexers, and (3) the accuracy of the admission control tests. In this section, we review the trade-offs involved in the selection of these components and their impact on a deterministic network service.

Deterministic Traffic Models

A traffic model for a deterministic service has several fundamental requirements. First, the model must be a worst-case characterization of the source to provide an absolute upper bound on a source's packet arrivals. Second, the model must be parameterized so that a source can efficiently specify its traffic characterization to the network. Next, the model should characterize the traffic as accurately as possible so that the admission control algorithms do not over-estimate the resources required by the connection. Finally, the model must be policable so that the network can enforce a source's traffic characterization. Packet Scheduling in a connection-oriented packet-switched network, packets from a particular connection traverse the network on a fixed path of switches and links. Each switch has a packet scheduler for each outgoing link. Since the packet scheduler can transmit only one packet at a time, it maintains a queue containing all packets waiting for transmission. Here we consider the following well-known scheduling disciplines at a packet scheduler for a set N of connections.

First-Come-First-Served (FCFS), Static Priority (SP), and Earliest-Deadline-First (EDF). Each of these disciplines has been investigated for use in bounded delay services. First-Come-First-Served schedulers transmit all packets in the order of their arrival. Since the maximum delay in a FCFS scheduler is the same for all connections j 2 N, all connections have an identical delay bound d. An EDF scheduler selects packets for transmission in increasing order of packet deadlines, where packet deadlines are calculated as the sum of the arrival time and the delay bound of a packet. The selection of a particular scheduling discipline for a packet scheduler involves a trade-off between the need to support a large number of connections with diverse delay requirements and the need for simplicity in the scheduling operations. For example, while a FCFS scheduler can be easily implemented, it can effectively support only one delay bound for all connections. On the other extreme, while an EDF scheduler can support a different delay bound for each connection, the scheduling operations of EDF are complex since they involve a search operation for the packet with the shortest deadline.

Admission Control Tests

While the number of admission control tests can be large, including tests for availability of transmission capacity, CPU power, buffer space, etc., the most crucial admission test in a network with a deterministic service is the delay bound test. The delay bound test verifies that, for all connections, the delay of each packet is less than its required delay bound. Most other admission control tests, including those that verify throughput and delay-jitter guarantees, can be directly derived from the delay bound test. Note that the complexity of a delay bound test depends on both the scheduling algorithm and the desired accuracy of the test. For certain packet schedulers the calculations required for accurate delay bound tests can be computationally expensive. Thus, less accurate but fast delay bound tests are often desirable.

Evaluation of Design Choices for Deterministic Services

Traces of MPEG-compressed video are used to empirically evaluate the fundamental limits and trade-offs of deterministic services. First, the theoretical limits on the efficiency of a deterministic network service are illustrated by combining the tightest traffic constraint function E, with an exact admission control test for the best packet scheduler, EDF.

Trade-offs in Packet Scheduling

There are three different packet schedulers namely EDF, SP and FCFS. The exact admission control tests are used with empirical envelopes as traffic constraint functions, and consider two types of connections : those carrying the Bride sequence and those carrying the Advertisements sequence. All connections of the same type have identical delay requirements.

A Comparison of Admission Control Tests

The achievable utilization is substantially lower. Since the admission test SP Sufficient 1 achieves utilization very close to that of SP Exact, it may be worthwhile to explore sufficient conditions for admission tests.

Summary of Trade-offs

Here we evaluate the utilization of a system that simultaneously considers practical choices for the traffic constraint functions, packet schedulers, and admission control tests, and compare this to the benchmark case. Advertisement connections requiring a delay bound of 30 msec and Bride connections requiring a delay bound of 50 msec, admission control tests are performed for the following two cases. The first benchmark case, shown by the upper curve, represents the case of exact analysis, EDF scheduling, and the empirical envelope for the source characterization. Reasonable network utilizations of 20% to 35% can be achieved for deterministic service to VBR video even when taking into account many practical considerations such as the need for simple schedulers, policing mechanisms, traffic models, and admission control tests. Moreover, these utilizations are considerably above the 15% utilization achievable with a peak rate allocation scheme.

Case Study : VBR Service with Deterministic Renegotiations

Dynamic resource allocation schemes are motivated by studies showing that correlations of VBR video traffic occur over long time scales due to the extended duration of scenes. By renegotiating the traffic characterization, for example, after each scene change, one can more accurately specify the traffic on a stream, resulting in a tighter characterization and hence higher network utilization. Since a renegotiations scheme requires multiple traffic characterizations for a single stream, a fast traffic characterization scheme such as the one described in this paper is needed to renegotiate traffic parameters. In this section we present and evaluate a new approach to dynamic resource allocation schemes, called deterministic renegotiations, that applies the traffic characterization method described in the previous sections.

Renegotiations of Traffic Characterizations

Most renegotiation schemes that have been proposed attempt to renegotiate the traffic characterization of a stream whenever its long-term rate changes significantly. Chong *et. al.* Address the problem of predicting the rate changes of a live video source. They consider both a recursive least-square method and a neural network approach for the prediction. A Renegotiated Constant Bit Rate (RCBR) scheme for both stored and live video which adds renegotiation and buffer monitoring to a static CBR service. They present algorithms for partitioning a video sequence into segments based on cost functions for both bandwidth allocation and number of renegotiations. Zhang and Knightly study a renegotiated VBR service for both stored and live video in. Their algorithm for stored video proceeds by identifying the worst-case segment of the video sequence, characterizing this worst-case segment, and then repeatedly applying the procedure on the remaining video sequence after this worst-case segment is removed. Although the above renegotiation schemes were shown to increase network utilization significantly, they all share a common drawback. Since these schemes calculate a traffic characterization independently for each video segment, it is possible that a stream needs to increase its resource allocation even if sufficient resources are not available. In such a scenario, the renegotiation requests cannot be accommodated, and either the video quality or the QoS must be compromised, resulting in a violation of the worst-case guarantees in a deterministic service. In contrast, the deterministic renegotiation scheme proposed here ensures that the traffic characterization for a stream does not increase. That is, renegotiation always involves a release of network resources. In this case, all renegotiation requests can be satisfied and deterministic QoS guarantees are always maintained.

Empirical Examples

The given examples are based on MPEG video sequences to demonstrate the impact of renegotiation on the achievable network utilization.

There are some factors to be addressed :

- What is the gain in utilization achievable with a deterministic negotiation scheme?
- What is the frequency of renegotiation needed to obtain a gain in network utilization?

Conclusion

The traffic characterization used for VBR video streams has a significant impact on the number of admissible streams in a multimedia network with a deterministic service. A method is presented for traffic characterization based on the empirical envelope of a video sequence that uses a two-step process. Using two MPEG-compressed video sequences, it is demonstrated that our characterization method determines accurate characterizations that admit a large number of streams. With the caveat that our experimental evaluation is based on only a small number of video traces, the experiments in this paper gave the following insights :

> For the MPEG video sequences as few as 200 parameters of the empirical envelope out of a total of 40,000 are sufficient to yield a characterization that admits the same number of streams as the empirical envelope. This observation suggests that the relevant information of an MPEG sequence is contained in a small segment of the empirical envelope. Using our heuristic algorithm, three leaky buckets were shown to be sufficient to admit nearly the same number of streams as the empirical envelope. Based on the good performance of our heuristic algorithm, it may not be worthwhile to investigate more complex algorithms for video characterization.

The deterministic resource renegotiation scheme that we describe is distinguished from previous approaches in that it is appropriate for services that provide constant video quality and deterministic QoS guarantees. Providing deterministic guarantees requires the network to allocate resources according to the worst-case scenario. A common belief is that this requires a peak-rate resource allocation scheme that would significantly under-utilize the network when sources have high peak-to-average-rate.

CHAPTER

17

Multimedia over Packet-Based Networks using VOIP Signaling Protocols

S. POORNA CHANDRIKA AND K.A. NEETHU

Introduction

The explosive growth of the Internet and the almost universal deployment of corporate LANs have made packet-based networks ubiquitous. Multimedia over packet-based networks has grown in rapid expansion and potential underlies the importance of an enabling and unifying standard such as H.323 which is an ITU-T recommendation for multimedia conferencing over packet-based networks. H.323 is broad and comprehensive in its scope yet flexible and practical in its applicability. This paper describes the components, protocols, and procedures in H.323; the challenges to the widespread adoption of H.323; the outlook for H.323 as a standard for multimedia conferencing.

The signaling protocols H.323 (ITU-T standard) and SIP (IETF standard). Then compared both the protocols and noted that although H.323 has more share of the market at present, but SIP is a much better protocol given its simplicity and scalability. Then also discussed MGCP, which is a gateway protocol whereby the Call Agent controls the signaling gateway. For both H.323 and SIP need some real-time protocols that does the actual transport. RTP and RTCP are used for the real-time transport and controlling. RTSP is used to provide controlled delivery of media streams. Some protocols that are required in conjunction with SIP so as to advertise the session (SAP) and give a description of the session (SDP). RSVP is used to reserve resources in the network and thereby provide some Quality of Service.

Voice over IP (VoIP) uses the Internet Protocol (IP) to transmit voice as packets over an IP network. So VoIP can be achieved on any data network that uses IP, like Internet, Intranets and Local Area Networks (LAN). Here the voice signal is digitized, compressed and converted to IP packets and then transmitted over the IP network. Signaling protocols are used to set-up and tear down calls, carry information required to locate users and negotiate capabilities. One of the main motivations for Internet telephony is the very low cost involved. Some other motivations are :

- ➢ Demand for multimedia communication, and
- ➢ Demand for integration of voice and data networks.

H.323 Protocol

H.323 is one of several video-conferencing recommendations issued by ITUT. The H.323 protocol stack is designed to operate above the transport layer of the underlying network. As such, H.323 can be used on top of any packet-based network transport like Ethernet, TCP/UDP/IP, ATM, and Frame Relay to provide real-time multimedia communication. H.323 uses the Internet Protocol (IP) for inter-network conferencing. The H.323 standard is designed to allow clients on H.323 networks to communicate with clients on the other video-conferencing networks.

Scope of H.323

H.323 is a broad and flexible recommendation. The scope of H.323, however, is much broader and encompasses inter-network multipoint conferencing among terminals that support not only audio but also video and data communication.

The scope of Recommendation H.323 can be summarized in the following broad categories :

- ➢ *Point-to-Point and Multipoint Conferencing Support* : H 323 conferences may be set-up between two or more clients without any specialized multipoint control software or hardware. However, when a multipoint control unit (MCU) is used H.323 supports a flexible topology for multipoint conferences.
- ➢ *Internetwork Interoperability* : H.323 clients are interoperable with switched circuit network conferencing clients such as those based on Recommendations.
- ➢ *Heterogeneousclient Capabilities* : H.323 client must support audio communication; video and data support is optional. This heterogeneity and flexibility does not make the clients incompatible.
- ➢ *Audio and Video Codecs* : H.323 specifies a required audio and video codec. However, there is no restriction on the use of other codecs and two clients can agree on any codec which is supported by both of them.

- *Management and Accounting Support* : H.323 calls can be restricted on a network based on the number of calls already in progress, bandwidth limitations, or time restrictions. Using these policies the network manager can manage H.323 traffic. Further, H.323 also provides accounting facilities that can be used for billing purposes.
- *Security* : H.323 provides authentication, integrity, privacy, and non-repudiation support.
- *Supplementary Services* : Recommendation H.323 recognizes the huge potential for applications based on IP telephony and multimedia. It provides a basic framework for development of such services. In version 2.0 of H.323, two services call transfer and call forwarding have been specified.

Importance of H.323

- *Standardization* : H.323 is a standard protocol that has been widely accepted. This will promote greater awareness, availability, and acceptability of multimedia conferencing over packet-based networks.
- *Inter-Networking* : H.323 bridges multimedia communications between packet-based and switched-circuit networks SCN.

H.323 makes possible the development of additional services such as e-mail, voice-mail, fax, call center functionality, and video-conferencing in an integrated environment.

- *Integrated Services* : H.323 makes possible the development of additional services such as e-mail, voice-mail, fax, call center functionality, and video-conferencing in an integrated environment.

H.323 Architecture : Components

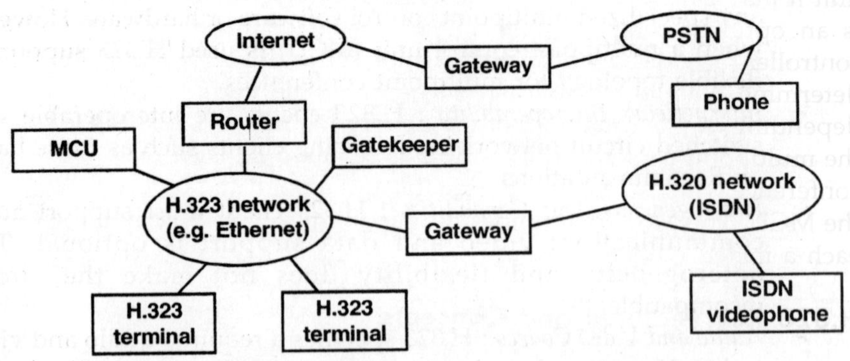

FIG. 17.1
Layout of H.323-enabled Inter-Network

In a general H.323 implementation four logical entities or components are required. These are terminals, gateways, gatekeepers, and multipoint control units (MCU). Terminals, gateways, and MCUs are collectively known as endpoints.

Terminal

A terminal, or a client, is an endpoint where H.323 data streams and signaling originate and terminate. It may be a multimedia PC with a H.323 compliant stack or a stand alone device such as a USB (Universal Serial Bus) IP telephone. A terminal must support audio communication; video and data communication support is optional.

Gateway

A gateway is an optional component in a H.323-enabled network. Through the provision of gateways in H.323 it is possible for H.323 terminals to inter-operate with other H.32X compliant conferencing terminals. A gateway provides data format translation, control signaling translation, audio and video codec translation, and call set-up and termination functionality on both sides of the network.

Gatekeeper

A gatekeeper is a very useful, but optional, component of an H.323-enabled network. Gatekeepers are needed to ensure reliable, commercially feasible communications. A gatekeeper is often referred to as the brain of the H.323. A gatekeeper provides several services to all endpoints in its zone. These services include Address translation, Admission and access control of endpoints, Bandwidth management and routing capability.

Multipoint Control Unit (MCU)

A multipoint control unit enables conferencing between three or more endpoints. It consists of a mandatory multipoint controller (MC) and zero or more multipoint processors (MP). Although the MCU is a separate logical unit it may be combined into a terminal, gateway, or gatekeeper. The MCU is an optional component of an H.323-enabled network. The multipoint controller provides a centralized location for multipoint call set-up. MC also determine whether to unicast or multicast the audio and video streams depending on the capability of the underlying network and the topology of the multipoint conference. The MCU is required in a centralized multipoint conference where each terminal establishes a point-to-point connection with the MCU. The MCU determines the capabilities of each terminal and sends each a mixed media stream.

H.323 Key Features and Concepts

- *Audio Codes* : H.323 specifies a series of audio codecs ranging in bit rates from 5.3-64 kb/s. Most H.323 terminals support G.723.1

which is much more efficient and produces good quality audio at 5.3 kb/s and 6.3 kb/s.

- *Video Codes* : Video communication is bandwidth intensive and bursty in nature. Therefore, efficient compression and decompression techniques are essential for good performance. Recommendation H.323 specifies two video codecs : H.261 and H.263.
- *Data Conferencing* : Real-time data conferencing capability is required for activities such as application sharing, whiteboard sharing, file transfer, fax transmission, and instant messaging. Recommendation T.120 provides this optional capability to H.323.
- *Multipoint Conferencing Support* : The MCU handles the mixing and switching of data in a similar manner to that used for video and audio.
- *Network and Platform Independence* : T.120 operates on top of the transport layer of the underlying network. As such, it is transparent and independent of the network hardware and software.
- *Interoperability* : T.120 is referenced in all the H.32X conferencing standards. This cross-referencing, together with the network and platform independence, ensures a high degree of interoperability at the application level.
- *Multicast Support* : T.120 supports multicast of data streams in multicast-capable networks. This support is flexible with mixed unicast and multicast also possible during a conference.

Control and Signaling Mechanisms

The flow of information in a H.323-enabled network consists of a mix of audio, video, data and control packets. Control information is essential for call set-up and tear down, capability exchange and negotiation, and administrative purposes. H.323 uses three control protocols : H.245 media control, H.225/Q.931 call signalling, and H.225.0 RAS.

Supplementary Services

Recommendation H.323 bridges traditional telephone networks with media rich packet-based networks. Services can range from value-added traditional telephone services such as call transfer and diversion to new services such as integrated messaging (e-mail, voice mail, fax, instant messaging, etc). H.323 provides a flexible architecture for supplementary services through the H.450X series of recommendations.

Security

Four security services are provided : authentication, integrity, privacy, and non-repudiation. Authentication is provided by admission control of endpoints. The gatekeeper that administers the zone handles this. Data integrity and privacy is provided by encryption. Non-repudiation ensures that no endpoint can deny that it participated in a call. This is also provided by gatekeeper services.

Alternatives to H.323

H.323 is not the only recommendation for multimedia transmission. A newer protocol is being developed by the Internet Engineering Task Force called SIP. SIP messages are text based and similar in format to existing Internet protocols such as HTTP. It has been argued that SIP is more suited to Internet applications and is easier to implement in software.

Session Initiation Protocol (SIP)

This is the IETF's standard for establishing VoIP connections. It is an application layer control protocol for creating, modifying and terminating sessions with one or more participants. Requests are generated by the client and sent to the server. The server processes the requests and then sends a response to the client. SIP depends on the Session Description Protocol (SDP) for carrying out the negotiation for codec identification. The services that SIP provide include :

- *User Location* : Determination of the end system to be used for communication.
- *Call Set-up* : Ringing and establishing call parameters at both called and calling party.
- *User Availability* : Determination of the willingness of the called party to engage in communications.
- *User Capabilities* : Determination of the media and media parameters to be used.

Call handling : The transfer and termination of calls.

Components of SIP

The SIP System Consists of two Components

- *User Agents* : A user agent is an end system acting on behalf of a user. There are two parts to it : a client and a server. The client portion is called the User Agent Client (UAC) while the server portion is called User Agent Server (UAS). The UAC is used to initiate a SIP request while the UAS is used to receive requests and return responses on behalf of the user.
- *Network Servers* : There are 3 types of servers within a network. A registration server receives updates concerning the current locations of users. A proxy server on receiving requests, forwards them to the next-hop server, which has more information about the location of the called party. A redirect server on receiving requests,

determines the next-hop server and returns the address of the next-hop server to the client instead of forwarding the request.

Overview of SIP operation.

- *SIP Addressing* : The SIP hosts are identified by a SIP URL. A SIP address can either designate an individual or a whole group.
- *Locating a SIP Server* : The client can either send the request to a SIP proxy server or it can send it directly to the IP address and port corresponding to the Uniform Request Identifier (URI).
- *SIP Transaction* : A request together with the responses triggered by that request make up a SIP transaction. The requests can be sent through reliable TCP or through unreliable UDP.
- *SIP Invitation* : A successful SIP invitation consists of two requests : a INVITE followed by ACK. The INVITE request asks the callee to join a particular conference or establish a two party conversation. The caller confirms that it has received that response by sending an ACK request.
- *Changing an Existing Session* : Sometimes we may need to change the parameters of an existing session. This is done by re-issuing the INVITE message using the same Call ID but a new body to convey the new information.

Comparison of H.323 with SIP

H.323 is inherently complex, and lacks the extensibility required of the signaling protocol for VoIP: SIP reuses most of the header fields, encoding rules, error codes and authentication mechanisms of HTTP. H.323 defines hundreds of elements while SIP has only 37 headers, each with a small number of values and parameters. H.323 uses a binary representation for its messages, which is based on ASNI while SIP encodes its messages as text, similar to HTTP. H.323 is not very scalable as it was designed for use on a single LAN and so has some problems in scaling though newer versions have suggested techniques to get around the problem. H.323 is still limited when performing loop detection in complex multi-domain searches. It can be done state fully by storing messages but this technique is not very scalable. On the other hand, SIP uses a loop detection method by checking the history of the message in the header fields, which can be done in a stateless manner. The advantage of SIP is that it is backed up by IETF, one of the most important standard bodies while the advantage of H.323 is that it has a much larger chunk of the market presently.

Supporting Protocols

Media Gateway Control Protocol (MGCP)

It is a protocol that defines communication between call control elements (Call Agents) and telephony gateways. Call Agents are also known as Media Gateway Controllers.

RTP and RTCP (Real-time Transport Protocol and Real-time Control Protocol).

RTP supports the transfer of real-time media (audio and video) over packet switched networks. It is used by both SIP and H.323.

Real-Time Streaming Protocol (RTSP)

RTSP, the Real Time Streaming Protocol, is a client-server protocol that provides control over the delivery of real-time media streams. RTSP acts as the "network remote control" between the server and the client.

Resource Reservation Protocol (RSVP)

RSVP can prioritize and guarantee latency to specific IP traffic streams. RSVP enables a packet-switched network to emulate a more deterministic circuit switched voice network. With the advent of RSVP, VOIP has become a reality today.

Session Description Protocol (SDP)

SDP is intended for describing multimedia sessions for the purpose of session announcement, session invitation, etc.

Session Announcement Protocol (SAP)

This protocol is used for advertising the multicast conferences and other multicast sessions.

Challenges

- *Interoperability and Implementation Issues* : H.323 is a large, complex, and flexible standard. Different interpretations and oversight in implementations have led to non-compliant and incompatible devices.
- *Lack of Value Added Services* : The vision of H.323 is global interoperability between packet and circuit switched networks. Global interoperability is still a problem.
- *Quality and Security Issues* : The quality of video on public networks like the Internet is poor. Even audio over the Internet does not compare favorably to the PSTN. Security of H.323 communications is also a big issue. Concerns over privacy have prevented businesses from moving over to H.323 for intra and inter-office communications. However, many products have not implemented the security recommendation.

Future Developments in H.323

The H.323 standard is still under development. The focus has shifted from LANs to larger networks such as the Internet and the challenges associated with it. Work is also being done to add mobile communication capability to H.323. Another initiative is the preparation of an implementation guide for H.323 to ease interoperability concerns. Interoperability issues and security are on-going initiatives. The other recommendations include H.310 for conferencing over broadband ISDN (B-ISDN), H.320 for conferencing over narrowband ISDN, H.321 for conferencing over ATM, H.322 for conferencing over LANs that provide a guaranteed quality of service, and H.324 for conferencing over public switched telephone networks (PSTN).

REFERENCES

1. Ulyess Black, "Voice over IP," 1999, 328 pages, Prentice Hall
2. W. Goralski, M Kolon, "IP Telephony," 1999, 468 pages, McGraw-Hill
3. Daniel Minoli, Emma Minoli, "Delivering Voice Over IP Networks," Second edition.
4. http ://www.databeam.com/h323/h323primer.html
5. http ://computer.org/internet/ic1999/w3053abs.htm
6. http ://www.cis.ohiostate.edu/~jain/talks/VoIP.htm

A Distributed Hierarchical Storage Manager for Video on Demand

I. RAJESHWARI

Introduction

Video on Demand (VoD) is the technology, which allows simultaneous access of viewers. I present here a distributed video on demand system is described. In this system, a large number of video can be stored on the tertiary storage devices. The system has a metadata database using which the user can select any video of his choice. As the user selects the video he wants to view, it is loaded onto a video file server who is close to the user's desktop from where it can be played. The system manages the distributed cache of videos on the file servers and schedules load requests to the tertiary storage devices. This paper describes the software architecture, storage organization, locating and loading videos, and distributed cache management algorithm used by the system.

Introduction

Video on Demand (VoD) is the technology, which allows simultaneous access of viewers to video content with the following basic functionalities :

- Every viewer has a dedicated video and audio channel.
- Every viewer can navigate and explore the audio-visual content in order to decide the material to be seen.
- Every user has complete VCR—like control over the content he is viewing.

VoD can be viewed as a distributed file system problem. As in a conventional network file system, users of a VoD system have *two basic needs* : locate relevant video and retrieve it for viewing on their local terminals. Providing widely distributed clients access to very large video databases poses the following *challenges* :

- Video data is *difficult both to store and deliver*. Hence meeting the real-time data delivery requirements of video is a difficult task. Better real-time scheduling and network bandwidth are required for video playback.
- Cost effective storage requires the use of *tertiary storage devices*, which provide access times too slow for interactive response.

Media playback requires that data be delivered at a *steady rate* without significant variations. If data is not delivered on time then audio output may be disrupted or video frames may be dropped, resulting in an unpleasant jerkiness in the presentation. Conventional network file systems, such as NFS and AFS may fail to deliver data on time, which will result in unacceptable playback quality. Real-time file servers address the problem of real-time delivery over local area networks by carefully scheduling I/O operations to meet the consumption constraints of their clients. Unfortunately, real-time delivery over WANs presents a new set of problems. In a WAN, packets of data sent by a real-time file server to remote clients must cross through network bridges, routers, and hubs, any of which could drop or delay packets, resulting in poor playback quality.

VoD requires a *high bandwidth* to play several videos simultaneously. A conventional ethernet LAN has a peak bandwidth of 10 Mbs, with observed performance typically being 6-8 Mbs. Thus, a LAN could support at most 4-5 viewers before reaching saturation. Newer network technologies, such as FDDI and ATM, hold greater promise. FDDI networks, for instance, offer a peak shared bandwidth of 100 Mbs, which can support 25 or more simultaneous users. ATM networks, on the other hand, offer between 25 and 250 Mbs on each link, with even higher aggregate bandwidth. Thus, a fast ATM switch could support simultaneous video transmission to every host on a LAN. The peak bandwidth out of a server to all of its clients cannot exceed the bandwidth of all intervening networks and hubs in case of WAN.

Storage Devices

Storage devices that can be used in VoD are Magnetic Tapes, Optical Storage and Magnetic Disks. The cheapest way to store larger volumes of information is on *magnetic tape*. A DAT tape can store 8 GB of data i.e., Two movies. Mechanical tape servers which can hold thousands of tapes with a robot arm for fetching any tape and inserting it into a tape drive can be used. The problems with these systems are the *access time* (especially for the second movie on a tape), *transfer rate* and the limited number of tape drives.

Next generation CDs will hold 4GB to make them suitable for

distributing MPEG movies. The main advantage of this type of storage is it cost less and is highly reliable. But its seek time is slow compared to magnetic disk.

Magnetic Disks have short access time, high transfer rates and substantial capacities which makes them well suited to hold movies that are actually being transmitted. Its main drawback is the high cost for storing movies that are rarely accessed.

Many video libraries require vast amount of storage. Magnetic disk storage is a costlier one for this case. A more cost effective solution is offered by tertiary storage, which uses robotic arms to serve a large number of removable tapes or disks to a small number of reading devices. Because of these long seek and media swap times, tertiary storage devices (especially tapes) are poor at performing random access within movies. Moreover, they can support only a single playback at a time on each reader. Thus, tertiary storage devices are inappropriate for direct video playback.

Storage Hierarchy

As each storage devices has its own advantages and disadvantages, a combination of these devices can be used. Not all movies are viewed with equal preference. Some movies are much popular than others. The following *storage hierarchy* (Figure 18.1) can be used for achieving better results. Performance increases as one move up the hierarchy. Based on the preference, the movie can be placed in the appropriate device. So the least preferred movies can be placed in the tape and the most preferred ones in the RAM.

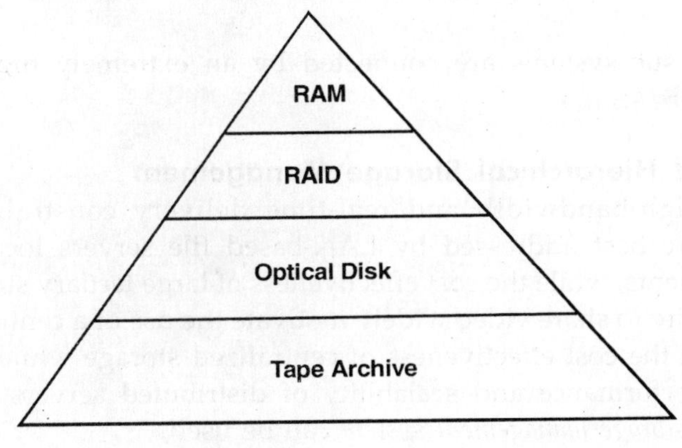

Fig. 18.1
Storage Hierarchy

Hardware Architecture of a Typical Video Server

Hardware architecture of a typical video server is shown in Figure 18.2. It has the following sub-systems :

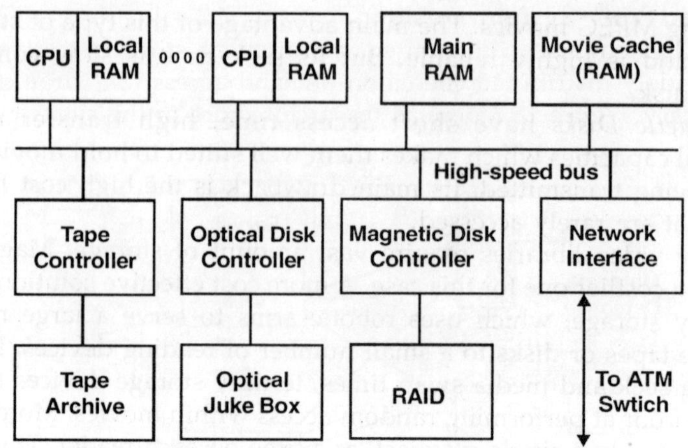

FIG. 18.2
The Hardware Architecture of a Typical Video Server

- One or more high performance RISC CPUs, each with some local memory,
- A shared main memory,
- A massive RAM cache for popular movies,
- A variety of storage devices for holding the movies, and
- Some networking hardware, normally an optical interface to ATM or SONET networks.

These sub-systems are connected by an extremely high-speed bus (atleast 1 GB/sec).

Distributed Hierarchical Storage Management

The high-bandwidth and real-time delivery constraints of video playback are best addressed by LAN-based file servers located close to playback clients, while the cost effectiveness of large tertiary storage devices and the desire to share video widely motivate the use of a central repository. To preserve the cost effectiveness of centralized storage while maintaining the high performance and scalability of distributed servers, a *distributed hierarchical storage management system* can be used.

A hierarchical storage manager applies the concept of caching to tertiary storage, using fast magnetic disks to cache frequently accessed data from large tertiary storage devices. Distributed hierarchical storage management extends this idea by allowing multiple caches to be distributed across a network. If a high percentage of client accesses are to data stored in a local cache, the perceived performance is very high and WAN traffic is limited.

Distributed VoD System Design

VoD System uses distributed hierarchical storage management to provide widely distributed clients on-demand access to a large continuous media library. Figure 18.3 depicts the architecture of the system.

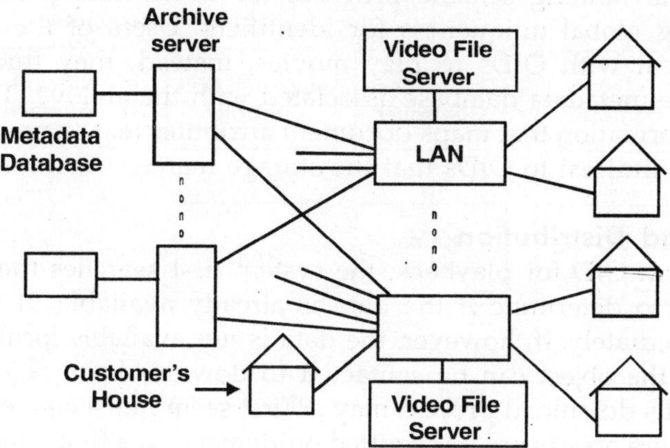

Fig. 18.3
Distributed VoD System

Archive servers (AS) act as central repositories for published objects, typically employing tertiary storage. Each AS has an accompanying catalog, or metadata database that stores information about the videos available on the archive. This information, which can range from simple bibliographical descriptions to sophisticated content indexes, can be queried by users using an *ad hoc* query interface, called a *video database browser* (VDB), to locate movies for playback. Real-time playback is provided by one or more video file servers (VFS) located on the client's LAN. When a client selects a video for viewing, the browser checks if it is already cached on one of the local VFSs. If so, no access to the archive is necessary, and playback can begin immediately. Otherwise, the client may request that the video be loaded from the archive.

Archive Server

The Archive Server (AS) plays the central role of a continuous media-publishing house. It handles the naming, storage, and distribution of movies.

Naming

A video first becomes accessible in the VoD system when it is published at an AS. They are assigned a globally unique object ID (OID) composed of the name of the publishing archive and a sequence number unique to the archive. The archive where an object is published, called its home archive, is guaranteed to have a copy of the object or to know of another server that does. Thus, given an OID, the system can always locate the corresponding object by contacting its home archive and following any forward references. Immutability greatly simplifies distributed cache coherency. Also, the use of a hierarchical naming scheme provides for decentralized naming while guaranteeing global uniqueness for identifiers. Users of the VoD system need not deal with OIDs to play movies. Instead, they find objects by querying the metadata database associated with the archive. This database contains information that maps document attributes (e.g., names, keywords, and content indices) to OIDs that the storage manager can manipulate.

Storage and Distribution

Given an OID for playback, the system first searches the user's local VFS caches to determine if the data is already available. If so, playback begins immediately. If, however, the data is not available locally, the home archive for the object can be contacted to download the object to a VFS. Although this download process may at first seem like a conventional "ftp" problem where objects are transmitted on-demand in a first-come, first-serve order, the size of video objects and the characteristic of tertiary storage devices motivate a different solution. Cost effective storage of large amounts of multimedia data mandate the use of tertiary storage devices such as a tape jukebox. While the transfer rate for these devices is quite high, the time to seek between non-contiguous objects may be large. Thus, achieving high performance from a tertiary device requires intelligent scheduling to avoid unnecessary tape swaps and seeks. The key to this scheduling knows as much information as possible about future access patterns of a client.

Server Arrays

While most systems rely on powerful single servers, employing a disk array can result in high scalability. An obvious design for such a system would place N independent servers on a network and allow clients to play movies from any one of them. While such a system does improve peak aggregate bandwidth, it can suffer load-balancing problems if many people simultaneously decide to watch a movie that is stored on only one of the servers. In this case, one server is overloaded while the others sit idle. A possible solution to this problem is to *replicate* popular movies across several servers, but this approach results in poor storage utilization and requires that the system choose the right material to replicate. A better approach to server parallelism is to *stripe* movies across servers, to form what we call a *software RAID*. Such systems have proven inappropriate for conventional distributed file systems because of the *high coordination overhead* between the distributed servers, the increased likelihood of independent *failures*, and the difficulties in achieving *distributed consistency*. For read-only caches, however, a software array does not suffer these problems. Because data on a VFS is read only and is already backed up at an archive server, issues of distributed consistency and independent failure do not arise. In addition, the predictable delivery characteristics of continuous media permit very low-overhead cooperation between servers.

Scheduling Object Loading

At any given time, the system has a list of objects that are in the cache and a list of objects that are reference by a directive, but are not cached. The system is said to be in equilibrium when the cache is full and contains all of the highest priority objects. If, however, a requested object has higher priority than the lowest priority objects in the cache, the system is out of equilibrium and the cache contents are non-optimal. Typical causes of disequilibrium include :

- A user has requested a new video for immediate loading (highest priority) and some objects in the cache are not presently being used (lower priority).
- A user finished watching a video, thereby downgrading its priority and making room for other requested material.
- The gradual escalation in priority of a movie scheduled for viewing some time in the future has made it more valuable than other data in the cache.

Equilibrium in the cache can be restored by replacing low priority objects with higher priority objects. Immediate correction of a slight disequilibrium, however, may be counter-productive since it places load on both the VFS and AS and generates large amounts of network traffic. Thus, the decision on whether to perform a load from the archive should reflect several factors :

- The priority of the object being fetched. A movie schedule for viewing several hours in the future may not warrant immediate action, while a request for immediate viewing might.
- The current load on the VFS. If the VFS is busy servicing video playbacks it may not have sufficient resources to receive and store a new move.
- The load on the archive server.
- Time of day. Heavy network usage is less likely to affect other users if performed late at night rather than early in the morning.

To allow these factors to influence the scheduling of object downloading, the cache manager allows administrators to specify a load threshold function that specifies the minimum priority that a requested object must have before it is loaded. Like functions for determining object priority, this threshold function can incorporate external variables and can be periodically re-evaluated, thereby allowing download criteria to change dynamically based on the time of day or the current VFS load.

The object priority values are also useful in performing scheduling at the archive server. Each VFS will log archive requests for all objects that meet its cache replacement criteria (not just the highest priority object) and include in the request the current object priority and deadline. By logging a large number of prioritized requests, the VFSs allow the archive to perform global optimization in picking a retrieval order that is most efficient for the tertiary storage device while still taking into account the relative priorities of the requested objects.

Conclusion

A distributed video on demand system in which a large number of video can be stored on the tertiary storage devices and how video can be retrieved from metadata database and viewed is discussed.

References

1. Craig Federighi and Lawrence A. Rowe, "A Distributed Hierarchical Storage Manager for a Video-on-Demand System".
2. Andrew S. Tanenbaum, "Computer Networks".
3. Douglas E. Corner, "Computer Networks and Internets".
4. John Freer, "Computer Communications and Networks".
5. http ://www.interactivestreams.com/web/vod/vod.html

Mobile Multimedia

ARUMUGAM RATHINAVELU AND ANNADURAI GOWRI SHANKAR

Introduction

The invention of Mobile technology is really a big boom in the telecommunication industry, which makes people more comfortable. It allowed the society to communicate from a mobile location at anywhere, anytime, which has forever changed the way people communicate with each other, do business, etc. Even though the mobile technology was introduced in 1970s, it has developed rapidly in the 1990s and is still developing today, where a large proportion of the population own and use mobile phones regularly. According to Voice and Data (July, 2003) the total mobile phone subscribers as on 31 March 2003 was 1,26,87,637 in India.

TABLE 19.1
Growth of Mobile Technology in India (Voice and Data, July 2003)

Category	*Revenue 2002-03*	*Revenue 2001-02*	*Growth (%)*
Cellular Services	8303	5516	50.5
GSM Phones	1795	1008	78.07
CDMA Phones	559.4	NA	

Generation of Mobile Communications

The mobile first commercial system was launched in Europe in late 1970's. The history of mobile communications divided into three generations as below :

- First Generation systems,
- Second Generation systems, and
- Third Generation systems.

First Generation Systems

It uses analog communication techniques for transmission over the radio spectrum. In this the main protocols are Nordic Mobile Telephone systems (NMT), Advanced Mobile Phone Services (AMPS), Total Access Communication System (TACS). These systems are in the field from 1970 to mid-1990's in few countries (It has not reached India).

Second Generation Systems

It uses digital radio techniques for transmission so it has higher capacity over first generation systems. Another advantage is frequency channel is spitted using Code division and time division (CDMA and TDMA). It was introduced in mid-1990's and follows 4 main standards :

Global System for Mobile (GSM),
Digital-AMPS, (D-AMPS)
Code Division Multiple Access (CDMA), and
Personal Digital Cellular (PDC).

These standards are adopted based on the country's technology level; India had chosen GSM, which is widely used throughout the world. GSM uses with 900 Mhz carrier frequency, when these frequencies are full, there are other frequencies like 1800, 1900 Mhz.

Generation Systems

Due to the very low data rate of around 10 Kpbs, it is difficult for the transmission. So the data rate is increased in this 2.5 Generation. It includes following standards :

High Speed Circuit Switched Data (HSCSD),
General Packet Radio Services (GPRS), and
Enhanced Data Rates for Global Evolution (EDGE).

Third Generation Systems

It provides high-speed mobile access to the amount of around 2M Bits/ Sec data rate. It provides the users to transmit voice, data and moving images to and from a mobile location at high speeds. 3G uses CDMA standard for transmission which provides high-speed access to the Internet, entertainment, movie trailers, music clips, weather, mapping information, banking, etc. at your hand.

CDMA—Code Division Multiple Access

CDMA is the technology, which is developed in the 2G, but the major

TABLE 19.2
Univsersity of New Castle, Australia,
http ://murray.newcastle.edu.au

Technology	*Features*	*Data Rate*	*Average time to download a 3 min. MP3 Song*
2G	Phone Calls Voice Mail Receive simple data files	10 K Bit/sec.	30 – 41 mins.
2.5G	Phone Calls Fax messages Voice mail Send/receive large data files Web browsing	64-144 K Bit/sec.	6-9 mins.
3G	Phone Calls Fax messages Global Roaming Send/Receive large data files High speed web navigation and browsing Video conferencing TV Streaming	144 K Bit/sec. for high mobility traffic (Moving in a car) 384 K Bits/sec. for low mobility traffic (travelling at walking pace) 2M Bits/sec. in good conditions (Stationery)	11 sec. - 1.5 min.

usage was introduced because of 3G Technology in 3GPP (Third Generation Partnership Project) and 3GPP2. Each mobile user transmission takes place by assigning a unique spreading code across the assigned spread spectrum. Whereas in the Frequency Division Multiple Access (FDMA) and Time Division Multiple Access (TDMA) the transmission is taken place by assigning a particular frequency or time for the user, which is limited. CDMA puts all the users on the same frequency spectrum at the same time, separating users with codes.

The advantages of CDMA (University of Newcastle, Australia)

- Takes advantage of multipath.
- Widespread signal structure, robust to fading (frequency diversity).
- Good frequency re-use, increasing system capacity.
- Users can operate asynchronously.
- Good tolerance to interference.
- "Soft Capacity Limit". This means that the more users the more background noise there will be, as opposed to FDMA and TDMA systems which have a "Hard Capacity Limit" where when this capacity is reached, new users will simply not be able to use the communication systems.

3GPP—Third Generation Partnership Project

It is the organization formed during 1998 that gives standards and specifications for the 3G worldwide for the creation, delivery and playback of multimedia over GSM and UTRA (Universal Terrestrial Radio Access).

UTRA

It consists of two modes :

- Frequency Division Duplex (FDD), and
- Time Division Duplex (TDD).

Frequency Division Duplex

It is the most commonly use system in 3GPP. In FDD, separate frequency band are used for Uplink (UL) and Downlink (DL), with a bandwidth of 5 Mhz and each carrier is divided into 10 ms radio frames, each frame is again sub-divided into 15 time slots. UL uses the frequency from 1920 to 1980 Mhz, whereas DL uses from 2110 – 2170 Mhz. So both UL and DL operate with a difference of 190 Mhz, the telecommunication will be good. It uses the same CDMA spreading code technique, so no two spreading codes are same.

Time Division Duplex

It uses the same carrier for UL and DL, but time slots can be dynamically allotted between UL and DL directions. The main problem, both UL and DL information can collide each other. So, it is not commonly used.

3GPP2—Third Generation Partnership Project

It is the next project in 3G, to cater to the North American and Asian mobile networks. It provides standards and specification for the following five areas :

- A-interface system,
- CDMA2000™,
- ANSI-41 (American National Standards Institute-41),
- Wireless packet data interworking, and
- Services and systems aspects.

In this CDMA 2000 is an important technology used worldwide that was developed by a US-based company called Qualcomm. In this the Uplink and Downlink uses the same carrier and bandwidth.

Because of the high transmission speed in 3G systems, it is widely used for applications like Multimedia, Video conferencing, audio streaming, etc.

Multimedia Applications on Mobile

Multimedia applications on mobile is developing like,

1. Video conferencing (FOMA).
2. Entertainment (QT).
3. Business (M Commerce).
4. Internet Communications (General).

This paper talks about Mobile Video as one of powerful multimedia applications.

Multimedia message service enable you to send images, audio clips and text from mobile to mobile, mobile to e-mail and *vice-versa.* Mobile communication gets re-shaping by using multimedia services. Users enjoy using multimedia content such as News, Entertainment, and other live services. We take 'mobile video' as a powerful upcoming multimedia application. Using current technologies, users can send and receive videos in various ways. Even video clips can be created and deliver to another end user.

Types of Mobile Video

There are two main types in mobile video

i.e., 1. Downloadable content.
2. Streaming content.

Downloadable content — Short video clips are downable and it requires storage memory in phone. It is like low MMS video messages saved.

Streaming content — It works more like a TV. Here
— Phone works like a display unit
— Phone doesn't require longer memory because no information stored

Few Mobile Video Services

1. Personalized video greetings.
2. Entertainment like movie trailers and music videos.
3. News including Weather, Travel and Sports and so on.

MMS is providing more joy with video capabilities. MMS enabled phone delivers short video content (Micro movies) via MMS.

MMS enabled mobile phones (specific models) support Audio/Video streaming in high speed circuit – switched data (HSCSD) networks.

Ex : NOKIA 6600 phone supports Realone™ player for streaming video and audio.

On introduction of 3G systems, multimedia in mobile is developing. In which Apple's Quicktime has created a standard for creation, delivery and play back of Multimedia content over mobile standards 3GPP and 3GPP2.

According to a Apple computers Quicktime (QT) with native 3GPP and 3GPP2 standards offers following multimedia solution :

Content Creation and playback solution,
QT editing and encoding tools on the Mac and PC Platform, and
Interoperability across 3G Networks.

Many distributed players for seamless playback of handset-generated multimedia on the desktop QT delivers MPEG-4 and H.263 video standards for 3G Standards. For Audio AAC (Advanced Audio Coding), AMR (Adaptive Multi Rate) and Qualcomm Code Exited Linear Predictive (QCELP).

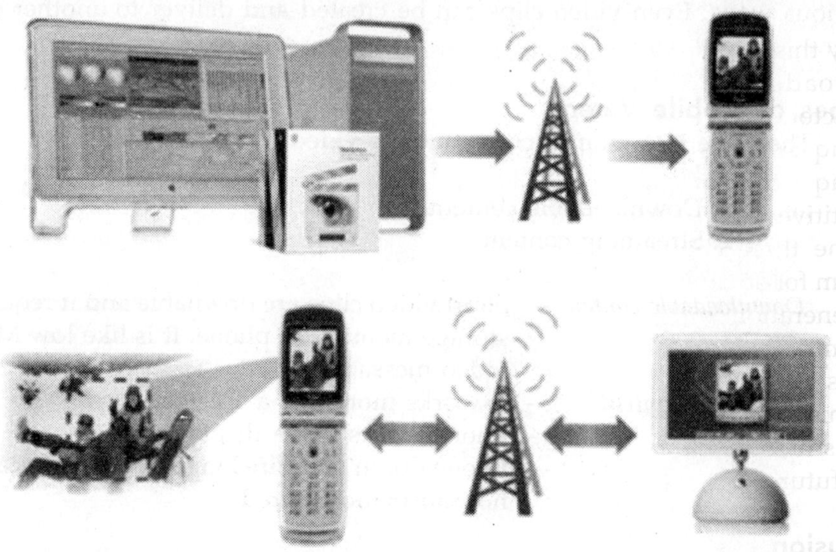

Latest Technologies

Based on the development in the field of mobile, lot of new technologies is coming out, which give rise to new applications FOMA (Freedom Of Mobile Multimedia Access) is developed by a Japanese company called as NTT DoCoMo during late 1990s. It works based on W-CDMA technology, which complies with IMT-2000, an international standard for third-generation (3G) mobile communications. Using this FOMA service the company is offering lot of applications like :

- i-mode – high speed packet transmission upto 384 Kbps,
- Video phone,
- Multiaccess – talk and transmit at same time,
- i-motion – access to exciting video content, and
- v-live – live streaming of video.

In the mobile inbuilt OS also developing, and today for instance the latest Symbian OS 7, which has the following features in the latest smart phone-sendo (www.sendo.com)

- Camera (still/video)
- Image editor
- Photo album
- Real one Video/Audio player
- Integral MP3 Player
- Document viewer
- WAP Browser
- Internet Browser
- Instant Messaging

By this we can clearly focus that the multimedia can be easily created, downloaded and transmit to anywhere. The latest news from newsfactor.com states that "Information technology giants Apple Computer (Nasdaq : AAPL), Ericsson (Nasdaq : ERICY) and Sun Microsystems (Nasdaq : SUNW) have announced a partnership designed to gain a competitive edge in the delivery of multimedia content to wireless devices.

The three companies are pushing a standardized content delivery platform for streaming media, widely recognized as a critical application for next-generation wireless networks being rolled out around the globe. The platform is based on MPEG-4 compression and decoding technology and Apple's Quick Time Multimedia Format."

This news clearly shows that lot of IT companies are now moving towards mobile applications, which makes mobile users to enjoy the usage in the future than what it is now.

Conclusion

To summarize our paper the multimedia and mobile can't be separated in near future, since need of multimedia and mobile for day-to-day Business and Entertainment. It is converging era. The mobile is slowly replacing TV, radio, recorders, newspapers, MP3 Players, etc. The major advantage is that anywhere, anytime the media can be reached in your hands apart from regular voice communications.

References

1. Naresh Chandra Laisharam, "Inflection Point", Voice and Data, July 2003.
2. Pravin Prashant, "Healthy, if not high", Voice and Data, July 2003.
3. Shyamanuja Das, "High Growth, Low Margin", Voice and Data, July 2003.
4. White Paper from Huges Software Systems and Adax Europe Ltd., "GSM to 3G : Evolution or Revolution?"
5. Chris Pearson, "The Power of TDMA-Based Technologies and the 3G Evolution", Universal Wireless Communications Consortium.

6. Apple site, "3GPP + 3GPP2 + Quick time : The Future is calling", http ://www.apple.com/mpeg4/3gpp, viewed on 2.1.2004.
7. Nttdocomo site, "FOMA", http ://foma.nttdocomo.co.jp/english/index.html., viewed on 4.1.2004.
8. Jay Wrolstad, "Apple, Ericsson, Sun Join Forces on Mobile Multimedia", http ://www.newsfactor.com/story.xhtml?story_id=16322#story-start, viewed on 5.1.2004.
9. Dan McDonough, Jr, "Nokia, DoCoMo Ally for Mobile Multimedia Standards", http ://www.newsfactor.com/story.xhtml?story_id=14774, viewed on 5.1.2004.
10. Symbian, "Sendo X", http ://www.symbian.com/phones/sendo_x.html, viewed on 6.1.2004.

Adaptive Call Admission Control for QoS Provisioning in Wireless/Mobile Multimedia Networks

S. Anitha, K. Sangeetha and R. Sumangali

Introduction

Recently there is a growing interest in the adaptive multimedia networking where the bandwidth of an ongoing multimedia call can be dynamically adjusted. In the wireless/mobile multimedia networks using the adaptive framework, the bandwidth of an ongoing call can be dynamically adjusted to adapt to the various communication environments, especially in overloaded situations. In the wireless/mobile multimedia networks using the adaptive framework, the existing QoS provisioning focused on the call blocking probability and the forced termination probability should be modified. In the adaptive multimedia framework, QoS provisioning is performed by two workhorse algorithms : a Call Admission Control (CAC) algorithm and a Bandwidth Adaptation Algorithm (BAA). In this paper, we redefine a QoS parameter—the *cell overload probability*—and propose the CAC algorithm that guarantees the upper bound of the *cell overload probability* in a cell. Also, we devise the BAA that allocates/reallocates bandwidth of ongoing calls in a cell. Here, "bandwidth adaptation" means the bandwidth allocation of incoming calls and/or the reallocation of bandwidth of the existing calls in a given cell. The proposed BAA seeks to minimize the *cell overload probability* at any time.

With the explosive demand on wireless/mobile communications and the emergence of bandwidth-intensive multimedia applications, Quality of Service (QoS) provisioning in wireless/mobile multimedia networks is becoming more and more important. The most significant QoS parameters in the existing wireless/mobile multimedia networks are the call blocking probability and the forced termination probability. It is widely accepted that the forced termination of an ongoing call (e.g., due to handoff failure) is much more unbearable to users than the blocking of a new call, so that there have been numerous schemes to provide satisfiable QoS by exclusively reserving the network resources for handoff calls. The key factor in QoS provisioning is a Call Admission Control (CAC) algorithm that provides acceptable QoS to users and utilizes the system resources (e.g., wireless link bandwidth) efficiently. So far, CAC algorithms in wireless/mobile multimedia networks have been focused on how to block originating calls to satisfy the QoS requirements.

We advocate in this paper that the adaptive multimedia-networking paradigm can play an important role to mitigate the highly varying resource availability in Wireless/mobile networks. Compared to wired networks, the fluctuation in resource availability in wireless/mobile networks is much more severe and results from two inherent features of such networks : fading and mobility. The adaptive multimedia-networking framework in this paper takes into consideration only mobility. Also, the cellular network environment is the focus of this paper. That is, an ongoing multimedia call in a given cell may change its bandwidth due to a new call arrival, a call completion, or an incoming/outgoing handoff call. In the existing non-adaptive wireless/mobile networks, an incoming call to a given cell will be forced to be terminated if there is not sufficient wireless bandwidth (e.g., channels) to accommodate the call. In the adaptive multimedia framework, QoS provisioning is performed by two workhorse algorithms : a CAC algorithm and a bandwidth adaptation algorithm (BAA). In this paper, we redefine a QoS parameter—the *cell overload probability*—and propose the CAC algorithm that guarantees the upper bound of the *cell overload probability* in a cell. Also, we devise the BAA that allocates/reallocates bandwidth of ongoing calls in a cell. Here, "bandwidth adaptation" means the bandwidth allocation of incoming calls and/or the reallocation of bandwidth of the existing calls in a given cell. The proposed BAA seeks to minimize the *cell overload probability* at any time.

Modeling the Adaptive Multimedia Networking

Recall that in the wireless/mobile multimedia network with the adaptive framework, the bandwidth of a multimedia call can be dynamically adjusted depending on the situation during its lifetime. We assume that the bandwidth of a call takes its discrete value from the set $B = \{b_1, b_2, \ldots, b_n\}$ where $b_i < b_i+1$ for $i = 1, \ldots, n-1$. We also assume that all calls belong to a single class and all of them take (varying) bandwidth values from the same set B. Here, bandwidth values in B are integers, all of which are assumed to be multiples of a basic bandwidth unit (e.g., a single channel). As for traffic characterization, we assume a simple model from a cell's perspective. The new call arrivals into a given cell are assumed to form a Poisson process with mean rate ë. Also, the call holding time is assumed to follow an exponential distribution with mean $1/\mu$. The cell residence time, the amount of time during which a call stays in a cell before handoff, is also assumed to follow an exponential distribution with mean $1/h$. Here h is also called as the handoff rate, which means how fast a call will handoff.

A call will be allocated bandwidth b_n (the maximum bandwidth) whenever possible. However, network congestion may occur, in which case a cell cannot accommodate all calls with their maximum bandwidth b_n. In this case, one or more calls should be allocated/reallocated lower bandwidth than b_n. To choose which calls and how much bandwidth of the chosen calls to be changed is the role of the BAA.

A BAA that manages the allocation/reallocation of bandwidth of each call is necessary in this adaptive multimedia framework. According to the different QoS objectives, there can be diverse BAAs. Here we adopt a simple objective to minimize the number of calls whose bandwidth is lower than predefined "target bandwidth". The target bandwidth will be denoted by b_{tar}, and it is assumed to take a predetermined value from the set B. Hereafter a call is referred to be "degraded" if and only if the bandwidth of the call is lower than b_{tar}.

Therefore, the proposed BAA in the adaptive multimedia framework seeks to allocate at least the target bandwidth to every call in a cell whenever possible. However, as the traffic load in the wireless/mobile multimedia network becomes higher, there are more "degraded" calls, and thus, users will become dissatisfied. Thus, for the adaptive multimedia framework to be successful, a CAC algorithm that prevents the cellular system from being highly overloaded is crucial. Here a cell is referred to be "overloaded" if there are one or more "degraded" calls in the cell. More precisely, the *cell overload probability*, PCO, is defined as the sum of probabilities for QoS provisioning in wireless/mobile multimedia networks 53 states where there are one or more "degraded" calls. The proposed CAC algorithm should therefore enforce the *cell overload probability* to be less than a predetermined value, P_{qos}, which will be given as QoS requirment.

The CAC Algorithm

Now the problem is how the proposed CAC algorithm can guarantee the upper bound of the *cell overload probability* in a cell. We basically adopt the distributed CAC algorithm proposed in [5], which considers the number of ongoing calls in adjacent cells when a call request arrives in a given cell. We consider one-dimensional cellular array such as one used in streets and highways. In addition, we assume that the cellular system uses a fixed channel allocation scheme and that each cell has the same bandwidth capacity (or the same number of channels).

Let us denote n, r, and l as the number of ongoing calls in the given cell (C_n), its right cell (C_r), and its left cell (C_l), respectively. Considering any test mobile in C_n, we assume that the test mobile remains in the same cell with probability p_r, and that it handsoff to one of its adjacent cells (either C_r or C_l)

with probability *ph/2* during time *T* which we refer to as the *estimation time*. Furthermore, we assume that the probability that a call hands off more than once during *T* is negligible. In our model, we approximately estimate *cell overload probability* of a radio cell after *estimation time* whenever a new call request arrives. Hereafter a cell is referred to be "overloaded" when the number of ongoing calls is greater than a threshold number (*N*th) which is the maximum number of calls all of which can be allocated at least b_{tar} in a cell. That is, if the number of calls in a cell is greater than *N*th, there are at least one or more calls whose bandwidth values are less than b_{tar}. Here *N*th is calculated by [C/ b_{tar}] where C is the total bandwidth capacity of a cell in basic bandwidth units.

Accordingly, the cell overload probability, *P*CO, is expressed by å$^{8}_{i=Nth+1}$ *P(i)* where *P(i)* represents the probability of having *i* calls in a radio cell. Let us denote *P*qos as the highest tolerable cell overload probability in wireless/ mobile multimedia networks where all calls requires the same P_{qos} throughout their connection.

The CAC algorithm of such system must take two factors into consideration when admitting a new call : (1) by admitting the new call, the desired QoS (in terms of P_{qos}) of existing calls in the system must be maintained; and (2) the system must provide the new call with its desired QoS. To achieve the above objectives, we estimate the state of the given cell after *T* units of time when the new call arrives. Therefore, a new call is admitted to the given cell at time t_0 if and only if the following condition is satisfied : At time $t_0 + T$, the overload probability of the given cell estimated by considering handoffs from its adjacent cells and handoffs from the given cell to adjacent cells must be smaller than P_{qos}.

The BAA

To support the proposed CAC algorithm for QoS requirements, the bandwidth adaptation algorithm (BAA) seeks to minimize the number of calls with lower than *target bandwidth*, b_{tar}. Alternately said, it seeks to maximize the number of calls with equal to or more than b_{tar} at any instant. There are broadly two cases where the BAA performs the bandwidth adaptation : for reduction and for expansion.

Notation for the BAA

b_{tar} target bandwidth

b_{min} minimum bandwidth (b_1)

b_{max} maximum bandwidth (b_n).

B_A available bandwidth in the given cell

B_T amount of squeezable bandwidth by changing all calls with more than b_{tar} into calls with b_{tar}

B_M amount of squeezable bandwidth by changing all calls with more than b_{min} into calls with b_{min}

The BAA for reduction applies to the case where a new call or an incoming handoff call arrives in the given cell and the cell is overloaded. Depending on the situation, the BAA allocates the suitable bandwidth to the incoming call (the new call or the handoff call) and reallocates the bandwidth of the existing calls, if necessary. The BAA for expansion may expand the bandwidth of calls with lower than target bandwidth to b_{tar} or more when there is an outgoing handoff call or a call completion in the given cell. The notation of the BAA is summarized in Table.

The description of the BAA for reduction when a call (new or handoff) arrives in the given cell is detailed below. There are six cases in the BAA for reduction. Below, the operation Reduce T (b_{wanted}) squeezes the calls with more than b_{tar} to b_{tar} and adds the squeezed bandwidth to B_A until B_A equals to or exceeds b_{wanted}. Similarly, Reduce M (b_{wanted}) squeezes the calls with more than b_{min} to b_{min} until B_A equals to or exceeds the b_{wanted}.

(a) if ($B_A >= b_{tar}$), allocate the maximum b_i to the incoming call ($b_i <= B_A$, $b_{tar} <= b_i <= b_{max}$)
(b) else if ($B_A < b_{tar}$ and $B_A + B_T >= b_{tar}$), Reduce T(b_{tar}) allocate the maximum b_i to the incoming call ($b_i <= B_A$, $b_{tar} <= b_i <= b_{max}$)
(c) else if ($B_A >= b_{min}$ and $B_A + B_T < =b_{tar}$), allocate the maximum b_i to the incoming call ($b_i <= B_A$, $b_{min} <= b_i < b_{tar}$)
(d) else if ($B_A < b_{min}$ and $B_A + B_T >=b_{min}$), Reduce T(b_{min}) allocate the maximum b_i to the incoming call ($b_i <= B_A$, $b_{min} <= b_i < b_{tar}$)
(e) else if ($B_A < b_{min}$ and $B_A + B_M >= b_{min}$), Reduce M(b_{min}) allocate the maximum b_i to the incoming call ($b_i <= B_A$, $b_{min} <= b_i < b_{tar}$)
(f) else drop/block the call

When a call leaves the cell, B_A increases. This change in B_A may make it possible for one or more calls to expand their bandwidth.

The Forced Termination Probability

In this section, we analyze the forced termination probability in the adaptive multimedia framework. The forced termination probability is almost directly proportional to the handoff dropping probability. Thus, we consider the handoff dropping probability instead of the forced termination probability. Here the handoff dropping probability means the probability that an attempt of handoff will fail.

As mentioned earlier, the handoff dropping probability in our adaptive framework is negligible in normal cases. However, theoretically it is possible that a handoff fails if a given cell is full of calls with b_{min} and there are not sufficient channels to allocate b_{min} to an incoming handoff call. That is, in the adaptive framework, the handoff dropping probability equals the steady state probability of $P(N_{max})$. Here N_{max} is the maximum possible number of calls in a cell with bandwidth adaptation.

Degradation Period Ratio

In this section, to quantify the level of the degradation of a call, we define another QoS parameter : the *degradation period ratio*. The *degradation period ratio* (DPR) is the portion of a call's lifetime during which the allocated bandwidth is lower than the target bandwidth with respect to the whole service time of the call. For example, if a call's DPR is 0.5, the period while the call's allocated bandwidth is less than the target bandwidth is half of the call's lifetime. Recall that a state is defined by the number of calls in each cell at a given instant. A call may experience a number of states throughout its lifetime. The residence time in a state represents the time interval between every instant of a new call arrival, a call departure, or an incoming/outgoing handoff call. We assume that the time between every state transition follows an exponential distribution with mean rate r. Here r is the state transition rate which reflects how fast the state of the system (a cell) will move to another state. The state transition rate is a function of the new call arrival rate *ë*, the handoff call arrival rate *ëh*, the call service rate μ, and the handoff rate h. More exactly, the rate r can be calculated from the effective new call arrival rate, the handoff call arrival rate, the call service rate, and the handoff rate as follows :

$$r = ë(1\ .\ PB) + ëh + E[n]\mu + E[n]h.$$

Here, $E[n]$ denotes the average number of calls in each cell.

Conclusion

It is anticipated that multimedia applications with the adaptive networking framework where the bandwidth of an ongoing call can be dynamically adjusted will become widespread in the near future. Although the forced termination probability can be reduced to a negligible level in this adaptive framework, a new kind of QoS provisioning is still required. In this paper, we have defined a QoS parameter, the *cell overload probability*, from the perspective of the adaptive multimedia networking paradigm. The key factor in QoS provisioning is a CAC algorithm, which enforces the upper bound of the *cell overload probability*. We have discussed how the proposed CAC algorithm can guarantee QoS in wireless/mobile multimedia networks. Also, we proposed the bandwidth adaptation algorithm to minimize the *cell overload probability* at any time. Even though the functional requirements of the adaptive multimedia networking framework are much more complicated than those of the non-adaptive multimedia framework, we believe that it is worthwhile to deploy the adaptive framework in the wireless/mobile multimedia networks, especially considering the scarcity and fluctuation of wireless link bandwidth. In this study, only a single class of the adaptive multimedia networking has been investigated.

As a future work, we will extend the proposed CAC algorithm for the case of multiple classes where there are various adaptive multimedia streams/encodings in integrated services networks.

REFERENCES

A. Alwan *et. al.*, Adaptive Mobile Multimedia Networks, *IEEE Communications Magazine*, 34(4) (April 1996) 34–51.

S.K. Das and S.K. Sen, Quality-of-Service Degradation Strategies in Multimedia Wireless Networks, in : *IEEE Vehicular Technology Conference (VTC'98)*, Ottawa, Canada (May 1998).

R. Howard, *Dynamic Probabilistic Systems*, Vol. 1, *Markov Models* (Wiley, 1971).

N. Yeadon, Filters : QoS Support Mechanisms for Multipeer Communications, *IEEE Journal on Selected Areas in Communications*, 14(7) (September 1996) 1245–1262.

M. Naghshineh and M. Schwarz, Distributed Call Admission Control in Mobile/Wireless Networks, in : *IEEE PIMRC'95* (1995) pp. 289–93.

S. Sen *et. al.*, Quality of Service Degradation Strategies in Multimedia Wireless Networks, in : *IEEE VTC'98*, Ottawa (1998) pp. 1884–88.

Part IV

Highspeed Networks

Asynchronous Transfer Mode

S. Anantha Krishnan

Introduction

The most important technical innovation on Broadband ISDN is Asynchronous Transfer Mode (ATM). ATM, also known as cell relay, is a transmission technique using fixed size cells. ATM is a packet-oriented transfer mode. The ATM layer consists of virtual channel and virtual path levels. The physical layer is divided into three functional levels shown below :

(a) *Transmission Path Level* : Extends between network elements that assemble and disassemble the payload of a transmission system.
(b) *Digital Section* : Extends between network elements that assemble and disassemble a continuous bit or byte stream. This refers to the exchange or signal transfer points in a network that are involved in switching data streams.
(c) *Regenerator Section Level* : A portion of digital section. An example of this level is repeater that is used simply to regenerate the digital signal along a transmission path that is too long to be used without such regeneration no switching is involved.

Virtual Channels and Virtual Paths

Logical connections in ATM are referred to as Virtual Channel Connections (VCCs). A Virtual Channel Connection is set-up between two end users through the network and a variable rate, full-duplex flow of fixed size cells are exchanged over the connection. A Virtual Path Connection (VPC) is a bundle of Virtual Channel Connections that have the same end points. The Virtual path technique helps contain the control cost by grouping connections sharing the common paths through the network into a single unit.

Several advantages can be listed for the use of virtual paths :

- Simplified network architecture,
- Increase network performance and reliability,
- Reduced processing and shift connection setup time, and
- Enhanced network services.

Virtual Channel Connection Uses

The endpoints of a Virtual Channel Connection may be end users, network entities or an end user and a network entity. In all cases call sequence integrity is preserved within a Virtual Channel Connection : That is, the cells are delivered in the same order in which they are sent. The main three uses of Virtual Channel Connections are :

- *Between End Users*—Can be used to carry end-to-end user data; can also be used to carry control signaling between end users. A Virtual Path Connection between end users provides them with an overall capacity.
- *Between an End User and a Network Entity*—Used for users-to-network control signaling. A user-to-network Virtual Path Connection can be used to aggregate traffic from an end user to a network exchange or network server.
- *Between Two Network Entities*—Used for network traffic management and routing functions. A network-to-network Virtual Path Connection can be used to define a common route for the exchange of network management information.

Virtual Path/Virtual Channel Characteristics

- *Quality of Service*—A user of a virtual channel is provided with quality of service specified by parameters such as cell loss ratio and cell delay variation.
- *Switched and Semi-permanent Virtual Channel*—Both switched connection, which require call control signaling, and dedicated connections can be provided.
- *Call Sequence Integrity*—the sequence of transmitted cells within a virtual channel is preserved.
- *Traffic Parameter Negotiation and Usage Monitoring*—Traffic parameters can be negotiated between a user and the network for each virtual channel. The input of the cell to the virtual channel monitored by the network to ensure that the negotiated parameters are not violated.

Control Signaling

For virtual channels, I.150 species four methods for providing an establishment by release facility. One or a combination of these methods will be used in any particular network.

- Semi-permanent VCCs may be used for user-to-user exchange in this case no control signaling is required.
- If there is no pre-established call control signaling channel, then none must be set-up. For that purpose, a control-signaling exchange must take place between user and network on some channel. Hence the need the permanent channel, probably of low data rate, that can be used to set up a virtual channel that because the channel is used to set-up signaling channels.
- The meta-signaling channel can be used to set-up the virtual channel between the user and the network for call control signaling. This user-to-network signaling virtual channel can then be used to virtual channel to carry user data.
- The meta-signaling channel can also to used to set-up a user-to-user signaling virtual channel. Such a channel must be set-up within a preestablished virtual path. It can then be used to allow to the end users, without network intervention, to establish and realize user-to-user virtual channel to carry user data.

For virtual part, three methods are defined in i.150 :

- A virtual path can be established on a semi-permanent basis by prior agreement. In this case, no control signaling is required.
- Virtual path is establishment/realize may be customer controlled. In this case, the customer uses a signaling virtual channel to request the virtual path from the network.
- Virtual path establishment/realize may be network controlled. In this case, the network establishes a virtual path for its own convenience. The path may be network-to-network, or user-to-user.

ATM Cells

The asynchronous transfer mode makes use of fixed-size cells, consisting of a 5-octet header and a 48-octet information field.

There are several advantages to the use of small, fixed-size cells. First, the use of small may reduce queuing delay for a high-priority cell, because the call waits less if it arrives slightly behind a lower less if it arrives slightly behind a lower priority cell that has gained to a resource. Second, it appears that fixed-size cells can be switched more efficiently, which is important for the very high data rates of ATM.

Header Format

- The virtual path identifier (VPI) consisting a routine field for the network.

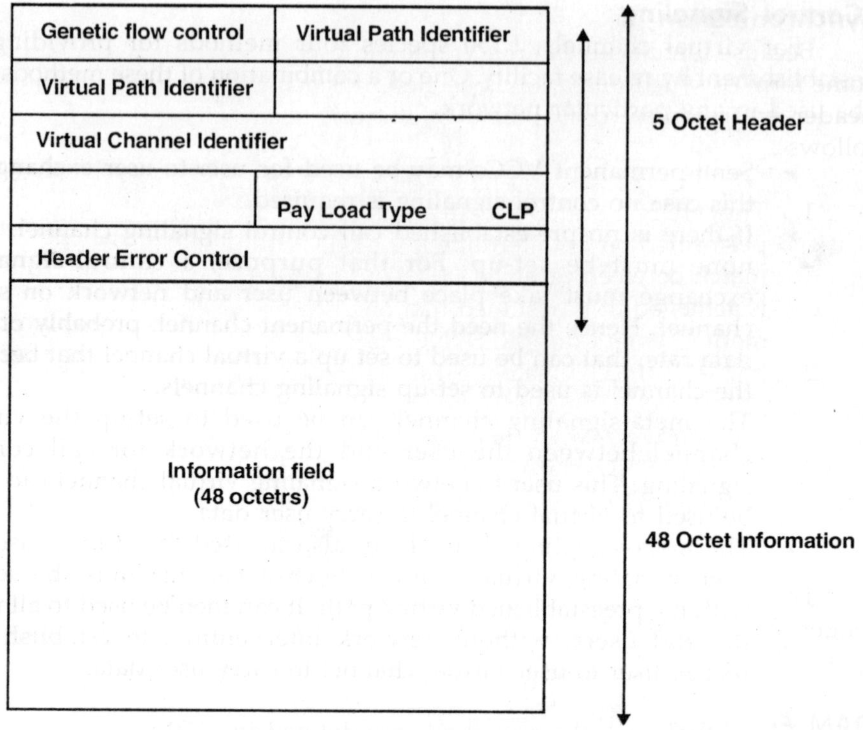

FIG. 21.1
ATM Header Format

- The virtual channel identifier (VCI) is used for routing to and from the end user.
- The payload type field indicates the type of information in the field.
- The cell loss priority (CLP) bit is used to provide guidance to the network in the event of congestion.
- The header error-control field is used for both error control and synchronization.

Transmission of ATM Cells

ATM cells may be transmitted at one of several data rates 622.08 Mbps, 155.52 Mbps, 51.84 Mpbs or 25.6 Mbps. As with the ISDN, we need to specify the structure that will be used to carry this payload. Two approaches are defined for this—A cell-based physical layer and an Synchronous Digital Hierarchy (SDH)-based physical layer.

Cell-Based Physical Layer

For cell-based physical layer, no framing is imposed. The interface structure consists of a continuous stream of 53-cetet cells.

Synchronization

Because there is no external frame imposed in the cell-based approach, some form of synchronization is needed. It is achieved on the basis of three header error control (HEC) field in the cell header. The procedure is as follows :

1. The HUNT state, a cell-delineartion algorithm is referred is performed bit to determine if the HEC coding law is observed (i.e., match between received HEC and calculated HEC). Once a match is achieved, it is assumed that one header has been found, and the method enters the PRESYNC state.
2. In the PRESYNC state, a cell-delineation algorithm is performed cell by cell until the encoding law has been confirmed *d* times consecutively; then there are a transition to the SYNC state.
3. In the SYNC state, the HEC is used for error detection and correction. Cell delineation is assumed to be lost if the HEC coding law is recognized as incorrect $ times consecutively.

The values *a* and *d* are design parameters. Greater value of $ results in longer delays in establishing synchronization but in greater robustness against false delineation. Greater robustness against false misalignment.

OAM Functions

ATM cells are used to convey operations, administration, and maintenance (OAM) information by preassigned cell header cell values, one for each level of information flow.

ATM Adaption Layer

The use of ATM creates the need for an adaption layer to support information transfer protocols not based on ATM. Two examples are PCM (Pulse-Code Modulation) voice and LAPD.

ALL Services :

- Handling of transmission errors,
- Segmentation and reassembly, to enable larger blocks of data to be carried in the information field of ATM cell,
- Handling of lost and misinserted cell conditions, and
- Flow control and timing control.

AAL Protocols

The AAL layer is organized in two logical sub-layers : the Convergence Sub-layer (CS) and the Segmentation and Reassembly Sub-layer (SAR). The convergence sub-layer provides the function needed to support specific applications using AAL. Each application attaches to AAL at a service access point (SAP), which is simply the address of the application. This sub-layer is thus service dependent.

The segmentation and reassembly sub-layer is responsible for packing information received from CS in to cells for transmission and unpacking the information at the other end. The following diagram indicated the general protocol architecture for ATM and AAL. In this a higher block of diagram is encapsulated in a single protocol data unit (PDU) consisting of the layer data and possibly a header and trailer containing protocol information at the CS level. This CS PDU is then passed down to the SAR layer and segmentation into number of blocks. Each of these blocks is encapsulated in a single 48-octet SAPDU, which may include as header of data and a trailer in addition to the block of data passed down from CS. Finally each SARPDU forms the payload of signal ATM Cell.

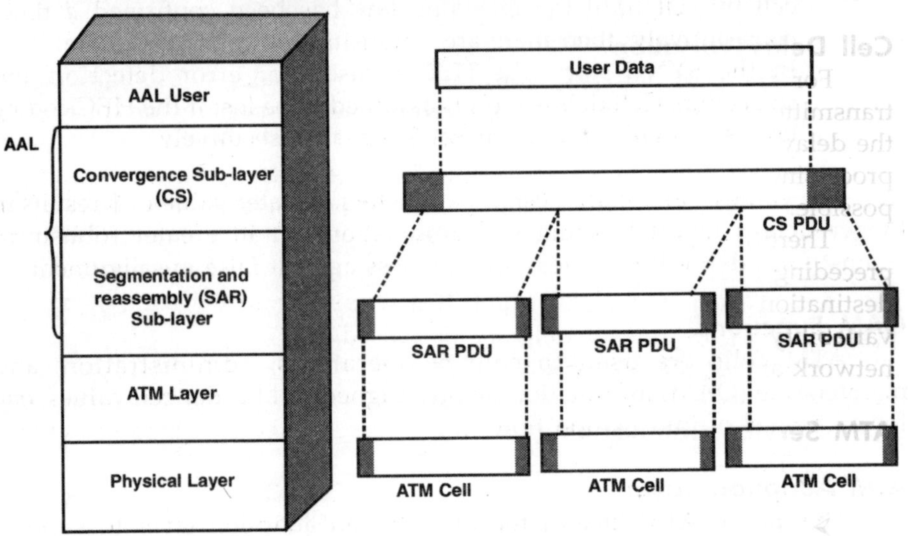

FIG. 21.2
AAL Protocol

ATM Traffic and Congestion Control

The types of traffic patterns imposed on ATM networks are differ from markedly from those of other switching networks.

A number of tools have been developed for control of congestion in packet switched and frame relay net works, as we have seen. These types of congesation control schemes are inadequate for ATM net works. Cites the following reasons :

1. Much of the traffic is not amenable to flow control.
2. Feedback is slow due to the drastically reduced cell transmission time compared to propagation delays across the network.
3. ATM networks typically support a wide range of applications

required capacity ranging from a few Kbps to several hundred Mbps.

4. Applications on ATM networks may generate very traffic patterns.
5. Different applications of ATM networks require different network services.
6. The very high speed in switching and transmission make ATM networks volatile in terms of congesation and traffic control.

Latency and Speed Effects

The time it takes to transfer the cell from source to the destination user will depend upon the number of intermediate ATM Switches, the switching time at each links in the path from source to destination.

Cell Delay Variation

For an ATM network, voice and video signal can be digitized and transmitted as stream of cells. A key requirement, especially for voice, is that the delay across the network to be sort. ATM is designed to minimize the processing to the network so that very fast cell switching and routing is possible.

There is another requirement that to some extent conflicts with the preceding to requirements—names that the rate of delivery of cell to the destination user must be constant. It is inevitable that there will be some variability in the rate of delivery of cells due both to efforts within the network and at the source UNI.

ATM Service Categories

The service categories of ATMs are :

➢ REAL TIME SERVICES
- ☐ Constant Bit Rate (CBR)
- ☐ Real Time Variable Bit Rate (rt-VBR)

➢ NON-REAL TIME SERVICE
- ☐ Non-Real Time Variable Bit Rate (nrt-VBR)
- ☐ Available Bit Rate (ABR)
- ☐ Unspecified Bit Rate (UBR)

Conclusion

In the above statement the ATM is very useful in all parts ISDN, to achieve the High speed networking without error free and easy flow of control.

Part V

Wireless/Mobile Computing

Generic Considerations Regarding Current and Future State of Wireless Technologies and Infrastructures

S. Anitha, P. Narendran, K. Sangeetha and R. Sumangali

Introduction

The use of wireless technologies is increasing significantly for local service applications in telecommunication networks for access and distribution in external plant and customer premise applications. The major advantages of wireless are communications to mobile subscribers, the opportunity for reducing infrastructure costs in fixed systems, the ability to rapidly deploy new systems, and the implementation of communications for sparsely populated areas and global users. A broad range of fixed and mobile, terrestrial and satellite systems and local area networks are used. This paper addresses the current state of the art of these technologies and infrastructures, projects where the field will be in the next decade, and discusses some of the challenges that must be met.

Service Considerations

Mobile and fixed local services provided by terrestrial and satellite systems are considered. Some services for the 2010 time frame are a continuation or an evolution of today's services. Other services will be totally new as a result of technology innovations. A key to the success of an entirely new infrastructure is lower costs than existing infrastructures.

Fixed Wireless Access (FWA)

Current FWA and local service implemented with duplex point-to-point (P-P) microwave and millimeter wave systems include fixed versions of mobile cellular systems, CLEC provided Broadband Wireless Access (BWA) up to OC-3 capacity from business premises to long distance carriers and satellite terminals, private industrial and local government networks, and VSAT links.

Future P-MP fixed services will include the duplex MMDS and 28/31 GHz Local Multipoint Distribution Service (LMDS) for industrial and residential subscribers. Future millimeter wave point-to-point systems include a greater variety of narrow band and broadband links from fiber network terminations to CLEC subscribers, and private networks.

Mobile Wireless Access (MWA)

The primary mobile systems for the local service today are cellular and PCS systems in the 800 MHz and 2 GHz bands respectively, 800 MHz low speed packet data (20kb/s) services such as Cellular Digital Packet Data (CDPD), and 800 MHz paging and messaging systems. Although all new cellular systems are digital, the digital service is not expected to exceed the analog AMPS service until the year 2000. US digital systems use IS-95 CDMA, IS-54/136 TDMA, and GSM technologies. The systems provide limited location information that is inadequate for fast 911 service.

The primary focus of future mobile systems will be to provide Internet access and higher speed data services to mobile subscribers and platforms. Both terrestrial and satellite systems will provide these services. Future mobile services will include the third generation (3G) and higher generation cellular systems which will permit data rates of 384kb/s to cellular mobile subscribers, accurate location systems which will greatly improve 911 service for cellphone subscribers, improved QoS, and higher voice quality than today's systems. Wideband CDMA access will be in most widespread use. Services and applications will include mobile computing, high speed Internet access, in-vehicle real time traffic data and optimum route selection, fleet and individual location information, email, video conferencing, video-game playing, music downloading, low tier service for wireless access to the home and walking speed subscribers, and common cordless and mobile handsets. These services will be introduced in Europe and Japan during the next two years and in the US several years later.

Competitive Approaches

Within the microwave technologies, there can be competition in terrestrial systems between the frequency bands, and also with satellite links, but for the short-term the primary approach will be the 1-2 GHz terrestrial access to the mobile subscriber. Future MWA systems will also use frequencies in the 6 GHz bands.

Fiber access, HFC, and broadband satellite will compete with LMDS and BWA wireless systems for high speed access in the 0.1 to 1.0 GB/s systems. Fixed 3G and higher generation wireless operating in the microwave and milliwave bands will compete with digital subscriber line

(DSL) and HFC for 1 to 10 MB/s access. By the year 2010 mobile cellular systems will provide access at rates above 2MB/s.

Technical Challenges and Requirements

Some of the primary technical challenges for the wireless systems envisioned for the 2010 time frame involve propagation issues related to the very difficult microwave multipath environment for the access systems in the 0.8 to 6 GHz frequency range. This environment plays a key role in the low QoS, the low data rate limitation because of delay dispersion problems, and the inability to use high-level modulation systems to achieve high spectral efficiency. Also for millimeter wave systems, losses due to rain, shrubs, trees, and polarization conversion can lead to significant fading. millimeter wave subscriber systems must be simple to instal without requiring significant system engineering for each subscriber site.

The higher data rate wireless systems of the future will make possible a significant mix of multimedia traffic including voice, high speed internet traffic, and video communications, which will introduce a wide range of latencies, burstiness, and holding times into the wireless networks.

Network Issues

There are many network issues that must be addressed by the future wireless networks. Since these will process and transport multimedia traffic, networking issues will be considerably more complex than in the past. Interoperability with all transport and switching elements of the infrastructure and seamless interconnection of the wireless network is required. In addition, the wireless networks must be compatible with the network management and billing systems encountered in internet working. The growth approach for the wireless networks is a key factor to address. If a new wireless service is to be added to an existing network, any changes to the infrastructure must be backwards compatible, at least for some reasonable time frame, and must allow those subscribers who do not elect to use the new service to continue operation with existing subscriber equipment. The strategy for the introduction of new services and network features must accommodate existing as well as future subscribers.

Regulatory and Standards Issues

Frequency spectrum being a limited natural resource, most frequency bands are allocated to more than one service. Spectrum sharing among different radio services is implemented where it does not impair service viability; it is accomplished through geographical and/or frequency separation between stations of the sharing services. Regulatory provisions are made for exclusive spectrum usage by services that would be excessively restricted by sharing. Generic examples of exclusive band usage for direct-to-user access systems include cellular terrestrial systems and mobile satellite systems; specific examples include LMDS and BWA terrestrial fixed systems and the Teledesic LEO FSS system. Significantly, there is also the problem of frequency band sharing among satellite systems themselves, both between satellites of the same kind, e.g. GEO-GEO or LEO-LEO, and of different kinds, e.g. GEO-LEO. Software Defined Radio (SDR), which aims at handset and base station versatility for operation with different standards. This standardization activity, and similar other, e.g. Wireless ATM (WATM), are progressed in an increasing number of forums and other industry organizations that effectively complement the work of the traditional standardization organizations.

The Technological Evolution

Fixed Services

The technological evolution on which fixed direct-to-user two-way wireless services will depend over the next decade is in the 20-100 GHz frequency range for fixed terrestrial services, and in the 18-50 GHz range for fixed satellite services.

Terrestrial Fixed Wireless Access (FWA)

Gallium Arsenide (GaAs) is the base active device material of choice in current commercial applications and promises to dominate over the next decade, especially in the more cost sensitive low-noise and power amplifiers, up- and down-converters, and oscillators. Indium Phosphide (InP) is a serious contender for some future commercial applications within the same time frame. Substantial improvements in commercially available components and sub-systems will be achieved toward the end of the next decade, such as higher device efficiency and reliability, high-performance non-hermetic operation, higher levels of circuit and sub-system integration including 3-dimensional Monolithic Microwave Integrated Circuits (MMICs), improved manufacturability and packaging, and cost effectiveness. New Micro Electromechanical (MEM) devices produced using integrated circuit technology will be used in the next decade for certain switching functions. Systems Point-to-Point (P-P) implementations using a low-level modulation method, e.g. QPSK.

Toward the end of the next decade, these can be expected to increase to 512-level modulations (which are being used in some frequency bands below 10 GHz) and to OC-12 or STM-4 transmission capacity. Mesh systems are under development and initial deployment is expected early in the next decade. These systems aim at higher network spectral efficiencies and flexible hubless network architecture.

Fixed Satellite Service (FSS)

Multimedia satellite communication systems are being developed to provide global, broadband communication services including high data rate Internet access, private Intranets, and TV broadcasting. Some of these systems will offer data communication services in the 20/30 GHz bands and digital broadcasting in the 12 GHz and 17 GHz.7 bands. Satellite communication networks can interoperate with the current major technology developments, e.g., Internet Protocol (IP) and Asynchronous Transfer Mode (ATM).

Major factors influencing the development of multimedia satellite networks at the 20/30GHz frequencies are : adaptive power control and adaptive coding technologies to minimize the impact of errors due to anomalous propagation; large bandwidth allocation to geosynchronous fixed satellite services (GSO FSS) and non-geosynchronous fixed satellite services (NGSO FSS) enabling high data rate services; advances in device technologies including 20 and 30GHz transistors, higher efficiency traveling-wave tubes (TWTAs).

The interest in ATM is also demonstrated by the architectures of some proposed new satellite systems. For example, some Ka-band (20/30 GHz) low earth orbit (LEO), medium earth orbit (MEO), and geosynchronous earth orbit (GEO) satellites plan to implement ATM on board processing (OBP) and switching capabilities.

A crucial requirement for any broadband network is the reliable transport of data traffic, namely, non-real-time loss-sensitive flows (as opposed to real-time voice/video streams). Examples include e-mail and file transfers, Web messages, and facsimile transmissions. Since reliable transmission is mandatory, the ubiquitous TCP/IP has emerged as the workhorse protocol for most data applications.

Many researchers have proposed a wide range of solutions to improve TCP/IP performance in satellite networks. These range from link-layer error control schemes and protocols to more elaborate TCP/IP versions, and advanced interworking. Although some solutions are more effective than others, it is likely that modern systems will draw from all the above.

Mobile Services

The technological evolution on which mobile direct-to-user two-way wireless services will depend over the next decade is in the 0.8-6 GHz frequency range for the terrestrial mobile service and in the 1-3 GHz range for the satellite mobile service.

Terrestrial Mobile Service (MS)

Silicon is the preferred base material in current commercial applications and promises to dominate over the next decade, particularly in CMOS and Silicon-Germanium (SiGe) integrated circuits. GaAs found widespread microwave applications, as well, primarily in low-noise and power amplifiers, where its superior noise performance and efficiency are at a premium. However, SiGe is now emerging as a serious competitor, especially because it facilitates the integration of handset transmitter-receivers on a single chip. This competition can be expected to intensify with time, and to result in substantial technology improvements over the next decade. Packaging is an important enabling technology in the manufacture of low cost, thermally efficient, miniaturized products for a wide range of wireless communication application. The dominant package options are the single chip plastic encapsulated and the ceramic package. A joint effort of six companies representing significant suppliers of technology to the ceramic packaging and interconnect industry has reported both performance and cost advantages.

Mobile Satellite Service (MSS)

Currently, mobile satellites are in the midst of the birth of providing Global Mobile Personal Communications via Satellite (GMPCS). The key advantage that mobile satellites provide over other networks is global access to network services. Current systems provide voice and data services on a global basis regardless of geographical location and local infrastructure. The current systems will grow to include the provision of enhanced and expanded services. These evolving services will include facsimile, e-mail, Internet access, video and multi-media.

Basic to the meaningful evolution of mobile satellite networks beyond their current status is the successful identification and allocation of increased spectrum space. Existing allocations will soon be exhausted by currently active and planned systems.

Providing more service with limited bandwidth will be an ongoing challenge to mobile satellite systems. This challenge will be met through improvements in source coding techniques that will allow lower transmission rates for the anticipated expanded services such as video and multi-media. Network protocol adaptations and improvements will be required to allow the transmission of high bandwidth applications such as web pages over low bandwidth channels. Improvements will also be necessary in transmission channel quality.

Upcoming Wireless Standards and Wireless Security

There are three wireless networking standards in relatively common use at this time :

- 802.11b—(11 Mb/second max speed, 2.4 GHz frequency)
- 802.11g—(54 Mb/second max speed, 2.4 GHz frequency)
- 802.11a—(54 Mb/second max speed, 5.5 GHz frequency)

New Security Option : SSL

Secure Socket Layer (SSL) encryption would be used to provide wireless users with simple access to a limited number of selected network services. At the moment, the proposed list includes :

- http (web pages)
- https (encrypted web pages)
- ssh (secure shell)
- sftp (secure file transfer)
- sPOP and sIMAP (secure email protocols)

Conclusions

The established major areas of commercial wireless access technology utilization ranked by deployment extent are : terrestrial mobile wireless access (MWA) using cellular systems in the 800 MHz and 1900 MHz bands, terrestrial broadband wireless access (BWA) using point-to-point (P-P) systems in the 38 GHz and 24 GHz frequency bands, the Iridium mobile satellite service (MSS) in the 1600 MHz band.

Future developments are expected during the coming decade : continuing introduction of enhanced 2G MWA systems, and subsequent introduction of 3G and 4G systems offering improved voice quality, higher data rates, mobile, 14 wireless IP, wireless ATM and some as yet unidentified new services and features in several frequency bands up to about 6 GHz.

All these systems aim to provide wireless IP and the ones with sufficiently large capacity also wireless ATM. The mobile satellite service (MSS) will be a component of the advanced generations of mobile telecommunication networks and will provide global coverage and access, in areas not served by the terrestrial wireless carriers, and for users whose primary needs are better served with a mobile satellite system

References

1. Budde, P. (1996), "Information Technology Management", *Paul Budde Communication*, Vol. 7 : 77-95.
2. Ericsson Inc (1996), *GSM : The Future*. Available at the URL :http ://www.ericsson.se/systems/gsm/future.htm.
3. Levesque, A. and Pahlavan, K. (1996) : Wireless Data, *"The Mobile communications Handbook"*, IEEE PRESS : 553-67.
4. Mcgladdery, W. and Clifford, R. (1993) : "Survey of current and emerging wireless data networks", *Proceedings of Canadian Conference on Electrical and Computer Engineering*, IEEE Canada : 1000-1003.

CHAPTER

23

Wireless Mobile Computing

S. VIMALA AND N. KAVITHA

Introduction

The term *mobile computing* is used to describe an array of technologies supporting personal mobility for computer users. Such mobility can take the form of users moving between fixed terminals anywhere in the world or users taking mobile devices with them wherever they move. In both cases, the user should have a consistent working environment with access to their usual files, email, and so on. Mobility should therefore support the seamless movement of people, data, and/or applications between different locations. The technologies required are a combination of various communications media, data servers, and (possibly portable) computers.

The explosion in mobile computing has been made possible through the continued advancement of certain key technological areas. It is possible to evaluate the past successes, current trends and future opportunities by considering the following areas : First, we need to consider the relationship between mobility, portability, human ergonomics and cost. For example, in order to make a device portable it must be small and lightweight, which precludes the use of most standard hard drive and keyboard designs. Second, a fundamental requirement of today's computer is network connectivity. This implies, mostly, radio-frequency wireless communications for mobile devices. Although infrared mobile computer communications can be also used, interference from the sun as well as the difficulty of non-line-of-sight communications make radio frequency the preferred method for location independent mobile communications. Third and most important are the power considerations of mobile computers. Mobility implies reliance on a mobile portable power source in the form of a battery. Since the power available from a battery is closely related to its size and weight, it is fundamental that all the parts of the mobile device are power-efficient. As battery capacities are not expected to increase more than 30% in the near future, while computing capabilities and features have ever increasing expectations, power efficiency has become a fundamental technology.

New wireless technologies offer more information, applications, and productivity tools to mobile workforce than ever before. But these enhanced capabilities can also involve expensive IT investments and complicate your infrastructure. The widespread deployment and use of wireless data communications in the mobile computing domain is generally recognized as being the next major advance in the information technology industry. Both mobility and wireless networking represent key enabling technologies underlying the vision of *ubiquitous computing*, where interconnected computers will be embedded in a wide range of appliances ranging in size from door locks to vehicle controllers performing tasks on behalf of their human users, such as automatically opening doors and routing vehicles to their intended destinations. Where *Wireless* refers to the method of transferring information between computing devices, such as a Personal Data Assistant (PDA), and a data source, such as an agency database server, without a physical connection. Not all wireless communications technologies are mobile. For example, lasers are used in wireless data transfer between buildings, but cannot be used in mobile communications at this time and *Mobile* simply describes a computing device that is not restricted to a desktop. A mobile device may be a PDA, a "smart" cell phone or Web phone, a laptop computer, or any one of numerous other devices that allow the user to complete computing tasks without being tethered, or connected to a network. Mobile computing does not necessarily require wireless communication. In fact, it may not require communication between devices at all.

There are some inherent challenges in using these technologies on a widespread basis. One particularly troublesome issue for wireless communications is security. For instance, some wireless technologies are not suitable for applications in which sensitive client information is exchanged between a central database and a remote device because the data signal can be intercepted. Furthermore, ensuring adequate security for such a situation could add significant expense to a wireless application.

In addition, both wireless and mobile devices incur support costs that exceed those of typical desktop equipment. Because of this, industry experts recommend that an organization standardizes its wireless and mobile application environment in order to reduce the burden on IT staff.

When deciding on whether to implement a wireless and/or mobile application, two key factors must be considered :

➢ *Usage* : How will the device or application be used? Is the application used for simple messaging, or does it re-engineer complex and sensitive processes? Usage and content determine the necessary complexity of the device, the level of security and reliability needed, and whether or not the application needs continuous, immediate access to data.

- *Amount of Data* : How much data must be exchanged between the device and the central data repository? Is the data cumbersome with intense bandwidth requirements? This factor determines which connectivity technologies would be the most fitting to use.

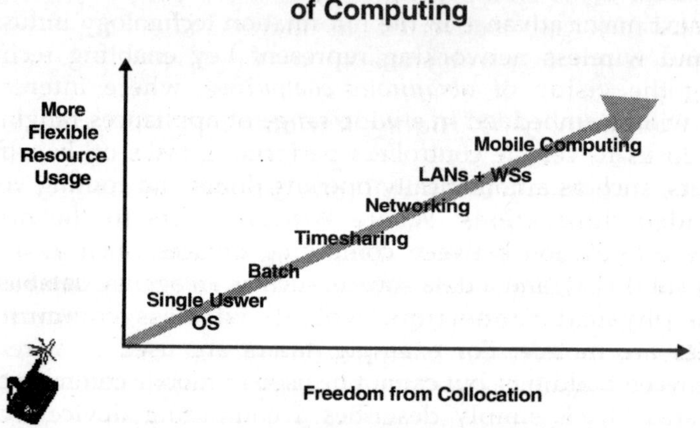

Fig. 23.1
Mobile Evolution

Definition

Wireless communication is simply data communication without the use of landlines. This may involve cellular telephone, two-way radio, fixed wireless, laser, or satellite communications.

Mobile, or "untethered," computing means that the computing device is not continuously connected to the base or central network. Mobile devices include PDAs, laptop computers, and many of today's cell phones (aptly called "smart phones"). These products may communicate with a base location with or without a wireless connection. An example of a wireless mobile application is using a modem-equipped PDA to receive text messages via satellite technology. A non-wireless mobile example could involve sending data from a laptop to a central database or network server over a temporary dial-up connection. In the latter example, the laptop can still be used as a mobile device regardless of whether or not it ever connects to another computing device.

Constraints of Mobility

Mobile computing is characterized by four constraints :

1. Mobile Elements are Resource-Poor Relative to Static Elements

For a given cost and level of technology, considerations of weight, power, size and ergonomics will exact a penalty in computational resources such as processor speed, memory size, and disk capacity. While mobile elements will improve in absolute ability, they will always be resource-poor relative to static elements.

2. Mobility is Inherently Hazardous

A Wall Street stockbroker is more likely to be mugged on the streets of Manhattan and have his laptop stolen than to have his workstation in a locked office be physically subverted. In addition to security concerns, portable computers are more vulnerable to loss or damage.

3. Mobile Connectivity is Highly Variable in Performance and Reliability

Some buildings may offer reliable, high-bandwidth wireless connectivity while others may only offer low-bandwidth connectivity. Outdoors, a mobile client may have to rely on a low-bandwidth wireless network with gaps in coverage.

4. Mobile Elements Rely on a Finite Energy Source

While battery technology will undoubtedly improve over time, the need to be sensitive to power consumption will not diminish. Concern for power consumption must span many levels of hardware and software to be fully effective. These constraints are not artifacts of current technology, but are intrinsic to mobility. Together, they complicate the design of mobile information systems and require us to rethink traditional approaches to information access.

Security

Security for mobile, wireless computing is a particularly difficult problem. Some technologies, such as Free Space Optics, have more security because of the physical characteristics of the media. However, other technologies, such as cell phones and digital pagers, have almost no security because of poorly designed communication protocols. There are options for bolstering security. For instance, industry analysts recommend firewalls for mobile devices wherever practical and anti-virus software developers have added extensions into their products to support the most common handheld devices. Even then, there are no fool-proof solutions.

According to Giga, the situation is made more complex because mobile workers tend to be less technically adept than tethered workers are. Therefore, security for their devices must be automatic and transparent in order to be effective.

Security Risk

Precisely because connection to a wireless link is so easy, the security of wireless communication can be compromised much more easily than that of wired communication, especially if transmission extends over a large area. This increases pressure on mobile computing software designers to include security measures.

Security is further complicated if users are allowed to cross-security domains. For example, a hospital may allow patients with mobile computers to use nearby printers but prohibit access to distant printers and resources designated for hospital personnel only.

Secure communication over insecure channels is accomplished by encryption, which can be done in software or more quickly, by specalised hardware such as the recently proposed clipper chip. Security depends on secret encryption key known only to the authorized parties. Managing these keys securely is difficult, but it can be automated by software such as the Massachusetts Institute of Technology's Kerberos.

Kerberos provides secure authentication services, as long as the Kerberos server itself is trusted. If authenticates users without exposing their passwords on the network and generates secret encryption keys that can be selectively shared between mutually suspicious parties. It also allow mobile units to authenticate themselves in domains where they are unknown, thus enhancing scale of mobility.

Challenges in Mobile Computing

The technical challenges that mobile computing to achieve this potential are hardly trivial, however, some of the challenges in designing software for mobile computing systems are quite different from those involved in the design of software for today's stationary network system. The many issues to be dealt with stem from essential properties of mobile computing : communication, mobility, and portability. Of course, special purpose system may avoid some design pressures by doing without certain desirable properties. For instance, portability would be less of a concern for mobile computers installed in the dashboards of cars than with hand-held mobile computers. However, we concentrate on the goal of large scale, hand-held mobile computing as a way to reveal a wide assortment of issues.

Communication

Mobile computing requires wireless network access, although sometimes—when in meeting rooms or at user desk—they remain stationary long enough to be physically attached to the network for a better or cheaper connection. Wireless networks communicate by modulating radio waves or pulsing infrared light. Wireless communication is linked to the wired infrastructure by stationary transceivers. The area covered by an individual by a individual transceivers signal is known as a cell. Cell size vary widely; for example, an infrared transceivers can cover a small meeting room, a cellular telephone transceivers has a range of a few miles, and a satellite beam can cover an area more than 400 miles in diameter.

Wireless communication faces more challenges than wired communication because the surrounding environment interacts with signal, blocking signal paths and introducing noise and echoes. As a result, low bandwidths, higher error rates, and more frequent spurious disconnections characterize wireless communication. These factors can in turn increase communication latency resulting from retransmission, retransmission time-out delays, error-control protocols processing, and short disconnections.

Mobility can also cause wireless connections to be lost or degraded. Users may travel beyond the coverage of network transceivers or enter areas of high interference. Unlike typical wired networks, the number of devices in the network cells varies dynamically, and large concentrations of mobile users, say, at convention and public event, may overload network capacity.

Mobility

Mobility Introduces Several Problems : A mobile computer network address changes dynamically, its current location affects configuration parameters as well as answers to user queries, and the communication path grows as it wanders away from nearby server.

Address Migration : As people move, their mobile computers will use different network access points, or "address". Today's networking is not designed for dynamically changing address. Active network connection usually cannot be moved to a new address. Once an address for a host name is known to a system, it is typically cached with a long expiration time and with no way to invalidate out of date entries. In internet Protocols, for example, a host IP name is inextricably bound with its network address; moving to a new location means acquiring a new IP name. Human intervention is commonly required to coordinate the use of address.

To communicate with a mobile computer, messages must be sent to its most recent address. The four basic mechanism to determine mobile computer's current address are : broadcast, central services, home base and forwarding pointers.

Portability

Today's desktop computers are not meant to be carried, so designers take a liberal approach to space, power, cabling, and heat dissipation. In contrast, designers of hand-held mobile computers should strive for the properties of a wrist watches : small, light, durable, operational under wide environmental conditions, and requiring minimal power usage for long battery life. Concessions can be made in each of these areas to enhance functionality, but ultimately the user must receive value that exceeds the trouble of carrying the device. Similarly, any specialized hardware to offload such task such as data compression or encryption from CPU should justify its consumption of power and space.

Conclusion

Mobile computing is technology that enables access to digital resources at any time, from any location. From a narrow viewpoint, mobile computing represents a convenient addition to wire-based local area distributed systems. Taken more broadly, mobile computing represents the elimination of time and place restrictions imposed by desktop computers and wired networks. In forecasting the impact of mobile technology, we would do well to observe recent trends in the use of the wired infrastructure, in particular, the Internet, in the past year; the advent of convenient mechanism for browsing has engendered an explosive growth in the use of those resources. The ability to access them at all times through mobile computing will allow their use to be integrated into all aspects of life and will accelerate the demand for network services. The challenge for computing designers is to adapt the system structures that have worked well for traditional computing so that mobile computing can be integrated as well.

REFERENCES

1. http ://www.cs.tcd.ie/publications/tech-reports/reports.03/TCD-CS-2003-23.pdf
2. http ://www.dir.state.tx.us/pubs/wireless/wireless.htm#_Toc12790129
3. http ://www.hp.com/hps/network/info/mws_brief.pdf
4. http://www.cs.colorado.edu/~rhan/CSCI_7143_002_Fall_2001/Papers/Forman94_Challenges.pdf
5. http ://www-2.cs.cmu.edu/afs/cs/project/coda/Web/docdir/podc95.pdf
6. http ://www.sss-mag.com/pdf/1mobicomp.pdf
7. http ://www.jasonredi.com/papers/mobile_computing_summary_distrib.pdf

Context-Aware Mobile Computing Architecture

T. AMUDHA AND S. ROHINI

Introduction

Information about the user's environment offers new opportunities and exposes new challenges in terms of time-aware, location-aware, device-aware and personalized applications. Such applications constantly need to monitor the environment—called context—to allow the application to react accordingly to this context. *Context-awareness is especially interesting in mobile scenarios* where the context of the application is highly dynamic and allows the application to deal with the constraints of mobile devices in terms of presentation and interaction abilities and communication restrictions.

Computer applications traditionally expect a static execution environment. However, this precondition is generally not possible for mobile systems, where the world around an application is constantly changing. More specifically, mobile systems advances the following goals : (1) enabling seamless interaction across devices; (2) creating physical spaces that are responsive to users; and (3) building applications that are aware of the context of their use. Examples of these goals are : continuing in an office a program started at home; automatically canceling phone forwarding upon return to office; having an airport overhead display highlight the flight information viewers are likely to be interested in; and automatically turning off a PDA's audible e-mail notification when in a meeting.

This paper proposes architecture to support context-aware computing; that is, application adaptation triggered by such things as the location of use, the collection of nearby people, the presence of accessible devices and other kinds of objects, as well as changes to all these things over time. It is extensible to consider all kinds of context information and comprises a layered architecture.

This paper describes system architecture for context-aware computing. The active components in this architecture use dynamic environments as a common data and communication interface. The kinds of information that our system manages can be broadly categorized as related to devices, people, and their context. It starts with a description of how this information is divided into components and how these components interact and a detailed presentation of the dynamic environment servers that compose the architecture : *device agent*, *active map*, and *user agent*.

System Organization

The minimal collection of information required for a context-aware system is people, devices, and context. Information about people is used to determine personal preferences and customizations as well as to permit adaptations according to who is nearby. Device is used in a generic sense for anything that can interact by messages, such as printers, displays, mobile hosts, thermostats, phones, etc. Finally, context, consisting of users' relationships to other objects in space, is necessary to tell not only what can be accessed but also whether access is desirable.

Logical Components and Interactions

An architecture providing these basic information categories can be organized in a variety of ways. The architecture presented here divides the world of information into three groups corresponding to the three types of information.

User information is private and individually customized, so it is encapsulated in a "user agent," one for each user. The user agent also publishes location information to the active map, subject to any privacy constraints the user has set. Dynamic device information should be stored

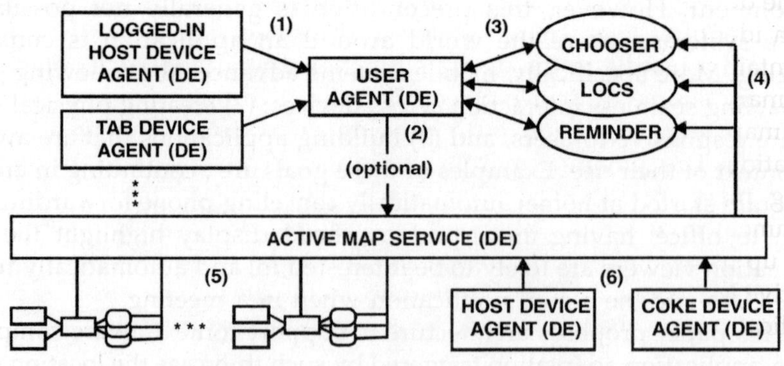

Fig. 24.1
Component and Their Interactions

close to a device making it is less likely for applications to have device connectivity but be partitioned from the information required to access them. Therefore, device information is encapsulated into a "device agent," that is responsible for monitoring or managing a device, for example, a workstation or palmtop.

The active map stores public information about a geographic region and allows queries and subscriptions of that information. The active map is kept up to date by the various device agents and user agents. These logical components of our system satisfy the needs for a basic level of context-aware functionality.

Device Agent

Device agents are dynamic environment servers specialized to monitor and provide information for workstations, printers, palmtops, or other particular devices. When the information about the device changes, an update message is sent. In a context-aware system there may be many kinds of device agents, for example, PDAs, hosts, and displays.

Name	The device name, e.g., Badge:38
Location	The location of the device
Agent	Connection information for the functional network interface of the device if one exists.
DE	Connection information for the Dynamic Environment network interface for the device.

Fig. 24.2
Device Agent Attributes

The device object includes a name identifying the type and instance. A location identifier tells where the device is located. The device object may also contain a handle to the device's functional interface. For applications, the primary source of device objects is indirect through the user agent or active map since their job is to provide an organized view of device information. The dynamic environment is also a convenient debugging and logging mechanism for device usage. The device agent's dynamic environment interface can be found in a number of ways. An agent can be looked up using the discover protocol or it may be looked up by location in the Active Map Server. Finally, a reference to the device agent can be passed to applications on their command lines when they are started.

Active Map Service

The *Active Map Server* (AMS) publishes dynamic environment objects having a location as well as other geographic information. Each AMS supports a set of locations called a *region*. The AMS acts as a location-oriented directory service : location serves as the key those clients use as a first step in determining most of a user's context. The kinds of information that the active map can provide are summarized below :

1. What is co-located with Ram?
2. Are Ram and Phone-3 on the same floor?
3. Is Ram in the building?

Service Organization

The approach here is to support regions that cover the geography over which context-aware applications naturally perform queries, e.g., a building or campus. The active map design consists of a collection of regional servers. Regions cover localized administrative or geographic domains, such as buildings or campuses. Although not strictly necessary, regions should be selected such that they reflect the locality of user movement. Shifting between multiple regions is not a frequent occurrence if regions are suitably defined. This is based on the observation that a user's access pattern is largely influenced by a "locality of reference." This locality is similar to the idea in computer memory systems : once an access is made to an object, future accesses tend to reference nearby rather than distant objects. Context-aware applications are more likely to monitor the contents of the room and building they are situated in than the contents of a building in the next town. In other words, located-information used by context-aware applications will have a high locality of reference based on physical proximity. Most AMS subscriptions will be within a campus, shopping center, work site, or other group of buildings, and probably within a single building. Organizing information into regions will generally not cause extra communication overhead in managing multiple regions as long as regions are big enough.

An important consequence of this approach is that the implementation of an AMS service must be able to scale to cover regions the size of buildings and small campuses so that "regional" queries can be implemented in an efficient fashion. There are a number of advantages to the regional approach. First, the service can be partitioned among servers each managing one or more regions. Second, regions provide a natural administrative barrier. The information pertaining to a domain can be maintained and access controlled according to the domain preferences.

Located Objects

The active map manages dynamic environment objects called *located-objects*. Any information that a client wishes to make publicly available can be entered into the active map with a located-object registration; however, every located-object must include a Location attribute that describes its current physical location. Examples of located-objects include persons, printers, terminals, telephones, PDAs, pagers, and workstations, as well as a store or building.

```
{[Name User:ragnap}
{Location LID:PARC-35-2-1-01}
[person Name "Ryle R. Ragnap"}
{unix Name ragnap}
{office LID:PARC-35-2-1-01}
{Agent sunrpc_2_0x31000041_1|tcp_13.2.116.64_3577}
{DE tcp_13.2.116.64_3579}}
```

Fig. 24.3
Examples for Location Object

The value of the Location attribute is called a *location identifier* or LID for short. Location identifiers represent real world places such as a room, hallway, building floor, building wing, building, street, town, and so on.

Location Information

In addition to providing a dynamic environment of located-objects, the AMS also manages information about the relationships that exist between locations. In people's daily lives two kinds of spatial relations are commonly used : containment and travel distance.

Containment

All locations known to the active map have a containment relation : rooms are contained in buildings and buildings are contained in a region.

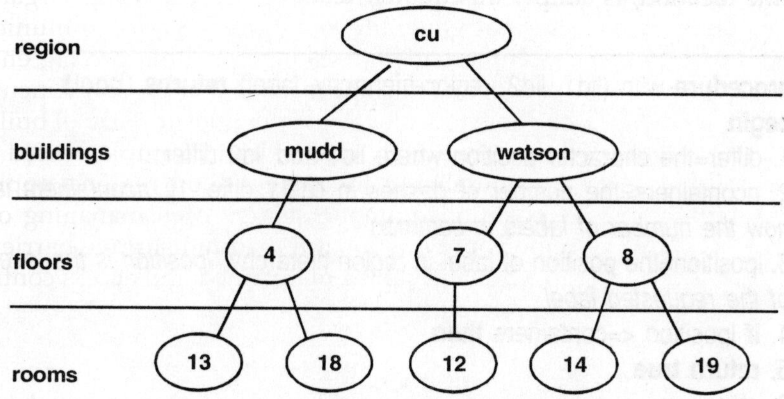

Fig. 24.4
Active Map Containment Hierarchies

The active map supports functions to describe the hierarchy, and the comparing of two locations to see if one is contained within another. A location is defined to be a spatial container—something having physical dimensions encompassing a domain. To be *in* a location means to be within a location's domain; to be *at* a location means to be in no smaller location's domain; and two objects *with* each other share a common location. For example, a person *at* location 2101, or *in* building 35. Additionally, containment tells us whether two objects share some common location domain, in which case they are "with" each other. This property can be used for questions such as "is John in the same building as Doug?"

```
procedure in (lid1,lid2)
begin
return substring (lid1,lid2);
end
```

FIG. 24.5
Computing "in"

For example : PARC-35-2-1-01,CSB-2-10

The first shows the PARC region, building 35, floor 2, pod 1, room 01. The dashes make the container structure explicit. The LID format is useful for figuring relations between two locations. So, to see if one object is "in" a location a procedure checks if the location is a prefix of the object's location. To be "at" a location, which is defined to mean situated at exactly the same location, is simply an equality test.

```
procedure with (lid1, lid2, region-hierarchy, label) returns (bool)
begin
1. differ=the character position where lid1 and lid2 differ;
2. ncontainers=the number of dashes in lid1[1..differ-1]; ncontainers is
now the number of labels in common
3. lposition=the position of label in region-hierarchy; lposition is the level
of the requested label
4. if lposition <=containers then
5. return true
6. else
7. return false
end
```

FIG. 24.6
Computing "with"

The algorithm for this computation takes as input the locations of two objects, e.g., PARC-35-1-02 and PARC-35-2-02, along with the region's hierarchy container labels (e.g., region, building, floor, pod, and room), and the container label for the query, e.g., building. Steps 1 and 2 use text operations to determine the index for the least common ancestor of the two locations. Steps 3 and 4 determine if the requested label, e.g., "floor," is a container that is part of the common prefix.

Travel Distance

It is useful to store distance information such as distances between locations and how to get from one place to another for adjacent objects. A graph-of-nodes representation captures the essential nature of distance in this system model because people generally move between two places by a single, shortest path. There are few desirable paths between locations because corridors and other architectural elements constrain how people move. Paths between distant places can be computed by combining information from these multiple scales. When the system administrator creates the AMS location-hierarchy they also define a graph of locations and the distances between them. A program takes this graph as input and produces a path table, which is loaded into the AMS during program initialization. For each location pair the table stores a distance that is a number for the length of the path from the source to the destination. Two uses for path information are to generate directions on how to move from one place to another, and to find objects within a certain distance.

activemap hierarchy (region) returns (labels)

Return the labels for each level in the region's hierarchy. For example "region building-floor-room" as a text string.

activemap distance (src, dst) returns (distance, step)

Return in distance *the number of feet between* src *and* dst. *Return in* step *the first step along the shortest path between* src *and* dst.

activemap path (src, dst) returns (path)

Return all the steps between src *and* dst *in a text list in* path. *The list consists of triplets (distance, left, next)*, *where* distance *is the number of feet for the current edge,* left *is the number of feet remaining for the path, and* next *is a location identifier for the next step.*

FIG. 24.7
Active Map Path API

This procedure is relatively easy because the step field of the path record contains the next location along the shortest path.

```
procedure path (source, destination)
begin
        activemap_distance (source,destination,
        distance, step);
while destination !=step
        output step;
        activemap_distance (step,destination,
        distance, step);
end
end
```

FIG. 24.8
Computing "path"

The path information that is loaded into the AMS at initialization time is computed using the shortest path algorithm. To manage this the AMS region is partitioned into multiple components each with shortest path information.

activemap query (location, pattern, maximum, options) returns (result)
    Query the active map server for up to maximum objects matching the pattern. The location specifies the active map container to search. Returns a list of objects.
activemap subscribe (location, pattern, options, fcn, arg)
    Initiate a subscription for objects matching the pattern within the container specified by location. Options may include situated-with *plus a located-object for positioning the query relative to some object. Invokes fcn with arg for each matching object.*
activemap unsubscribe (location, pattern, fcn, arg)
    Delete an existing subscription.
activemap move (location, object-name, object)
    Direct the active map to move an object from one location to another. The object name *is the concise object name. The object parameter is optional and used to rewrite the contents of the object.*

FIG. 24.9
Active Map Query API

Query and Subscribe Operations

The AMS query interface is an extension of the generic dynamic environments interface. The AMS permits two options for queries that assist in exploring the hierarchical structure of located-objects. Queries can have a target container and they can be "situated-with" a located-object. When a query has a target, only located-objects within that container are returned. When a query is situated-with a particular located-object, the query follows that object as it moves within the active map.

Move Operation

Agent processes that manage objects are responsible for updating the object's state within the active map. When an object's location or attributes change the agent issues an active map move operation. The move places the object at a new location in the active map and causes a post-processing stage. During this post-processing, the active map may send update messages reporting the changes to subscribers that have posed standing queries.

Active Map Scaling

A key issue in building active maps is that of scale. A variety of issues must be dealt with to avoid overloading the AMS, its clients, and the communication facilities that join them : Large meetings of mobile users may cause considerable traffic because context-aware clients at the meeting as well as remote applications may need to be informed of the frequent occupant changes. High message volume may also occur in high traffic locations such as building lobbies. Low bandwidth links (usually wireless) limit the amount of information that can be sent to some clients. Mobile hosts have significantly stricter resource budgets and hence cannot do as much work as other hosts. The worst-case usage scenario that our architecture is designed to handle is the "meeting scenario" in which several hundred people, all using context-aware applications, converge on an auditorium over a period of several minutes. To illustrate some of the issues involved, consider how location information about this scenario might be disseminated to the people involved : the simplest—a naive unicast approach—would result in updates going to each of clients, which quickly gets out of hand. Using broadcast or multicast for the updates would reduce the aggregate message traffic even further, but would likely *increase* the traffic seen by some clients, since not all clients are interested in exactly the same information.

Active Map Availability

Our design relies on a centralized active map server, implying that the AMS will stop functioning whenever the server crashes. This is not a problem in practice for two reasons : The active map server is host-independent and hence can be run on any available server machine. A distributed watch-dog facility can monitor and restart the server if it fails. A well-known multicast channel allows a newly restarting AMS to obtain current location information from all located-objects agents (i.e., device and user) currently in its region. Agents are expected to be listening to this channel address for a SERVER message in order to re-publish their located-objects with the AMS. AMS clients starting up new instances of the server in their partition when they notice its absence and having servers watch for each other and perform re-integration whenever partitions heal.

User Agent

In our system, each user's information is logically centralized in a user agent. This provides a well-known place for a user's own applications, as well as applications run by others, to find out about the user. This section describes the user agent from a functional viewpoint and proceeds with a presentation of the agent's distributed organization and protocols.

Functional Description

The user agent performs two functions. First, it manages a dynamic environment, called the *user environment*, containing user-specific information. Second, analogous to a device agent that creates a device-object, the user agent creates a user-object giving details about the user including their last known location. The user environment allows applications to share user-specific state across devices. In addition to updates from the user, the environment is also updated by device agents. Specifically, when a device is "owned" (i.e., in use) by the user, the device agent sends device-object updates to the user agent. For example, once a user logs into a host, a host device agent monitors the keyboard and mouse, and upon sensing activity will forward the sightings (a device object) to the user agent. Device objects contain various attributes including the time and type of interaction, and the device location. By updating the user environment, device agents keep the environment populated with a collection of device-objects. This is useful because applications supplied with information about the collection of devices in use by a user can more easily employ multiple devices. For example, when a user returns to his office and logs into a workstation, applications running on a laptop might switch over to use the larger display. The second function of the user agent is to manage it's own user-object. This object is updated in the user environment and provides the best estimate of the user's location. The reported location is only an estimate because device agents may produce multiple streams of potentially conflicting location sightings. This might occur when a user leaves their active badge on their desk, or someone types on a workstation logged-in to another user. It is the job of the user agent to weigh the accuracy of incoming reports and to compute a best estimate of the user's current location. When the user agent computes a new location it updates the user-object in the user environment.

User Agent Organization

The user agent is an abstraction that provides user-specific information.

It can be implemented in a variety of ways, such as a logically centralized server. This approach makes it easy to locate information and

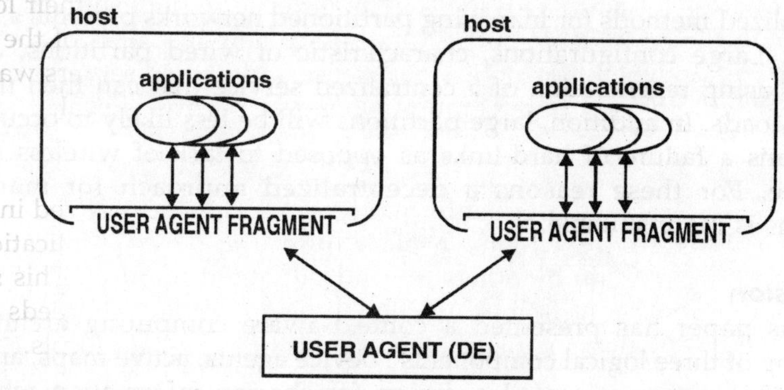

FIG. 24.10
User Agent Organizations

has only a single place to introduce new policies that use a variety of information. Instead of a completely centralized approach, our user agent design employs a backend "user agent" process plus a front-end "user agent fragment" (UAF) process running on each host executing a user's applications. Under normal conditions, the front-end user agent fragment acts as a smart pass through for communicating with dynamic environments, and in particular, the user agent and active map. The second advantage of a user agent fragment residing on each host is to manage dynamic environment information during a network partition. Specifically, when multiple applications exist, either on the same or different hosts, they can potentially share their global environment variables.

It can be concluded that centralized traffic routing is less important for partitions of a small number of cells. This supposes that all clients are able to filter all queries, which is the case in wireless-partitions.

Message	Response	Description
any	Server	Dynamic environment server hearing any trafficcredirects sender to use central server
UPDATE		Update of a dynamic environment to peers
QUERY	UPDATE	Client request of matchng objects from peers
CHECK	UPDATE	Client request of update of a dynamic environment

FIG. 24.11
Summary of Decentralized Message Exchanges

An alternative to server regeneration is to decentralize the management of dynamic environment using broadcast (or multicast) to send updates and queries. A distributed multiple group assignment method is another way to manage the overload problem. The choice between centralized and decentralized methods for managing partitioned networks presents a design tradeoff. Large configurations, characteristic of wired partitions, can be handled using regeneration of a centralized service that can then manage systems loads. In addition, large partitions will be less likely to occur since this means a failure of hard-links as opposed to lack of wireless service coverage. For these reasons a decentralized approach for managing partitions is more suitable.

Conclusion

This paper has presented a context-aware computing architecture consisting of three logical components : device agents, active maps, and user agents. This paper presented a design for sharing information when the fragment is separated from the back-end but still in contact with other devices and hosts.

Ant-Based Routing Schemes for Mobile Ad Hoc Networks

MANGARAJ SAHOO AND B. MAJHI

Introduction

In general case, *ad-hoc* networks are defined as networks formed by users or devices wishing to communicate, without the necessity for the help or existence of any infrastructure or previously established relationship between the potential network members. *Ad-hoc* communication can take place in different scenarios and is independent of any specific device, wireless transmission technology, network or protocol. Some examples of the possible uses of *ad-hoc* networking include sensor networks, search and rescue operations, vehicle communication networks, and possible military applications, etc.

Overview

In particular, we expect that *ad-hoc* networks will be formed in situations where no infrastructure is available. As for the mode of operation, they are basically peer-to-peer multi-hop wireless networks where information packets are transmitted in a store-and-forward manner from a source to an arbitrary destination, via intermediate nodes. The network topology changes dynamically and in an unpredictable manner since the nodes can move freely. Therefore, outdated topology information must be updated or removed. Since there is no centralized entity to keep the topology up-to-date, a *distributed algorithm* is required.

Finding a route to a destination requires exchange of control information among the nodes. Thus, the amount of update traffic can be quite high when the number of highly mobile nodes is large. Thus, the highly dynamic nature of *ad-hoc* networks motivates the study of routing protocols, which aim at achieving *routing stability*.

Again the wireless communication media has a limited bandwidth, which is susceptive to various interferences that can lead to establishment of useless routes, low throughput and other problems. Some of the protocols assume that the communication links are symmetric. Although this assumption is not always valid, it is usually made because routing in asymmetric networks is a relatively hard task. In certain cases, it is possible to find routes that could avoid asymmetric links, since it is quite likely that these links imminently fail. The issue of symmetric and asymmetric links is one among the several challenges encountered in *ad-hoc* networks. Mobile hosts are powered by battery. Hence, energy efficient routing protocols are required to minimize power consumption.

Desirable Properties of *ad-hoc* Routing

As for the mode of operation, *ad-hoc* networks are basically peer-to-peer multi-hop mobile wireless networks where information packets are transmitted in a store-and-forward manner from a source to an arbitrary destination, via intermediate nodes. In such networks, routing decision depends on many factors including topology, selection of routers, initiation of request, and specific underlying characteristic that could serve as a heuristic in finding the path quickly and efficiently. The desirable properties of a routing protocol for *ad-hoc* networks supposed to include the following[1] :

- *Distributed Operation* : The routing algorithm should not be dependent on a centralized controlling node to cope with topological changes.
- *Loop Free* : The routing protocol must guarantee that the routes supplied are loop-free. This avoids any waste of bandwidth or CPU consumption.
- *Demand-based Operation :* To minimize the control overhead in the network and thus not wasting network resources more than necessary, the protocol should be reactive.
- *Multiple Routes :* To reduce the number of reactions to topological changes and congestion multiple routes could be used.
- *Uni-directional Link Support :* The radio environment can cause the formation of uni-directional links. Utilization of these links along with the bi-directional links can improve the routing protocol performance.
- *Security :* The radio environment is especially vulnerable to impersonation attacks. So to ensure the wanted behaviour from the routing protocol, we need some sort of preventive security measures.

- *Power Conservation* : The nodes in an ad-hoc network are very limited in battery power. Nodes use some sort of stand-by mode to save power. The routing protocol must have support for these sleep-modes.
- *Quality of Service Support* : Some sort of Quality of Service support is probably necessary to incorporate into the routing protocol. It could for instance be real-time traffic support.

There are several routing protocols proposed for usage in *ad-hoc* networks. None of the proposed protocols have all the desirable properties.

Ad-hoc Routing Schemes

Most of these protocols are designed for IP (Internet Protocol) based, homogenous, mobile *ad-hoc* networks.[2] Each node in the network has identical capability (identical communication devices and ability to perform functions from the common set of services). It is assumed that each node has a unique address (IP address for example). Number of hops is used as the only route selection criteria. These protocols focus on *fast route establishment* and re-establishment and route *maintenance with minimal overhead*.

A majority of these *ad-hoc* routing protocols can be classified as either proactive (table-driven) protocols or reactive (demand-driven) protocols. In either case, the routing protocols typically specify that each node periodically advertise current routing information to its neighbours. The neighbour is then able to calculate routes to network nodes based on the received information. The node can also incorporate the information it has received into its own advertisements, as necessary according to the protocol. In the case of proactive protocols, the advertisements can contain information about every known link between other routing agents in the network. Reactive protocols, on the other hand, supply next-hop information about all destinations in the network. However, due to high mobility of nodes such periodic advertisements may impact route maintenance overhead of routing protocols in such a way that no bandwidth might remain leftover for the transmission of data packets. Two techniques for solving this problem are to limit the amount of information advertised and to establish routes only on demand so that periodic advertisements are no longer mandatory.

Routing schemes solely inspired from the biological swarm intelligence can adapt to the changing network requirements by means of the principle of *emergence* via "stigmergy". There are few routing schemes based on swarm intelligence proposed for *ad-hoc* networks.

Swarm Intelligence and *Ad-hoc* Routing

Swarm intelligence[3] refers to the "intelligent" behaviours arising from the interactions among a swarm of social insects, such as ants, when working collectively towards a common goal, e.g., food foraging. Ants can find shortest paths through a process called "stigmergy", which could be described as indirect communication between individuals through the environment.

Basic Ant Algorithm

The basic idea of the ant algorithm is taken from the food searching behaviour of real ants. When ants search for food, they start from their nest and walk toward the food. When an ant reaches an intersection, it has to decide which branch to take next. While walking ants deposit *pheromone* which marks the selected route. The concentration of pheromone on a certain path is an indication of its usage. Other ants are attracted by these pheromone trails and in turn reinforce them even more. As a result of this *autocatalytic* reaction, the shortest path emerges rapidly.

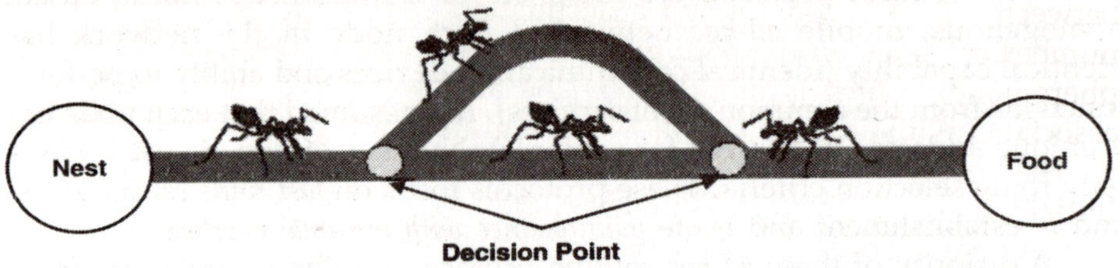

FIG. 25.1
All Ants take the Shortest Path after an Initial Searching Time

Figure 25.1 shows a scenario with two routes from the nest to the food. At the intersection the first ants randomly select a branch. Since the lower route is shorter than the upper one, the ants, which take this path, will reach the food place first. On their way back to the nest, the ants again have to select a path. After a while the pheromone concentration on the shorter path will be higher than on the longer path, because the ants using the shorter path will increase the pheromone concentration faster. Thus, eventually all ants will only use this path. This behaviour of the ants can be used to find the shortest path in networks. Especially the dynamic component of this method provides for a high degree of adaptation to changes in mobile *ad-hoc* network topology, since in these networks the existence of links is not guaranteed and link changes occur frequently.

Swarm intelligence boasts a number of advantages due to the use of mobile agents and stigmergy.[4] These include :

- *Scalability* : Population of the agents can be adapted according to the network size. Scalability is also promoted by local and distributed agent interactions.
- *Fault Tolerance* : Swarm intelligent processes do not rely on a centralized control mechanism. Therefore the loss of a few nodes or links does not result in catastrophic failure, but rather leads to graceful, scalable degradation.

- *Adaptation* : Agents can change, die or reproduce, according to network changes.
- *Modularity* : Agents act independently of other network layers.[11]
- *Autonomy* : Little or no human supervision is required.
- *Parallelism* : Agent's operations are inherently parallel.

These properties make swarm intelligence very attractive for ad-hoc wireless networks.

A simple Ant-Based Scheme

Let G = (*V, E*) be a connected graph with n = | *V* | nodes. The simple ant colony optimization meta-heuristic can be used to find the shortest path between a source node v_S and a destination node v_D on the graph G. The number of nodes on the path gives the path length. A variable j_{ij} (artificial pheromone), which is modified by the ants when they visit the node is associated with an edge *e(i, j)* Î *E* of the graph connecting the nodes v_i and v_j . The pheromone concentration j_{ij} is an indication of the usage of this edge. Initially j_{ij} is constant for each edge *e*(*i*, *j*).

An ant located in node v_i uses pheromone j_{ij} of node v_j Î N_i to compute the probability of node v_j being the next hop. N_i is the set of one-step neighbours of node v_i. The transition probabilities $P_{i,j}$ of a node v_i, i.e. the probability that the ant selects node v_j after it has visited v_i, are defined as follows :

$$p_{i,j} = \begin{cases} \dfrac{\varphi_{i,j}}{\sum_{j \in Ni} \varphi i,j} & \text{if } j \in N_i \\ 0 & \text{if } j \notin N_i \end{cases} \qquad \sum_{j \in Ni} p_{i,j} = 1, \quad i \in [1, N]$$

During the route finding process, ants deposit pheromone on the edges. In the simplest version of the algorithm, the ants deposit a constant amount Dj of pheromone, i.e. the amount of pheromone of the edge e(v_i, v_j) when the ant is moving from node v_i to node v_j is changed as follows :

$j_{ij} := j_{ij} + \mathrm{Dj}$

Like real pheromone the artificial pheromone concentration decreases with time. In the simple ant algorithm this is described by :

$j_{ij}\,(t{+}t) := (1{-}q).j_{ij}(\mathrm{t}),\ q$ Î (0, 1] ....(1)

The simple ant algorithm shown in this section illustrates different reasons why this kind of algorithms could perform well in mobile multi-hop *ad-hoc* networks. These include the following :

- Ant-based can show better adaptation to continuously changing network topologies in multi-hop *ad-hoc* networks.[4, 5]

- In contrast to other routing approaches, the ant-based algorithm is based only on local information, i.e. no routing tables or other information blocks have to be transmitted to other nodes of the network.
- It is possible to integrate the link quality into computation of the pheromone concentration, especially into the evaporation process. This will improve the decision process with respect to the link quality. It may be noted that the approach can be modified so that nodes can also manipulate the pheromone concentration independent of the ants, e.g. if a node detects a change of the link quality.
- Each node has a routing table with entries for all its neighbours, which also contains the pheromone concentration. The decision rule for selection of the next node is based on the pheromone concentration at the current node, which is provided for each possible link. Thus, the approach supports multi-path routing.

Ant-based Routing in *Ad-hoc* Networks

Several variations of AntNet[5,6] have been developed but all of them rely on the same concept where forward ants are launched towards destinations and backward ants travel back and update pheromone along the backward paths. The amount of added pheromone is proportional to the goodness of the path measured by the forward ant. In the following sections some of these routing schemes are discussed.

Ant-Colony-based Routing Algorithm (ARA)

ARA is an on-demand routing protocol[7] and it performs routing in three phases : Route discovery, Route maintenance, and Route failure handling. Each of these phases is discussed briefly in this section.

A. Route Discovery

In ARA new routes are created in the *route discovery* phase by means of a *forward ant* (FANT) and a *backward ant* (BANT). A *forward ant* is an agent, which establishes the pheromone track back to the source node. In analogous, a *backward ant* establishes the pheromone track back to its origin, namely, the destination node.

The FANT is a small packet with a unique sequence number. Nodes are able to distinguish duplicate packets on the basis of the sequence number and the source address. A node that receives a FANT for the first time creates a record in its routing table. The node interprets the source address of the FANT as destination address, the address of the previous node as the next hop, and computes the pheromone value depending on the number of hops it took the FANT to reach the node. The node then relays the FANT to its neighbours. Duplicate FANTs are identified through the unique sequence number, and are removed. The destination node extracts the information of the FANT, creates a BANT and returns it to the source node. The BANT's task is to establish a track to source node. When the sender receives the BANT from the destination node, the path is established and data packets can be sent.

Figure 25.2 shows the establishment of the pheromone track back to the source node *S*. The forward ant only creates one pheromone track to the source node in node 6, but two tracks in node 5, via node 3 and node 4. Figure 25..3 depicts analogous situation for the backward ant. It only creates one pheromone track to the destination node *D* in node 5 and two tracks in node 6. Thus, ARA also supports *multi-path* routing.

B. Route Maintenance

For *maintenance of the routes* during the communication ARA does not need any special packets. Once the FANT and BANT have established the pheromone tracks for the source and destination nodes *regular data packets* are used to maintain the path. As in biological systems, established paths do not keep their initial pheromone values forever. When a node v_i relays a data packet to destination v_D to a neighbour node v_j, it increases the pheromone value of the entry (v_D, v_j, j) by Dj, i.e. this path to the destination is strengthened by the data packet. Likewise, the next hop v_j increases the pheromone value of the entry (v_D, v_j, j) by Dj, i.e. the backward path to the source node is also strengthened. The evaporation process of the real pheromone is modeled by decreasing the pheromone values according to equation 1.

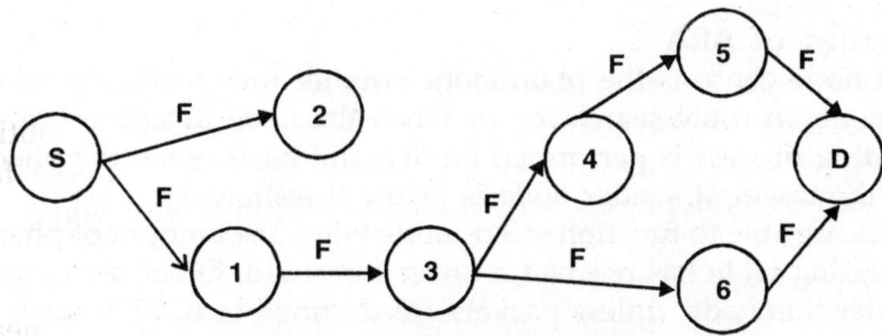

FIG. 25.2
Route Discovery Phase

A forward ant (F) is send from the sender (S) toward the destination node (D). The forward ant is relayed by other nodes, which initialize their routing table and the pheromone values.

The backward ant (B) has the same task as the forward ant. It is send by the destination node toward the source node.

C. Handling Route Failure

Routing failures, which are especially caused by node mobility, are very common in *ad-hoc* networks. ARA assumes IEEE 802.11 on the MAC layer.

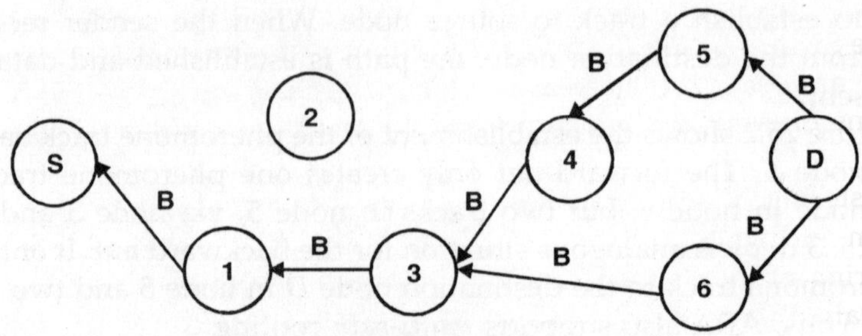

Fig. 25.3
Route Discovery Phase

This enables ARA to recognize a route failure through a missing acknowledgement on the MAC layer.

If a node receives a ROUTE_ERROR message for a certain link, it first deactivates this link by setting the pheromone value to 0. Subsequently, the node searches for an alternative link in its routing table. If there is another route to the destination it will send the packet via this path. Otherwise, the node informs its neighbours, hoping that they can forward the packet to the destination. Either the packet can be transported to the destination node or the backtracking continues to the source node. If the packet does not reach the destination, the source node has to initiate a new route discovery process.

D. Properties of ARA

Each node controls the pheromone counter independently when ants visit the node on route search for, or when the node detects a link failure. Route finding process is performed on-demand basis when the pheromone entry for the target at sender node is below threshold.

Nodes are able to function sleep-mode when the amount of pheromone in their routing table has reached a lower threshold. Other nodes will then not consider this node, unless packets are destined to it. This saves energy and power.

ARA supports multipath routing. Each node can have several paths to a destination and the choice of a certain route depends on the environment, e.g. link quality to the relay node. In case of link failure the alternative routes when available can be used without going for a costly route discovery process.

ARA, however, because ants are broadcasted into the network for on-demand route-discovery, may not scale for large-scale mobile *ad-hoc* networks.

Scalable Ant-based Routing Protocols

A. Adaptive-SDR Protocol

The same concept as in AntNet[6] has been extended and applied to

Adaptive Swarm-based Distributed Routing (Adaptive-SDR)[8] for routing in wireless and satellite networks. Adaptive-SDR resolves the *scalability* limitations of AntNet by incorporating a mechanism to cluster nodes into colonies.

Clustering is performed less frequently, in the beginning stage of the algorithm and whenever the network topology changes enough to justify a re-clustering of the nodes. Then, it finds routes in network by using special agents called ants and forwards the network traffic using the routes discovered by the ants. The route discovery (by ants) and the network data traffic forwarding are performed constantly as part of regular network operation.

Adaptive-SDR is scalable and can avoid routing loops. In addition, this scheme performs well with high utilization of the network capacity. By monitoring the state of the queues of the links to all outgoing neighbours, the next-hop probabilities are adjusted according to the load in each queue. Then, the node with the highest adjusted probability is selected as next-hop. This probability adjustment is only temporary and for the purpose of forwarding data at that specific time instant. It does not permanently change the routing table probabilities. The advantage of this method is that the best next-hop is penalized when it is congested, while it is still the best, and thus always chosen, when there is no congestion.

B. GPS/Ant-Like Routing Algorithm

GPS-AL is a *source routing* scheme in which the network relies on location information and support from fixed infrastructure.[9]

The routing protocol is based on the physical location of a destination host *d* stored in the routing table. If there is an entry in the routing table for host *d*, the best possible route is chosen using a shortest path algorithm. The route, comprised of a list of nodes and the corresponding TTLs, is attached to the packet, which is sent to first host in the list. If host *d* is not found in the routing table, the mobile node sends a message to the nearest fixed node that tries to find the destination node. GPS-AL employs ants during route discovery only to accelerate the dissemination of routing information, and hence, does not make use of the above-described *"auto-catalytic"* effect for finding shortest paths.

Hence, ants are not used as feedback agents to reinforce routes positively (in the case when a route is still good), negatively (when a route is no longer good) or explore new routes randomly—ants in this approach are unicasted to specified direction, not allowing for amplification of fluctuations, and depending on known metrics such as timestamp of a route in the routing table. Further, a shortest path algorithm is applied to determine the best possible route to a destination, therefore assuming that a node knows a lot about the links currently present in the network, and as well a lot about positions of other nodes, which certainly will not be true for the large scale *ad-hoc* networks.

C. *Mobile Agent-Based Routing (MABR)*

MABR is a *proactive* approach[10] for routing in large-scale mobile *ad-hoc* networks. The nodes are assumed to be aware of their position by means of a positioning service (e.g., GPS) and are able to determine other nodes position accurately enough through a location management scheme.

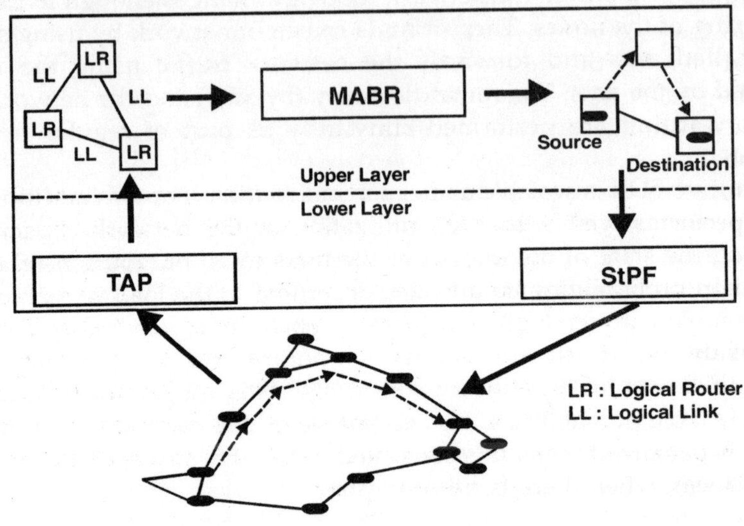

FIG. 25.4
Two-Layer Architecture Proposed for Ant-Based Routing[10]

This scheme uses a two-layered architecture, as shown in Figure 25.4, where TAP (Topology Abstracting Protocol) is used to supply a simplified topology with fixed "logical routers" and fixed "logical links". A logical router represents an aggregated collection of mobile hosts, which all together build and share among each other the same routing tables. A logical link represents a path along a roughly straight line to a distant logical router over possibly multiple hops. On top of this abstract topology the actual routing protocol MABR (Mobile Ants-Based Routing) runs and is responsible for updating the routing tables of logical routers and determining logical paths for routing packets over this abstract topology MABR. Finally, the StPF (Straight Packet Forwarding) protocol is applied in order to transmit packets over a logical link. Therefore, it forwards packets along this logical link in a greedy manner.

Each node is at every moment part of a specific logical router and, hence, makes uses of the corresponding routing tables. So when a node whishes to send a packet to another node, it first discovers that node's location through any location management scheme[10] and stores these coordinates in the header fields of the packet. By applying MABR, it determines to which zone the destination coordinates belong in its view and selects any logical link with the probability given in the routing table R for that zone. The packet is tagged as well with the corresponding logical router k (geographical coordinates) as a next logical hop. Then SPF is employed in order to route the packet to these coordinates; i.e. the source node transmits the packet to a node closer to logical router k and so forth. Any node at logical router k in turn carries out the same procedure again, first determining a next outgoing logical link by MABR, and then routing the packet to these coordinates by SPF. Eventually the packet will arrive at the logical router for the destination coordinates. The receiving node finally sends the packet to the intended destination node.

The advantages include the ability to react and deal quickly with local and global changes, not only in the network topology, but as well in the communication bandwidth, in the transmission delay, etc. However, with this approach no random exploration of routes is possible. Also, in a network where the topologies change frequently, the overhead of doing proactive routing may far outweigh the benefits of doing so.

Conclusion

In this paper, we have presented an overview of *swarm intelligence* applied to routing schemes in *ad-hoc* networks. Inherent properties of swarm intelligence as observed in nature include : massive system scalability, emergent behaviour and intelligence from low complexity local interactions, autonomy, and *stigmergy*, or communication through the environment. These properties are desirable for many types of networks. Ant-based approaches hold great promise for solving numerous problems of *ad-hoc* power aware networks. *Swarm intelligence* however is a new field and much work remains to be done. Comparison of the performance of swarm-based algorithms has been done by emulation. Analytic proof and models of the swarm-based algorithm performance remain topics of ongoing research.

References

1. Toh C., *Ad-hoc mobile wireless networks : protocols and systems*. Prentice Hall, 2002.
2. IETF MANET Working Group, http ://www.ietf.org/html.charters/manet-charter.html
3. Eric Bonabeau, Marco Dorigo, and Guy Theraulaz. "*Swarm Intelligence—From Natural to Artificial Systems*." Oxford University Press, New York, 1999.
4. S. Lipperts and B. Kreller, "Mobile agents in telecommunications networks—a simulative approach to load balancing", *Proc. 5th Intl. Conf. Information Systems, Analysis and Synthesis, ISAS'99*, 1999.
5. Gianni Di Caro and Marco Dorigo. "AntNet : A Mobile Agents Approach to adaptive Routing." Technical Report IRIDIA/97-12, Universite Libre de Bruxelles, Belgium.
6. G. Di Caro and M. Dorigo, "AntNet : Distributed stigmergetic control for communications networks," *Journal of Artificial Intelligence Research*, Vol. 9, 1998.
7. Mesut Gunes, Udo Sorges, and Imed Bouazizi. "ARA : The Ant-colony-based Routing Algorithm for MANETs." In *International Conference on Parallel Processing Workshops (ICPPW'02)*, Vancouver, B.C., Canada, August 2001.
8. Ioannis N. Kassabalidis, *et. al.* "Adaptive-SDR : Adaptive Swarm-based Distributed Routing." In *IEEE WCCI 2002, Signal Processing for Wireless Communications*, Honolulu, Hawaii, May 2002.

9. Daniel Camara and Antonio Alfredo F. Loureiro. "A GPS/Ant-Like Routing Algorithm for Ad Hoc Networks." In *IEEE Wireless Communications and Networking Conference (WCNC'00)*, Chicago, IL, September 2000.
10. Heissenbttel and T. Braun. "Ants-based Routing in Large Scale Mobile Ad-Hoc Networks". Technical report, University of Bern, 2003.
11. K. Oida and M. Sekido, "An agent-based routing system for QoS guarantees", *Proc. IEEE International Conference on Systems, Man, and Cybernetics*, Oct. 12-15, pp. 833-38, 1999. September 28-29, 1998.

IEEE 802.11a,b, and 802.11g—A Smart Choice for Wireless Networks

G. SUDHARSAN

Introduction

With the ever-growing trend in the wireless and mobile communication, the indoor wireless communication has drawn extensive attention of many researchers. An important feature of WLAN is that it can be used independently of a wired network. It can be used anywhere as a stand-alone network to link multiple computers together without having to build or extend a wired network. WLAN communication takes place in a part of the radio spectrum that is designed as license free. The range of WLAN depends on actual usage and environment of the system and varies form 100 feet inside a solid walled building to several thousand feet outdoors, with a direct line of sight. WLAN is capable of roaming from the AP and reconnecting to the network through other APs residing at other points in the network.

Some of the advantages of deploying WLAN are :

- Mobility improves productivity with the real-time access to information, regardless of worker location, for faster and more efficient decision-making.
- Cost-effective network set-up for hard-to-wire locations such as older buildings and solid wall structures.
- Reduced cost of ownership, particularly in dynamic environments requiring frequent modifications due to minimal wiring and installation costs per device and per user.

WLAN can have any of three topologies :

- Peer to peer topology,
- AP–based topology, and
- Point to multipoint topology.

In a peer to peer topology, client devices within a cell communicate directly to each other. An AP-based topology uses access points to bridge traffic onto a wired (Ethernet or Token ring) or a wireless backbone. The AP enables a wireless client device to communicate with any other wired or wireless device on the network. The AP topology is more commonly used, demonstrating that WLANs do not replace the wired LANs; instead they extend connectivity to mobile devices. In point to multipoint wireless bridges connect a LAN in one building to a LAN in another building. There should be a line–of–sight between any two transceivers. The line–of–sight varies based on the type of wireless bridges and antenna used as well as the environmental conditions.

IEEE 802.11a

IEEE 802.11a, a new specification that represents the next generation of enterprise-class wireless LANs. Among the advantages it has over current technologies are greater scalability, better interference immunity, and significantly higher speed, up to 54 Mbps and beyond, which simultaneously allows for higher bandwidth applications and more users. This part provides an overview, in basic terms, of how the 802.11a specification works, and its corresponding benefits.

Physical Layer

802.11a utilizes 300 MHz of bandwidth in the 5 GHz band. Though the lower 200 MHz is physically contiguous, the FCC has divided the total 300 MHz into three distinct 100 MHz domains, each with a different legal maximum power output. The "low" band operates from 5.15—5.25 GHz, and has a maximum of 50 mW. The "middle" band is located from 5.25—5.35 GHz, with a maximum of 250 mW. The "high" band utilizes 5.725—5.825 GHz, with a maximum of 1 W. Because of the high power output, devices transmitting in the high band will tend to be building-to-building products. The low and medium bands are more suited to in-building wireless products. One requirement specific to the low band is that all devices must use integrated antennas. The frequency range used currently for most enterprise-class unlicensed transmissions, including 802.11b, is the 2.4 GHz ISM band. This band offers only 83 MHz of spectrum for all wireless traffic, including cordless phones, building-to-building transmissions, and micro-wave ovens. In comparison, the 300 MHz offered in the U-NII band represents a nearly four-fold increase in spectrum.

OFDM Modulation Scheme

802.11a uses Orthogonal Frequency Division Multiplexing (OFDM), a new encoding scheme that offers benefits over spread spectrum in channel availability and data rate. The high data rate is accomplished by combining many lower-speed sub-carriers to create one high-speed channel. 802.11a uses OFDM to define a total of 8 non-overlapping 20 MHz channels across the 2 lower bands; each of these channels is divided into 52 sub-carriers, each (Figure 26.1) approx. 300KHz wide. By comparison, 802.11b uses 3 non-overlapping channels.

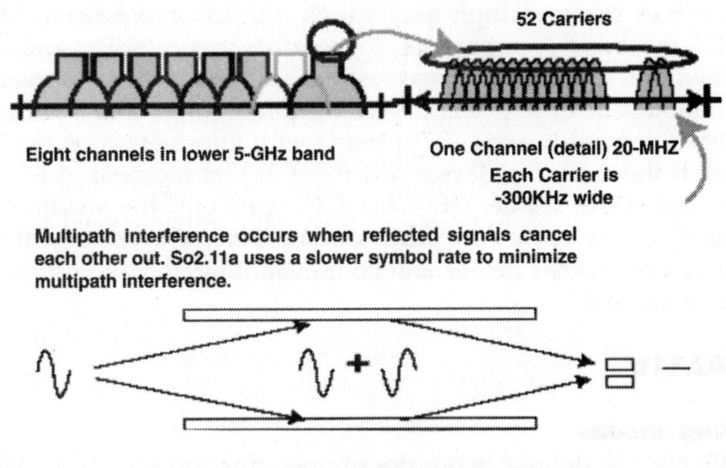

FIG. 26.1
Multipath Interference

A large (wide) channel can transport more information per transmission than a small (narrow) one. 802.11a utilizes channels that are 20 MHz wide, with 52 sub-carriers contained within. The sub-carriers are transmitted in "parallel". The receiving device processes these individual signals, each one representing a fraction of the total data that, together, make up the actual signal. With this many sub-carriers comprising each channel, a large amount of information can be sent at once. With so much information per transmission, it becomes important to guard against data loss. Forward Error Correction (FEC) was added to the 802.11a specification for this purpose (FEC does not exist in 802.11b). At its simplest, FEC consists of sending a secondary copy along with the primary information. If part of the primary information is lost, insurance then exists to help the receiving device recover (through sophisticated algorithms) the lost data. This way, it eliminates the need to retransmit. Because of its high speed, 802.11a can accommodate this overhead with negligible impact on performance. Another threat to the integrity of the transmission is multipath reflection, also called delay spread. When a radio signal leaves the "sending" antenna, it radiates outward, spreading as it travels. If the signal reflects off a flat surface, the original signal and the reflected signal may reach the "receiving" antenna simultaneously. Depending on how the signals overlap, they can either augment or cancel each other out. A baseband processor, or equalizer, unravels the divergent signals. However, if the delay is long enough, the delayed signal spreads into the next transmission. OFDM specifies a slower symbol rate to reduce the chance a signal will encroach on the following signal, minimizing multipath interference.

MAC Layer

802.11a uses the same Media Access Control (MAC) layer technology as 802.11b, carrier sense multiple access with collision avoidance (CSMA-CA). CSMA-CA is a basic protocol used to avoid signals colliding and canceling each other out. It works by requesting authorization to transmit for a specific amount of time prior to sending information. The sending device broadcasts a request to send (RTS) frame with information on the length of its signal. If the receiving device permits it at that moment, it broadcasts a clear to send (CTS) frame. Once the CTS goes out, the sending machine transmits its information. Any other sending devices in the area that "hear" the CTS realize another device will be transmitting and allow that signal to go out uncontested.

IEEE 802.11b

Operating modes

IEEE 802.11b defines two types of operating modes which is usually a PC equipped with wireless network interface (NIC) and an AP. The 802.11b standard defines two modes : infrastructure mode and *ad-hoc* mode. In the infrastructure mode, the wireless network consists of at least one access point connected to the wired network infrastructure and a set of wirteless end stations. This configuration is called basic service set. An extended service set (ESS) is a set of two or more basic set forming a single sub-network. Since most WLANs require access to the wired LAN for service (file servers, internet links) they operate in infrastructure mode.

Ad-hoc mode is simply a set of wireless stations that communicate directly with one another without using any access point or any connection to a wired network. This mode is useful for quickly and easily setting up a wireless network anywhere, such as hotel room, convention centre or airport where access to wired network is barred.

Physical Layer

The three physical layers originally defined in 803.11b included two spread spectrum techniques and a diffuse infrared specification. The radio–based standard operate within the 2.4Ghz unlicensed ISM band. The original 802.11b wireless standard defines data rates of l Mbps and 2 Mbps via radio waves using FHSS or DSSS. FHSS and DSSS are fundamentally different mechanisms and will not interoperate with one another. In the FHSS, the 2.4

Ghz band is divided into 751 Mhz sub-channels. The sender and receiver agree on a hopping pattern and data is sent over a sequence of the sub-channels. Each conversation within 802.11b network occurs over a different hopping pattern are designed to minimize the chance of two senders using the same sub-channels simultaneously.

FHSS techniques allow for a relatively simple radio design, but are limited to speeds of no higher than 2 Mbps. This limitation is driven primarily by FCC regulations that restrict sub-channels bandwidth to 1 Mhz. These regulations force FHSS systems to spread their usage their across the entire 2.4 Ghz band, meaning they must hop often, which leads to a high amount of hopping overhead. In contrast, the DSSS techniques divide the 2.4 Ghz band into 14-22 Mhz channels. Adjacent channels overlap one another partially, with three of the 14 channels being completely non-overlapping. Data is sent across one of these 22 Mhz channels. To compensate for noise on a given channel, spreading is used. Each bit of user data is converted into a series of bit patterns called chips. The strength of the DSSS system is that when the ratio between the original signal bandwidth and the spread signal bandwidth is large, the system offers a great immunity to interface.

The infrared physical layer operates in the near–visible light range of 850–950 nm. Diffuse transmission is used so the transmitter and receiver do not have to point to each other. The transmission distance is limited to the range of 10 to 20 meters, and the signal is contained by the walls and windows. This feature has the advantage of isolating the transmission systems in different rooms. The system cannot operate outdoors.

IEEE 802.11g

Introduction to IEEE 802.11g

With low cost and high-speed data rate capabilities, the popularity of IEEE 802.11-based WLANs is growing exponentially. Currently, the two most important IEEE standards are : 802.11b in the 2.4 GHz Industrial-Scientific-Medical (ISM) band, which uses *Complementary Code Keying* (CCK) at the higher data rates, and 802.11a in the 5 GHz Unlicensed National Information Infrastructure (U-NII)/ISM bands and license-free 5 GHz bands, which uses *Orthogonal Frequency Division Multiplexing* (OFDM). The former offers data rates of 1, 2, 5.5, and 11 Mbps, while the latter is capable of supporting higher data rates : 6, 9, 12, 18, 24, 36, 48 and 54 Mbps. IEEE 802.11g is drawing attention recently based on the use of the same data rates and OFDM technology as employed in 802.11a, plus backward compatibility with 802.11b devices. Actually, both 802.11g and 802.11a use almost the same PHY specification and, therefore, should have similar throughput performance, but actually 802.11g throughput performance is significantly different from 802.11a based on the following reasons :

- 802.11g mandates the use of a 20 μs slot time in order to be compatible with current 802.11b devices. The use of a 9 μs slot time as is used in 802.11a is optional.

- 802.11g shares the same 2.4GHz spectrum as 802.11b. When both 802.11g and 802.11b devices are present, there should be coordination between .11b and .11g users.
- Frequency-dependent propagation loss favours 802.11g, that is, free space path loss is greater at 5 GHz than at 2.4 GHz. But encounter interference from non-WLAN devices e.g., Bluetooth devices, cordless phones, microwave ovens, etc.
- There are fewer available channels in the 2.4 GHz band than in the 5 GHz bands.

Co-existence with 802.11b Devices

One of the benefits of 802.11g is that the standard is being prepared so that 802.11g devices have built-in backwards compatibility with 802.11b devices. Simultaneous operation of these two types of devices, however, affects the overall network performance, and it is discussed in this section.

Framing and the Preamble

The first detail that requires explanation is how data is transmitted within an 802.11 network. While it is relatively well known that the 802.11

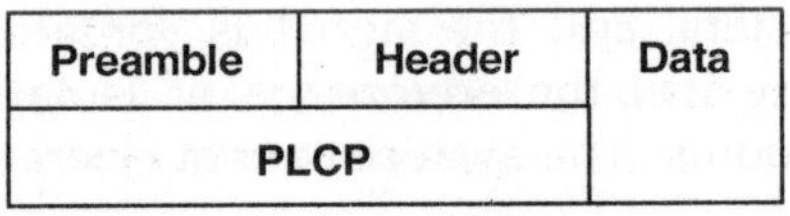

Preamble	Header	Data
PLCP		

FIG. 26.2
IEEE 802.11 Data Packet

standards define a data modulation that determines the rates at which data can be transmitted (for example, in 802.11b, the highest data rate of 11 Mbps is achieved using CCK modulation); less well known are the "overheads" that accompany each of these data packet transmissions. The term "overhead" refers to information that must be sent in order for the network to operate properly, but which is not part of the data that the user is transmitting. Since the network must still spend time to send this information, but since it is not recognized by the end user as part of his traffic stream, the total throughput of the network will appear to be lower than the peak data rate that is quoted. It is partly for this reason that even the highest performing 802.11 networks do not achieve user throughput results much in excess of 50% of the peak data rate (about 5 Mbps for an 11 Mbps 802.11b network using long preambles, and 30 Mbps for a 54 Mbps 802.11a network.). Also, while actual throughput measurements are taken using the result of some higher layer application (like FTP for example), we will confine our discussion to the 802.11 protocol layer.

First part is known as PLCP (Physical Layer Convergence Protocol) field in 802.11. There are three different preambles. For 802.11b there is the

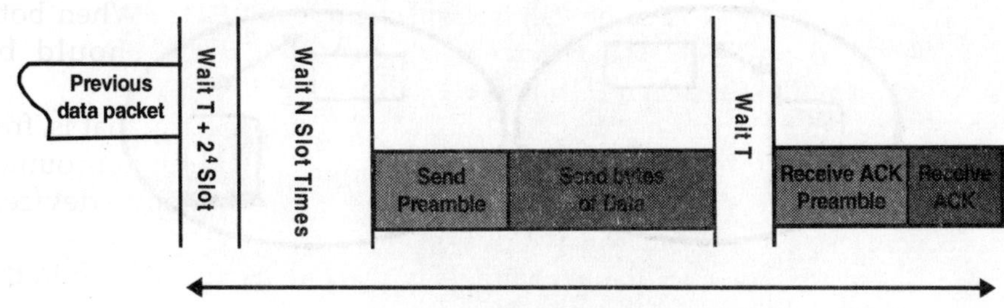

FIG. 26.3
802.11 Preamble, Slot, and Acknowledgement (ACK) Frame Overheads

long preamble (192 μsec) and the short preamble (96 μsec), and for 802.11a and 802.11g there is the OFDM preamble (20 μsec). The effect of this preamble can be estimated in the following way. If 1500 bytes of data are sent at 11 Mbps, this takes 1091 μsec (1500 8/11). If this data were sent with the long preamble attached, it would take an extra 192 μsec for a total of 1283 μsec. Sending 1500 bytes of data in 1283 μsec means that the user will see a throughput of 9.5 Mbps, a reduction of 13.6% from the quoted 11 Mbps rate. On the other hand, if the short preamble is used, then 1500 bytes is sent in 1187 μsec, for an effective rate of 10.2 Mbps. The use of the long preamble lowers the effective data rate.

Channel Access and the Slot Time

In this section describes how, once it is created, a data packet like that shown in the above figure gets transmitted in 802.11. The 802.11 media access protocol attempts to avoid having different devices send their data packets at the same time. When this does happen it is known as a collision, and it usually results in neither packet being correctly received. This requires the data to be retransmitted, and the effect is a lowered average system throughput. In order to attempt to avoid these collisions, 802.11 devices access the channel in the following way. While any one device is transmitting, no other devices will transmit. The other devices will wait until the channel is clear before transmitting. But after they determine that the channel is clear, and before they transmit their data packets, they will wait a random period of time in order to decrease the statistical likelihood that any two devices that have been waiting for the channel to become clear will transmit at the same time. The period of time that a device waits before accessing the channel (The "backoff time") is counted in integer units of what is known as the "slot time". The slot times are shown schematically in Figure 26.3.

In the 802.11b standard, the slot time is defined to be 20 μsec. In 802.11a, the slot time is defined to be 9 μsec. The effect of these times can

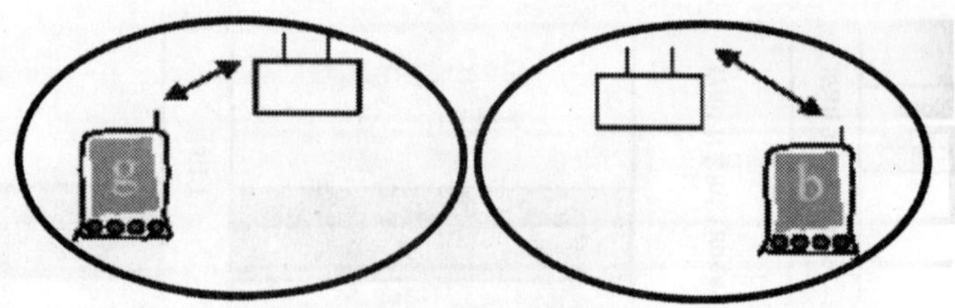

FIG. 26.4
Schematic Diagram of an Overlapping

be estimated in the same way that we estimated the effects of the preamble, above. If a device is transmitting a 1500 byte packet at 11 Mbps, this will take 1091 μsec. In 802.11b, the slot time is 20 μsec, and the number of slots used is a random number between 0 and 31. Using 15 slot times as an average, this adds an additional 300 μsec to the transmission time, for an effective throughput of 1500 bytes in 1391 μsec, or 8.6 Mbps. So the backoff times reduce the throughput by about 22% in this case. As can be seen, the magnitude of this effect will change depending on the data rate, because while the time required to send a packet will change, the time spent backing off will not.

This will be a very important issue in understanding the throughput of 802.11g devices in the presence of 802.11b devices. Because 802.11g is based on the 802.11a standard, it uses a 9 μsec slot time with a random number of slots between 0 and 15. Using the same calculation as above, this can be seen to reduce a 54 Mbps data rate by 22% to 42 Mbps. The channel access mechanism cannot operate correctly unless all devices in a network use the same slot timing to determine when they should send their packets. If different slot times were used, the devices with the smaller slot time would have preferential access to the wireless medium. (If an 802.11g device chose a backoff value of 10 slots, and an 802.11b device in the same network chose a backoff value of 5 slots, the 802.11g device would *still* access the channel first if it was using 9 μsec slots [90 μsec total] while the 802.11b device was using 20 μsec slots [100 μsec total].)

Overlapping BSS Case

We now analyze some of the issues surrounding 802.11g system deployment in the presence of 802.11b devices. First we take the case of Overlapping BSSes on the same channel. This refers to the situation, depicted in Figure 26.4, in which two systems, unrelated to each other, are in close enough proximity to hear each other.

As shown, we make this situation as simple as possible and designate that one of the networks has only 802.11g devices in it, and the other network has only 802.11b devices. Given the ideal circumstances, what would be the effect of this case? In the ideal case, the 802.11b devices and

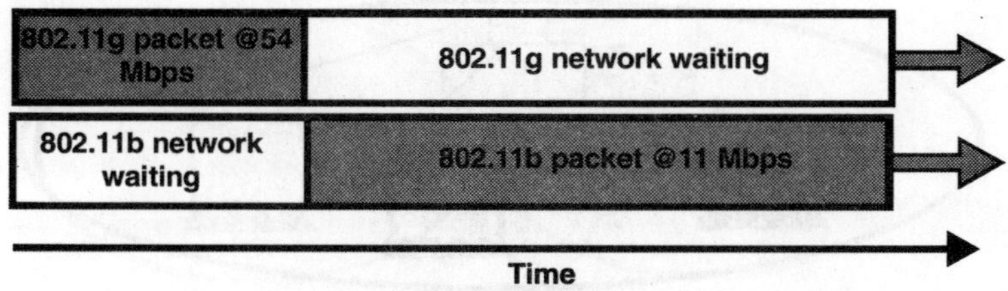

FIG. 26.5
Demonstration of Device Throughout

802.11g devices will not transmit at the same time since that would cause packet collisions. Rather, the devices would sense each other and would only transmit when the other devices were not transmitting. This is shown schematically in Figure 26.4.

Take a simple example of the effective throughput in this case, as above. Ignoring overheads (as mentioned several times, the calculations shown here indicate the magnitude of the effect, but do not include the full complexity of the 802.11 protocol), the 802.11g network at 54 Mbps can send a 1500 byte packet in 222 µsec. The 802.11b network at 11 Mbps can send a 1500 byte packet in 1091 µsec. Therefore, from the point of view of each network (or from the point of view of a device on each network) it will require 1313 µsec to transmit a packet of 1500 bytes. From the point of view of the 802.11b device this translates into an effective throughput of 9.1 Mbps, or about a 17% reduction in throughput due to the presence of nearby 802.11g devices.

From the point of view of the 802.11g device, however, the picture is far worse. That device also sees that it takes 1313 µsec to transmit 1500 bytes, so its throughput is the same as that of the 802.11b device. (This should actually be obvious from a glance at Figure 26.9. It takes the same amount of time or a device on each network to transmit the same amount of data, so the effective data rate must be the same.) The 802.11g devices, therefore, see a reduction in their effective data rate by about 83% due to the presence of nearby 802.11b devices.

Mixed-Mode Networks

In mixed mode networks the situation is even more complicated due to the fact that the 802.11b devices and the 802.11g devices will operate in a compatible mode. An example of a mixed mode network is shown in Figure 26.6.

In this network, not only will the devices, ideally, back off to each other creating the same situation as described above, but there will be other effects as well. First, in order for the devices to operate in conjunction with each other, the slot times must be equivalent. Since the 802.11b devices can only operate with a 20 µsec slot time, the 802.11g devices must use this as well. The magnitude of this effect, which can be as large as a 20% reduction in the

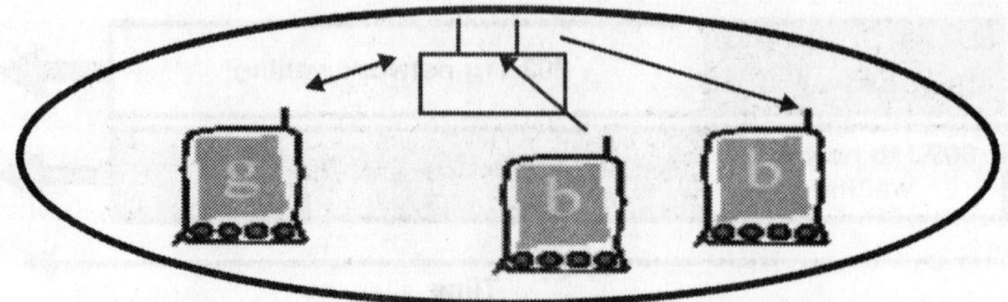

FIG. 26.6
Schematic Diagram of a Mixed-mode Configuration

throughput of the 802.11g devices, depending on the data rate at which the devices are operating. Requiring that 802.11g and 802.11b devices to backoff in the presence of one another means, as shown above, that the effective throughput for any devices can be limited by the slowest device on the network.

Protection Mechanisms

The situation I have described at the moment is that, in an environment with both 802.11g and 802.11b devices,

- The devices will ideally defer to each other, causing the effective throughput of any given device to be determined by the slowest active device in the area at a given time.
- In order to operate in a compatible mode, the 802.11g devices must use the longer slot time of 802.11b, causing a further degradation to the throughput performance.

In fact, there is one further complication that we have not yet described. As we have mentioned numerous times, the 802.11b and 802.11g devices will ideally defer to each other in order to avoid having their packets collide over the air. These devices, however, may not defer to each other, because the 802.11g OFDM modulation may not be received properly by the 802.11b receivers. The result of completely uncoordinated devices operating within range of each other will be a reduction in effective throughput for a different reason—over the air packet collisions.

When an 802.11b device is brought into the area, that device will not be able to recognize, nor will it be recognized by the 802.11g network. According to the 802.11 protocol, this 802.11b device can begin to send messages called probe requests, trying to locate an 802.11b network. Those requests (using 802.11b signaling) will collide with the 802.11g devices, and will cause the throughput degradation shown here. As more and more devices enter the area, the increased number of probes will degrade the 802.11g performance further. It is important to recognize that, in this simulation, the 802.11b devices are not even sending any data. They are only sending 802.11 probe requests, and already they have degraded the 802.11g network throughput. If they were sending data packets in an uncoordinated fashion, the collisions would be far worse causing even more degradation. There is a mechanism for dealing with this problem as well, and this is the protection mechanism known as RTS/CTS (Request-to-Send and Clear-to-Send.) RTS can be thought of as a reservation request sent by a device on the network. CTS is a response to this message, informing the device making the request that its request has been received, and that it is OK to send its data packet. In its traditional mode, RTS/CTS was used in the following way. When there are devices on the network that cannot hear other devices on the network (the so-called "hidden node problem"), those devices do not transmit their data to the AP immediately when they sense that the channel is quiet. Rather, it sends an RTS message to the AP. If the AP receives that RTS message, it sends the CTS, which will be heard by all of the devices on the network, even those that the RTS-sending device may not be able to hear.

	802.11a	**802.11b**	**802.11g**
Operating frequencies	5 GHz U-NII/ISM Bands	2.4 GHz ISM Band	2.4 GHZ ISM Band
FCC regulation	Part 15.407/15.247	Part 15.247	Part 15.247
Modulation techniques	OFDM	Barket Code/CCK	Barket Code/CCK/OFDM
Data rates (Mbps)	**6, 9, 12, 18, 24, 36, 48, 54**	**1, 2 5, 5, 11**	**1, 2, 5, 5, 11 6, 9, 12, 18, 24, 36, 48, 54**
Slot time	9 qs	20 qs	9 qs (optional)
Preamble	OFDM	Long Short (optional)	Long/Short./OFDM

FIG. 26.7
Different WLAN System Characteristics

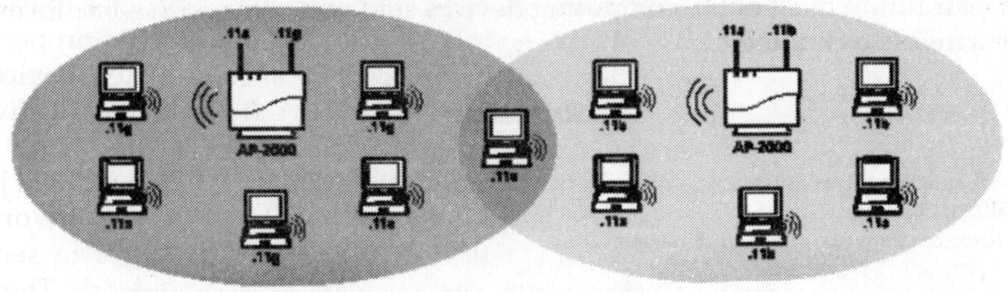

FIG. 26.8

(By definition, there are no devices in an infrastructure-based network that cannot be heard by the AP). All the devices hearing the CTS will know to cease transmissions for a period of time (defined by the CTS) and this will result in fewer collisions. The mechanism is shown in Figure 26.7.

The benefit of reduced packet collisions is not at zero cost, however. As is clear in Figure 26.7 it now takes more time to transmit the same amount of data, this reducing the effective throughput seen by the user. In the case of 802.11g/802.11b co-existence, there is a provision which allows for the sending of only a CTS packet by the AP; that is, the CTS packet can be sent by the AP when it needs to send a downlink packet, and that CTS does not need to be in response to an RTS. This protection mechanism is referred to as "CTS-Only". Figure 26.7. a illustration of 802.11 preamble, slot, acknowledgement (ACK), and RTS/CTS frameoverheads.

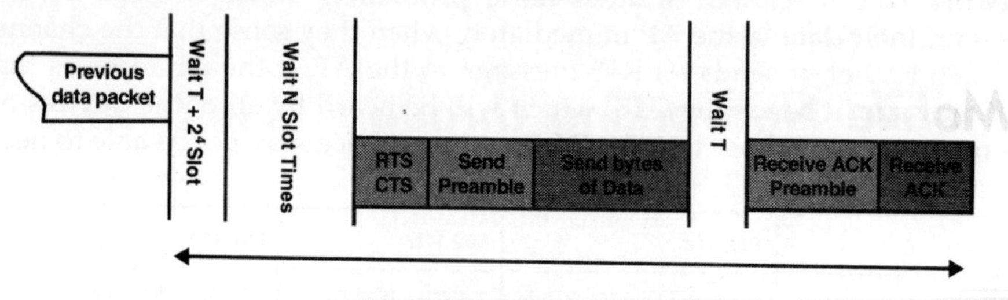

FIG. 26.9
Mixed Environment where 802.11b, 802.11a, and 802.11g are Deployed Side-By-Side

Conclusion

Thus in this paper, I have discussed about the various IEEE 802.11 standards such as 802.11a, 802.11b and 802.11g and its interoperability with each other. The advent of WLAN opens up a whole new definition of what a network infrastructure can be. Due to its convenience (mobility and scalability), wireless networking is becoming more popular and it seems that in near future most of the computing devices sold will come with some form of wireless technology.

REFERENCES

www.intermec.com/datactr/
William Stallings,
"wireless communication and networks".

Mobile Networking through Mobile IP

S. RAMESH AND R. ARAVIND BABU

Introduction

Mobile IP is a proposed standard protocol that builds on the Internet Protocol by making mobility transparent to applications and higher level protocols like TCP.

Although the Internet offers access to information sources worldwide, typically we do not expect to benefit from that access until we arrive at some familiar point—whether home, office, or school. However, the increasing variety of wireless devices offering IP connectivity, such as PDAs, handhelds, and digital cellular phones, is beginning to change our perceptions of the Internet.

Mobile IP

To understand the contrast between the current realities of IP connectivity and future possibilities, consider the transition toward mobility that has occurred in telephony over the past 20 years. An analogous transition in the domain of networking, from dependence on fixed points of attachment to the flexibility afforded by mobility, has just begun.

In mobile networking, computing activities are not disrupted when the user changes the computer's point of attachment to the Internet. Instead, all the needed reconnection occurs automatically and non-interactively.

Truly, mobile computing offers many advantages. Confident access to the Internet anytime, anywhere will help free us from the ties that bind us to our desktops. Consider how cellular phones have given people new freedom in carrying out their work. Taking along an entire computing environment has the potential not just to extend that flexibility but to fundamentally change the existing work ethic. Having the Internet available to us as we move will give us the tools to build new computing environments wherever we go. Those who have little interest in mobility will be still benefited from the ability to resume previous applications when they reconnect. This is especially convenient in a wireless LAN office environment, where the boundaries between attachment points are not sharp and are often invisible.

The evolution of mobile networking will differ from that of telephony in some important respects. The endpoints of a telephone connection are typically human; computer applications are likely to involve interactions between machines without human intervention. Obvious examples of this are mobile computing devices on airplanes, ships, and automobiles. Mobile networking may well also come to depend on position-finding devices, such as a satellite global positioning system, to work in tandem with wireless access to the Internet

Another difference may well be rate of adoption. It took many years for mobile phones to become cheap and light-weight enough to be perceived as convenient. Because wireless mobile computing devices such as PDAs and pocket organizers have already found user acceptance, mobile computing may become popular much more quickly.

However, there are still some technical obstacles that must be overcome before mobile networking can become widespread. The most fundamental is the way the Internet Protocol, the protocol that connects the networks of today's Internet, routes packets to their destinations according to IP addresses. These addresses are associated with a fixed network location much as a non-mobile phone number is associated with a physical jack in a wall. When the packet's destination is a mobile node, this means that each new point of attachment made by the node is associated with a new network number and, hence, a new IP address, making transparent mobility impossible.

Mobile IP (RFC 2002), a standard proposed by a working group within the Internet Engineering Task Force, was designed to solve this problem by allowing the mobile node to use two IP addresses : a fixed home address and a care-of address that changes at each new point of attachment. There is a great deal of interest in mobile computing and apparently in Mobile IP as a way to provide for it. A quick Web search for items related to Mobile IP returned over 60,000 hits impressive even given the notorious lack of selectivity for such procedures. Mobile IP forms the basis either directly or indirectly of many current research efforts and products. The Cellular Digital Packet Data (CDPD), for example, has created a widely deployed communications infrastructure based on a previous draft specification of the protocol. In addition, most major router vendors have developed implementations for Mobile IP.

However, once the security solutions are solid, nomadic users may finally begin to enjoy the convenience of seamless untethered roaming and effective application transparency that is the promise of Mobile IP.

How Mobile IP Works

IP routes packets from a source endpoint to a destination by allowing routers to forward packets. The routing tables typically maintain the next-hop information for each destination IP address, according to the number of networks to which that IP address is connected. The network number is derived from the IP address by masking off some of the low-order bits. Thus, the IP address typically carries with it information that specifies the IP node's point of attachment.

To maintain existing transport-layer connections as the mobile node moves from place to place, it must keep its IP address the same. In TCP, connections are indexed by a quadruplet. On the other hand, correct delivery of packets to the mobile node's current point of attachment depends on the network number contained within the mobile node's IP address, which changes at new points of attachment. To change the routing requires a new IP address associated with the new point of attachment.

Mobile IP has been designed to solve this problem by allowing the *mobile node* to use two IP addresses. In Mobile IP, the *home address* is static and is used, for instance, to identify TCP connections. The *care-of address* changes at each new point of attachment and can be thought of as the mobile node's topologically significant address; it indicates the network number and thus identifies the mobile node's point of attachment with respect to the network topology. The home address makes it appear that the mobile node is continually able to receive data on its *home network*, where Mobile IP requires the existence of a network node known as the *home agent*. Whenever the mobile node is not attached to its home network, the home agent gets all the packets destined for the mobile node and arranges to deliver them to the mobile node's current point of attachment.

Whenever the mobile node moves, it *registers* its new care-of address with its home agent. To get a packet to a mobile node from its home network, the home agent delivers the packet from the home network to the care-of address. This modification can be understood as a packet transformation or, more specifically, a *redirection*. When the packet arrives at the care-of address, the reverse transformation is applied so that the packet once again appears to have the mobile node's home address as the destination IP address. When the packet arrives at the mobile node, addressed to the home address, it will be processed properly by TCP or whatever higher level protocol logically receives it from the mobile node's IP processing layer. In Mobile IP the home agent redirects packets from the home network to the care-of address by constructing a new IP header. This new header then shields or encapsulates the original packet, causing the mobile node's home address to have no effect on the encapsulated packet's routing until it arrives at the care-of address. Such *encapsulation* is also called *tunneling*, which suggests that the packet burrows through the Internet, bypassing the usual effects of IP routing.

Mobile IP, then, is best understood as the cooperation of three separable mechanisms :

- Discovering the care-of address;
- Registering the care-of address; and
- Tunneling to the care-of address.

Discovering the Care-of Address

The Mobile IP *discovery* process has been built on top of an existing standard protocol, Router Advertisement, specified in RFC 1256. Mobile IP discovery does not modify the original fields of existing router advertisements but simply extends them to associate mobility functions. The mobile node can broadcast or multicast a solicitation that will be answered by any foreign agent or home agent that receives it.

Home agents use agent advertisements to make themselves known, even if they do not offer any care-of addresses. The IETF working group was concerned that dynamic preference values might destabilize the operation of Mobile IP. Because no one could defend static preference assignments except for backup mobility agents, which do not help distribute the routing load, the group eventually decided not to use the preference assignments with the care-of address list.

Thus, an agent advertisement performs the following functions :

- allows for the detection of mobility agents;
- lists one or more available care-of addresses;
- informs the mobile node about special features provided by foreign agents, for example, alternative encapsulation techniques;
- lets mobile nodes determine the network number and status of their link to the Internet; and
- lets the mobile node know whether the agent is a home agent, a foreign agent, or both, and therefore whether it is on its home network or a foreign network.

If advertisements are no longer detectable from a foreign agent that previously had offered a care-of address to the mobile node, the mobile node should presume that foreign agent is no longer within range of the mobile node's network interface. In this situation, the mobile node should begin to hunt for a new care-of address.

Registering the Care-of Address

Once a mobile node has a care-of address, its home agent must find out about it. The process begins when the mobile node, possibly with the assistance of a foreign agent, sends a registration request with the care-of address information. When the home agent receives this request, it adds the necessary information to its routing table, approves the request, and sends a registration reply back to the mobile node. Although the home agent is not required by the Mobile IP protocol to handle registration requests by updating entries in its routing table, doing so offers a natural implementation strategy and all implementations

Authentication : Registration requests contain parameters and flags that characterize the tunnel through which the home agent will deliver packets to the care-of address. The triplet that contains the home address, care-of address, and registration lifetime is called a *binding* for the mobile node. A registration request can be considered a *binding update* sent by the mobile node.

A binding update is an example of a *remote redirect*, because it is sent remotely to the home agent to affect the home agent's routing table. The home agent must be certain that registration was originated by the mobile node and not by some other malicious node pretending to be the mobile node. A malicious node could cause the home agent to alter its routing table with erroneous care-of address information, and the mobile node would be unreachable to all incoming communications from the Internet.

The need to authenticate registration information has played a major role in determining the acceptable design parameters for Mobile IP. To secure the registration request, each request must contain unique data so that two different registrations will in practical terms never have the same MD5 hash. Otherwise, the protocol would be susceptible to *replay attacks*, in which a malicious node could record valid registrations for later replay, effectively disrupting the ability of the home agent to tunnel to the current care-of address of the mobile node at that later time. To ensure this does not happen, Mobile IP includes within the registration message a special identification field that changes with every new registration. The exact semantics of the identification field depend on several details, which are described at greater length in the protocol specification. Briefly, there are two main ways to make the identification field unique.

One is to use a timestamp, and then each new registration will have a later timestamp and thus differ from previous registrations. The other is to cause the identification to be a pseudorandom number; with enough bits of randomness. When randomness is used, Mobile IP defines a method that protects both the registration request and reply from replay, and calls for 32 bits of randomness in the identification field. If the mobile node and the home agent get too far out of synchronization for the use of timestamps, or if they lose track of the expected random numbers, the home agent will reject the registration request and include information to allow resynchronization within the reply. The identification field is also used by the foreign agent to match pending registration requests to registration replies when they arrive at the home agent and to subsequently be able to relay the reply to the mobile node. The foreign agent can limit registration lifetimes to a configurable value that it puts into its agent advertisements. The home agent can reduce the registration lifetime.

In Mobile IP foreign agents are mostly passive. The foreign agent also decapsulates traffic from the home agent and forwards it to the mobile node. The node that foreign agents do not have to authenticate themselves to the mobile node or home agent. A bogus foreign agent could impersonate a real foreign agent simply by following protocol and offering agent advertisements to the mobile node.

Automatic home agent discovery : When the mobile node cannot contact its home agent, Mobile IP has a mechanism that lets the mobile node try to register with another unknown home agent on its home network. This method of *automatic home agent discovery* works by using a broadcast IP address instead of the home agent's IP address as the target for the registration request. When the broadcast packet gets to the home network, other home agents on the network will send a rejection to the mobile node; however, their rejection notice will contain their address for the mobile node to use in a freshly attempted registration message.

Tunneling to the Care-of Address

The default encapsulation mechanism that must be supported by all mobility agents using Mobile IP is IP-within-IP. Using IP-within-IP, the home agent, the *tunnel source*, inserts a new IP header, or *tunnel header*, in front of the IP header of any datagram addressed to the mobile node's home address. The new tunnel header uses the mobile node's care-of address as the destination IP address, or *tunnel destination*. The tunnel source IP address is the home agent, and the tunnel header uses 4 as the higher level protocol number, indicating that the next protocol header is again an IP header.

Problems Facing Mobile IP

The most pressing outstanding problem facing Mobile IP is that of security. Work is continuing to refine and extend the protocol within the academic and commercial communities.

Security issues : A great deal of attention is being focused on making Mobile IP coexist with the security features coming into use within the Internet. Firewalls, in particular, cause difficulty for Mobile IP because they block all classes of incoming packets that do not meet specified criteria. Enterprise firewalls are typically configured to block packets from entering via the Internet. It presents difficulties for mobile nodes wishing to communicate with other nodes within their home enterprise networks.

Slow growth in the wireless LAN market : Mobile IP has been engineered as a solution for wireless LAN location management and communications, but the wireless LAN market has been slow to develop.

Issues in IP addressing : Mobile IP creates the perception that the mobile node is always attached to its home network.

Current Development Efforts

Mobile IP has been studied in a number of wireless communication research projects. At the University of California at Berkeley, Mobile IP is being used to construct vertical handoffs between dissimilar media (for example, infrared, radio LANs, wide-area cellular, and satellite), depending upon error rates and bandwidth availability. Other factors such as cost and predictive service might also be taken into account. CMU's Monarch project has been the focus of investigation into campus wireless networks, Mobile IP, Mobile IPv6, and *ad-hoc* networking. Other academic efforts have been proceeding at the University of Portland, University of Alabama, University of Texas, UCLA, Macquarie University, SUNY Binghampton, University of Singapore, Swedish Royal Institute of Technology, and many others. Two books about Mobile IP have recently been published.

Current IETF drafts that employ Mobile IP include the Tunnel Establishment Protocol and Mobile IP Local Registration with Hierarchical Foreign Agents. The latter uses the ability to advertise multiple foreign agents to arrange hierarchies of mobility agents. This may help cut the number of registrations that must transit the global Internet between the home and foreign networks. DHCP for Mobile Networking with TCP/IP investigates the suitability of using the Dynamic Host Configuration Protocol to provide care-of addresses to mobile nodes. Mobile IPv4 Configuration Option for PPP IPCP is a new extension to PPP that will enable dial-up users to more efficiently employ their dynamic IP addresses as care-of addresses.

Conclusion

As this brief introduction to mobile networking has shown, Mobile IP has great potential. Security needs are getting active attention and will benefit from the deployment efforts underway. Within the IETF, Mobile IP is likely to move from a proposed standard to a draft standard in the near future.

Test results have given added confidence that the Mobile IP specification is sound, implementable, and of diverse interest throughout the Internet community. Only a few minor revisions are needed by the network protocol engineers and programmers who must implement it.

It is possible that the deployment pace of Mobile IP will track that of IPv6 or that the requirements for supporting mobility. Since both IPv6 and Mobile IP have little direct effect on the operating systems of mobile computers outside of the network layer of the protocol stack, application designers should find this to be an acceptable programming environment. Of course, everything depends heavily on the willingness of platform and router vendors to implement Mobile IP and/or IPv6, but indications are strong that most major vendors already have implementations either finished or underway.

References

1. www.computer.org
2. www.eecs.hardvard.edu
3. www.devx.com

A Simulation Study on the Performance of Mobile IP

V.K. KARUNAMOORTHY

Introduction

The proliferation of portable computing devices within the past few years has led to an increase in mobility of such devices and the consequent problems are not encountered with static computing. The problem lies with the need to maintain seamless connectivity to the Internet while the computer moves from one network to another and movement within the same network. The problems encountered arise from the current Internet addressing service itself, which routes data according to the network to which a host is connected. If a host becomes mobile and is connected to a network other than its home network, IP packets addressed to the host continue to be delivered to its home network. A classic example is the need to retrieve e-mail addressed to the host while connected to any network in the world.

The purpose of this research was to create a simulation of an IP-based data network which supports the Mobile IP protocol and to test different approaches to Mobile IP. The route optimization for a Mobile IP network is also simulated and the results are compared with the results of base Mobile IP simulation.

Mobile IP

The key feature of Mobile IP design is that all required functionalities for processing and managing mobility information are embedded in well-defined entities—the Home Agent (HA), Foreign Agent (FA), and Mobile Nodes (MN).

Mobile Node

A host or router that changes its point of attachment from one network or sub-network to another. A mobile node may change its location without changing its IP address; it may continue to communicate with other Internet nodes at any location using its (constant) IP address, assuming link-layer connectivity to a point of attachment is available.[1]

Home Agent

A router on a mobile node's home network that tunnels datagram for delivery to the mobile node when it is away from home, and maintains current location information for the mobile node.

Foreign Agent

A router on a mobile node's visited network provides routing services to the mobile node. The foreign agent detunnels and delivers datagram to the mobile node that were tunneled by the mobile node's home agent. A simple Mobile IP network is shown in Figure 28.1. For datagram sent by a mobile node, the foreign agent may serve as a default router for registered mobile nodes.

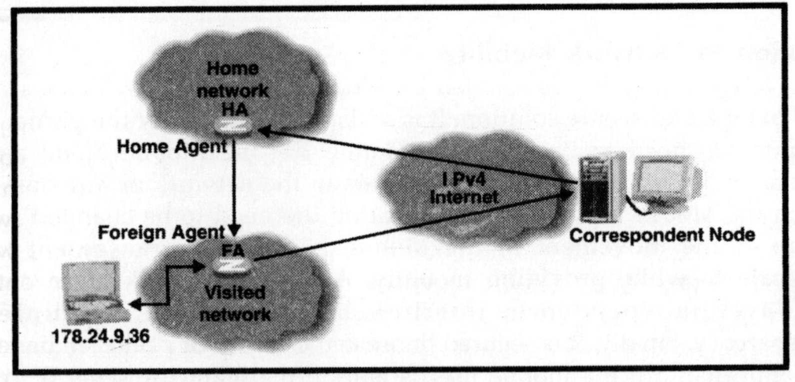

FIG. 28.1
A Simple Mobile Network

Suppose a mobile node moves from its home network to a foreign network, the correct delivery of packets to its current point of attachment depends on the IP address contained within the mobile node's IP address, which changes at new points of attachment. The change of routing requires a new IP address associated with the new point of attachment. Mobile IP has been designed to solve this problem by allowing the mobile node to use two IP addresses. In Mobile IP, the home address is *static* and is used for instance to identify TCP connections. The *care-of-address* changes at each new point of attachment and can be thought of as the mobile node's topological significant address. Whenever the mobile node is not attached to its home network, the home agent gets all the packets destined for the mobile node and arranges to deliver them to the mobile ode's current point of attachment.

How Mobile IP Works

This section explains how Mobile IP works. The Mobile IP process has three main phases which are discussed in the following sections.[2]

Agent Discovery

A Mobile Node discovers its Foreign and Home Agents during agent discovery.

Registration

The Mobile Node registers its current location with the Foreign Agent and Home Agent during registration.

Tunneling

A reciprocal tunnel is set-up by the Home Agent to the care-of address (current location of the Mobile Node on the foreign network) to route packets to the Mobile Node as it roams.

Solution to Network Mobility

Network mobility is enabled by Mobile IP, which provides a scalable, transparent, and secure solution. It is scalable because only the participating components need to be aware of Mobile IP—the Mobile Node and the endpoints of the tunnel. No other routers in the network or any hosts with which the Mobile Node is communicating the need to be changed or even aware of the movement of the Mobile Node. It is transparent to any applications while providing mobility. Also, the network layer provides link-layer independence; interlink layer roaming, and link-layer transparency. Finally, it is secured because the set-up of packet redirection is authenticated. Since a mobile user is able to maintain the same IP address even while roaming across networks, a live IP connection can be maintained without having to stop and restart as it would be with a mechanism like Dynamic Host Configuration Protocol (DHCP). This is the real power of Mobile IP that offers the potential to leverage Mobile IP with applications such as voice over IP (VoIP) and streaming media (video) to IP devices while the user is changing location.

Introduction to Network Simulator

NS2 is an open-source simulation tool that runs on Linux. It is a discreet event simulator targeted at networking research and provides substantial support for simulation of routing, multicast protocols and IP protocols, such as UDP, TCP, RTP and SRM over wired and wireless (local and satellite) networks. It has many advantages that make it a useful tool, such as support for multiple protocols and the capability of graphically detailing network traffic. Additionally, NS2 supports several algorithms in routing and queuing. LAN routing and broadcasts are part of routing algorithms. Queuing algorithms include fair queuing, deficit round-robin and FIFO.[6]

NS2 started as a variant of the REAL network simulator in 1989.[6] REAL is a network simulator originally intended for studying the dynamic behaviour of flow and congestion control schemes in packet-switched data network. Currently NS2 development by VINT group is supported through Defence Advanced Research Projects Agency (DARPA) with SAMAN and through NSF with CONSER, both in collaboration with other researchers including ACIRI.[6] NS2 is available on several platforms such as Free BSD, Linux, SunOS and Solaris. NS2 also builds and runs under Windows.

Simulation Design

Flow of Simulation

The Flow chart for the simulation of Mobile IP is given in Figure 28.2.

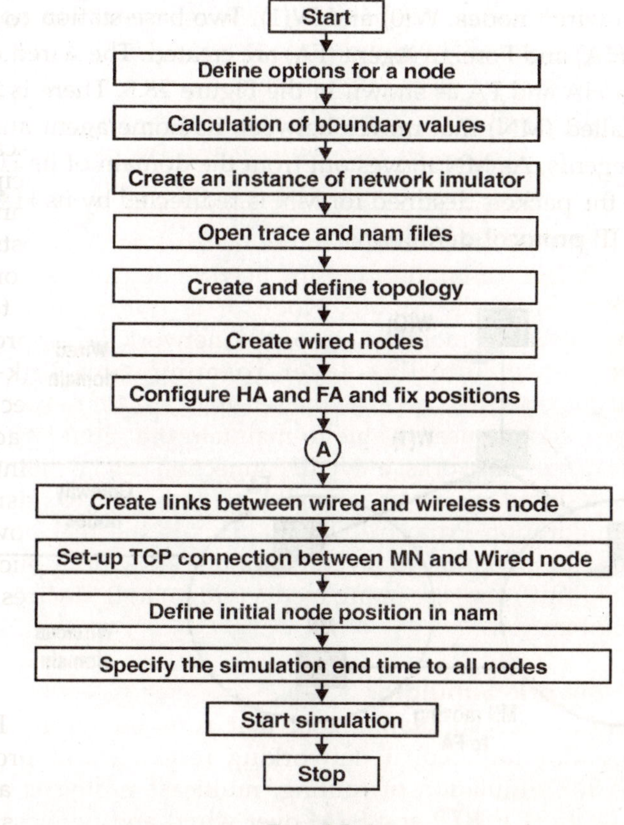

FIG. 28.2
Flow Chart for the Simulation of Mobile IP

Post-Simulation Process

The following graphs are drawn using the trace files :

- One-way delay *Vs.* Time
- Throughput *Vs.* Time

The One-way delay is concerned in the project because the packet delay is impacted by the Triangle routing. So, in order to extract the end-to-end delay information from the ns trace file, a trace viewer *nans*[8] is used.

Simulation-I : Withput RO

Scenario-I : Wired-cum-Wireless Network with Single FA

In this section, a mixed scenario consisting of a wireless and a wired domain, where data is exchanged between the mobile and non-mobile nodes, is going to be created. For the mixed scenario, a wired domain consists of two wired nodes, W(0) and W(1). Two base-station nodes called Home Agent (HA) and Foreign Agent (FA) are created. The wired node W(1) is connected to HA and FA as shown in the Figure 28.3. There is a roaming mobile node called (MN) that moves between its home agent and any one of the foreign agents. As MN moves out from the domain of its HA into the domain of FA, the packets destined for MN is redirected by its HA to the FA as per mobile IP protocol definitions.

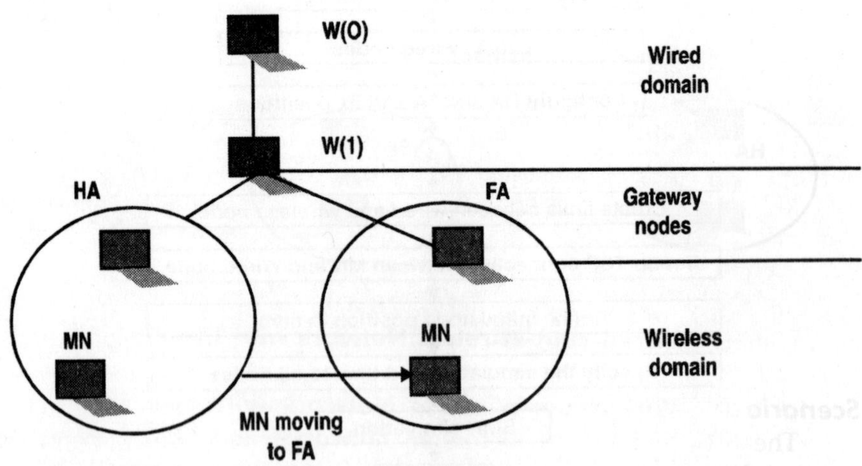

Fig. 28.3
Scenario-I : Wired-cum-Wireless Network with Single FA

Results of Scenario-I

(a) One-way Delay Vs. Time

	MN with HA	*MN with FA*
Minimum Throughput (Packets)	600	450
Maximum Throughput (Packets)	2700	1600

(b) Throughput Vs. Time

		MN with HA	*MN with FA*
Minimum Delay	(ms)	38	66
Maximum Delay	(ms)	205	237

This is a wired-cum-wireless network like scenario-I described in section with an additional FA (FA2). The Figure 28.4 shows scenario-II : Wired-cum-wireless network with two FAs.

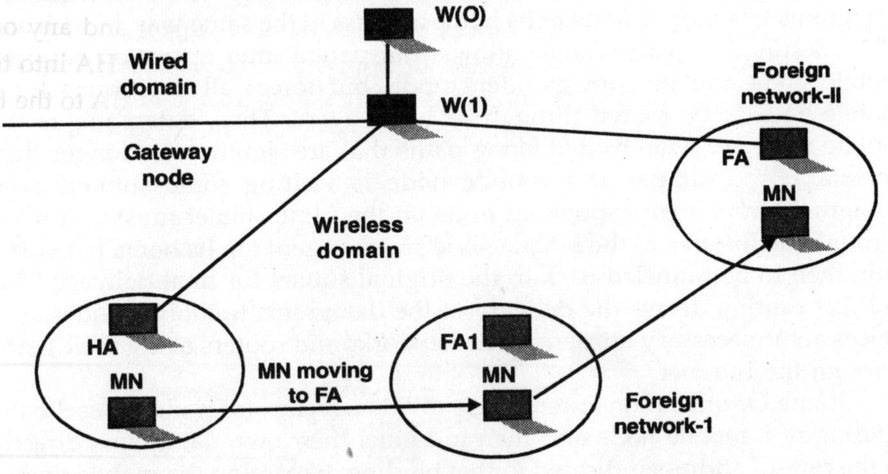

FIG. 28.4
Wired-cum-Wireless Network with Two FAs

Scenario-II : Wired-cum-Wireless Network with two FAs

The MN first moves to foreign network-I and then goes to foreign network-II. Hence, the CN that wants to communicate with the MN sends packets to the HA first. The HA will then checks the MN location. If the MN is in the HA network, then it simply sends the packets to the MN. If the MN is in foreign network-I, then HA tunnels the packet to the FA1. Similarly, the packet is sent to FA2 when the MN is in foreign network-II.

Results of Scenario-II

(a) One-way Delay Vs. Time

	MN in HA	*MN with FA1*	*MN with FA2*
Minimum Delay (ms)	38	72	66
Maximum Delay (ms)	205	220	215

(b) Throughput Vs. Time

	MN in HA	*MN with FA1*	*MN with FA2*
Minimum Throughput (Packets)	560	500	500
Maximum Throughput (Packets)	2700	1400	1560

Route Optimization

The base Mobile IP protocol allows any mobile node to move about changing its point of attachment to the Internet, while continuing to be identified by its home IP address. The Correspondent nodes send IP datagrams to a mobile node at its home address in the same way as with any other destination. This scheme allows transparent inter operation between mobile node and its correspondent node, but forces all datagrams for a mobile node to be routed through its home agent. Thus, datagrams to the mobile node are often routed along paths that are significantly longer than optimal. For example, if a mobile node is visiting some subnet, even datagrams from a correspondent node on the same subnet must be routed through the Internet to the mobile node's home agent (on its home network), only then to be tunneled back to the original subnet for final delivery. This indirect routing delays the delivery of the datagrams to mobile nodes, and places an unnecessary burden on the networks and routers along their paths through the Internet.[7]

Route Optimization Extensions provide a means for nodes to cache the binding of a mobile node and then to tunnel their own datagrams directly to the care-of address indicated in that binding, bypassing the mobile node's home agent. Extensions are also provided to allow datagrams in flight when a mobile node moves, and datagrams sent based on an out-of-date cached binding, to be forwarded directly to the mobile node's new care-of address.

Simulation-II : With Route Optimization

Scenario-I : With Single FA

The scenario-I described in section 6.1 is used to simulate a wired-cum-wireless network with route optimization. The results of the simulation are illustrated on next page.

Results of Scenario-I : With Single FA

(a) One-way Delay *Vs.* Time

		MN in HA	*MN with FA*
Minimum Delay	(ms)	38	24
Maximum Delay	(ms)	210	210

(b) Throughput *Vs.* Time

	MN in HA	*MN with FA*
Minimum Throughput (Packets)	600	500
Maximum Throughput (Packets)	2700	4500

Scenario-II : With Two FAs

The scenario-II described in section 5.2 is used here to simulate mobile a wired cum wireless network with route optimization.

The results of the simulation-II are illustrated below.

Results of Scenario-II : With Two FAs

(a) One-way Delay *Vs.* Time

	MN in HA	*MN with FA1*	*MN with FA2*
Minimum Delay (ms)	38	30	24
Maximum Delay (ms)	215	215	173

(b) Throughput *Vs.* Time

	MN in HA	*MN with FA1*	*MN with FA2*
Minimum Throughput (Packets)	560	500	600
Maximum Throughput (Packets)	2700	3650	4500

Conclusion

The development of Mobile IP has been going on for the past few years. This project simulates two scenarios of a wired-cum-wireless mobile network with and without route optimization. The results are obtained from the simulator trace files and analyzed. The benefits of route optimization for a mobile network are summarized on next page.

TABLE 28.1
Minimum End-to-End Delay

Scenario	*MN with HA*	*MN with FA*
MIP without RO	38	66
MIP with RO	38	24

TABLE 28.2
Maximum Throughput without and with RO

Scenario	*MN with HA*	*MN with FA*
MIP without RO	2700	1700
MIP with RO	2700	4500

From the Tables 28.1 and 28.2 it is concluded that the minimum delay is reduced from 66 ms to 24 ms and the Throughput is increased from 1700 to 4500 packets when RO is implemented in a Mobile IP network.

REFERENCES

1. Perkins, C.E., *IP Mobility Support* (*RFC* 2002), October 1996.
2. ———, (*RFC* 3220) January 2002.
3. ———, "Mobile IP : Design Principles and Practices", Addison-Wesley, 1997.
4. James D. Solomon, "Mobile IP : The Internet Unplugged", Prentice Hall, 1998.
5. Johnson D. and Perkins C., "Mobility Support in Ipv6", Internet Draft draft-ietf-mobileipipv6-12.txt, April 2000. Work In Progress.
6. Network simulator-2, http ://www.isi.edu
7. Charles E. Perkins, "Route Optimization in Mobile IP—draftietf-mobileip-optim-11.txt" Internet draft, September 2001, Work in Progress
8. Ankur Jain, "A Trace File Analyzer Utility", January 2003, http ://www.geocities.com/ankurjain009/projects.htm
9. Nokia White Paper, "Introducing Mobile IPv6 in 2G and 3G Mobile Networks", http ://www.nokia.com, January 2003.

Quantitative Analysis of a Hybrid Replication with Forwarding Strategy for Efficient and Unifrom Location Management in Mobile Wireless Networks

N. RADHIKA, R. RATHINAPRIYA AND S. ARUMUGAM

Introduction

In Personal Communication Services (PCS) network, a location management scheme must handle two-user location operation efficiently, update and search. The former operation occurs when a mobile host moves to a new location; the latter operation occurs when there is a call for the Mobile host and the network must find the mobile host to deliver the call. A well-known basic and simple scheme is to update the location of each MH at its Home Location Register (HLR) whenever it moves to a new Visitors Location Registration (VLR) area.

An important research issue is to minimize the network signaling cost associated with location update and search operations under location management strategies, as these operations need to be performed frequently. Search operations are related to how often a MH is called, call arrival rate, while update operations related to the MH's mobility rate. Thus in general, the Call to Mobility Ratio (CMR) parameter is defined as the ratio between a MH's call arrival rates to its mobility rate.

We develop and analyze a hybrid scheme that combines replication and forwarding techniques. Replication is known to be most effective in reducing user search and update cost when CMR is high because when the call arrival rate to the user is much higher than the mobility rate, communication cost would be dominated by search operations and search cost can be reduced by replicating the location of frequently called MH at selective VLRs from which most calls to mobile user originate, thus avoiding the cost of querying the HLR for the location of the called MH. Conversly forwarding is known to be most effective when CMR is low because when the mobility rate is much higher than the call arrival rate, the communication cost would be dominated by location update operations and the update cost can be reduced by simply forming a forwarding chain of VLRs through which the location of the MH can be found from the HLR, thus avoiding updating the HLR upon every update operation. HLR is updated only when the forwarding chain becomes too long. Hybrid scheme take advantages of the benefits of replication and forwarding techniques at high and low CMR values, respectively.

A Key concept of hybrid scheme design is that it will degenerate into the forwarding scheme. When the CMR value is sufficiently low and on the other hand, into the replication scheme when the CMR value is sufficiently high. Under the hybrid scheme, the system applies the optimal number of replicas and optimal forwarding chain length in order to minimize the total signaling cost, when given the user profile as input. A lookup table is built at static time and applied to all users at runtime to identify the optimal number of replicas and the optimal forwarding chain length to be used for each user.

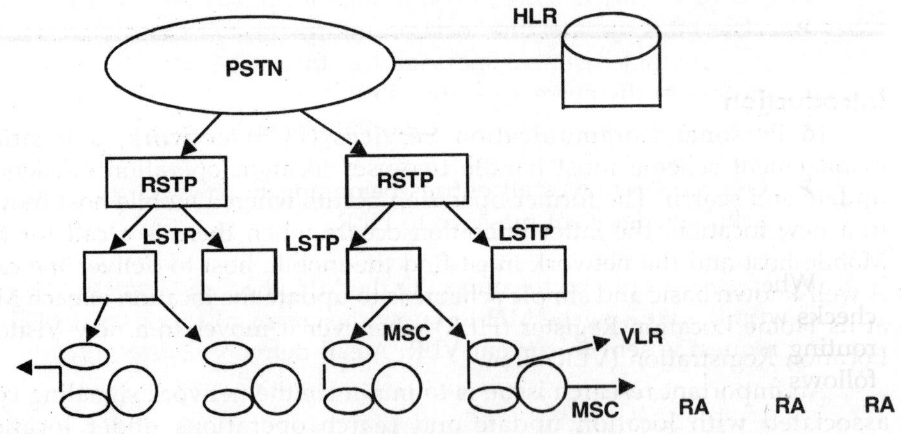

Fig. 29.1
PCS Signaling Network Architecture

System Description

A Registration Area (RA) can cover a single cell (or) group of cells. A Mobility-Switching Center (MSC) is used to connect all the cells in one RA. HLR is responsible for keeping track of a MH's current location as well as its profile. Each MH is permanently associated with a HLR. Conceptually the HLR of a MH is at higher level, while all VLR's that the MH wanders in to from time to time are at lower level. There may be some network switches connecting the HLR to VLRs in the mobile network. Each VLR (or) HLR is connected to the rest of the signaling network through a local signal transfer point; one or more LSTPs belonging to one region may be connected to a Regional Signal Transfer Point (RSTP). Separate RSTPs may be connected by a Public Switched Telephone Network (PSTN). We assume that each VLR corresponds to one RA. When a mobile user moves to new RA, the mobile user sends the registration information to the new VLR which, in turn can perform appropriate update actions, depending on the location management scheme used. We assume the average communication cost between a VLR and the HLR is equal to communication cost between any two randomly placed VLRs represented AST. Average communication cost between two neighbouring VLR's is represented by T.

Location Management Scheme

IS-41 Basic HLR/VLR : When a MH enters a new VLR area, it reports to new VLR, which in turn informs its HLR by means of location update operation under IS-41 scheme and proceeds as follows :

- When a MH moves in to new RA, it sends a location update message to current base station, which forwards this message to current serving VLR.
- Current serving VLR forwards the message to MH's VLR.
- The HLR updates the location information of the MH and sends an acknowledgement message together with a copy of the MH's profile to the current serving VLR.
- The HLR sends a location cancellation message to the old serving VLR.
- Old VLR removes all entries belonging to the MH and sends an acknowledgement message to HLR.

When a call is placed to connect to the MH, the PCS signaling network checks with the HLR of the MH to know the current VLR of the MH and a routing request is sent to current VLR. A call delivery scheme proceeds as follows :

- The Calling MH sends a call initiations message through its base station to its currently serving VLR.
- VLR determines the associated HLR serving the called MH and sends a location request message to the HLR.
- HLR determines the callee VLR and sends a route request message to this VLR/MSC.
- Cal lee VLR sends the route information to the HLR.
- HLR forwards the route information to the calling VLR. Now the calling VLR can set-up a connection to the callee VLR via the ss7-signaling network using the usual call set-up protocol.

Forwarding

A per user forwarding strategy was proposed to reduce the total signaling network cost. In the forwarding strategy when a user moves to new RA, it updates the HLR only when the current forwarding chain length reaches a predefined constant K. Otherwise a forwarding pointer is set-up from the old VLR to new VLR. Update procedure is described :

- When a MH moves in to new RA, it sends a location update message to current base station, which then forwards this message to its associated VLR.
- If the current forwarding length is less than the maximum forwarding chain length k, then
- New VLR deregisters the MH at the old VLR but asks the old VLR to keep a pointer to point to new VLR.
- Old VLR sends an acknowledgement to new VLR.
- Forwarding length is increased by one.

Otherwise, IS-41 basic strategy is followed and the forwarding chain is reset after which the HLR points to new VLR directly. When servicing a call to a MH, the HLR is queried first to determine the first VLR at which the MH was registered, then a current chain of forwarding pointers is followed to reach the MH's current VLR. A call delivery under the forwarding strategy proceeds as follows :

- First VLR is obtained from the callees HLR as in the IS-41 scheme.
- Callees current VLR is reached by following the forwarding chain.
- Callees current MSC/VLR sends user route information to the HLR.
- The HLR forwarding route information to the calling MSC. Now, the calling MSC can set-up a connection to the callee MSC via the ss7-signaling network using the usual call set-up protocol.

Replication

Location update operation due to mobility proceeds as follows :

- The MH sends a location update message to the serving MSC/VLR which forwards it to the MH's VLR as in IS-41.
- HLR updates the location of the MH in its table. In addition, it also sends an update message to all VLR's where a replica of the MH's profile is stored.
- A call delivery operation under the replication strategy proceeds as follows.
- Calling MH sends a call initiation message to its currently serving MSC/VLR through its base station.
- If MSC/VLR stores a location replica, it contracts the callees current MSC directly and gets the routing information.

Hybrid Replication With Forwarding Strategy

Replication strategy attempts to exploit locality in calling patterns to reduce the call delivery cost and it most beneficial when the users CMR value is above a threshold. A hybrid strategy that combines purchaser replication and forwarding are analyzed. The basic idea is that under a low CMR, the hybrid strategy attempts to reduce the total cost by replacing expensive HLR updates operating with adjacent VLR forwarding pointer operations, thus behaving like forwarding strategy. Under a modest CMR, the hybrid strategy combines the benefits from both forwarding and replication strategies. Finally, under a high CMR, the hybrid strategy exploits call locality to reduce the total signaling cost.

A location update under our hybrid strategy proceeds as follows :

1. When a MH moves in to a new visitors location area, it sends a location update to the new VLR/MSC via its current base station.
2. The new VLR/MSC examines the current forwarding chain length. If it reaches k, the HLR is updated to point to the new VLR as in IS-41, the forward chain is reset as in forwarding scheme, and all N replicas are updated to store the location of the new VLR as in replication scheme. This is the only condition under which replicas are being updated upon location update operation since the first VLR of the forwarding chain has been changed as a result of reset operation being executed when the maximum forwarding chain length K is reached.

Otherwise

- ➢ The MH registers at the new VLR and the new VLR deregisters MH at the old VLR.
- ➢ Old VLR sets a pointer to point to the new VLR, and then sends an acknowledgement and MH's location profile to the new VLR.
- ➢ The current forwarding chain length is increased by one.
- ➢ The replicas are not changed.

When a call is placed to a MH, the callees local VLR is searched first to see if it stores a location replica. If Replica is found the caller will use the local information to get the first VLR at which the callee was registered, and then the chain of forwarding pointers is followed to reach the current VLR. A Call delivery in the hybrid strategy proceeds as follows :

- ➢ Calling MH sends a call initiation message to its current serving VLR/MSC through its base station. The VLR/MSC checks if it has a location replica of the callee. If a replica is found, the callees VLR sends a routing request message directly to reach the first VLR in the forwarding chain. Otherwise, the callees HLR is contacted which sends a routing request message to the first VLR.

- ➢ Query message reaches the callee's current serving VLR/MSC by following the forwarding chain.
- ➢ The callees current serving VLR/MSC sends routing information to the calling VLR/MSC, which forwards it to the calling VLR/MSC. Now, the calling MSC can set-up a connection to the called MSC via the ss7-signaling network using a usual call set-up protocol.

Conclusion

We have analyzed a hybrid replication with forwarding location management scheme which can be uniformly applied to all MHs with different CMR values in wireless networks. The most striking feature of hybrid scheme is that it can determine and apply the optimal N and K values on a per user basis to minimize the communication cost due to location management operations while still being able to use the same data structures and Algorithms to execute location management operations in a uniform way for all users.

References

1. I.F. Akyildiz, J. McNair, J.S.M. Ho, I.U. Zunalioglu, "Mobility Management in next Generation Wireless Systems".
2. L.R. Chen and B.G.U., "A Comparative Cost Analysis of Location Management Algorithms in Wireless Networks".
3. G. Cho and L.F. Marchall, "An efficient Location and Routing Scheme for Mobile Computing Environments".
4. S. Rajagopalan and B.R. Badrinath, "An adaptive Location Management Strategy for Mobile IP", 1995.
5. M. Mouly and M.B. Pautel, "The GSM System for Mobile Communications", 1992.

An Approach to Spontaneous Service Discovery in Mobile Ad Hoc Networks

T. SANTHA AND S. UMAMAHESWARI

Spontaneous Service Discovery

Spontaneous networking[4] is the integration of services and devices into network environments with the objective of instantaneous service availability without any manual user intervention. The requirements for the Spontaneous networking are :

- *Effective Service Discovery,* which interprets the context of the situation easier and narrow the choice of services.
- *Presence and Availability,* which means that the services that are available should be projected to the person's device and the availability of a service needs to be managed, based in policies defined by the context of the interaction among members.
- *Simple "User-friendly" Task Specification,* which specifies the actions that they want, performed in a relatively simple manner.

Need for Presence Awareness

A wide range of distributed application scenarios requires presence awareness.[2] Presence awareness provides information like the location, idendity, activities and the neighbours of someone or something who or which is present somewhere. The goal is to provide the necessary services to the various applications that make use of presence information.

Currently there are already a lot of applications, which need presence awareness information, and in the near future there will be more. Well known today's application areas are messengers like from AOL, Yahoo or Microsoft. Future use cases could be location-based services in the area of mobile phones like friend finder or applications which coordinate a fleet of vehicles. Other examples are collaborative browsing environments or e-shops enriched with presence awareness information to name only a few. What all these application scenarios have in common is that they are in need of presence awareness. Each application implements its own proprietary solution, which extends the time necessary to develop such kind of software and raises the costs. To achieve the presence and awareness a Presence Association model and a Secure Service Presence Model are introduced and a Presence Avaliability Policy Language (PAL) is also designed.

Session Initiation Protocol (SIP)/Simple Protocol

Presence, also known as presence information, conveys the ability and willingness of a user to communicate across a set of devices. A presence protocol is a protocol for providing a presence service over the Internet or an IP network. The Session Initiation Protocol (SIP) can be used as a presence protocol. SIP is extended as SIMPLE, i.e. SIP for Instant Messaging and Presence Leveraging Extensions.[5] IETF Applications Area Working Group—Focuses on the application of the SIP Protocol (RFC 3261) to the suite of services collectively known as instant messaging and presence.

The Components of SIP Simple are :

- Presence Event Package (–draft-ietf-simple-presence-10.txt (July 2003).)
- Extents the SIP Event Package RFC 3265
- The package is identified by : Event : presence header field.

The Presence Event Package has the core extensions to SIP to support Presence and Awareness. This package contains

- Presentity and Watcher.
- Presence User Agent (PUA).
- Presence Agent (PA).

Presentity and Watcher

Presentity is the entity that is projecting its presence information. More often this is a user identified with a SIP address. Watcher is the entity that is receiving presence information. More often this is a user identified with a SIP address.

Presence User Agent

A Presence User Agent manipulates presence information for a presentity.

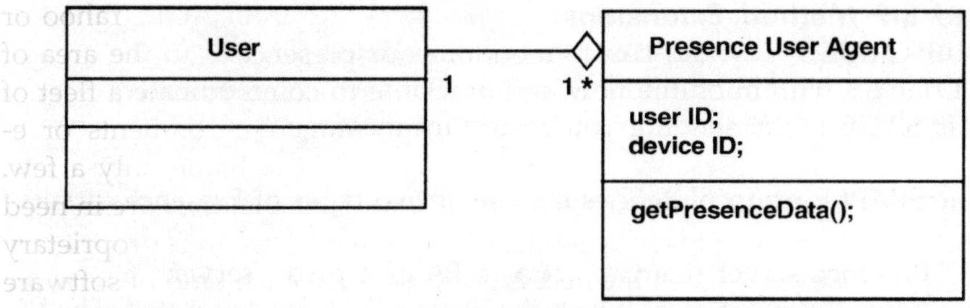

FIG. 30.1
Presence User Agent

Presence Agent

A presence agent is a SIP user agent which is capable of receiving SUBSCRIBE requests, responding to them, and generating notifications of changes in presence state which is depicted in Figure 30.2.

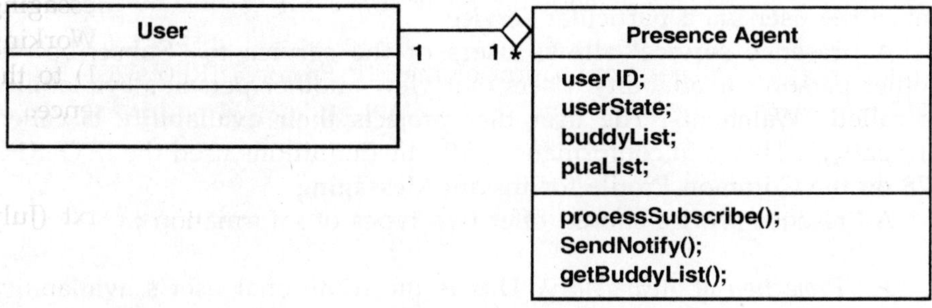

FIG. 30.2
Presence Agent

Figure 30.3 shows the relationship between the Presence Agent and the Presence User Agent.

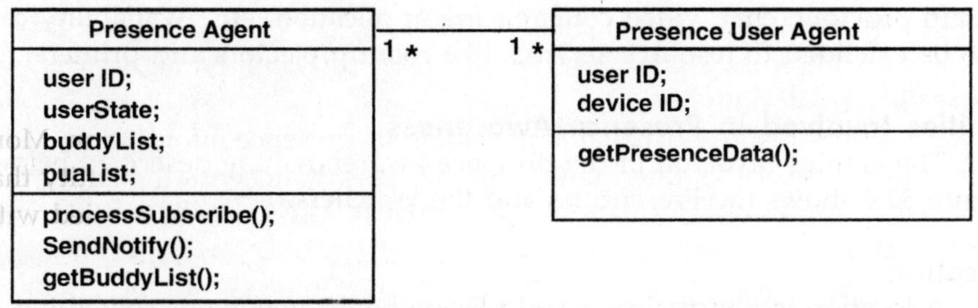

FIG. 30.3
Presence Agent and Presence User Agent Relationship

Defined SIP Method Extensions

SUBSCRIBE : "I would like to monitor your presence."
NOTIFY : "Hi!I'm online now and available to communicate."
MESSAGE : "I'm sending you an instant message."

The SIMPLE protocol defines the use of two types of Presence servers.

- Presence server that can act as a PA or a proxy server.
- Edge Presence Server where the PA and PUA are co-located. The PA is aware of the presence information that is available from the PUA.

Presence and Availability

The spontaneous service discovery can be achieved by the Presence and Availability of the services. The Presence for network communications is the concept of knowing whether a resource or person is registered with the system. The monitoring system will be kept away that do not require user identification. Availability is the concept of allowing other persons to contact the user via a particular service.

A presence service[1] allows users of the service to "Subscribe" to another person's availability. Users that view another person's availability are called "Watchers". The user that projects their availability is called "Presentity". This is in conformance with the definitions used the IETF RFC 2778 on the Common Profile for Instant Messaging.

A Presence service should offer two types of information :

- *Projection of Availability*. This is the traditional user's availability information.
- *Communication Contact Information*. This second type of information reflects how the person is available for immediate communication. The contact information describes different media that the person is currently available on—the devices, software applications, etc.

Examples of such would be—a telephone, an Instant Messaging via a certain provider, chat, video conferencing application, etc. Availability can also be extended to resource services like room projectors and printers.

Entities Involved in Presence Awareness

The entities involved in the presence awareness[2] are described below. Figure 30.4 shows the Presentities and the Watchers.

Location

A location is a virtual or a real place where someone or something is located at or *is present*. Examples of locations in the virtual world are documents (HTML pages, text documents, ...) or hosts. In the case of a document, being present might mean that someone has opened a document.

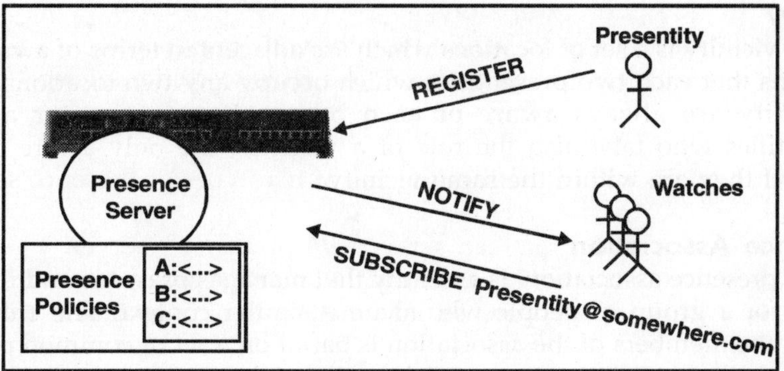

Fig. 30.4
Presentity and Watcher

Locations can be specified here by using e.g. URLs. In case of hosts, being present could mean someone is logged on to the host. Locations in this case can be specified by using IP addresses, maybe augmented by a port number.

Presentity

A presentity is present at a location. Each presentity has a unique identifier. In the real world a unique identifier could be the postal address of someone. In the virtual world a unique identifier could be of the form user@domain. A presentity needs not to be of flesh and blood but may also be a running program, may be a bot or a user agent. Like locations a presentity provides presence information. It is represented as a tuple in the following way :

PI = { PD, L, S }
PD = {P, D}

Whereby P is the presentity to which the presence information is associated. D is a *discriminator* between multiple instances of the same presentity.

Watcher

A watcher is interested in presence information. There are different ways a watcher can get this information : First, a watcher can fetch presence information once. In this case it gets a snapshot of current presence information. Second, a watcher can poll presence information at regular intervals. Third, a watcher can subscribe to presence information. A watcher can take the role of a presentity at the same time and *vice versa*. Like for instance in a collaborative browsing application where each participant is present at some web page (or web site) and at the same time interested in who else is present there.

Vicinity

A vicinity is a set of locations which are adjacent in terms of awareness. It means that each two presentities which occupy any two locations within a vicinity are always aware of each others. Presentities (or actually presentities who take also the role of a watcher) are only aware of each others if they are within the same vicinity.

Presence Association

A presence association[3] is an entity that manages presence and resource access for a group of people who share a similar context. The behaviour among the members of the association is based on a set of common policies. Although the association can contain policies that restrict communication among members, we primarily would like to keep an open communication policy among association members and resources. One of the first types of associations we envisioned is location-based associations, for example room associations. A room association is a persistent object with the resources of the room already registered with it. This is not an unreasonable assumption, since many resources in meeting rooms are generally stationary. Mobile resources most often belong to users and need to be dynamically registered with the association. Location associations will most likely be the primary association that users will indirectly interact with. They behave as a first entry point for users to a corporate network. All users in a particular location will be subjected to a particular set of policies for network and resource access.

Presence Association Model

The basic components of our Presence Association Model are shown in Figure 30.5 and consist of an Association Manager, Presence Associations, a Presence Service, Services and Presence Clients and an Association Client.

The *Association Manager* is the entity that creates and manages the associations. Each *Association* manages three different types of policies. These are membership, presence, and service access policies. The membership policies, which will accept or reject a registration request to the association. An example of a membership policy might be that the creator must confirm each new member. The second set of policies, the presence policies controls the projection of availability among members and services of an association. The third set of policies, the resource access policies control the access to those services shared among the members. Since other users on the network can physically access networked resources, it is necessary to prevent access to these resources when in use by members of the association.

The *Presence Service* projects the properties of associations like the availability of their members and services. The projection is done according to a set of notification policies that determine for example which members and under what context the member sees the availability of other members. The presence service uses the SIP SIMPLE protocol for communication with the presence clients.

The *Services* can be any form services that support access control policies and secure communication. The Services can be registered and are placed in a particular association.

The *Association Client* serves as an interface to the Association Manager. The *Presence Client* serves as an interface to the Presence Service.

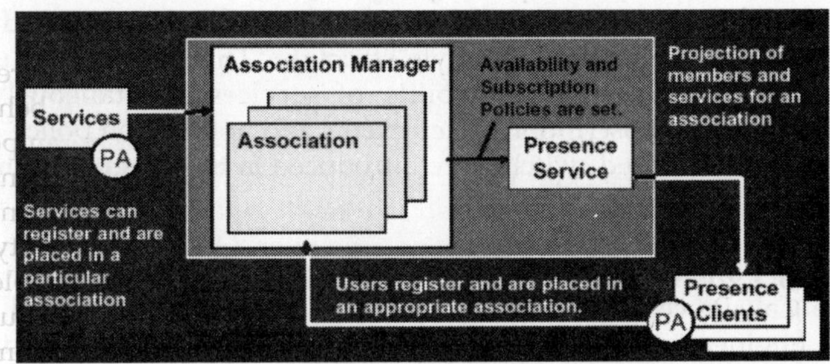

FIG. 30.5
Presence Association Model

Advantages of the Presence Association Model

This model combines the services and users into a group that shares a common set of subscription and notification policies. The Group-based presence services manage the users and access control policies that directly impact the subscription and notification policies. The service discovery is done without the user's knowledge (i.e.) spontaneous service discovery.

The Secure Service Presence Model

There should be a proper mechanism available for managing the policies to the services. A Security Service profile is to be developed that identifies the Security Protocol or security mechanism used for each service. The concept of this framework is given below.

The Secure service registers the Association Manager as a Service Location Protocol (SLP) service. There is an SLP service template associated with it that defines any special arguments that correspond to the Secure Service Profile (SSP).

The Association Manager places the service with a particular association and generates a master key or password required to use the service.

The Presence Service sets the availability and subscription policies. The user (Presence client) communicates with the Association. The availability of services and members of an association are projected to the Presence Client by the Presence Service. Password or a Key is passed as an argument with the service URL.

The client then tries to set-up the Secure Session. The SSP consists of all the secure mechanisms and protocols which are to be used for a Secured communication. The SSP opens the Common Open Policy Service (COPL) for its reference.

Presence Availability Policy Language

A Presence Availability policy Language (PAL) is defined based on the Call Processing Language (CPL) style structure. This language is used to identify the presence and availability of services spontaneously. This languages uses the subscription policy events and notification policy events. Some new context-based switches are introduced in this language which are not available in the CPL.

Specifying Policies Using Call Processing Language (CPL)

The Call Processing Language (CPL)[9] is a language designed by the Internet Engineering Task Force (IETF) for the Internet Telephony. This language is used to describe and control the Internet Telephony Services and is designed to be implemented on either Network Servers or User Agent Servers. This language describes the services as a Decision Graph based on XML syntax.

The CPL scripts are verifiable, well-formed and executable. They are guaranteed to complete, i.e. no loops are there. The scripts have standardized representation which is readable and producible. This language is a platform independent one.

A CPL script runs in a network system, and controls that system's proxy, redirect, or rejection actions for the set-up of a particular call.

Features of Presence and Availability Policy Language

The Presence and Availability Policy Language is defined based on the Call Processing Language (CPL) style structure with new context-based switches like role, location, time/date, activity, relationship. The syntax of the PAL script is shown below.

Syntax Of The PAL Script
<pal id='11089'name ='College'
priority='2'>
<notification-event>
<role-switch> <role name='Lecturer'>
<location-switch><location is='College'>
<availability value='available' status='current activity' location= 'current location'>
<notify/> ....
</pal>

The Role Switch
<pal id='16571' name='test1' priority='1'>

```
<notification-event><role-switch>
  <role name='personal, test'>
<availability value='available' status='current activity'
location='current location'>
<notify/></availability></role>
</role-switch></notification-event>
</pal>
```

The Watcher Switch

```
<papl id='19160' name='test3' priority='2'>
<notification-event>
<watcher-switch>
<watcher name='watcher@example.com'>
<availability value='available' status='current activity' location='
current location'>
<notify/></availability></watcher>
</watcher-switch>
</notification-event>
</pal>
```

The Subscription

```
<pal id='31383' name='subscribe policy' priority='1'>
<subscribe>
<watcher-switch>
<watcher name='ram@mitel.com'>
<role-switch>
<role name='personal, test'>
<subscribe-reply reply='confirmed'>
<send-reply/></subscribe eply></role>
</role-switch></watcher>
</watcher-switch></subscribe>
</pal>
```

Conclusion and Suggestions for Further Work

This paper highlights the need for the spontaneous service discovery in the mobile *ad-hoc* networks and introduces a Presence Association model and a Secure Service Presence Model and defines a Presence and Availability Policy language (PAL) for the spontaneous service discovery.

The concept of Presence and Awareness of services is an enabling technology for spontaneous service discovery. This concept overcomes the problems involved in the existing service discovery protocols and the proximity-based protocols.

The future work on the introduced presence association model includes the completion and refinement of the system model. Implementing incomplete or missing components especially for policy and security management inside the association would be the main focus of the work. Another milestone would be incorporating different types of secure group-based services in the system, like chat, audio and video. For this task it will be necessary to implement prototype services or extend the existing ones to integrate them in the system.

References

1. *Ghavam, A., Liscano, R. Barbeau M., Gray, T., Georganas, N.*, "Secure Presence-based Services".
2. *Holger Christein, Peter Schulthess*, "A General Purpose Model for Presence Awareness", Distributed Systems Department, University of Ulm, Germany.
3. *Liscano, R., Ghavam, A., Barbeau, M., Gray, T., and Georganas, N.*, "Enabling Secure *ad-hoc* Communications in the Enterprise", Proceedings of the 1st International Conference on *Ad-hoc* Networks and Wireless. Toronto, Ontario, Sep. 2002.
4. *Preuss, S. and Clemens, H.*, "Spontaneous Networking," Workshop on Future Services for Networked Devices (FuSeNetD 1999), In Conjunction with Eurescom 1999, Heidelberg, Gernamy, Nov. 8-9 1999.
5. http ://www.ietf.org/internet-drafts/draft-ietf-simple-presence-10.txt
6. *SIMPLE on the Web* http ://www.ietf.org/html.charters/simple-charter.html
7. *SIP on the Web* http ://www.ietf.org/html.charters/sip-charter.html
8. *RFC 2778* 'A Model for Presence and Instant Messaging'—http ://www.ietf.org/rfc/rfc2778.txt
9. http ://www.ietf.org/internet-drafts/draft-ietf-iptel-cpl-framework-00.txt

Part VI

Network Routing

Part VI

Network Routing

CHAPTER

31

Dynamic Routing in a Mesh Network

R.S.D. WAHIDA BANU AND G. VARAPRASAD

Introduction

The routing decisions are based on assigning routing priorities to the links such that packet is forwarded to the highest priority links which is not blocked. Routing priorities are assigned using a local greedy metric, which minimize the distance (number of hops) to the destination. This shows that routing decision using a local greedy metric are not optimal, and the performance of the routing can be improved substantially by new measures. Thus, various look-ahead metrics, which take into account the potential gain on the other switching nodes toward the destination of a packect, are suggested.

The contribution of this work are : (1) a new model to capture the behaviour of switching node; (2) an iterative optimization technology to set routing priority according to various look-head measures; and (3) heuristic to ensure the stability of the routing priorities. The optimization objective is to maximize throughput by minimizing the maximum total flow carried on a link in the network under static traffic model. The performance is studied computationally on various networks and traffic metrics. It is shown that up to a 50% performance increase can be obtained by optimizing the routing priories.

In recent years, we have witnessed considerable accomplishments in the design, development, and development of broadband communication networks. The Internet grow at remarkable rate. At the same time, a phenomenal growth in data traffic and wide range of new requirements of emerging applications called for new mechanisms for the control and management of communication networks. This poses some major challenges. Not only are many problems intrinsically difficult, but also there are also additional constraints, such as limitations on the computational capabilities of network elements. In additional, any such control and management mechanism must scale well with network growth and provide fast response to internal (e.g., link failure) and external events.

A scheduling displaçe to decide which requests to serve next, it is very important because they are the key to fair sharing network resources and providing performance-critical applications, such as telephone and interactive multi-participant games, with performance guarantees. Actually scheduling has two orthogonal components. First, it decides the order in which requests are served. Second, it manages the service queue of request awaiting services.

In circuit switching networks, source traffic is smooth and without significant fluctuations. Therefore, scheduling is not important problem in such networks, when you considering packet switching networks scheduling is required. Two types of services one best effort service and other one is guaranteed service Scheduling discipline must satisfy four sometime contradictory requirements.

In static routing problem, a pair-wise traffic function and link capacities problem are given. Thus, the problem is to choose routes and assigns fractions to the links in order to minimize delay or maximize throughput. This problem can be solved a multicommodity flow problem. In static routing, the section of routes and the assign of lows on the links are detected before the routing tables are downloaded into the network's switches and remain unchanged in time.

In dynamic problem, requires changing routing decision continuously, according to the change in traffic and congestion conditions in the network. Earlier models of dynamic and static routing problem have been studied by Gallager,[14] Bertsekas,[15] Segall,[16] and others. These models mainly consider the shortest path routing problem to minimize expected delay; however, congestion and packet loss (due to the congestion occur) problem are not presented. In dynamic routing techniques such as ho-potato,[13] deflection routing,[3,5,8,10] and congestion routing,[11,8] ensure no packet loss due to congestion inside with minimum buffer requirements. Such routings, the online routing decision with the instant traffic load inside the network

Unlike deflection and hot potato routings, which packet are deflected away from the shortest path, in convergence routing, packet are deflected toward the shortest paths. As a result, convergence routing ensures that packets will reach their destinations without being routed on the same link twice. Thus, it ensures a dynamic bound on the maximum route length in an arbitrary topology network

In this paper, we showed that the performance of optimum delay routing could be improved. The performance considers in this work does minimizing the maximum total low carry maximization of throughput by minimizing the maximum total low on a link in the mesh network under the load. We define a new iterative optimization problem to assign routing priorities to maximize the throughput of optimum delay routing.

Source Availability

As the network size goes to infinity, the cost may also go to infinity. It is obvious that, even if the network size approaches infinity, we should only be concerned with the relative cost performance. That is, the algorithm should be considered to have "converged" if the cost lies within a small percentage of the optimal cost. We are considering two types of source availability.

Many parameters associated with delay requirements are affected by temporal conditions, such as congestion. Parameters advertised by a link might be based, for example, on average behaviour or on worst-case behaviour. In either case, the advertised parameters are not accurate. This inaccuracy can be eliminated by rapidly advertising the current, updated, accurate conditions. Unfortunately, this is impractical when the network is highly dynamic and changes are frequent. Thus, advertised values should be considered as uncertain. The precise probability distributions associated with each value depends on *a priori* knowledge on the frequency of updates and the dynamics of the network.

In this section, we present an iterative algorithm, based on the routing metrics. The objective function of the optimization problem is to minimize the maximum values of congestion, defined as total flow on a link, for a given expected traffic matrix. Minimization of maximizes throughput. Each node can execute the algorithm independently (distributed) or by a central site.

1. How to captures the existence of such routing alternatives?, and
2. How to predict the availability of links?

A. Source Equal Capacity

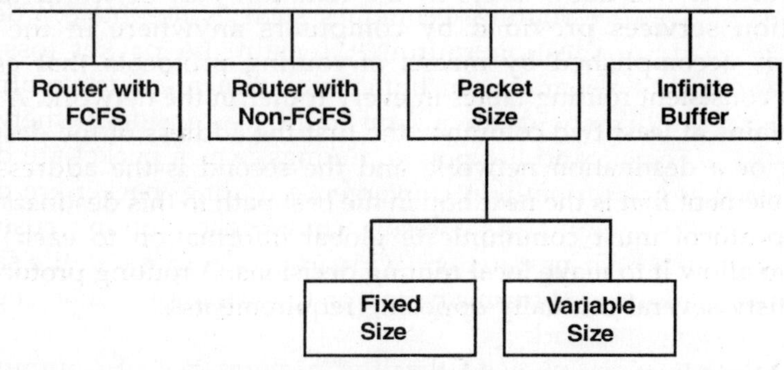

FIG. 31.1
Source Equal Capacity

B. Source Non-Equal Capacity

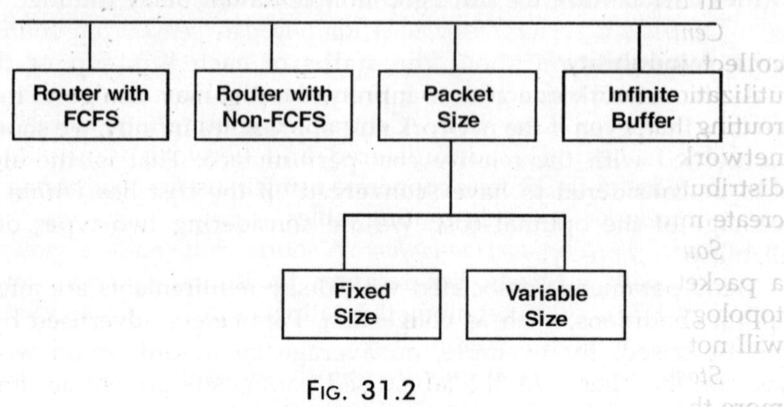

FIG. 31.2
Source Equal Capacity

Routing

What is Routing?

The determination to path that a data unit (frame, packet, message) will traverse from source to destination. Telephone network routing differs from Internet routing in many ways, because telephone networks are much better connected and have more reliable links and switches, and telephone network, such as predicate traffic flow, and a relatively small network core. Large packet networks, such as the Internet, present a very different environment. In the Internet, links and router are unreliable, alternative paths are scare, and traffic patterns can change unpredictably within minutes.

What is Need for Routing Algorithms?

Routing is the process of finding a path from source to destination in the network. It will allow users in the remotest part of world to get to information services provided by computers anywhere in the world. Routing is accomplished by means of routing protocols that establish mutually consistent routing tables in every router in the network. A routing table contains at least two columns : the first the address of the destination endpoint or a destination network, and the second is the address of the network element that is the next hop in the best path to this destination. Any routing protocol must communicate global information to each routing element to allow it to make local routing decisions. A routing protocol must try to satisfy several mutually opposing requirements :

- Minimizing routing table space;
- Minimize control message; and
- Robustness.

Classification of Routing Algorithms

In this section we discuss commonly available routing.[9]

Centralized versus Distributed Routing : in centralized routing process collect information about the status of each link (up or down link, utilization, and capacity) and processes this information to compute a routing table for every node. Centralized routing is reasonable when the network is centrally administered and network is not too large. In distributed routing, routers cooperate using a distributed routing protocol to create mutually consistent routing tables.

Source-based versus Hop-by-hop : A source route allow a sender to specify a packet path precisely, but requires the source to aware of the entire topology. If link or router along the path goes down, a source-routed packet will not reach its destination.

Stochastic versus Deterministic : Stochastic routing, each router maintains more than one next hop for each possible destination. Deterministic route, each router forwards packet toward a detonation along exactly one path.

Single versus Multiple Path : In Single-path routing, a router maintains only one path to each destination. Single-path routing is used for on Internet, because maintaining alternative path require more routing table pace. In multiple-path routing, a routing, a router maintains a primary path to a destination, along with alternative paths. Telephone networks usually use multiple-path routing, because this reduces the call blocking probability, which is very important for the customer stratifications.

State Dependent versus State Independent : State dependent or *dynamic* routing, the choice of route dependents on the current network state. State independent or *Static* routing, the route ignores the network state. Internet use state dependent *versus* state independent telephone network use state dependent.

Optimization Algorithms

The objective function of the optimization problem is to minimize the maximum values of dynamic, defined as total flow on a link, for a given expected traffic matrix. Minimization of maximum congestion prevents bottlenecks in the network and maximizes throughput. Each node can execute the algorithms independently.

Algorithm I

```
For each node, each link

    Check the queue-length
    If (queue-length >=0) then
        C-Bandwidth=Active-Bandwidth
    Else
        C-Bandwidth=bandwidth/queue-length.
    End if
        Broad cast (C-Bandwidth)
    End for
```

Algorithm II

Step 1 : Receive the Broad cast from each node, link
Step 2 : Construct topology
Step 3 : Calculate multiple path
Step 4 : Check the no. of shortest path
Step 5 : If (no. of shortest path>1) then
c-shortest path=prob (no. of shortest path)
else
c-shortest path=shortest path;
end if
Step 7 : route the shortest path (c-shortest path)
Step 8 : Check the no acknowledgements (ACK)
Step 9 : If (ACK< Digtrct-level)
Go to Step 4
else
Go to Step 1
End if

Summary of Flow of Packets

Minimize Z such that

$$Z=fij^k \qquad i, j, k$$

$$fij^k=tij\ Pij^{k}+\Sigma \qquad fij^k+Pij^k \qquad i, j, k$$

$$fij^k=0 \qquad i, j, k$$

The solution to this multi-commodity flow problem will assign to the flow variable fij^k and calculate Z. thus, based on this solution, it is possible to compute new utilization values $\tilde{n}_{i,j}$ for each link (i,j) as follows :

$$\rho_{i,j}=\frac{\Sigma_k fij^k}{Z}$$

since z is the maximum total flow on a link the network, always ensure that the utilization takes values i.e., $o=\tilde{n}_{i,j}=1$.

Conclusion

This research work presents the design and implementation of source routing in mesh network topology. Delay time for each channel is calculated and is stored in the routing table. Shortest path from each node to each destination is identified and it is also stored in the routing matrix. When a request exists from a node, the required information is routed through the shortest path, which is taken from the routing matrix. Thus, the information is routed successfully.

The usual assumptions are made so that each channel could model as an *FCFS* Queue. The average delay time 'waiting time' is computed for each channel involved in the mesh network topology by applying queuing theory. Finally, the problem has been formulated as an optimization problem where the decision variables are the intermediate nodes in the network topology. The main objective of routing is that intermediate nodes need not keep route information because the path is explicitly specified in the data packet.

References

1. G. Varaprasad, R.S.D. Wahida Banu, "Shortest Path between Source to Destination in A Mesh Network", *ICET 2004*, Bhuwaneswar, p. 67.
2. G. Varaprasad, R.S.D. Wahida Banu, "Adaptive Routing in a Wide Area Network", *NCON 2003*, Srivillupuram, PP 120-28.
3. G. Varaprasad, R.S.D. Wahida Banu, "Flexible Routing in a Mesh Network", *SIS 2004*, IITM, Chennai.
4. G. Varaprasad, R.S.D. Wahida Banu, "Routing in Communication Network Using Neural Network", National Conference on Intelligent Systems, Automation Signal Processing *NCISASP'03*, March 1, 2003. pp. 58-63.
5. George Apostolopoulos, Roch Guerin, Sanay Kamat and S.K. Tripathi, "Intradomain QOS Routing in the IP Networks, Feasibility and Cost/Benefit Analysis", *IEEE Networks*. Sep./Oct. 1999, pp. 42-52.
6. Reuven Cohen, Yoram Ofek and Adrrian Segall, "A New Label-Based Source Routing For Multi-Ring Networks", *IEEE transactions* Vol. 3, June 1995, pp. 320-28.
7. Roger Chen, C.V., Georges A. Makhoul and Dikran S. Meilisetain, "A Queuing Analysis of the Performance of DQDBS", *IEEE/ACM Transactions on Networking*, Vol. 3, No. 6, Dec. 1995, pp. 872-81.
8. Adre Giraro, Redouance Ziadance, "Revenue Optimization of B-ISDN Networks", *IEEE Transaction on Communications*, Vol. 43, Mar. 1995, pp. 1992-97.
9. China-jin Wang, Paul N. Weissler, "The Use of Artificial Neural Network for Optimal Message Routing", *IEEE Network*, Mar./April pp. 16-24.
10. Joseph Bannister, Flaminio Borgonovo, Luigi Fratta and Mario Gerla, "A Performance Model Deflection Routing in Multi Buffer Networks with Non-Uniform Traffic", *IEEE Transactions Networking*, Vol. 3, No. 5, Oct. 1995.
11. Kapoor, K.V., "Problem and Solution In Operations Research", New Delhi, Sultan Chand & Sons Educational Pub., 1998.
12. Krishana Bala, Thomas, E. Stern, David Simchi-Levi, Kavitha Bala, "Routing an a Linear Light Ware Network", *IEEE/ACM Transactions on Networking*, Vol. 3, No. 4, Aug. 1995, pp. 459-69.
13. Whay C. Lee, Michael G. Hluchy and Pierre A. Humblet, "Routing Subject to Query of Service Constraints in Integrated Communication Networks", *IEEE Network*, July/April 1995.
14. Andrew S. Tenenbaum, "Computer Network", Delhi, PHI Pvt. Ltd., 1990.
15. Emmanouel A. Varvarigos and Dimitri P. Bertekas, "Performance of Hyper-cube Routing Schemes without Buffering", *IEEE/ACM Transaction on Networking*, Vol. 2, No. 3, June 1994.
16. D. Johnson and D. Maltz, "Dynamic source Routing in *Ad-Hoc* Wireless Networks", from Mobile Computing, Norwood (MA) : Kluwer, 1996.
17. Charles Perkins and Pravin Bhagwat, "DSDV Routing over a Multihop Wireless Network of Mobile Computers", from Mobile Computing, Norwood (MA) : Kluwer, 1996.
18. D.P. Bertsekas, "Dynamic Models of Shortest Path Routing Algorithms for Communication Networks with Multiple Destinations," *in Proc. 1979 IEEE Conf. Decision Contr.*, Dec. 1979, pp. 127-33.

CHAPTER

32

MPLS—Exploring the Dimensions and Capabilities

V.S. Dhenesh, K.K. Suresh Kumar,
P. Ramesh and N. Senthilkumaran

Introduction

IT is a heaven and the customers are the key idols for the Internet Service Providers (ISPs). The large and small ISPs constantly face the challenges of adapting their networks to support the rapid growth and customer demand for more reliable and differentiated services. The IP over ATM provided many ISPs, a solution for delivering excellent performance through traffic engineering, but the Multi Protocol Label Switching (MPLS) offers simpler mechanisms for packet-oriented traffic engineering and multi-service functionalities with the added benefit of greater scalability.

The MPLs addresses the scalability issues associated with the IP-over-ATM. It significantly reduces the complexity of network operators. It also facilitates the delivery of new routing capabilities that enhance conventional IP routing techniques. It offers a standard-based solution that promotes multi-vendor interoperability.

The MPLs is applied in traffic engineering, the Class of Services (CoS) and the Virtual Private Network (VPN) to enhanced routing in the public networks.

Both large and small Internet Service Providers (ISPs) constantly face the challenges of adapting their networks to support rapid growth and customer demand for more reliable and differentiated services.

Multiprotocol Label Switching (MPLS) offers simpler mechanisms for packet-oriented traffic engineering and multi-service functionality with the added benefit of greater scalability. MPLS emerged from the IETF's effort to standardize a number of proprietary multilayer switching solutions that were initially proposed in the mid-1990s.

The first half of this paper describes the forces that motivated the development and evolution of these different solutions. The second half of this paper builds on the understanding of multilayer switching, focusing on the specifics of MPLS. The benefits of MPLS for the core of the Internet, and the most popular applications for MPLS are also highlighted.

Multiprotocol Label Switching (MPLS) is the latest step in the evolution of routing/forwarding technology for the core of the Internet.[3] MPLS delivers a solution that seamlessly integrates the control of IP routing with the simplicity of Layer 2 switching. Furthermore, MPLS provides a foundation that supports the deployment of advanced routing services because it solves a number of complex problems :

- MPLS significantly reduces the complexity of network operation.
- MPLS facilitates the delivery of new routing capabilities that enhance conventional IP routing techniques.
- MPLS offers a standard-based solution that promotes multi-vendor interoperability.

Evolution

Fundamental Blocks

MPLS emerged from the IETF's effort to standardize a set of proprietary multilayer switching solutions.[3] The emergence of the multilayer switching solutions and MPLS is part of the evolution of the Internet to decrease complexity by combining Layer 2 switching and Layer 3 routing into a fully integrated solution.

The basic blocks for Enhanced Routing using MPLS include :

- Separation of the control and forwarding components.

All multilayer switching solutions, including MPLS, are composed of two distinct functional components namely a control component and a forwarding component as in Fig. 32.1 The control component uses standard routing protocol like OSPF to exchange information with other routers to build and maintain a forwarding table. When packets arrive, the forwarding component searches the forwarding table maintained by the control component to make a routing decision for each packet. Later, the forwarding component examines information contained in the packet's header, searches the forwarding table for a match, and directs the packet from the input interface to the output interface across the system's switching fabric.

By completely separating the control component from the forwarding component, each component can be independently developed and modified.

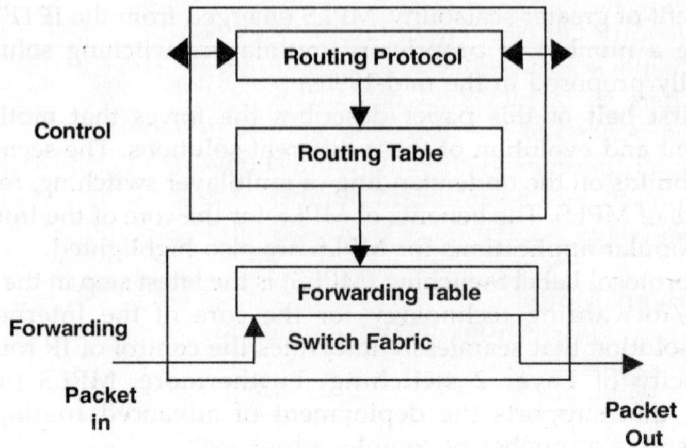

FIG. 32.1

Routing Functional Components : Control and Forwarding

Multilayer Switching

The fundamental approach adopted by these strategies was to take the control software from an IP router, integrate it with the forwarding performance of a label-swapping ATM switch, and create an extremely fast and cost efficient IP router as shown in Figure 32.2.

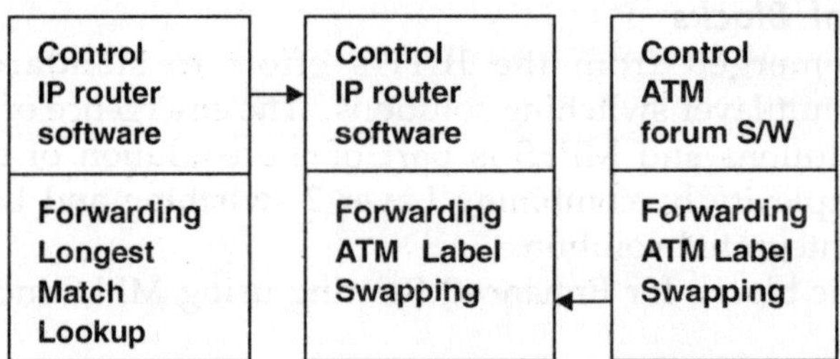

FIG. 32.2

Multilayer Switch as a Fast IP-router

Data Driven Model

In the data-driven model, label bindings are created when user data packets arrive. A flow is a sequence of packets that have the same source and destination IP addresses and TCP or UDP port numbers.[2] A multilayer switch can either create a label binding as soon as it sees the first packet in traffic flow or wait until it has seen a number of packets in the flow. The benefit of waiting for a number of packets ensures that the flow is long enough to merit the overhead of assigning and distributing a label. The advantage of the data-driven model is that a label binding is created only when there is a traffic flow that uses the label binding.

Each multilayer switch must provide sophisticated and high-performance packet classification capabilities to identify traffic flows. Typically, there is latency between the recognition of a flow and the assignment of a label to the flow. The amount of control traffic needed to distribute label bindings is directly proportional to the number of traffic flows. The presence of a significant number of relatively short-lived flows can impose a heavy burden on network operations.

Control Driven Model

In the control-driven model, label bindings are created when control information arrives.

Benefits

- Labels are assigned and distributed before the arrival of user data traffic. This means that if a route exists in the IP forwarding table, a label has already been allocated for the route, so traffic arriving at a multilayer switch can be label swapped immediately.
- Scalability is significantly better than in the data-driven model, because the number of label switched paths is proportional to the number of entries in the IP forwarding table, not to the number of individual traffic flows.
- In a stable topology, the label assignment and distribution overhead is lower than in the data-driven model because label-switched paths are established only after a topology change or the arrival of control traffic, not with the arrival of each new traffic flow.
- Every packet in a flow is label switched, not just the tail end of the flow as in the data-driven model.

MPLS

MPLS is the latest step in the evolution of multilayer switching in the Internet.[3] It is an IETF standard-based approach built on the efforts of the various proprietary multilayer switching solutions.

MPLS uses the control-driven model to initiate the assignment and distribution of label bindings for the establishment of label-switched paths (LSPs). LSPs are simplex in nature duplex traffic requires two LSPs, one LSP to carry traffic in each direction. Concatenating one or more label switched hops creates an LSP, allowing a packet to be forwarded from one label-switching router (LSR) to another LSR across the MPLS domain. An LSR is a router that supports MPLS-based forwarding.

The MPLS control component centers around IP functionality, which is similar to proprietary multilayer switching solutions. However, MPLS defines new standard-based IP signaling and label distribution protocols, as well as extensions to existing protocols, to support multi-vendor interoperability. MPLS does not implement any of the ATM Forum signaling or routing protocols so the complexity of coordinating two different protocol architectures is eliminated. In this way, MPLS brings significant benefits to a packet-oriented Internet.

The MPLS forwarding component is based on the label-swapping algorithm.[6] If the Layer 2 technology supports a label field the native label field encapsulates the MPLS label. However, if the Layer 2 technology does not support a label field, the MPLS label is encapsulated in a standardized MPLS header that is inserted between the Layer 2 and IP headers.

The 32-bit MPLS header contains the following fields :

- The label field (20-bits) carries the actual value of the MPLS label.
- The CoS field (3-bits) can affect the queuing and discard algorithms applied to the packet as it is transmitted through the network.
- The Stack (S) field (1-bit) supports a hierarchical label stack.
- The TTL (time-to-live) field (8-bits) provides conventional IP TTL functionality.

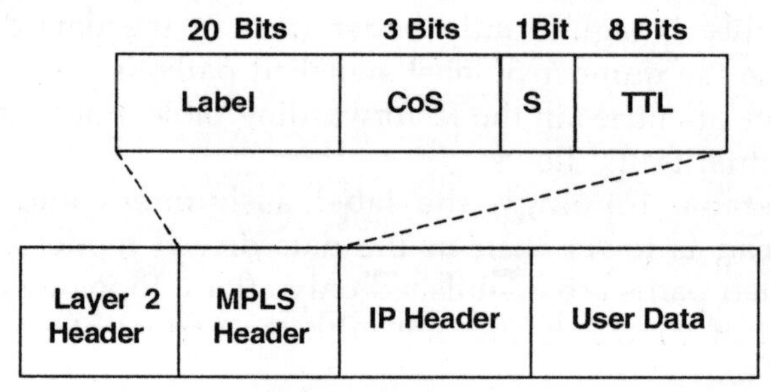

FIG. 32.3
MPLS Header

Objectives

The purpose of the MPLS working group is to standardize a base technology that combines the use of label swapping in the forwarding component with network layer routing in the control component. To achieve its objectives, the MPLS working group has to deliver a solution that satisfies a number of requirements, including :

- MPLS must run over any link layer technology, and not just ATM.
- MPLS core technologies must support the forwarding of both unicast and multicast traffic flows.
- MPLS must scale to support constant Internet growth.
- MPLS must support operations, administration, and maintenance facilities at least as extensive as those supported in current IP networks.

Enhanced Routing Functionalities

Figure 32.4 illustrates how MPLS provides more than just destination-based forwarding. Assume that the routers in the core of the network perform conventional, longest-match IP forwarding. If either Host A or Host B transmits a packet to Host C, the packet follows Path 1 across the core of the network because this is the shortest path computed by the IGP.

Suppose that the network administrator has been monitoring traffic statistics and needs to implement a policy to control congestion at Router B. The policy would reduce congestion at Router B by distributing the traffic load along different paths across the network. Traffic sourced by Host A and destined for Host C would follow the IGP shortest path, Path 1. Traffic sourced by Host B and destined for Host C would follow another path, Path 2. Using conventional IP routing, this policy cannot be implemented because all forwarding at Router A is based on the packet's destination address.

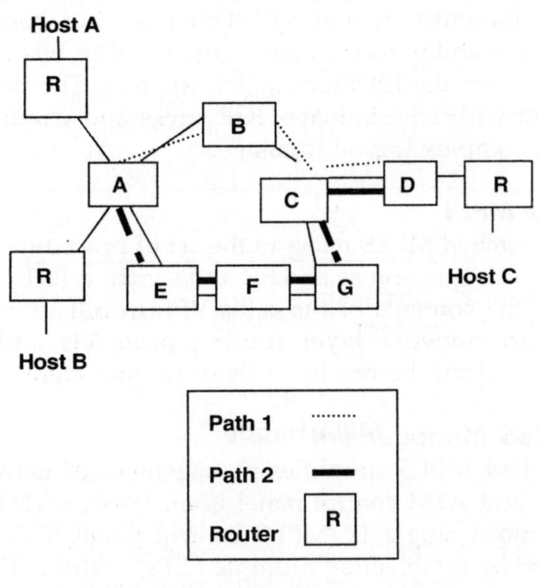

FIG. 32.4
Enhanced Routing Functionality

Now, if the routers in the core of the network function as LSRs, it is easy to implement a policy to reduce congestion at LSR B. The network administer configures LSP 1 to follow Path 1. The network administer configures LSP 2 to follow Path 2. Finally, the network administer configures LSR A to put all traffic received from Host A and destined for Host C into LSP 1. Likewise, LSR A is configured to place all traffic received from Host B and destined for Host C into LSP 2.

MPLS Types

IP-Routed MPLS

IP routed MPLS refers to the set of procedures that define how an IP router can function as an LSR to switch packets based on the label carried in the packets header. The IP-routed MPLs is superior to cell-switched MPLS in the following ways :

The IP differentiated services approach to CoS does not map well to existing ATM quality of service mechanisms. IP over ATM requires the deployment of routing adjancies that would lead to IGP stress during failure scenarios.

IP-Routed MPLS eliminates the potential for SAR bottleneck because it does not rely on ATM as a transport. It eliminates the complexity of managing two separate control planes and two fundamentally different types of networking equipment. It provides more efficient use of network bandwidth. It support IPDifferserv CoS because frame-based LSR have the ability to read and write the EXP bits in the MPLS label stack that carry the IPDifferserv information. The peer-to-peer nature of IP-Routed MPLS eliminates IGP stress and eliminates the need to manage a complex logical topology.

Cell-Switched MPLS

The cell-switched MPLS refers to the set of procedures that define how an ATM switch can function as an LSR and switch cells by inferring the top label based on the contents of the cell's VPI. In cell switched MPLS ATM switches execute network layer routing protocols and all forwarding decisions are based on the results of these routing algorithms.

Simplifying CoS Management

Cell switched MPLS simplifies management of network because the dual IP/MPLS and ATM control panel in an IP-over-ATM network can be consolidated into a single IP/MPLS control panel. Cell switched MPLS supports IP CoS by establishing multiple LSPs, with each LSP dedicated to a specific traffic class.

Cell switched MPLS offers an enhancement to IP-over-ATM for providers that :

- ➢ Want to keep the existing ATM infrastructures.
- ➢ Do not have the budget to purchase new frame based LSRs.
- ➢ Believe in the future of cell-based networks.
- ➢ Transmit mostly cell-based traffic, not frame based.

Reducing IGP Stress

The major problem when trying to scale IP-over-ATM is that the deployment of PVCs leads to IGP stress during failures. The peer-to-peer nature of cell switched eliminates the need to establish an overlay network consisting of a full mesh of n-squared routing adjacencies. By doing so the IGP stress during failures is eliminated.

Comparison of IP-Routed and Cell-Switched MPLS

SAR Bottlenecks

Cell switched MPLS requires SAR interfaces to communicate with cell-based switches in the core of the network. But IP-routed MPLS does not require SAR interfaces because it does not run over cell switching. Hence, IP-routed MPLS eliminates SAR bottlenecks.

Limitations for Faster Reroute

MPLS fast reroute can significantly reduce packet losses during periods of network instability. However, the fast reroute mechanism supported by IP-routed MPLS is generally not supported by cell switched MPLS.

Exhaustion of a Finite Label Space

Both the label space used by IP-routed MPLS and cell switched MPLS are finite resources if the label space exhausted cell switched MPLS degrades less gracefully for certain applications than for IP-routed MPLS. The use of arbitrary label stacking allows the creation of a hierarchy to conserve a finite label space to eliminate exhaustion problems while it is very easy for IP-routed MPLS to support arbitrary label stacks. It is difficult with cell switched MPLS.

Cell Tax

Cell switch MPLS does not support the most efficient use of network bandwidth due to the ATM cell tax. It means that cell switch MPLS can consume up to 25% more bandwidth than IP-routed MPLS. In fact TCP/IP is one of the worst protocols to run over the ATM transport because the transmission of the single ACK requires not one but two ATM cells.

It is more efficient to move towards IP-routed MPLS and not to cell switch MPLS because the transition from IP over ATM to cell switch MPLS will not significantly enhance the operation of the network but it requires a second transition to IP-routed MPLS to reach the ultimate goal.

Applications

Traffic Engineering

Traffic engineering allows ISPs to move traffic flows away from the shortest path calculated by the IGP and onto potentially less congested physical paths across the network (Figure 32.5). Traffic engineering is currently the primary application for MPLS because of the unprecedented growth in demand for network resources, the mission-critical nature of IP applications, and the increasingly competitive nature of the service provider

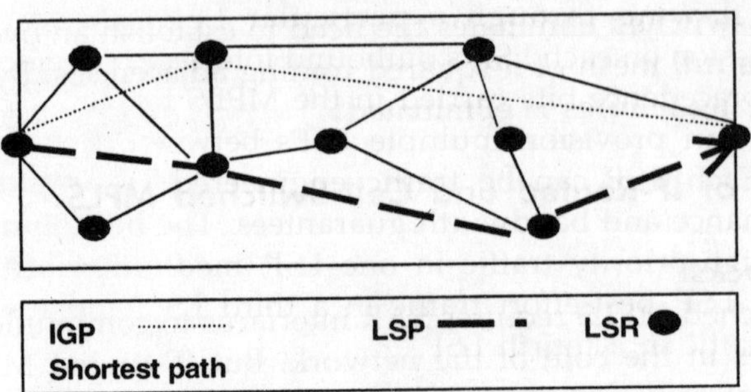

FIG. 32.5
Traffic Engineering LSP vs. IGP Shortest Path Across a Service Provider's Network

marketplace. A successful traffic engineering solution can balance a network's aggregate traffic load on the various links, routers, and switches in the network so that none of its individual components is over-utilized or under-utilized. This results in a network that is more efficiently operated and provides more predictable service.

MPLS is Suited for Traffic Engineering for the Following Reasons

- Support for explicit paths allows network administrators to specify the exact physical path that an LSP takes across the service provider's network.
- Per-LSP statistics can be used as input to network planning and analysis tools to identify bottlenecks and trunk utilization, and to plan for future expansion.
- Constraint-based routing provides enhanced capabilities that allow an LSP to meet specific performance requirements before it is established.
- An MPLS-based solution can run over packet-oriented networks and is not limited to ATM infrastructures.

CoS

MPLS can benefit service providers as they begin to roll out support for differentiated services (DiffServ). The differentiated services model defines a variety of mechanisms for classifying traffic into a small number of service classes. Subscribers are motivated to use the Internet as a public transport for a number of different applications ranging from traditional file transfer to delay sensitive services such as voice and video. To meet customer requirements, ISPs need to adopt not only traffic engineering techniques but also traffic classification technologies.

An ISP can take two approaches to support MPLS-based class of service forwarding :

- Traffic flowing through a particular LSP can be queued for transmission on each LSR's outbound interface based on the setting of the precedence bits carried in the MPLS header.
- An ISP can provision multiple LSPs between each pair of edge LSRs. Each LSP can be traffic engineered to provide different performance and bandwidth guarantees. The head end LSR could place high-priority traffic in one LSP, medium-priority traffic in another LSP, best-effort traffic in a third LSP, and less-than-best-effort traffic in a fourth LSP.

VPN

A Virtual Private Network (VPN) simulates the operation of a private Wide Area Network (WAN) over the public Internet. To offer a viable VPN service for its customers, an ISP must solve the problems of data privacy and support the use of non-unique, private IP addresses within a VPN. MPLS provides a simple and efficient solution to both of these challenges because it makes forwarding decisions based on the value of the label, not the destination address in the packet header.

VPNs are typically constructed using four fundamental building blocks :

- Firewalls to protect each customer site and provide a secure interface to the Internet.
- Authentication to verify that each customer site exchanges data with only validated remote sites.
- Encryption to protect data from examination or manipulation as it is transported across the Internet.
- Tunneling encapsulation to provide a multiprotocol transport service and enable the use of the private IP address space within a VPN MPLS allows ISPs to offer VPN services by providing a simple, flexible, and powerful tunneling mechanism.

An ISP can deploy a VPN by provisioning a set of LSPs to provide connectivity among the different sites in the VPN. Each VPN site then advertises to the ISP a set of prefixes that are reachable within the local site. The ISP's routing system distributes this information by piggybacking labels in routing protocol updates or by using a label distribution protocol. VPN Identifiers allow a single routing system to support multiple VPNs whose internal address spaces overlap with each other. Finally, each ingress LSR places traffic into LSPs based on a combination of a packet's destination address and VPN membership information.

Conclusion

MPLS is the latest step in the evolution of the multiplayer switching to enhance the public networking and to the core of internet. MPLS combines the use of label swapping in the forwarding component with IP routing and standards of label distribution protocols in the control component. MPLS can run over any link-layer technology—not just on the ATM infrastructure.

One of the core benefits of MPLS is that it permits ISPs to deliver new services that cannot be readily supported by conventional IP routings. MPLS enhances routing capabilities by supporting more than just destination-based forwarding, which will support the internet and service providers for their explosive growth. The paper opens the inroads for the MPLS functionality and can be extended towards the adaptability and flexibility of MPLS that has put it on the upbeat.

References

1. Davie, B., Doolan, P., and Rekhter, Y., "Switching in IP Networks : IP Switching, Tag Switching, and Related Technologies", Morgan Kaufmann, 1998, ISBN 1-55860-505-3.
2. Metz, Christopher, "IP Switching : Protocols and Architectures", McGraw-Hill, New York, 1999, ISBN 0-07-041953-1.
3. Newman, P., Edwards, W., Hinden, R., Hoffman, E., Ching Liaw, F., Lyon, T., and Minshall, G., "Flow Management Protocol Specification for IPv4 Version 1.0", May 1996.
4. Newman, P., Edwards, W., Hinden, R, Hoffman, E., Ching Liaw, F., Lyon, T. and Minshall, G., "Transmission of Flow Labelled IPv4 on ATM Data Links Ipsilon Version", May 1996.
5. Newman, P., Edwards, W., Hinden, R., Hoffman, E., Ching Liaw, F., Lyon, T., and Minshall, G. "Ipsilon's General Switch Management Protocol Specification Version 2.0", March 1998.
6. Rekhter, Y., Davie, B., Katz, D., Rosen, E., and Swallow, G., "Cisco Systems Tag Switching Architecture Overview", February 1997.

PART VII

Network Security : Threads and Solutions

Network Security

A. Agilandeeswary and S. Narmatha

Introduction

Network security is a complicated subject; historically it's tackled by well-trained and experienced experts. However, as more and more people become "wired", an increasing number of people need to understand the basics of security in a networked world. This paper explains the introduction to firewall, and establishing a security perimeter and generations of firewall architectures.

A firewall is a gateway that restricts and controls the flow of traffic between networks, typically between an internal corporate network and the Internet. A very secure firewall must be in place to ensure that only authorized users access the network. We can establish a security perimeter by using perimeter networks, trusted networks, untrusted networks and unknown networks. When we deploy a network security policy, we want it to be strategically enforced at defensible boundaries within our network.

These strategic boundaries are called perimeter networks. Trusted networks are the networks inside our network security perimeter. These networks are the ones that we are trying to protect. Untrusted networks are the networks that are known to be outside of our security perimeter. Unknown networks are those networks that are neither trusted nor untrusted. Firewalls inspected network traffic using one of four architectural models, which are defined by the information that they examine to make security-relevant decisions.

Application layer firewalls also implement the broadest set of security data checks, which increases the processing time required. Throughout the industry, application layer firewalls are generally considered to provide the best security.

Evolution of Firewall Industry

- Any business that has contemplated connecting to the Internet has been forced to deal with the issue of network security.
- A firewall provides a single point of defense between two networks; it protects one network from the other.
- Usually, a firewall protects the company's private network from the public or shared networks to which it is connected.
- A firewall can be as simple as a router that filters packets or as complex as a multi-computer, multi-router solution that combines packet filtering and application-level proxy services.
- The first generation of firewall architectures has been around almost as long as routers, first appearing around 1985 and coming out of Cisco's IOS software division. These firewalls are called packet filter firewalls.
- During the 1989-90 timeframe, Dave Presotto and Howard Trickey of AT&T Bell Laboratories pioneered the second generation of firewall architectures with their research in circuit relays, which are also known as circuit level firewalls. They also implemented the first working model of the third generation of firewall architectures, known as application layer firewalls.
- Around 1991, Bill Cheswick and Steve Bellovin began researching dynamic packet filtering. Check Point Software released the first commercial product based on this fourth generation architecture in 1994.

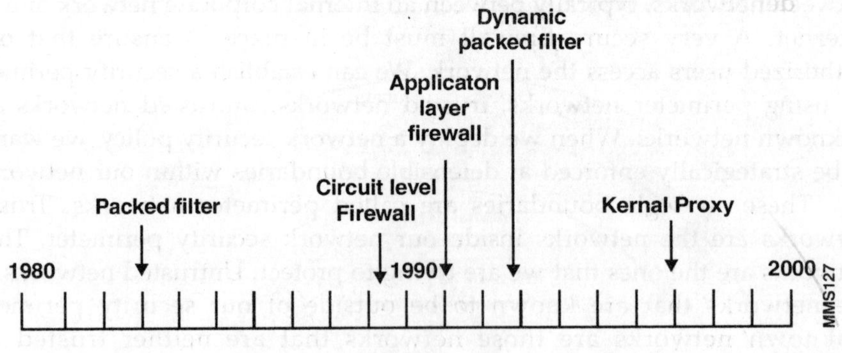

FIG. 33.1
Time Line of Firewall Architecture

- The firewall industry's initial innovations resulted from Department of Defense research and funding projects. However, the demand from the public sector for Internet-based security solutions has new and old security companies researching new architectures to meet the ever-expanding requirements for high-speed security solutions that are extensible, flexible, and maintainable.

Establishing a Security Perimeter

- A network security policy focuses on controlling the network traffic and usage.
- It identifies a network's resources and threats, defines network use and responsibilities, and details action plans for when the security policy is violated.
- There are four types :
  1. Perimeter Networks
  2. Trusted Networks
  3. Untrusted Networks
  4. Unknown Networks

(1) Perimeter Networks

- When we deploy a network security policy, we want it to be strategically enforced at defensible boundaries within our network. These strategic boundaries are called perimeter networks.
- To establish our collection of perimeter networks, we must designate the networks of computers that we wish to protect and define the network security mechanisms that protect them.

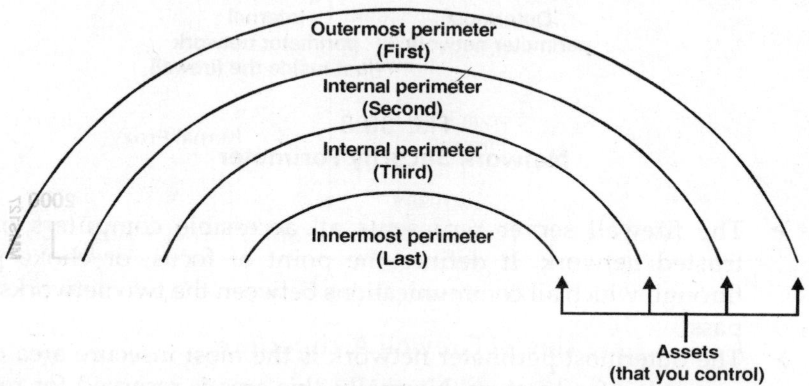

FIG. 33.2
Perimeter Networks

- To have a successful network security perimeter, the firewall server must be the gateway for all communications between trusted networks, untrusted and unknown networks.
- Each network can contain multiple perimeter networks within it.
- Three types of perimeter networks : the outermost perimeter, internal perimeter, and the innermost perimeter.
- The outermost perimeter network identifies the separation point between the assets that we control and we do not control, usually this point is the router that we use to separate our network from our Internet service provider's network.
- Internal perimeter networks represent additional boundaries where we have other security mechanisms in place, such as intranet firewalls and filtering routers.
- The following figure depicts two perimeter networks (an outermost perimeter network and an internal perimeter network) defined by the placement of the internal and external routers and the firewall server.

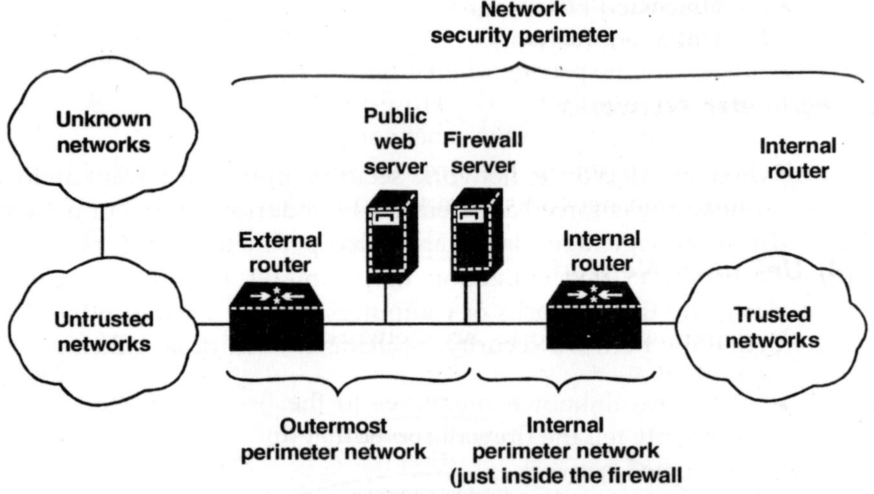

FIG. 33.3
Network Security Perimeter

- The firewall server represents all accessible computers on the trusted network. It defines the point of focus, or choke point, through which all communications between the two networks must pass.
- The outermost perimeter network is the most insecure area of our network infrastructure. Normally, this area is reserved for routers, firewall servers, and public Internet servers, such as HTTP, FTP, and Gopher servers.

- Sensitive company information that is for internal use only should not be placed on the outermost perimeter network.

(2) Trusted Networks

- Trusted networks are the networks inside our network security perimeter.
- These networks are the ones that we are trying to protect.
- A trusted network refers to a network comprising hosts that can only accept network packets specifically labeled for that host.
- When we set-up the firewall server, we explicitly identify the type of networks that are attached to the firewall server through network adapter cards. After the initial configuration, the trusted networks include the firewall server and all networks behind it.

(3) Untrusted Networks

- Untrusted networks are the networks that are outside of our security perimeter.
- They are the private, shared networks from which we are trying to protect our network. However, we still need and want to communicate with these networks even though they are untrusted.
- When we set-up the firewall server, we explicitly identify the untrusted networks from which firewall can accept requests.

(4) Unknown Networks

- Unknown networks are networks that are neither trusted nor untrusted.
- They are unknown quantities to the firewall because we cannot explicitly tell the firewall server that this network is a trusted or an untrusted network.
- Unknown networks exist outside of our security perimeter.
- All non-trusted networks are considered as unknown networks, and the firewall applies the security policy that is applied to the Internet node in the user interface, which represents all unknown networks.

Four Generations of Firewall Architecture

1. Packet Filter Firewall
2. Circuit Level Firewall
3. Application Layer Firewall
4. Dynamic Packet Filter Firewall

(1) Packet Filter Firewall

- A packet filter firewall is a first-generation firewall technology that analyzes network traffic at the transport protocol layer.
- Packet filters typically enable us to manipulate the transfer of data.
- The complete network packet inspection adheres to the following general algorithm :
  - If no matching rule is found, then drop the network packet.
  - If a matching rule is found that permits the communication, then allow peer-to-peer communication.
  - If a matching rule is found that denies the communication, then drop the network packet.

Advantages

- Packet filters are generally faster than others because they perform fewer evaluations. They can easily be implemented.
- A single rule can protect an entire network by connections between specific Internet sources and internal computers.
- Packet filters do not require client computers to be specifically configured.
- We can use packet filter firewalls to shield internal IP addresses from external users.

(2) Circuit Level Firewall

- A circuit level firewall is a second-generation firewall technology that validates the fact that a packet is either a connection request or a data packet belonging to a connection, or virtual circuit, between two peer transport layers.
- Circuit level firewall checks the header information contained within each network packet to determine whether the transmitting computer has permission to send data to the receiving computer and whether the receiving computer has permission to receive that data.

Advantages

- Circuit level firewalls are generally faster than application layer firewalls because they perform fewer evaluations.
- It helps to protect an entire network by prohibiting connections between specific Internet sources and internal computers.
- In conjunction with network address translation, we can use circuit level firewalls to shield internal IP addresses from external users.

(3) Application Layer Firewall

- An application layer firewall is a third-generation firewall technology that evaluates network packets for valid data at the application layer before allowing a connection.
- Most application layer firewalls include specialized application software and proxy services.

Advantages of Proxy Services

- Proxy services understand and enforce high-level protocols, such as HTTP and FTP.
- Proxy services maintain information about the communications passing through the firewall server.
- Proxy services are also capable of processing and manipulating packet data.
- By providing transparency, proxies provide users with the appearance that they are communicating directly with external servers.
- Proxy services can be used to deny access to certain network services, while permitting access to others.
- Proxy services do not allow direct communications between external servers and internal computers, so the names of internal computers do not have to be made known to external computers. In other words, proxy services shield internal IP addresses from the external world.
- Proxy services can route internal services, as well as external-to-internal requests.
- Proxy services can provide value-added features, such as HTTP object caching, URL filtering, and user authentication.
- Proxy services are good at generating audit records, allowing administrators to monitor attempts to violate the firewall's security policies.

(4) Dynamic Packet Filter Firewall

- A dynamic packet filter firewall is a fourth generation firewall technology that allows modification of the security rule.
- This type of technology is most useful for providing limited support for the UDP transport protocol.
- This firewall accomplishes its functional requirements by associating all UDP packets that cross the security perimeter with a virtual connection.

Advantages

- Dynamic Packet filters can easily be implemented.
- A single rule can protect an entire network by connections between specific Internet sources and internal computers.
- Dynamic Packet filters do not require client computers to be specifically configured.
- It does not allow unsolicited UDP packets onto our internal network.

Conclusion

- When considering alternative firewall technologies, we have to establish the common trade-offs between performance and security.
- To find this, we must consider how far a network packet must travel, as well as what level of security checks are being performed on each packet.
- Packet filter firewalls generally provide the highest performance, followed by circuit level firewalls, dynamic packet filter firewalls, and application layer firewalls.
- The level of security checks generally follows the reverse pattern because as network packets pass through more protocol layers, they are inspected in more detail.
- In general, application layer firewalls are the slowest architecture due to the fact that all network packets are sent up one network stack and down a different one, thus being treated as two separate network sessions.
- Application layer firewalls also implement the broadest set of security data checks, which increases the processing time required.
- Throughout the industry, application layer firewalls are generally considered to provide the best security.

References

1. www.Hotbrick.com
2. www.Networksecurity.com
3. www.Networkevalution.com
4. www.NetworkIntroduction.com

Network Security Concepts

R. Vijayalakshmi and S. Sampath

Introduction

Viruses or other malicious code may corrupt data on a wireless device and subsequently be introduced to a wired network connection.

- Malicious entities may, through wireless connections, connect to other agencies or organizations for the purposes of launching attacks and concealing their activities.
- Interlopers, from inside or out, may be able to gain connectivity to network management controls and thereby disable or disrupt operations.
- Malicious entities may use third party, untrusted wireless network services to gain access to an agency's or other organization's network resources.
- Internal attacks may be possible via *ad-hoc* transmissions.

This paper provides an overview of wireless networking technologies and wireless handheld devices most commonly used in an office environment and with today's mobile workforce. This paper seeks to assist agencies in reducing the risks associated with 802.11 wireless Local Area Networks (LAN), Bluetooth wireless networks, and handheld devices.

Network security is a complicated subject, historically only tackled by well-trained and experienced experts. However, as more and more people become "wired", an increasing number of people need to understand the basics of security in a networked world. This document was written with the basic computer user and information systems manager in mind, explaining the concepts needed to read through the hype in the marketplace and understand risks and how to deal with them. Some history of networking is included, as well as an introduction to TCP/IP and internetworking. We go on to consider risk management, network threats, firewalls and more special-purpose secure networking devices.

Organizations are increasingly using Information Technology to improve communication and increase profitability. Although companies can benefit from the application of IT, the increased use of IT also increases the risk of a security breach. The convenience associated with IT increases the need for security. Once security is compromised, the benefits of IT pale into insignificance and IT becomes a curse rather than a blessing. Many organizations don't enjoy a healthy return on their IT investment because of their inability to manage IT risks. People must therefore be concerned with how they can use IT without putting themselves at risk. This discourse attempts to identify possible threats to IT security.

The Internet revolution has opened the door to millions of end users, exposing Web sites, valuable corporate information, mission-critical business applications, and consumers' private information to more risk than ever before. As corporations move ever more corporate data to central servers and intensify the use of the Internet to allow for more efficient business processes, they become increasingly vulnerable to malicious attacks.

Hackers gaining access to companies systems via the Internet, or people within the organization obtaining unauthorized access to company data and applications, is the order of the day. Worse still, these attacks are increasing at an alarming rate, and because of an organization's increased reliance on the Internet and new business apps, the corresponding downtime cost and information security loss is becoming enormous.

Besides a firewall, we will need an intrusion detection tool, content filtering of email, web and FTP, and security scanning and reporting of your network. Computer system threats are many and varied.

A threat is a danger, which could affect the security (confidentiality, integrity, availability) of IT assets, leading to a potential loss or damage. Power loss, can cause data loss; fluctuations in power supply damage both data and equipment. Power problems may also affect air-condition systems which are required to maintain proper environmental conditions in the computing equipment. Fire is also a major threat. There could also be saboteurs from within an organization or those who infiltrate a company's computing network from outside to destroy valuable data, or introduce virus. There are also threats that arise from careless mistakes of staff. "Often, the cases of deliberate acts are the most serious, as they have been planned to avoid detection and cause the maximum damage".

To ensure the most comprehensive level of protection possible, every network should include security components that address the following five aspects of network security.

Identity

Identity is the accurate and positive identification of network users, hosts, applications, services, and resources. Identity mechanisms are important—ensuring that authorized users gain access to the enterprise computing resources they need, while unauthorized users are denied access. Cisco networks use the Authentication, Authorization, and Accounting (AAA) capabilities of the Cisco Secure Access Control Server to provide a foundation that authenticates users, determines access levels, and archives all necessary audit and accounting data.

Perimeter Security

Perimeter security solutions control access to critical network applications, data, and services so that only legitimate users and information can pass through the network. This access control is handled by routers and switches with Access Control Lists (ACLs) and by dedicated firewall appliances. A firewall provides a barrier to traffic crossing a network's perimeter and permits only authorized traffic to pass, according to a predefined security policy. Complementary tools, including virus scanners and content filters, also help control network perimeters. Firewalls are generally the first security products that organizations deploy to improve their security postures. Cisco provides organizations considerable flexibility in firewall choices. The Cisco PIX® Firewall is the world's leading firewall, providing network customers of all sizes with unmatched reliability, scalability, and functionality. The Cisco IOS® Firewall provides embedded firewall capabilities in the routing and switched infrastructures.

Secure Connectivity

Companies must protect confidential information from eavesdropping or tampering during transmission. By implementing Virtual Private Networks (VPNs), enterprises can establish private, secure communications across a public network usually the Internet and extend their corporate networks to remote offices, mobile users, telecommuters, and extranet partners. Encryption technology ensures that messages traveling across a VPN cannot be intercepted or read by anyone other than the authorized recipient by using advanced mathematical algorithms to "scramble" messages and their attachments.

Security Monitoring

To ensure that their networks remain secure, companies should continuously monitor for attacks and regularly test the state of their security infrastructures. Network vulnerability scanners can proactively identify areas of weakness, and Intrusion Detection Systems (IDSs) can monitor and reactively respond to security events as they occur. IDS and vulnerability scanners provide an additional layer of network security. While firewalls permit or deny traffic based on source, destination, port, or other criteria, they do not actually analyze traffic for attacks or search the network for existing vulnerabilities. In addition, firewalls typically do not address the internal threat presented by "insiders." The Cisco Intrusion Detection System (IDS) is the industry's first real-time, network intrusion detection system that can protect the network perimeter, extranets, and increasingly vulnerable internal networks. The system uses sensors, which are high-speed network appliances, to analyze individual packets to detect suspicious activity. Cisco also offeres IDS host sensors to provide pervasive protection on servers throughout the network. If the data stream in a network exhibits unauthorized activity or a network attack, the sensors can detect the misuse in real time, forward alarms to an administrator, and remove the offender from the network.

Different Types of Threats

General Threat

This could result from human error. Human error results in accidental destruction, modification, disclosure, or incorrect classification of information. In this category errors occur due to ignorance. Ignorance could be due to inadequate security awareness, lack of security guidelines, lack of proper documentation, lack of knowledge (even on the part of systems staff). Often lack of knowledge results in incorrect system configuration. It is a low level of security awareness that makes users inadvertently give information on security weaknesses to attackers.

IT related fraud is on the increase. If staff are dishonest, the fruits are IT fraud, theft, embezzlement, illegal selling of confidential corporate information and systems. Dishonest employees have been known to use IT to bring organizations to their knees.

Related to earlier mentioned threats is that of inferior security management. It isn't enough to acquire sophisticated IT equipment. Exposure to IT-related failure is high, if the security policy is inadequate, or not enforced. Common sources of these threats are hackers. Hacking is the process of accessing computer systems by persons who have no legitimate access to the system, or at least not to that part of the system. It may be carried out by people outside the organization or by insiders who are users of the system but who attempt to gain access to parts of the system they are not authorized to access. Access may mean exploiting facilities provided by the system, or exploiting flaws in the security mechanism of the system, or guessing or obtaining the log-on names and password of legitimate users.

The aims of hackers are to obtain confidential information; to commit fraud; to cause disruption to the target organization; or for intellectual amusement. There've been several well-publicized examples of hacking in the US and in Europe. In quite a number of banks with huge IT investments, system availability is quite low. For many it is the usual "the system is down" refrain that seems to be the norm. ROS threats include natural disasters such as fire, flood, earthquake, etc. ROS is equally affected by man-made disasters such as war, bombs, civil disturbance, dangerous chemicals, nuclear accidents, etc. Any disaster will affect our ability to benefit from the IT investment.

Constant equipment failure due to defective hardware, cabling, or communications system, NITEL, etc. will definitely result in ROS problems. If equipment fails due to malfunctioning air-conditioning system, or poor environmental conditions, again ROS is affected. Where quality of service delivered by public infrastructure is poor, ROS will always be a major threat. A common ROS problem in Nigeria is Power supply failure. Which is the backup, NEPA, or generator? ROS threats can result from the failure of either. ROS is a major threat to IT security if IT service provision is poor. What is the quality of IT service, i.e. from an IT or Internet provider? If your business is dependent on Internet access, your ISP must always provide high quality Internet service. Sabotage is another threat that can affect ROS.

Malicious damage of information or information processing functions such as physical destruction of network interface devices, cables, physical destruction of computing devices or media, theft, deliberate electrical overloads or shutting-off electrical power can all affect reliability of service. Bugs in software can cause ROS problems. This is especially so if the software is relatively new and if it didn't undergo rigorous testing before it was released. Hostile computer programs such as viruses have seriously affected organizations' ability to use IT. An attack can render an organization's IT infrastructure impotent for a significant amount of time. As it is said, time is money, don't let viruses waste your money. There is an alarming increase in the development viruses (in programs, documents and email attachments). With the advent and widespread use of the Internet, virus attacks are having immediate worldwide impact. Other hostile computer programs are Trojan horse, logic bomb and worm.

Privacy Threats

These are the unauthorized monitoring of sensitive data crossing the Internal network, unknown to the data owner, or unauthorized reading of electronic mail. If you use IT, how private is your data, or your customer's data? How easy is it for your sensitive information to get into the wrong hands? Integrity/Accuracy threats are those that result from deliberate damage of information or information processing functions from internal or external sources. Integrity/accuracy problems occur when there is deliberate modification of information, either done externally or internally. Examples include creating phony account balances, unauthorized deletion of transactions, or modification of accounting procedures. Does your system produce exception reports, or have audit facilities? IT security is nil if information produced by the system is of doubtful value.

Access Control Threats

These can result from password cracking. Security is compromised through careless handling of password files, or use of bad passwords. Access control threats could be through attack programs allowing internal access, or external access to systems. Developers can also cause access control problems by creating unsecured maintenance modes in the software. Bugs in network software can open unknown/unexpected security holes. Access control problems can occur from unauthorized physical access to systems. Where are systems kept? Are they in a free for all zones, without any physical security cover?

Repudiation (Denial) Threats

Receivers of confidential information may refuse to acknowledge receipt. Senders of confidential information may refuse to acknowledge the source. The last group of threats is legal threats. Companies run into problems when they fail to comply with regulatory or legal requirements. Also many countries' law forbids (especially over the Internet) incitement to racism, gambling, money laundering or the use of, or distribution of, pornographic or violent material. You may be liable if internal users or attackers abuse your systems to these ends. The impact of these threats differs. But after a threat impacts heavily on your bottom line, it is no longer a threat but a disaster.

In the last decade, the number of computers in use has exploded. For quite some time now, computers have been a crucial element in how we entertain and educate ourselves, and most importantly, how we do business. It seems obvious in retrospect that a natural result of the explosive growth in computer use would be an even more explosive (although delayed) growth in the desire and need for computers to talk with each other. Two separate forces have driven the growth of this industry which until recently have had different goals and end products. The first factor has been research interests and laboratories; these groups have always needed to share files, email and other information across wide areas. The research labs developed several protocols and methods for this data transfer, most notably TCP/IP. Business interests are the second factor in network growth. For quite some time, businesses were primarily interested in sharing data within an office or campus environment, this led to the development of various protocols suited specifically to this task.

Within the last five years, businesses have begun to need to share data across wide areas. This has prompted efforts to convert principally LAN-based protocols into WAN-friendly protocols. The result has spawned an entire industry of consultants who know how to manipulate routers, gateways and networks to force principally broadcast protocols across point-to-point links (two very different methods of transmitting packets across networks). Recently (within the last 2 or 3 years) more and more companies have realized that they need to settle on a common networking protocol. Frequently the protocol of choice has been TCP/IP, which is also the primary protocol run on the Internet. The emerging ubiquitousness of TCP/IP allows companies to interconnect with each other via private networks as well as through public networks.

Businesses, governments and individuals communicate with each other across the world. While reality is rapidly approaching this utopian picture, several relatively minor issues have changed status from low priority to extreme importance. Security is probably the most well known of these problems. When businesses send private information across the net, they place a high value on it getting to its destination intact and without being intercepted by someone other than the intended recipient. Individuals sending private communications obviously desire secure communications. Finally, connecting a system to a network can open the system itself up to attacks. If a system is compromised, the risk of data loss is high.

It can be useful to break network security into two general classes :

- methods used to secure data as it transits a network, and
- methods which regulate what packets may transit the network.

While both significantly affect the traffic going to and from a site, their objectives are quite different.

Transit Security

Currently, there are no systems in wide use that will keep data secure as it transits a public network. Several methods are available to encrypt traffic between a few coordinated sites. Unfortunately, none of the current solutions scale particularly well. Two general approaches dominate this area :

Virtual Private Networks

This is the concept of creating a private network by using TCP/IP to provide the lower levels of a second TCP/IP stack. This can be a confusing concept, and is best understood by comparing it to the way TCP/IP is normally implemented. In a nutshell, IP traffic is sent across various forms of physical networks. Each system that connects to the physical network implements a standard for sending IP messages across that link. Standards for IP transmission across various types of links exist, the most common are for Ethernet and Point-to-Point links (PPP and SLIP). Once an IP packet is received, it is passed up to higher layers of the TCP/IP stack as appropriate (UDP, TCP and eventually the application). When a virtual private network is implemented, the lowest levels of the TCP/IP protocol are implemented using an existing TCP/IP connection. There are a number of ways to accomplish this which tradeoff between abstraction and efficiency. The advantage this gives you in terms of secure data transfer is only a single step further away. Because a VPN gives you complete control over the physical layer, it is entirely within the network designer's power to encrypt the connection at the physical (virtual) layer. By doing this, all traffic of any sort over the VPN will be encrypted, whether it be at the application layer (such as Mail or News) or at the lowest layers of the stack (IP, ICMP). The primary advantages of VPNs are : they allow private address space (you can have more machines on a network), and they allow the packet encryption/ translation overhead to be done on dedicated systems, decreasing the load placed on production machines.

Packet Level Encryption

Another approach is to encrypt traffic at a higher layer in the TCP/IP stack. Several methods exist for the secure authentication and encryption of telnet and rlogin sessions (Kerberos, S/Key and DESlogin), which are examples of encryption at the highest level of the stack (the application layer). The advantages to encrypting traffic at the higher layer are that the processor overhead of dealing with a VPN is eliminated, inter-operability with current applications is not affected, and it is much easier to compile a client program that supports application layer encryption than to build a VPN. It is possible to encrypt traffic at essentially any of the layers in the IP stack. Particularly promising is encryption that is done at the TCP level, which provides fairly transparent encryption to most network applications.

It is important to note that both of these methods can have performance impacts on the hosts that implement the protocols, and on the networks which connect those hosts. The relatively simple act of encapsulating or converting a packet into a new form requires CPU-time and uses additional network capacity. Encryption can be a very CPU-intensive process and encrypted packets may need to be padded to uniform length to guarantee the robustness of some algorithms. Further, both methods have impacts on other areas (security-related and otherwise—such as address allocation, fault tolerance and load balancing) that need to be considered before any choice is made as to which is best for a particular case.

Traffic Regulation

The most common form of network security on the Internet today is to closely regulate which types of packets can move between networks. If a packet which may do something malicious to a remote host never gets there, the remote host will be unaffected. Traffic regulation provides this screen between hosts and remote sites. This typically happens at three basic areas of the network : routers, firewalls and hosts. Each provides similar service at different points in the network. In fact the line between them is somewhat ill-defined and arbitrary. In this regard, the following definitions are used :

Router traffic regulation : Any traffic regulation that occurs on a router or terminal server (hosts whose primary purpose is to forward the packets of other hosts) and is based on packet characteristics. This does not include application gateways but does include address translation.

Firewall traffic regulation : Traffic regulation or filtering that is performed via application gateways or proxies.

Host traffic regulation : Traffic regulation that is performed at the destination of a packet. Hosts are playing a smaller and smaller role in traffic regulation with the advent of filtering routers and firewalls.

Filters and Access Lists

Regulating which packets can go between two sites is a fairly simple concept on the surface—it shouldn't be and isn't difficult for any router or firewall to decide simply not to forward all packets from a particular site. Unfortunately, the reason most people connect to the Internet is so that they may exchange packets with remote sites. Developing a plan that allows the right packets through at the right time and denies the malicious packets is a thorny task, which is far beyond this article's scope. A few basic techniques are worth discussing, however.

- *Restricting access in, but not out* : Almost all packets (besides those at the lowest levels which deal with network reachability) are sent to destination sockets of either UDP or TCP. Typically, packets from remote hosts will attempt to reach one of what are known as the well known ports. These ports are monitored by applications which provide services such as Mail Transfer and Delivery, Usenet News, the time, Domain Name Service, and various login protocols. It is trivial for modern routers or firewalls only to allow these types of packets through to the specific machine that provides a given service. Attempts to send any other type of packet will not be forwarded. This protects the internal hosts, but still allows all packets to get out. Unfortunately this isn't the panacea that it might seem.
- *The problem of returning packets* : Let's pretend that you don't want to let remote users log into your systems unless they use a secure, encrypting application such as S/Key. However, you are willing to allow your users to attempt to connect to remote sites with telnet or ftp. At first glance, this looks simple : you merely restrict remote connections to one type of packet and allow any type of outgoing connection. Unfortunately, due to the nature of interactive protocols, they must negotiate a unique port number to use once a connection is established. If they didn't, at any given time, there could only be one of each type of interactive session between any given two machines. This results in a dilemma : all of a sudden, a remote site is going to try to send packets destined for a seemingly random port. Normally, these packets would be dropped. However, modern routers and firewalls now support the ability to dynamically open a small window for these packets to pass through if packets have been recently transmitted from an internal host to the external host on the same port. This allows connections that are initiated internally to connect, yet still denies external connection attempts unless they are desired.
- *Dynamic route filters* : A relatively recent technique is the ability to dynamically add entire sets of route filters for a remote site when a particular set of circumstances occur. With these techniques, it is possible to have a router automatically detect suspicious activity

(such as ISS or SATAN) and deny a machine or entire site access for a short time. In many cases this will thwart any sort of automated attack on a site.

Filters and access lists are typically placed on all three types of systems, although they are most common on routers.

Address Translation

Another advancement has been to have a router modify outgoing packets to contain their own IP number. This prevents an external site from knowing any information about the internal network, it also allows for certain tricks to be played which provide for a tremendous number of additional internal hosts with a small allocated address space. The router maintains a table which maps an external IP number and socket with an internal number and socket. Whenever an internal packet is destined for the outside, it is simply forwarded with the routers' IP number in the source field of the IP header. When an external packet arrives, it is analyzed for its destination port and re-mapped before it is sent on to the internal host. The procedure does have its pitfalls; checksums have to be recalculated because they are based in part on IP numbers, and some upper layer protocols encode/depend on the IP number. These protocols will not work through simple address translation routers.

Application Gateways and Proxies

The primary difference between firewalls and routers is that firewalls actually run applications. These applications frequently include mail daemons, ftp servers and web servers. Firewalls also usually run what are known as application gateways or proxies. These are best described as programs, which understand a protocol's syntax, but do not implement any of the functionality of the protocol. Rather, after verifying that a message from an external site is appropriate, they send the message on to the real daemon, which processes the data. This provides security for those applications that are particularly susceptible to interactive attacks. One advantage of using a firewall for these services is that it makes it very easy to monitor all activity, and very easy to quickly control what gets in and out of a network.

Even indiscriminate attacks, such as viruses and worms, can result in the loss of valuable data, high repair costs, negative publicity, legal liability, and the loss of hours or even days of productivity.

When designing security into our network, four things to consider :

1. Layers

With the many types of security threats today, companies put themselves at great risk by implementing a point product, such as a firewall, and thinking the network is safe. However, a firewall alone may not be sufficient to prevent against external threats. Sometimes companies are not even aware that their security has been breached because they have not incorporated the right monitoring and analysis tools as part of their overall security solution. With a multilayered approach, even if an intruder is able to bypass one access point, overlapping layers of security ensure that the break-in will be stopped by another mechanism. In addition, overlapping security can prevent either accidental or intentional harm to information resources or the network by employees.

2. *Modular Approach*

A modular approach means that we can implement security features that meet our unique exposure and budget requirements, at the same time maintaining the flexibility and scalability to layer in other security mechanisms as your needs grow and change.

3. *Manageability*

Security is a dynamic, ever-changing requirement. New security threats come along frequently. It is extremely important to implement a security system that is adaptable and easy to manage.

When companies buy point products from different vendors, security becomes difficult to manage. Each mechanism has to be programmed to distribute and enforce security policies, and then synchronized with every other security appliance in the network. If all of the products don't act in concert, there likely will be gaps and therefore greater exposure to malicious mischief.

4. *Inclusiveness*

When point security devices such as firewalls were first developed, they were created with conventional Ethernet LANs in mind. Over the past few years however, more small companies have started taking advantage of mobility and remote access, wireless LANs, and converged networks, meaning those carrying both voice and data over the same network.

Some point-product security vendors are still focused on the world of Ethernet LANs. Their products have not evolved to support Virtual Private Networks (VPNs), wireless LANs (WLANs), IP telephony, or other up-and-coming technologies. Thus, security for these areas of the network must be managed separately. If any of these technologies are in our future, make sure that security extends to these parts of the network as well.

Conclusion

There are two basic types of network security, transit security and traffic regulation, which when combined can help guarantee that the right information is securely delivered to the right place. It should be apparent that there is also a need for ensuring that the hosts that receive the information will properly process it, this raises the entire specter of host security : a wide area which varies tremendously for each type of system. With the growth in business use of the Internet, network security is rapidly becoming crucial to the development of the Internet. Soon, security will be an integral part of our day-to-day use of the Internet and other networks.

Network Security

S. KAVITHA, K. TAMIL SELVI,
M. RATHAMANI AND E. NIRMALARAJESWARI

Introduction

Over the past few years, Internet-enabled business, or e-business, has drastically improved companies' efficiency and revenue growth. E-business applications such as e-commerce, supply-chain management, and remote access allow companies to streamline processes, lower operating costs, and increases customer satisfaction. Such applications require mission-critical networks that accommodate voice, video, and data traffic, and these networks must be scalable to support increasing number of users and the need for greater capacity and performance. However, as networks enable more and more applications and are available to more and more users, they become ever more vulnerable to a wider range of security threats. To combat those threats and ensure that e-business transactions are not compromised, security technology must play a major role in today's networks. The widespread use of computers and networks environments has emphasized the necessity to study the secure operating systems and network security mechanisms. Current commercial solutions for network security, such as firewalls, cannot defend against insider attacks, nor can they support sophisticated trust relationships with external entities. This paper presents a more comprehensive and flexible network security solution. It enforces a mandatory access control policy and encryption on network-related operations and traffic. This proposed paper is a prime description for a contribution to the advance of the security of interconnected open systems. The first part of the article is a panorama over the different network security architectures. The second one is a description of the CHIAERA model and an implementation of the adopted architecture measures on a network. We propose a general facility for the distribution and handling of asymmetric "public" key, and integrate it in applications like MHS, FTAM, RPC and Directory service. The third part is a conclusion on some hanged problems and open questions on the reliability of the adopted model and some future intended works on this trend. A basic understanding of computer networks is requisite in order to understand the principles of network security. We'll cover some of the foundations of computer networking, then move on to an overview of some popular networks.

What is a Network?

A "network" has been defined as "any set of interlinking lines resembling a net, *a network of roads,* an interconnected system, *a network of alliances*." a computer network is simply a system of interconnected computers.

The ISO/OSI Reference Model

The *International Standards Organization* (ISO), *Open Systems Interconnect* (OSI) Reference Model defines seven layers of communication types, and the interfaces among them. (See Figure 35.1) Each layer depends on the services provided by the layer below it, all the way down to the physical network hardware, such as the computer's network interface card, and the wires that connect the cards together.

An easy way to look at this is to compare this model with something we use daily : the telephone. (In the ISO/OSI model, this is at the application layer.) The telephones, of course, are useless unless they have the ability to translate the sound into electronic pulses that can be transferred over wire and back again. (These functions are provided in layers below the application layer.) Finally, we get down to the physical

Application
Presentation
Session
Transport
Network
Data Link
Physical

FIG. 35.1
The ISO/OSI Reference Model

connection : both must be plugged into an outlet that is connected to a switch that's part of the telephone system's network of switches.

If I place a call to you, I pick up the receiver, and dial your number. This number specifies which central office to which to send my request, and then which phone from that central office to ring. Once you answer the phone, we begin talking, and our session has begun. Conceptually, computer networks function exactly the same way.

Security

UUCP (Unix-to-Unix Copy), like any other application, has security tradeoffs. Some strong points for its security is that it is fairly limited in what it can do, and it's therefore more difficult to trick into doing something it shouldn't; it's been around a *long* time, and most its bugs have been discovered, analyzed, and fixed; and because UUCP networks are made up of occasional connections to other hosts, it isn't possible for someone on host E to directly make contact with host B, and take advantage of that connection to do something naughty.

On the other hand, UUCP typically works by having a system-wide UUCP user account and password. Any system that has a UUCP connection with another must know the appropriate password for the UUCP or UUCP account. Identifying a host beyond that point has traditionally been little more than a matter of trusting that the host is who it claims to be, and that a connection is allowed at that time. More recently, there has been an additional layer of authentication, whereby both hosts must have the same *sequence number*, that is a number that is incremented each time a connection is made.

Hence, if I run host B, I know the UUCP password on host A. If, though, I want to impersonate host C, I'll need to connect, identify myself as C, hope that I've done so at a time that A will allow it, and try to guess the correct sequence number for the session. While this might not be a trivial attack, it isn't considered very secure.

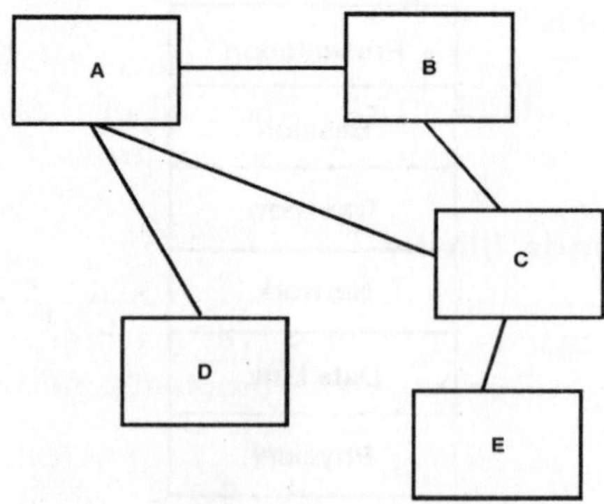

Fig. 35.2
A Sample UUCP Network

Risk Management : The Game of Security

It's very important to understand that in security, one simply cannot say "what's the best firewall?" There are two extremes : absolute security and absolute access. The closest we can get to an absolutely secure machine is one unplugged from the network, power supply, locked in a safe, and thrown at the bottom of the ocean. Unfortunately, it isn't terribly useful in this state. A machine with absolute access is extremely convenient to use : it's simply there, and will do whatever you tell it, without questions, authorization, passwords, or any other mechanism.

This is no different from our daily lives. We constantly make decisions about what risks we're willing to accept. When we get in a car and drive to work, there's a certain risk that we're taking. It's possible that something completely out of control will cause us to become part of an accident on the highway. When we get on an airplane, we're accepting the level of risk involved as the price of convenience. However, most people have a mental picture of what an acceptable risk is, and won't go beyond that in most circumstances. If I happen to be upstairs at home, and want to leave for work. It would be more convenient, but the risk of injury outweighs the advantage of convenience.

Every organization needs to decide for itself where between the two extremes of total security and total access they need to be. A policy needs to articulate this, and then define *how* that will be enforced with practices and such. Everything that is done in the name of security, then, must enforce that policy uniformly.

Types and Sources of Network Threats

Now, we've covered enough background information on networking that we can actually get into the security aspects of all of this. First of all, we'll get into the types of threats there are against networked computers, and then some things that can be done to protect you against various threats.

Unauthorized Access

"Unauthorized access" is a very high-level term that can refer to a number of different sorts of attacks. The goal of these attacks is to access some resource that your machine should not provide the attacker.

Executing Commands Illicitly

It's obviously undesirable for an unknown and untrusted person to be able to execute commands on your server machines. There are two main classifications of the security of this problem : normal user access, and administrator access.

Data Destruction

Some of those perpetrate attacks are simply twisted jerks who like to delete things. In these cases, the impact on your computing capability—and consequently your business—can be nothing less than if a fire or other disaster caused your computing equipment to be completely destroyed.

Backups

This isn't just a good idea from a security point of view. Operational requirements should dictate the backup policy, and this should be closely coordinated with a disaster recovery plan. These can be useful in recovering your data in the event of an electronic disaster : a hardware failure, or a break-in that changes or otherwise damages your data.

Have Someone on Staff be Familiar with Security Practices

Having at least one person who is charged with keeping abreast of security developments is a good idea. This need not be a technical wizard, but could be someone who is simply able to read advisories issued by various incident response teams, and keep track of various problems that arise. Such a person would then be a wise one to consult with on security-related issues, as he'll be the one who knows if web server software version such-and-such has any known problems, etc.

Firewalls

Internet provides a two-way flow of traffic. This is clearly undesirable in many organizations, as proprietary information is often displayed freely within a corporate *intranet* (that is, a TCP/IP network, modeled after the Internet that only works within the organization).

In order to provide some level of separation between an organization's Intranet and the Internet, *firewalls* have been employed. A firewall is simply a group of components that collectively form a barrier between two networks.

Application Gateways

The first firewalls were application gateways, and are sometimes known as proxy gateways. These are made up of bastion hosts that run special software to act as a proxy server. (Figure 35.3)

Packet Filtering

Packet filtering is a technique whereby routers have *ACLs* (Access Control Lists) turned on. By default, a router will pass all traffic sent it, and will do so without any sort of restrictions. Figure 35.4 shows a packet-filtering gateway.

In some of these systems, new connections must be authenticated and approved at the application layer. Once this has been done, the remainder of the connection is passed down to the session layer, where packet filters watch the connection to ensure that only packets that are part of an ongoing (already authenticated and approved) conversation are being passed.

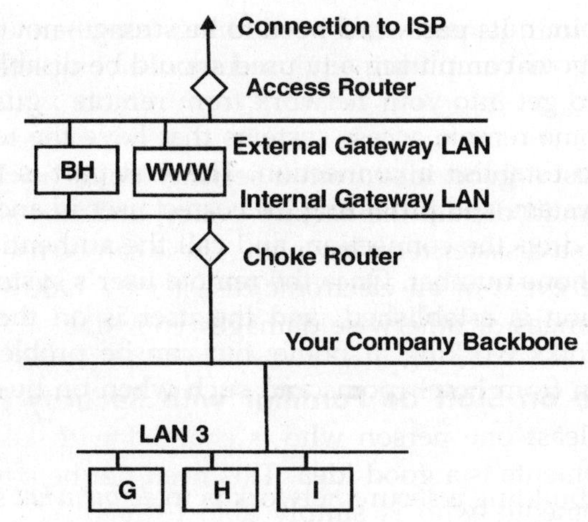

FIG. 35.3

A Sample Application Gateway

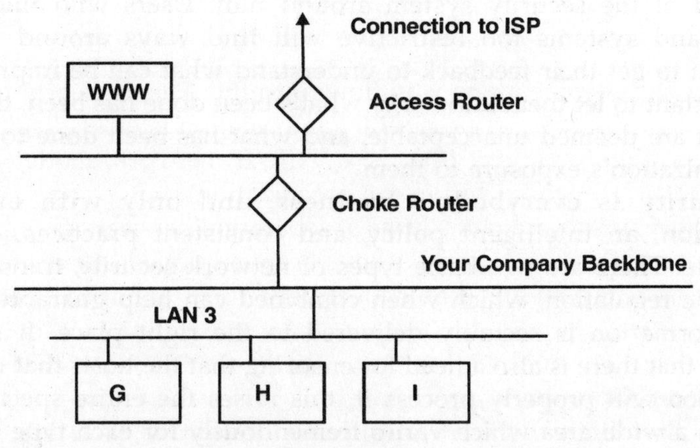

FIG. 35.4

A Sample Packet-Filtering Gateway

Secure Network Devices

Modems, if we allow them to answer incoming calls, can provide an easy means for an attacker to sneak *around* (rather than *through*) your front door (or, firewall). Just as castles weren't built with moats only in the front, your network needs to be protected at all of its entry points.

Secure Modems : Dial-Back Systems

If modem access is to be provided, this should be guarded carefully. The *terminal server*, or network device that provides dial-up access to your network needs to be actively administered, and its logs need to be examined for strange behaviour. Its password need to be strong—not ones that can be guessed. Accounts that aren't actively used should be disabled. In short, it's the easiest way to get into your network from remote : guard it carefully.

There are some remote access systems that have the feature of a two-part procedure to establish a connection. The first part is the remote user dialing into the system, and providing the correct user-id and password. The system will then drop the connection, and call the authenticated user back at a known telephone number. Once the remote user's system answers that call, the connection is established, and the user is on the network. This works well for folks working at home, but can be problematic for users wishing to dial in from hotel rooms and such when on business trips.

Conclusion

The key for building a secure network is to *define what security means to your organization*.

Many people pay great amounts of lip service to security, but do not want to be bothered with it when it gets in their way. It's important to build systems and networks in such a way that the user is not constantly reminded of the security system around him. Users who find security policies and systems too restrictive will find ways around them. It's important to get their feedback to understand what can be improved, and it's important to let them know *why* what's been done has been, the sorts of risks that are deemed unacceptable, and what has been done to minimize the organization's exposure to them.

Security is everybody's business, and only with everyone's cooperation, an intelligent policy, and consistent practices, will it be achievable. There are two basic types of network security, transit security and traffic regulation, which when combined can help guarantee that the right information is securely delivered to the right place. It should be apparent that there is also a need for ensuring that the hosts that receive the information will properly process it, this raises the entire specter of host security : a wide area which varies tremendously for each type of system. With the growth in business use of the Internet, network security is rapidly becoming crucial to the development of the Internet. Soon, security will be an integral part of our day-to-day use of the Internet and other networks.

Approaches to Network Security

K.R. VALLIMAAN AND V. ROOPA

Introduction

Network Security is the surveillance, protection, containment, and deterrence of abuse against assets. This should be within the context of a risk management framework. It is the property of the network that ensures Protection, Accountability, Availability. It is both a term and an attribute related to the protection, detection and containment of physical and logical threats to network information, network resources and communication including data. Systems, applications, centers and human/machine interfaces with respect to availability, confidential, integrity, access control, authentication, audit and recovery. It is also an attribute of quality and reliability in relation to the value of the asset to be protected or the criticality of asset to the business. Network Security in essence is an extension of the internal set of controls reflective of both industry standards and best practices. It involves inferred trust, roles, relationships, responsibilities, and accountabilities for intra-network as well as inter-networks. One kind of solution for security threats is *KERBEROS*.

Need for Kerberos

In addition to the security concern, password-based authentication is inconvenient; users do not want to enter a password each time, they access a network service. This process is termed as *authentication by assertion* with authentication by assertion, applications assert the identity of the user and the server believes it. Such authentication is easily thwarted by modifying the application. This may require privileged access to the system, which is easily obtained on PCs and personal workstations. While most uses of authentication by assertion require that a connection originate from a "trusted" network address, on many networks, addresses are themselves simply assertions.

Stronger authentication methods based on cryptography are required. When using authentication based on cryptography, an attacker listening to the network gains no information that would enable it to falsely claim another's identity. Kerberos is the most commonly used example of this type of authentication technology. Unfortunately, strong authentication technologies are not used as often as they should be, although the situation is gradually improving.

Kerberos Authentication Service

Kerberos is a distributed authentication service that allows a process (a client) running on behalf of a principal (a user) to prove its identity to a verifier (an application server, or just server) without sending data across the network that might allow an attacker or the verifier to subsequently impersonate the principal. Kerberos optionally provides integrity and confidentiality for data sent between the client and server.

Kerberos Encryption

Though conceptually, Kerberos authentication proves that a client is running on behalf of a particular user, a more precise statement is that the client has knowledge of an encryption key that is known by only the user and the authentication server. In Kerberos, the user's encryption key is derived from and should be thought of as a password; we will refer to it as such in this article. Similarly, each application server shares an encryption key with the authentication server; we will call this key the server key.

Encryption in the present implementation of Kerberos uses the Data Encryption Standard (DES). It is a property of DES that if ciphertext (encrypted data) is decrypted with the same key used to encrypt it, the plaintext (original data) appears. If different encryption keys are used for encryption and decryption, or if the ciphertext is modified, the result will be unintelligible, and the checksum in the Kerberos message will not match the data. This combination of encryption and the checksum provides integrity and confidentiality for encrypted Kerberos messages.

The Kerberos Ticket

The client and server do not initially share an encryption key. Whenever a client authenticates itself to a new verifier it relies on the authentication server to generate a new encryption key and distribute it securely to both parties. This new encryption key is called a *session key* and the Kerberos ticket is used to distribute it to the verifier. The Kerberos ticket is a certificate issued by an authentication server, encrypted using the server key. Among other information, the ticket contains the random session key that will be used for authentication of the principal to the verifier, the name of the principal to whom the session key was issued, and an expiration time after which the session key is no longer valid. The ticket is not sent directly to the verifier, but is instead sent to the client who forwards it to the verifier as part of the application request. Because the ticket is encrypted in the server key, known only by the authentication server and intended verifier, it is not possible for the client to modify the ticket without detection.

Application Request and Response

Messages 3 and 4 in Figure 36.1 show the application request and response, the most basic exchange in the Kerberos protocol. It is through this exchange that a client proves to a verifier that it knows the session key embedded in a Kerberos ticket. There are two parts to the application request, a ticket (described above) and an authenticator. The authenticator includes, among other fields : the current time, a checksum, and an optional encryption key, all encrypted with the session key from the accompanying ticket.

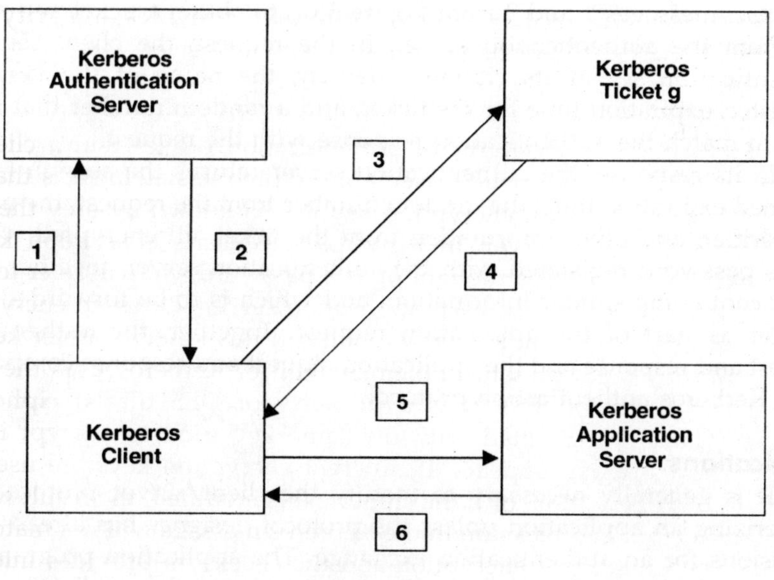

FIG. 36.1
Message Transfer

Upon receipt of the application request, the verifier decrypts the ticket, extracts the session key, and uses the session key to decrypt the authenticator. If the same key was used to encrypt the authenticator as used to decrypt it, the checksum will match and the verifier can assume the authenticator was generated by the principal named in the ticket and to whom the session key was issued. This is not by itself sufficient for authentication since an attacker can intercept an authenticator and replay it later to impersonate the user. For this reason the verifier additionally checks the timestamp to make sure that the authenticator is fresh. If the timestamp is within a specified window (typically 5 minutes) centered around the current time on the verifier, and if the timestamp has not been seen on other requests within that window, the verifier accepts the request as authentic. A discussion of the benefits and drawbacks to the use of timestamps in authentication protocols can be found in. At this point the identity of the client has been verified by the server. For some applications the client also wants to be sure of the server's identity. If such mutual authentication is required, the server generates an application response by extracting the client's time from the authenticator, and returns it to the client together with other information, all encrypted using the session key.

Authentication Request and Response

The client requires a separate ticket and session key for each verifier with which it communicates. When a client wishes to create an association with a particular verifier, the client uses the authentication request and response, messages 1 and 2 from Figure 36.1, to obtain a ticket and session key from the authentication server. In the request, the client sends the authentication server its claimed identity, the name of the verifier, a requested expiration time for the ticket, and a random number that will be used to match the authentication response with the request.

In its response, the authentication server returns the session key, the assigned expiration time, the random number from the request, the name of the verifier, and other information from the ticket, all encrypted with the user's password registered with the authentication server, together with a ticket containing similar information, and which is to be forwarded to the verifier as part of the application request. Together, the authentication request and response and the application request and response comprise the basic Kerberos authentication protocol.

Applications

It is generally necessary to modify the client/server protocol when Kerberizing an application unless the protocol designer has already made provisions for an authentication exchange. The application program must generate and send a Kerberos application request to the application server during the protocol initialization phase, and the server must verify the Kerberos authentication information. The request must be transmitted within the client/server protocol. The Kerberos library provides routines that generate and verify these messages.

More recent implementations of Kerberos provide a Generic Security Services Application Programmer Interface (GSSAPI). The GSSAPI provides a standard programming interface which is authentication mechanism independent. This allows the application programmer to design an application and application protocol which can used alternative different authentication technologies, including Kerberos. The use of the GSSAPI in application programs is recommended wherever possible.

Because it is a generic authentication interface, the GSSAPI does not support all of the functionality provided by Kerberos. For example, Kerberos's notion of user-to-user authentication is not currently supported. Hence, an application programmer will not always be able to use the GSSAPI in all cases, and may have to use the Kerberos API in order to use some features.

Other Approaches for Improving Security

Kerberos is not a complete solution to network security problems. Other tools can also provide partial solutions to network security problems, and when combined with Kerberos, stronger security can be attained. Among these other tools are one-time passcodes and public-key cryptography.

One-Time Passcodes

A one-time passcode authentication mechanism uses a different passcode each time authentication is required. Kerberos does not protect against the theft of a password through a Trojan horse login program on the user's workstation, but if the user's password were to change each time it was entered, a password stolen in this manner would be useless to an attacker. One-time passcode authentication methods typically use a credit card sized device that either displays a time varying password (called a passcode), or returns a passcode when a challenge is entered on a small keypad. Some methods use a printed list of passcodes that can be used one after another. When a user logs in using one of these devices, the user is prompted for the passcode. The user enters the passcode from the device in much the same way as a normal password.

One-time passcode devices are not by themselves sufficient for securing distributed systems because the information needed to verify the passcode might not be present on all servers with which the client interacts during a session, and because it is not practical to require entry of the passcode on every server access. However, one-time passcode methods can be combined with Kerberos so that knowledge of both the passcode and a password-based encryption key are required to successfully complete the initial authentication exchange. Commercial products that combine one-time passcodes with Kerberos are available.

Public-key Cryptography

In public-key cryptography, encryption and decryption are performed using a pair of keys such that knowledge of one key does not provide knowledge of the other key in the pair. One key is published and is called the public key, and the other key is kept private. This second key is called the private key, not to be confused with a secret key which is shared by the parties to communication in a conventional cryptosystem (it takes two to share a secret, but once you tell something to anyone else it is no longer private). Public-key cryptography has several advantages over conventional cryptography when used for authentication. These include more natural support for authentication to multiple recipients, support for non-repudiation (since the verifier does not know the private key, it can't generate a message that purports to be from the authenticated principal), and the elimination of secret encryption keys from the central authentication server.

While public-key encryption is well suited for use in authentication by store and forward applications such as electronic mail, and it is required by applications where a signature is verified by many readers, performance is a problem for high-performance servers that perform many authentication operations. Public-key encryption may also be used by authentication servers to exchange conventional cross-realm keys on-demand between authentication servers, with the cost amortized over many requests.

Conclusion

Authentication is critical for the security of computer systems. Without knowledge of the identity of a principal requesting an operation, it's difficult to decide whether the operation should be allowed. Traditional authentication methods are not suitable for use in computer networks where attackers monitor network traffic to intercept passwords. The use of strong authentication methods that do not disclose passwords is imperative. The Kerberos authentication system is well suited for authentication of users in such environments.

There are a variety of antivirus software packages that operate in many different ways, depending on how the vendor chose to implement their software. They look for patterns in the files or memory of our computer that indicate the possible presence of a known virus. Antivirus packages know what to look for through the use of virus profiles called "signatures" provided by the vendor. New viruses are discovered daily. The effectiveness of antivirus software is dependent on having the latest virus profiles installed on our computer.

Basis of Network Threats and its Solutions

P. Felcy Judith and S. Rajeswari

Introduction

Industrial communications is yet another area in which electronic networking is becoming increasingly important. Computer systems, networks and data system installations are indispensable resources, but at the same time they represent an enormous security risk, as a result of which enormous damage may be inflicted on companies. Unfortunately, it is beyond dispute that the change from centralized to distributed computing has not made life simpler for security officers and network planners with regard to their control tasks.

Even in-house networks are no longer safe, since potential security risks may come from within. And that with the continuous rise in espionage in trade and industry, to which an increasing number of companies is resorting as a proven weapon in times of fierce competition in order to gain a competitive edge. The first section of this document describes potential security risks and weaknesses with regard to networks. The section after that introduces the most important protection mechanisms. The final section describes the network topologies, which can typically be found in an industrial environment and presents the different security concepts.

Security Risks and Types of Assault

The sophisticated architectures of today's information systems feature a large number of points of attack : information is routed through a wide range of stations on its way from the source address to the destination address, including mobile workstations, field offices, network nodes and sub-networks.

It is understandable that with the new open systems architecture access and resource usage control is slackening. The rising number of computer crimes provides evidence of the increasing risk. A particular source of potential danger is the Internet in this context. The rise in the number of hosts on the Internet continues to be exponential, as is therefore the rise in the number of potential intruders.

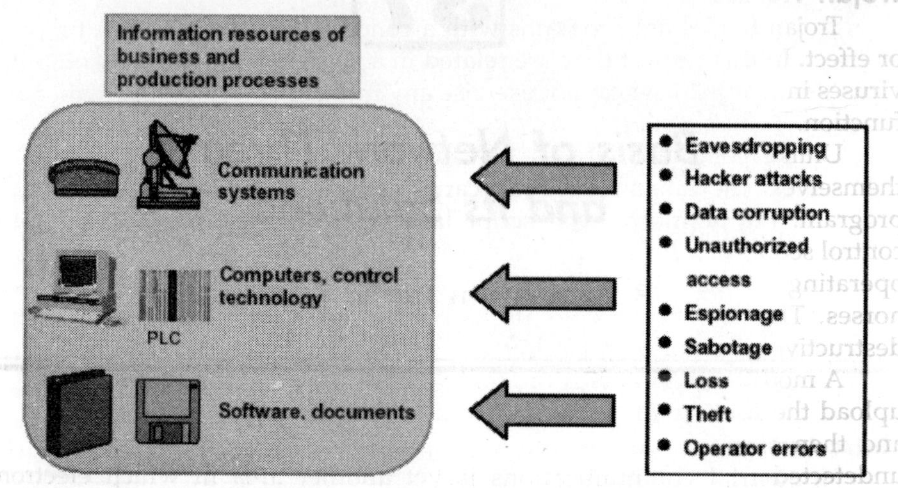

FIG. 37.1
Network Threads

But not only the hackers on the Internet corrupt information security. An increasing number of enterprises is being confronted with industrial espionage. The most common methods of industrial espionage are probably the theft or duplication of confidential documents, the gleaning of knowledge from persons having access to confidential material and information, or the tapping of telephones, fax machines and computer systems.

Computer Viruses

A computer virus is a non-autonomous program routine, which propagates itself and, as a result, performs manipulations that the user cannot control in parts of the system, on other programs or their environment.

Its property of propagation is responsible for the name "virus", as in the case of its biological archetype. The possibilities of manipulation are manifold. Particularly frequent are overwriting or clinging of the virus code to other programs and sectors of the operating system, this always happening so that the virus code is executed before the original program.

Boot viruses overwrite this data sector with their program. As a result, the virus code is executed when the computer starts up and is resident in RAM on the computer as long as the computer is operating.

In contrast to boot viruses, file viruses cling to program files. This happens as a result of the virus code being executed before the original program when the file is opened. As a result, the program then runs in its customary manner and the virus is not detected all that quickly.

Trojan Horses

Trojan horses are programs with a concealed, undocumented function or effect. In this respect they are related in a specific manner with computer viruses in that the user cannot exercise any influence on the execution of this function.

Unlike computer viruses, however, Trojan horses do not propagate themselves. They are attached to a carrier, which can be a quite normal user program. Furthermore, even script languages, such as batch files, ANSI control sequences, Postscript and the like, which are being interpreted by the operating system or user program concerned, can be abused as Trojan horses. The more privileges its carrier program has, the greater is the destructive effect of a Trojan horse.

A modified login program, for example, containing a Trojan horse can upload the user's name and password to the perpetrator over the network and then forward them to the login program proper in order to remain undetected.

Sniffer Assaults

One method of determining highly confidential data is to monitor the data packets at the Internet Protocol (IP) level. Various protocol analyzers support the use of a normal network station as a LAN analysis system. As a result, perpetrators can avail themselves of a large number of passwords and other confidential information in a very short time.

Spoofing Assaults

IP Spoofing

IP spoofing is a commonly used method to climb under firewall systems and simultaneously forms the basis for a whole number of other methods of assault. With IP spoofing, the perpetrator fakes the originator's IP address of the IP packets in order to identify himself as an authorized user. This form of assault is particularly dangerous when the firewall system is a packet filter that is merely in a position to determine the origin of the data packets from their source address. In this instance, the information relating to whether the data packet concerned is an ordinary or a fake packet is lost. The data packet is treated as if it had presumably originated from an authorized user and is switched forward.

DNS Spoofing

Computers connected to the Internet can be clearly identified by their IP addresses. A physical IP address consists of 32 bits, which are normally represented by four decimal figures between 0 and 255-198.22.156.94, for example. Since these numbers are not very easy to remember, it is recommended that a name be assigned to this kind of IP address. The procedure for doing this is known as the Domain Name System (DNS).

So-called name servers have databases at their disposal in which the corresponding IP addresses are assigned to the computer names and the corresponding names to the IP addresses. To translate a name into an IP address, a program sends a UDP packet with a suitable query to a DNS server, which searches for the name in the database and returns it to the inquirer.

We talk of DNS spoofing when a perpetrator succeeds in faking the assignment between a computer name and its corresponding IP address—in other words, a name is resolved into a wrong IP address, or the other way round.

ICMP Assaults

The purpose of the Internet Control Message Protocol (ICMP) as a component of the TCP/IP protocol stack is, among other things, to display error and diagnostic information to the originator of IP packets in the event of problems occurring on the network. The sender can then react to the error. In many implementations, the TCP/IP stack's automatic reaction to specific messages is immediate, as is necessary. A perpetrator who sends corrupted ICMP protocol elements is thus in a position to manipulate specific computer systems on the network that we have to protect.

Routing Assaults

Routing is the name given to the process of finding the correct path for transmitting a data packet. Protocols such as OSPF (Open Shortest Path First) or RIP (Routing Information Protocol) supply the necessary information, detect changes of network topology and inform the participating systems about such changes. This use of dynamic routing makes it possible to send current routing information to the computer, it then being used by the computer, without prior checking, to compile its routing tables. If a perpetrator sends corrupted RIP packages, he can manipulate specific transmission paths as a result and thus reconfigure undesired routes.

Denial of Service Assaults

One of the greatest dangers on the Internet is what is known as "denial of service assaults". In these assaults, computers or individual services on the Internet are made to crash or resources are overloaded in such a manner that they are then temporarily unavailable to other users (this is why we speak of "denial of service"). One of the reasons for such assaults being possible is software error.

Protection Mechanisms

Those responsible for the security of computer systems and information will already know that a single security procedure is frequently insufficient to preclude all risks. On the contrary, a comprehensive security solution consists of a combination of different protection mechanisms in order to safeguard confidential information from unauthorized third parties.

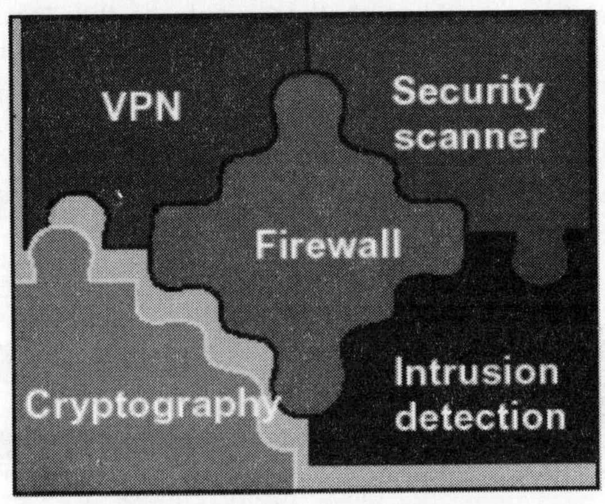

FIG. 37.2
Network Protection Methods

Firewall

The function of a firewall system is to support, to the extent possible, uninterrupted user access from a private network (Intranet) to the public network (Internet) and simultaneously to safeguard the private data network from external intruders. Generally speaking, a firewall system consists of several hardware and software components, which are configured individually, depending on the requirement concerned for the services available to in-house users and the degree of security that has to be guaranteed. As a result, the firewall prevents unauthorized or non-authenticated access to the Local Area Network (LAN) and supports controlled access to distributed data stocks and network resources while simultaneously creating a log of access activities.

Architecture and Design of Firewalls

The access to in-house data networks from external networks is defined by access control systems.

Packet Filter Access Control System

Packet filters are capable of filtering data packets according to criteria such as :

- source and destination addresses,
- protocols,
- ports, and
- user-defined bit masks.

for example. If necessary, the MAC address is evaluated to prevent a kind of "IP spoofing" like that an external user identifies himself as an internal user. The packet filter checks whether a rule of the "security policy" is applicable to a packet. If this is the case, the check is interrupted and the appropriate rule is applied to the packet. Following that, the next packet is examined. The "security policy" consists of a number of formal rules, which determine what actions are allowed, and by which side the establishment of a connection may be initiated. This mechanism makes it possible to check all the data packets and then to discard or forward them.

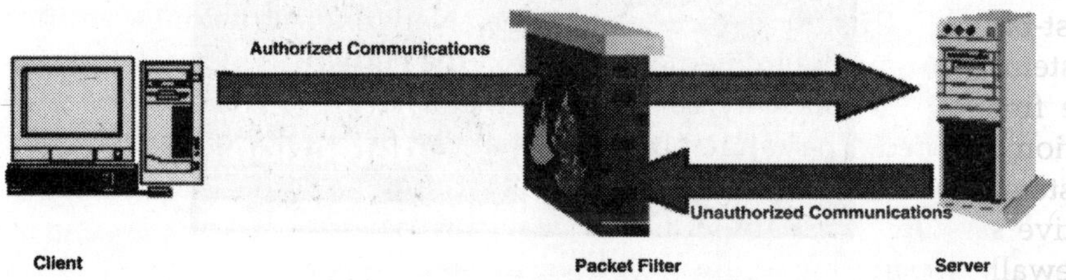

Fig. 37.3
Packet Filter Access Control System

According to this principle, everything that is not expressly allowed is prohibited. Suitable packet filters might be dedicated network components such as routers and computer systems with suitable software. Implementation of the filter conditions is performed by an entry in what are known as "filter tables" (router access lists).

Security Scanners

Security scanners are designed to trace security risks attributable to defective software products, administration and user activities before they can be abused. Security scanners therefore operate proactively. An assessment of the security risk concerned as to whether corrective action has to be taken by the system administrator in the event of a weak point is therefore made on the basis of the individually specified security guidelines. The result of a security check, generally speaking, is a detailed report of the weak points, with the help of which the system administrator can customize the firewall, operating system and application configuration. In this particular instance, we make a distinction between two types of scanner—network scanners and host scanners. A network scanner allows a quick, in-depth analysis of the critical network and system infrastructure within a company from the viewpoint of the perpetrator. It results in a comprehensive picture of all the operating systems present and the active services on the network. In this context, the scanner frequently acts as an assault simulator and uses, in doing so, methods of assault and tools as developed and propagated in the hacker world. Unlike these systems, host-based scanners are installed directly on the system that has to be scanned. They supply information about the devices connected to the system, details of their configuration—deactivated virus scanners, for instance—and also installed software.

Intrusion Detection Systems

In implementing the security strategy, there are also other components such as intrusion detection systems. These identification systems look out for assault signatures, specific patterns which might be used as an indication of malicious or suspicious activities on the network and systems. As is also the case with security scanners, we differentiate between network-based and host-based intrusion detection systems. Network intrusion identification systems examine the immediate traffic on the network—in front of or behind the firewall. In this way assaults can be detected in real time and other action initiated. The range of actions that can be taken extend from alerting system support by e-mail, pager or SNMP trap to active interruption of an active session by means of a TCP reset or dynamic reconfiguration of the firewall, depending on the solution, in order to block undesired activities without a long delay. With host-based systems, the focus is on checking the protocol files for indications of suspicious activities. Since undesired actions have been executed already with this method, these intrusion identification systems frequently act merely as post-analyzers.

Cryptography

Data are encrypted by means of cryptographic mechanisms and thereby transformed into an incomprehensible form for any person who does not have the secret decryption code in his possession. This means that highly confidential data can be transmitted over insecure networks or rendered illegible on storage media. Apart from confidentiality due to the encryption of plain text, cryptographic methods can be used to safeguard the authenticity of a message or the integrity of a file. Integrity—the certainty of having received data in unmodified form—is achieved with the help of "Message Digests (MD)", which are special checksums formed via a data packet.

Conclusion

The significance of information and data at the corporate level has increased rapidly over the past few years. An assault on the integrity and availability, up to and including sabotage on systems, frequently results in enormous financial losses. Hence, Securing Network is highly necessary in these days.

Fold Head Cryptography

V. KALAICHELVI AND R.M. CHANDRASEKARAN

Introduction

Communication generally needs privacy and security while communicating. Nowadays, with the technologic progress and as our dependency on electronic systems has increased we need more sophisticated techniques. The aim of this paper is to create an enhanced version of cryptography. In today's world where data has come to be considered the most important entity, it has become very much necessary to protect data by using various security measures of data security. For this reason they have, many algorithms that implements encryption and decryption procedures for the purpose of data security. These standard algorithms are difficult to crack but are published ones and require that the consultancy or manufacturer which provides data security be trusted upon for providing security for vital data. This paper stands different that the development of our own algorithm addresses the user needs in specific, thereby more flexibility. This paper also features dynamic generate Cipher text unlike the standard algorithms. The main objective of this paper is to provide an ideal cipher, simple, fast, compact, portable, and secure information.

The FHC algorithm is based on the folding technique and this technique described in Section 3. Folding is the origin of paper folding nature. The space in the editor is divided into number of zones. Mixing of various zones like folding helps to create the cipher text. For example, demarcation can be the exact center of the editor. So that the partition of the text on the lower half is transferred to the text in the upper half and *vice-versa*. Similarly, the line of demarcation can be vertically centered, diagonally connected or according to complexity of usage. This algorithm takes lesser time for execution.

The rest of the paper is organized as follows : Section 2 gives the detailed information about the Radix 64 Conversion. Section 3 explains the Folding technique. Section 4 explains the Implementation Details. Section 5 concludes the paper.

Radix 64 Conversion

Normally before any encryption procedure starts there must some one preprocess conversion takes place. Usually this may be the hexadecimal conversion process. Disadvantage of this type of conversion is there must be some standard replacement for the characters available in the original text. So this paper tries to avoid such type of difficulty with the help of radix 64 conversion.

Radix 64 initially fixes 64 characters. These 64 characters may be alphabets, numbers, special symbols, ASCII symbols or any other. In addition the = character is used for padding. Plain text is initially converted into these 64 radix characters.

This simple example of converting a small binary string into radix 64 notation.

' 001100110011 '

This 12 bit binary string can be divided into two sets of 6 bits.

' 001100 ' and '110011'

Converting the 6 bit binary number to base 10 notation, then getting 12 and 51.

$$0 * 32 + 0 * 16 + 1 * 8 + 1 * 4 + 0 * 2 + 0 * 1 = 12$$
$$1 * 32 + 1 * 16 + 0 * 8 + 0 * 4 + 1 * 2 + 1 * 1 = 51$$

Looking up 12 and 51 in the radix 64 alphabet, they are 'M' for 12 and 'z' for 51. So we can effectively represent this binary sequence in two human readable characters.

' Mz '

Uses of Padding Character

In the case where a binary sequence is not an integral size of 3 bytes , then we have a representation problem. There are two cases to consider. The first case where we have one byte remaining, we should pad two additional bytes with all zeros onto the end of the binary sequence. We can then represent the one byte with two radix 64 characters followed by two padding characters.

Let consider an example

00000001

Pad the single byte instance with two more bytes of zeros.

00000001 00000000 00000000

Now break up the binary sequence in sets of six bytes.

000000 010000 000000 000000

Take the first two radix 64 characters and pad two ' = ' characters to the end of the sequence.

" AQ = = "

The second case is where we have two bytes remain.

00000010 00000001

Here we should pad one additional zero byte to the end of the binary sequence.

00000010 00000001 00000000

Now break up the binary sequence in sets of six bytes.

000000 100000 000100 000000

We then take 3 radix 64 characters and pad with one " = " sign.

' AgE= '

Advantages Over Hexadecimal Conversion

➢ Less Space, Efficient—Compression

Most computers group binary files in sets of 8 bits, called a byte. The problem with this grouping is that it cannot be represented in one character and also be human readable. Often bytes are represented in the hexadecimal data representation format (4 bits) that is maybe a little more human readable than radix 64 , but also slightly less space efficient.

The binary string would be '1C7' in hexadecimal notation, or three hexadecimal characters. The equivalent radix 64 notations is 'HH', only two radix 64 characters. So, as you can see, radix 64 has a special efficiency (compression) advantage over the more popular hexadecimal notation.

➢ Avoid chosen cipher text attack

This generation deals with avoiding redundant characters into a plain text. Because cryptanalysis point of view the plain text redundant characters are important. In hexadecimal conversion deals some standard replacement for the character available in the original text.

For example,

a = 61, aa = 6161

So, hexadecimal conversion surely produces redundant code generation. Radix 64 conversion avoids this type of difficulty.

Plain text				
A	B	C	D	E
F	G	H	I	J
K	L	M	N	O
P	Q	R	S	T
U	V	W	X	Y

Cipher text				
U	V	W	X	Y
P	Q	R	S	T
K	L	M	N	O
F	G	H	I	J
A	B	C	D	E

Proposed Folding Technique

The origin of folding is from paper folding nature. This folding is broadly divided into 3 angles of processing :

1. Horizontal Folding
2. Vertical Folding
3. Diagonal Folding

The horizontal folding method finds the mid-row of whole text. With respect to that mid-row subsequent rows are exchanged,

Consider there are 5 rows present in the plain text document. Cipher text created with respect to

$$1 \longleftrightarrow 5$$
$$2 \longleftrightarrow 4$$
$$3 \longleftrightarrow 3$$

Fig. 38.1
Horizontal Folding Technique

Note : Exchange occurs.

In the case of vertical folding method columns are exchanged dynamically. It is same as horizontal folding using column processing instead of row processing.

Plain text				
A	B	C	D	E
F	G	H	I	J
K	L	M	N	O
P	Q	R	S	T
U	V	W	X	Y

Cipher text				
E	D	C	B	A
J	I	H	G	F
O	N	M	L	K
T	S	R	Q	P
Y	X	W	V	U

FIG. 38.2
Vertical Folding Technique

The diagonal folding method must be implemented in square matrix arguments. If not proper padding must be added to get the appropriate solution. On the side of decryption padding must be eliminated after processing.

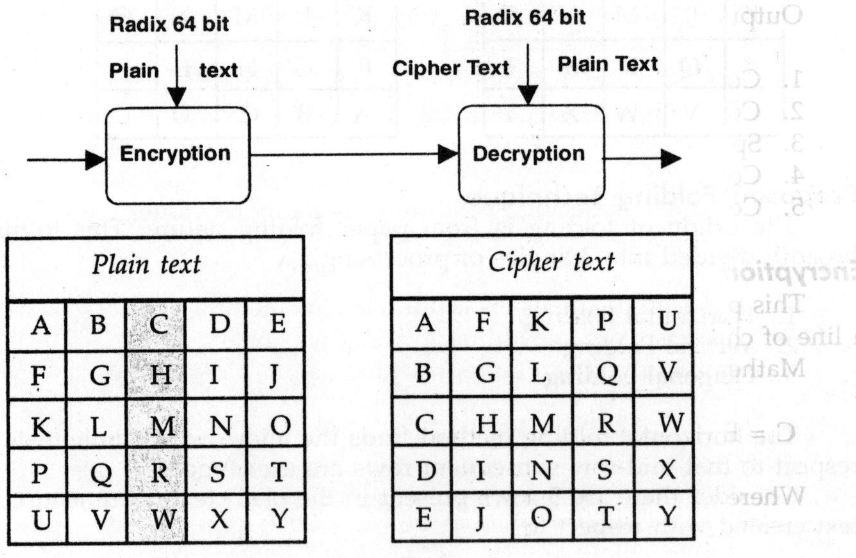

Plain text				
A	B	C	D	E
F	G	H	I	J
K	L	M	N	O
P	Q	R	S	T
U	V	W	X	Y

Cipher text				
A	F	K	P	U
B	G	L	Q	V
C	H	M	R	W
D	I	N	S	X
E	J	O	T	Y

FIG. 38.3
Diagonal Folding Technique

Implementation Details

The designing phase is the most crucial for any paper. The entire goal can be split into four modules each of which proceeds sequentially and finally achieves the objective.

Proposed Methodology

The goal is divided into four modules. So the implementation goes with

- Radix 64 encoding
- Encryption
- Decryption
- Radix 64 decoding

Fold Head Cryptography Model

Radix 64 Encoding

In this plain text is initially converted into Radix 64 character. It is done by the following algorithm.

Algorithm 4.2.1

Input : The original message file
(Plain text)
Output : Radix 64 value.

1. Convert the text string into US-ASCII value.
2. Convert US-ASCII value into binary.
3. Split this string up into groups of 6 bits (starting from left to right).
4. Convert each 6 bit binary value into a decimal number.
5. Convert this decimal value into its Radix 64 value.

Encryption

This paper implements encryption by the method of folding where in a line of characters are substituted by another line.

Mathematically, It can be represented as

$$C = E\ (R_{64}(P))$$

Where C — is the Ciphertext
P — is the Plaintext
E — Encryption process
R_{64} — Radix 64 conversion

Decryption

This is essentially the encryption algorithm run in reverse. Mathematically, it can be represented as

$P = R_{64}(D(C))$

Where C — is the Ciphertext
P — is the Plaintext
D — is the Decryption process
R_{64} — Radix 64 conversion

Proposed Encryption/Decryption Algorithm

Algorithm 4.2.3

(1) Count the total number of radix 64 characters.
(2) Find the exact or nearest square root value to form the square matrix.
(3) The matrix is filled by the radix 64 characters from left to right and then the remainder of the matrix filled by the padding character ('='). On the side of decryption padding must be eliminated after processing.
(4) Apply horizontal folding technique to that matrix.
(5) Apply vertical folding technique to the output of the step 4.
(6) Apply diagonal folding technique to the output of the step 5.

Radix 64 Decoding

In this the radix 64 value is converted into original Plain text. It is done through the following algorithm.

Algorithm 4.2.4

Input : Radix 64 value.
Output : The original message file
(Plain text)

1. Convert the character to it's Radix 64 decimal value.
2. Convert this decimal value into binary.
3. Squash the 6 bits of each character into one big string of binary digits.
4. Split this string up into groups of 8 bits (starting from left to right).
5. Convert each 8 bit binary value into a decimal number.
6. Convert this decimal value into its US-ASCII equivalent.

Conclusion

The aim of this paper is to create an enhanced version of cryptography. Using this cryptographic technique it is hardly impossible for the hacker to break the code to get into the data. High level security is provided by using the fold head cryptography. The symmetry axis for folding the data is generated by the system itself; hence it is highly difficult to decipher how the cryptography is carried out. Normal cryptography technique may involve keys which might be broken but in Fold head cryptography the system is even more secure by fixing the key at the same time folding along the symmetric line is which increases the security options to the highest degree possible. Radix 64 conversion eliminates the redundant data occurred in the plaintext pattern. So this improves the complexity of the cipher text. This idea further enhanced into this will be implemented with the block cipher modes.

References

1. Bruce Schenier, "Applied Cryptography", John Wiley and Sons Inc, 2001.
2. William Stallings, "Cryptography and Network Security", Pearson Education (Singapore) Pte. Ltd., 2003.
3. Charles P. Pleeger, "Security In Computing", PHI, 1989.
4. Hans, "Information and Communicaton Security", Springer Verlag, 1998.
5. Simonds, "Network Security", McGraw Hill, 1998.
6. Derek Atkins, "Internet Security", echmedia, 1998.
7. Baxer, "Networking Security", McGraw, Hill, 1996.

CHAPTER 39

Steganography : The Art and Science of Hidden Communication

K. Duraiswamy and R. Uma Rani

Introduction to Information Hiding

Steganography literally means covered writing. Its goal is to hide the fact that communication is taking place. This is often achieved by using a (rather large) cover file and embedding the (rather short) secret message into this file. The result is a innocuous looking file (the stego file) that contains the secret message. It has until recently been the poor cousin of cryptography. Now, it is gaining new popularity with the current industry demands for digital watermarking and fingerprinting of audio and video. A message in ciphertext may arouse suspicion while an *invisible* message will not. In contrast to cryptography, where the "enemy" is allowed to detect, intercept and modify messages without being able to violate certain security premises guaranteed by a cryptosystem, the goal of steganography is to hide messages inside other "harmless" messages in a way that does not allow any "enemy" to even detect that there is a second secret message present.

Introduction to Terms Used

In the field of steganography, some terminology has been developed, as explained below. The adjectives *cover*, *embedded* and *stego* were defined at the Information Hiding Workshop held in Cambridge, England. The term "cover" is used to describe the original, innocent message, data, audio, still, video and so on. When referring to audio signal steganography, the cover signal is sometimes called the "host" signal. The information to be hidden in the cover data is known as the "embedded" data. The "stego" data is the data containing both the cover signal and the "embedded" information. Logically, the processing of putting the hidden, or embedded data, into the cover data, is sometimes known as embedding. Occasionally, especially when referring to image steganography, the cover image is known as the *container*.

Types of Steganography

Steganography has been classified into two types :

1. Technical Steganography.
2. Linguistic Steganography.

The *technical steganography* methods are,

Invisible Ink : One of the methods with the longest tradition.

Hiding-places : Suitcases, heels.

Microdots : A method that can be used to hide up to one page in a dot.

Computer-based Methods : Uses redundant information in texts, pictures, sounds, videos.

Linguistic Steganography : Linguistic steganography is any form of steganography where the carrier media is text. The modification can be done in very different ways. The modification can be done graphically, by changing the structure of the text or even by creating a new text only for the purpose to hide data in it.

The *linguistic steganography* methods are :

Open Codes : The secret message appears in an openly readable but harmless message. Masking, cues, null-ciphers or grilles can do this.

Semagrams : The secret message is hidden in tiny (but visible) details of the open text.

Cryptography, Steganography and Digital Watermarking—A Comparison

While *cryptography* is about protecting the content of messages (their meaning), *steganography* is about concealing their very existence. It comes from Greek roots, literally means 'covered writing', and is usually interpreted to mean hiding information in other information. Examples include sending a message to a spy by marking certain letters in a newspaper using invisible ink, and adding sub-perceptible echo at certain places in an audio recording. It is often thought that communications may be secured by encrypting the traffic, but this has rarely been adequate in practice. Eneas the Tactician, and other classical writers, concentrated on methods for hiding messages rather than for enciphering them; and although modern cryptographic techniques started to develop during the Renaissance, we find in 1641 that John Wilkins still preferred hiding over ciphering because it arouses less suspicion. This preference persists in many operational contexts to this day. For example, an encrypted email message between a known drug dealer and somebody not yet under suspicion, or between an employee of a defense contractor and the embassy of a hostile power, has obvious implications.

As the purpose of *steganography* is having a covert communication between two parties whose existence is unknown to a possible attacker, a successful attack consists in detecting the existence of this communication (e.g., using statistical analysis of images with and without hidden information). *Watermarking,* as opposed to steganography, has the (additional) requirement of robustness against possible attacks. In this context, the term 'robustness' is still not very clear; it mainly depends on the application. Copyright marks do not always need to be hidden, as some systems use *visible digital watermarks,* but most of the literature has focused on imperceptible (e.g., invisible, inaudible) digital watermarks which have wider applications. Visible digital watermarks are strongly linked to the original paper watermarks which appeared at the end of the 13th century to differentiate paper makers of that time. Modern visible watermarks may be visual patterns (e.g., a company logo or copyright sign) overlaid on digital images. The intent of use is also different : the payload of a watermark can be perceived as an attribute of the cover-signal (e.g., copyright information, license, ownership, etc.). In most cases the information hidden using steganographic techniques is not related at all to the cover. These differences in goal lead to very different hiding techniques.

Steganography Under Various Media

1. Text

In studying steganography in text, we examine three main techniques : line-shift coding, word-shift coding, and feature coding. Each is designed to fight illegal distribution of text documents by stamping some recognizable feature into the text, either by shifting the lines, shifting the word spacing, or altering characteristics of the letters themselves. We find that some of these methods are quite strong, proving resistant to even 10 levels of photocopying.

We also look at some more interesting, alternative methods, such as using grammar to encode data.

2. Images

Steganography in images has truly come of age with the invention of fast, powerful computers. Software is readily available off the Internet for any user to hide data inside images. The most popular technique is Least Significant Bit insertion. There are also more complex methods such as masking and filtering, and algorithms and transformations, which offer the most robustness to attack, which exploits the human eye's weakness to luminance variation.

3. Audio

The final medium, audio, is first explained through a look at how audio is stored and transmitted. It is then explored through four main methods of data-hiding : Least significant bit insertion, phase coding, spread spectrum coding, and echo hiding.

PC Software that Provide Steganographic Services

Steganographic software is new and very effective. Such software enables information to be hidden in graphic, sound and apparently "blank" media.

AppendX is a simple Steganography tool. It's purpose is not to give enormous security. It simply can hide data for inexperienced users. There is no cryptography used by AppendX. It appends data to an other data file (e.g. .png,.jpg,.gif) so that if viewed normally the data is not detected.

Steghide is a steganography program, which embeds a secret message in a cover file by replacing some of the least significant bits of the cover file (JPEG, BMP, WAV and AU files) with bits of the secret message. After that, the secret message is imperceptible and can only be extracted with the correct pass phrase.

ShadowJPEG is a steganography tool. It hides a file at the end of a JPEG image file. Cryptography is implemented using a simple private-key system, which is used to encrypt the data before the injection.

Hide 4 PGP is another steganographic toos which, hides data in BMP, WAV, and VOC files.

Steganalysis

Whereas the goal of steganography is the avoidance of suspicion to hidden messages in other data, steganalysis aims to discover and render useless such covert messages.

Two aspects of attacks on steganography are detection and destruction of the embedded message. Some authors propose to use a public watermark detector as an oracle to estimate a secret spread spectrum watermark with a complexity quadratic in the number of samples. The image is first degraded until no watermark can be found, then random signals are added while the watermark cannot be detected.

A wide range of further literature on steganalysis is available, but is beyond the scope of this paper.

Conclusion

Until recently, information hiding techniques received very much less attention from the research community and from industry than cryptography. Steganography has its place in security. It is not intended to replace cryptography but supplement it. Hiding a message with steganography methods reduces the chance of a message being detected. However, if that message is also encrypted, if discovered, it must also be cracked (yet another layer of protection). There are an infinite number of steganography applications. This paper explores a tiny fraction of the art of steganography. It goes well beyond simply embedding text in an image.

Steganography does not only pertain to digital images but also to other media (files such as voice, other text and binaries; other media such as communication channels, the list can go on and on).

REFERENCES

1. Neil F. Johnson, Zoran Duric, Sushil Jajodia, *Information Hiding : Steganography and Watermarking—Attacks and Countermeasures*
2. J. Brassil, S. Low, N. Maxemchuk, L. O'Goram, "Hiding Information in Document Images."

WEB Page Resources

1. http ://www.research.att.com/.
2. http ://nsi.org/Library/Library.html.
3. http ://www.trcone.com/t_links.html

Wireless LAN Security

R. Vijayalakshmi and S. Sampath Kumar

Introduction

This paper provides best-practice information for designing and implementing Wireless LAN (WLAN) security in networks utilizing elements of the network security to provide best-practice information on network security designs.

This paper frames the WLAN implementation within the context of the overall security design. It represents a system-based approach to security. This type of approach focuses on overall design goals and translates those goals into specific configurations and topologies. In the context of wireless, it is recommended to also consider network design elements such as mobility and Quality of Service (QoS) when deciding on an overall WLAN design. This paper begins with an overview of the architecture, and then details the specific designs under consideration. The designs are :

- Large-network WLAN design
- Medium-network WLAN design
- Small-network WLAN design
- Remote-user WLAN design

Each design may have multiple modules that address different aspects of WLAN technology.

The Need for Wireless

Standard 802.11-based Wireless LANs (WLANs) provide mobility to network users while maintaining the requisite connectivity to corporate resources. As laptops become more pervasive in the workplace, users are more prone to use laptops as their primary computing device, allowing greater portability in meetings and conferences and during business travel. WLANs offer organizations greater productivity per employee by providing constant connectivity to traditional networks in venues where previously unavailable.

Wireless network connectivity is not limited to enterprise use. WLANs offer increased productivity not only before and after meetings, but also outside the traditional office environment. Numerous Wireless Internet Service Providers (WISPs) are appearing in airports, coffee shops, hotels, and conference and convention centers, enabling enterprise users to connect in public access venues.

Types of Wireless Technology

Wireless local-area networking has existed for many years, providing connectivity to wired infrastructures where mobility was a requirement to specific working environments. These early networks were based on both frequency-hopping and direct-sequencing radio technologies (described later). These early wireless networks were non-standard implementations, with speeds ranging between 1 and 2 MB. Without any standards driving WLAN technologies, the early implementations of WLAN were relegated to vendor-specific implementation, with no provision for interoperability, inhibiting the growth of standards-based WLAN technologies. Today, several standards exist for WLAN applications : 802.11, HiperLAN, HomeRF SWAP, and Bluetooth.

Functional View

From a functional viewpoint, WLANs can be categorized as follows : peer-to-peer wireless LANs, multiple-cell wireless LANs, and building-to-building wireless networks (point to point and point to multipoint). In a peer-to-peer wireless LAN, wireless clients equipped with wireless Network Interface Cards (NICs) communicate with each other without the use of an access point. Coverage area is limited in a peer-to-peer LAN, and wireless clients do not have access to wired resources. A multiple-cell wireless LAN extends the coverage through the use of overlapping cells. Coverage area of a cell is determined by the characteristics of the access point (a wireless bridge) that coordinates the wireless clients' use of wired resources.

Building-to-building wireless networks address the connectivity requirement between LANs (buildings) in a campus-area network. There are two different types of building-to-building wireless networks : point to point and point to multipoint. Point-to-point wireless links between buildings are radio or laser-based point-to-point links. A radio-based point-to-point bridged link between buildings uses directional antennas to focus the signal power in a narrow beam, maximizing the transmission distance. A laser-based point-to-point bridged link between buildings uses laser light (usually infrared light) as a carrier for data transmission. A radio-based point-to-multipoint bridged network uses antennas with wide beam width to connect multiple buildings (LANs) in a campus-area network.

Technology View

Though most of this paper focuses on 802.11 WLANs (described below), it is relevant to understand other wireless standards currently in the market.

HiperLAN

HiperLAN is a European Telecommunications Standards Institute (ETSI) standard ratified in 1996. HiperLAN/1 standard operates in the 5-GHz radio band up to 24 Mbps. The ETSI has recently approved HiperLAN/2, which operates in the 5-GHz band at up to 54 Mbps using a connection-oriented protocol for sharing access among end-user devices.

HomeRF SWAP

In 1988, The HomeRF SWAP Group published the Shared Wireless Access Protocol (SWAP) standard for wireless digital communication between PCs and consumer electronic devices within the home. SWAP supports voice and data over a common wireless interface at 1 and 2-Mbps data rates using frequency-hopping and spread-spectrum techniques in the 2.4-GHz band.

Bluetooth

Bluetooth is a Personal-Area Network (PAN) specified by the Bluetooth Special Interest Group for providing low-power and short-range wireless connectivity using frequency-hopping spread spectrum in the 2.4-GHz frequency environment.

802.11 Wireless Technology

The IEEE maintains the 802.11-based standard, as well as other 802-based networking standards, such as 802.3 Ethernet. A non-profit, vendor-neutral organization known as the Wi-Fi Alliance provides a branding for 802.11-based technology known as Wi-Fi. A Wi-Fi compliant device must pass interoperability testing in the Wi-Fi laboratory. All vendor products that are Wi-Fi certified are guaranteed to work with all other Wi-Fi certified products—regardless of the vendor.

Standard 802.11-based wireless technologies take advantage of the radio spectrum deemed usable by the public. This spectrum is known as the Industrial, Scientific, and Medical (ISM) band. The 802.11 standard specifically takes advantage of two of the three frequency bands, the 2.4 GHz-to-2.4835 GHz UHF band used for 802.11 and 802.11b networks, and the 5.15 GHz-to-5.825 GHz SHF band used for 802.11a-based networks.

The spectrum is classed as unlicensed, meaning there is no one owner of the spectrum, and anyone can use it as long as that user's device complies with FCC regulations. Some of the areas the FCC governs include the maximum transmit power of the radios and the type of encoding and frequency modulations that can be used.

Wireless LAN Components

Components of a WLAN are access points, NICs or client adapters, bridges, and antennas.

- *Access Point*—An access point operates within a specific frequency spectrum and uses a 802.11 standard specified modulation technique. It also informs the wireless clients of its availability and authenticates and associates wireless clients to the wireless network. An access point also coordinates the wireless clients' use of wired resources.
- *NIC or Client Adapter*—A PC or workstation uses a wireless NIC to connect to the wireless network. The NIC scans the available frequency spectrum for connectivity and associates it to an access point or another wireless client. The NIC is coupled to the PC or workstation OS using a software driver.
- *Bridge*—Wireless bridges are used to connect multiple LANs (both wired and wireless) at the Media Access Control (MAC) layer level. Used in building-to-building wireless connections, wireless bridges can cover longer distances than access points (IEEE 802.11 standard specifies 1 mile as the maximum coverage range for an access point).
- *Antenna*—An antenna radiates the modulated signal through the air so that wireless clients can receive it. Characteristics of an antenna are defined by propagation pattern (directional versus omnidirectional), gain, transmit power, and so on. Antennas are needed on both the access point and bridge and the clients.

Network Availability

The following sections describe in detail items that should be considered when deploying services in order to secure wireless LANs (WLANs). Note that in the remote, small, and medium network designs, high availability is not provided in the Cisco SAFE Blueprint for network security wired network, so it is not expected to be present for wireless.

Dynamic Host Configuration Protocol

- *Requests per second*—The Dynamic Host Configuration Protocol (DHCP) server hardware and software must be able to accommodate the projected number of new DHCP requests per second that will be offered by introducing WLANs. If the DHCP servers are overburdened, wireless users will not be able to acquire DHCP addresses, denying Extensible Authentication Protocol (EAP) users from gaining IP connectivity after authentication and denying IP security (IPsec) users from setting up a secure tunnel with the Virtual-Private-Network (VPN) gateways.

- *DHCP Safe Failover Protocol*—Network designers should implement DHCP servers that provide redundancy on dual servers via the draft RFC DHCP Safe Failover Protocol. By implementing this protocol, network designers can increase network availability for their wireless end users.
- *Address Management*—Network designers should consider the additional IP addressing requirements that are introduced by implementing WLANs. Also, if the network designer chooses to use IPsec VPNs to secure the wireless environment, additional IP addressing is required for the VPN tunnels that are built. If DHCP services are not available in either case, wireless users will be denied access to the corporate network.
- *Network Design Considerations*—Network designers must consider where the DHCP services are located in relation to the end users accessing the services. A redundant network is required between the two locations in order to achieve high availability. Also, it is recommended that network designers not group all their DHCP services in one subnet because a denial-of-service (DoS) attack against the subnet can deny DHCP service to all wireless users.

RADIUS

- *Requests per second*—The Remote Access Dial-In User Service (RADIUS) server hardware and software must be able to accommodate the projected number of new RADIUS requests per second that will be offered by introducing WLANs. If the RADUIS servers are overburdened, wireless access point and VPN gateways will not be able to authenticate users, denying wireless users connectivity to the corporate network. Also, it should be noted that if the network designer elects to use a back-end database for user authentication, the back-end database must also be designed to accommodate the projected number of user authentication requests per second that will be offered by introducing WLANs.
- *Redundant Server Deployment*—Multiple RADIUS servers should be deployed in order to give the authenticating device (wireless access point or VPN gateway) redundant options for servicing authentication requests. Network designers should also group the authenticating devices to alternate the listing of primary and secondary RADIUS servers. This set-up accomplishes two goals : it limits the failure domain in the case of a server failure and also enables each RADIUS server to scale more effectively.
- *User Management*—RADIUS servers need to provide high-availability access to the user database required for user authentication. Network designers should consider implementing

servers that synchronize data if the user database is to be stored locally. This set-up allows a single point of administration and eliminates the possibility of a user definition being on one RADIUS server but not the other. If the user database is stored externally (Lightweight Directory Access Protocol [LDAP], NT domain), network designers should consider the location of the RADIUS servers to the back-end database because a network outage between the two resources can deny wireless users access to the corporate network.

IP Security Protocol

- *Connections per second*—The VPN gateway hardware and software must be able to accommodate the projected number of new IPsec connections per second that will be offered by introducing WLANs.
- *Encryption throughput*—The VPN gateway hardware and software must be able to accommodate the projected encryption throughput that will be offered by introducing WLANs. VPN gateways work harder to encrypt several smaller packets than one larger packet, causing lower encryption throughput numbers for the VPN gateway. It is important that network designers understand the packet size distribution of their wired networks in order to properly size the VPN gateway for the wireless network environment.
- *Simultaneous IPsec Sessions*—The VPN gateway hardware and software must be able to accommodate the projected number of simultaneous IPsec sessions that will be offered by introducing WLANs. VPN gateways are designed to handle a finite limit of simultaneous IPsec sessions.

Failure to design the IPsec environment with these considerations in mind will cause the wireless users to be unable to access the corporate network, or when they do so, performance will be severely degraded. VPN vendors have addressed the previous three items by introducing proprietary clustering technologies. The clustering technologies load balance new IPsec connections to the least-loaded VPN gateway in order to give the new IPsec connection the best possible service.

More in-depth information on designing IPsec networks can be found in "SAFE VPN : IPsec Virtual Private Networks in Depth."

Architecture Overview

Design Fundamentals

Implementation decisions vary, depending on the network functionality required. However, the following design objectives, listed in order of priority, guided the decision-making process :

- Security and attack mitigation based on policy.
- Authentication and authorization of users to wired network resources.
- Wireless data confidentiality.
- User differentiation.
- Access point management.
- Authentication of users to network resources.
- Options for high availability (large enterprise only).

Wireless needs to provide a secure WLAN connectivity option to enterprise networks. As a connectivity option, WLAN access must adhere to an organization's security policy as closely as possible. In addition, it must provide this access as securely as possible while recognizing the need to maintain as many of the characteristics of a traditional wired LAN as possible. Finally, WLANs must integrate with existing network designs based on the security architecture.

802.1X/EAP

An alternative WLAN security approach focuses on developing a framework for providing centralized authentication and dynamic key distribution. This approach is based on the IEEE 802.11 Task Group "i" end-to-end framework using 802.1X and the Extensible Authentication Protocol (EAP) to provide this enhanced functionality. Cisco has incorporated 802.1X and EAP into its WLAN security solution—the Cisco Wireless Security Suite. The three main elements of an 802.1X and EAP approach follow :

- Mutual authentication between client and authentication (Remote Access Dial-In User Service [RADIUS]) server.
- Encryption keys dynamically derived after authentication.
- Centralized policy control, where session time-out triggers reauthentication and new encryption key generation.

When these features are implemented, a wireless client that associates with an access point cannot gain access to the network until the user performs a network logon. After association, the client and the network (access point or RADIUS server) exchange EAP messages to perform mutual authentication, with the client verifying the RADIUS server credentials, and *vice versa*. An EAP supplicant is used on the client machine to obtain the user credentials (user ID and password, user ID and one-time password [OTP], or digital certificate). Upon successful client and server mutual authentication, the RADIUS server and client then derive a client-specific WEP key to be used by the client for the current logon session. User passwords and session keys are never transmitted in the clear, over the wireless link.

The sequence of events follows (refer to Figure 40.1).

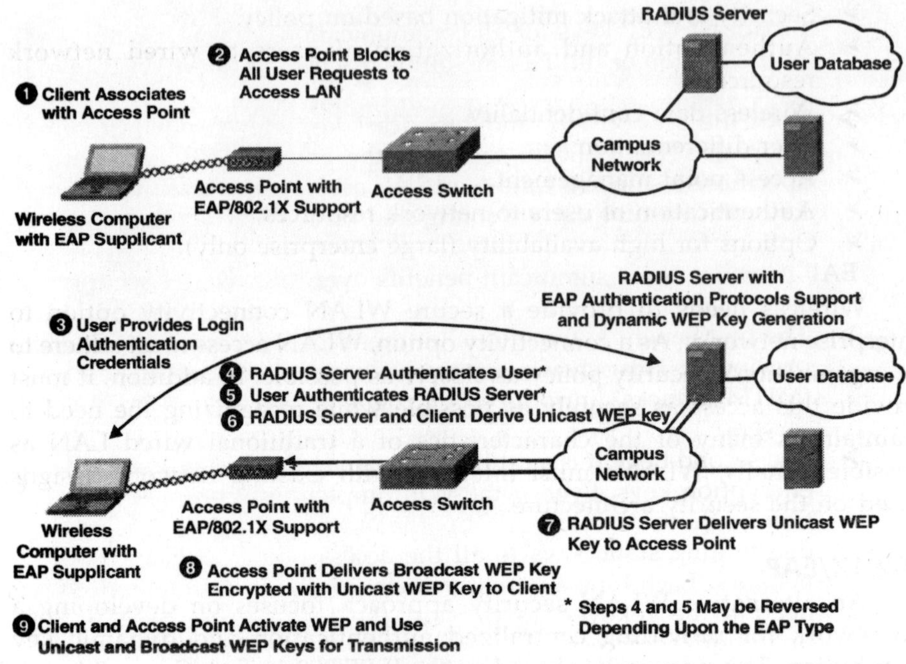

FIG. 40.1
EAP Authentication Process

- A wireless client associates with an access point.
- The access point blocks all attempts by the client to gain access to network resources until the client logs on to the network.
- The user on the client supplies network login credentials (user ID and password, user ID and OTP, or user ID and digital certificate) via an EAP supplicant.
- Using 802.1X and EAP, the wireless client and a RADIUS server on the wired LAN perform a mutual authentication through the access point in two phases. In the first phase of EAP authentication, the RADIUS server verifies the client credentials, or *vice versa*. In the second phase, mutual authentication is completed by the client verifying the RADIUS server credential, or *vice versa*.
- When mutual authentication is successfully completed, the RADIUS server and the client determine a WEP key that is distinct to the client. The client loads this key and prepares to use it for the logon session.
- The RADIUS server sends the WEP key, called a session key, over the wired LAN to the access point.
- The access point encrypts its broadcast key with the session key and sends the encrypted key to the client, which uses the session key to decrypt it.
- The client and access point activate WEP and use the session and

broadcast WEP keys for all communications during the remainder of the session or until a time-out is reached and new WEP keys are generated.

➢ Both the session key and broadcast key are changed at regular intervals. The RADIUS server at the end of EAP authentication specifies session key time-out to the access point and the broadcast key rotation time can be configured on the access point.

EAP provides three significant benefits over basic 802.11 security :

➢ The first benefit is the mutual authentication scheme, as described previously. This scheme effectively eliminates "Man-In-The-Middle (MITM) attacks" introduced by rogue access points and RADIUS servers.

➢ The second benefit is a centralized management and distribution of encryption keys. Even if the WEP implementation of RC4 had no flaws, there would still be the administrative difficulty of distributing static keys to all the access points and clients in the network. Each time a wireless device was lost, the network would need to be rekeyed to prevent the lost system from gaining unauthorized access.

➢ The third benefit is the ability to define centralized policy control, where session time-out triggers reauthentication and new key derivation.

EAP Authentication Protocols

Numerous EAP types are available today for user authentication over wired and wireless networks. Current EAP types include :

- EAP-Wireless (LEAP)

➢ EAP-Transport Layer Security (EAP-TLS).
➢ Protected EAP (PEAP).
➢ EAP-Tunneled TLS (EAP-TTLS).
➢ EAP-Subscriber Identity Module (EAP-SIM).

LEAP

LEAP is the widely deployed EAP type in use today in WLANs. LEAP supports all three of the 802.1X and EAP elements mentioned previously. With LEAP, mutual authentication relies on a shared secret, the user's logon password, which is known by the client and the network. As shown in Figure 40.2, the RADIUS server sends an authentication challenge to the client. The client uses a one-way hash of the user-supplied password to fashion a response to the challenge and sends that response to the RADIUS server. Using information from its user database, the RADIUS server creates its own response and compares that to the response from the client. When the RADIUS server authenticates the client, the process repeats in reverse, enabling the client to authenticate the RADIUS server. When this is complete, an EAP-Success message is sent to the client and both the client and the RADIUS server derive the dynamic WEP key.

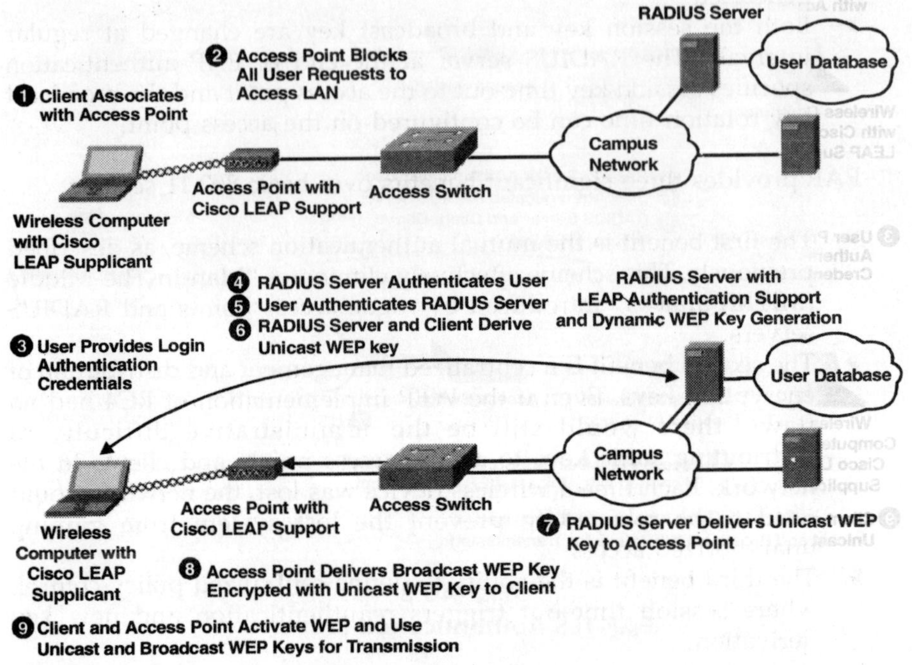

FIG. 40.2
LEAP Authentication Process

EAP-TLS

EAP-TLS is an Internet Engineering Task Force (IETF) standard (RFC 2716) that is based on the TLS protocol (RFC 2246). EAP-TLS uses digital certificates for both user and server authentication and supports the three key elements of 802.1X/EAP mentioned previously. As shown in Figure 40.3, the RADIUS server sends its certificate to the client in phase 1 of the authentication sequence (server-side TLS). The client validates the RADIUS server certificate by verifying the issuer of the certificate—a certificate authority server entity—and the contents of the digital certificate. When this is complete, the client sends its certificate to the RADIUS server in phase 2 of the authentication sequence (client-side TLS). The RADIUS server validates the client's certificate by verifying the issuer of the certificate (certificate authority server entity) and the contents of the digital certificate. When this is complete, an EAP-Success message is sent to the client and both the client and the RADIUS server derive the dynamic WEP key.

Conclusion

Maintaining a secure wireless network and associated devices requires significant effort, resources, and vigilance and involves the following steps :

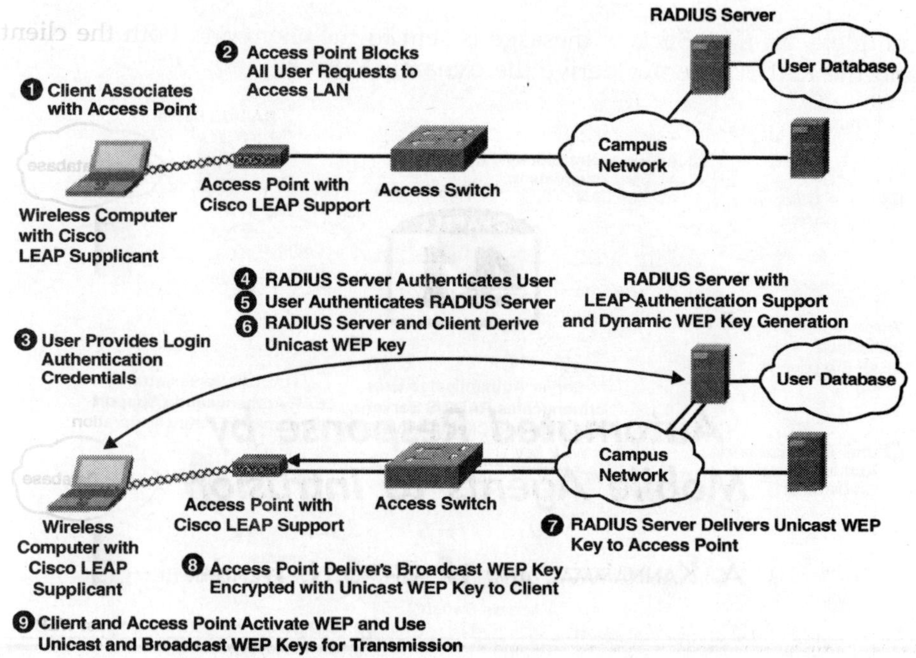

FIG. 40.3
EAP-TLS Authentication Process

- Maintaining a full understanding of the topology of the wireless network.
- Labeling and keeping inventories of the fielded wireless and handheld devices.
- Creating backups of data frequently.
- Performing periodic security testing and assessment of the wireless network.
- Performing ongoing, randomly timed security audits to monitor and track wireless and handheld devices.
- Applying patches and security enhancements.
- Monitoring the wireless industry for changes to standards that enhance security features and for the release of new products.
- Vigilantly monitoring wireless technology for new threats and vulnerabilities.

REFERENCES

http ://www.isaac.cs.berkeley.edu/isaac/wep-faq.html
http ://www.cs.umd.edu/~waa/wireless.pdf
http ://www.cs.umd.edu/~waa/class-pubs/rc4_ksaproc.ps
http ://www.cs.rice.edu/~astubble/wep/wep_attack.pdf
http ://airsnort.sourceforge.net/
Borisov *et. al.*, "Security of the WEP Algorithm".

Automated Response by Mobile Agents to Intrusion

A. Kannammal and N. Ch. S.N. Iyengar

Introduction

Intrusion Detection System (IDS)

Intrusion Detection is defined as the problem of identifying individuals called "crackers" who are using a computer system without authorization and those who have legitimate access to the system but are abusing their privileges, known as "insider threat". Hence intrusion is any set of actions that attempt to comprise the integrity, confidentiality, or availability of a resource.

Requirements of IDS

As the network-computing environment increases in complexity, so do the functional requirements of IDSs. Common functional and performance requirements of IDS are described below. The IDS must continuously monitor and report intrusions. It must supply enough information to repair the system, determine the extent of damage, and establish responsibility for the intrusion. It should be modular and configurable. It must be able to operate in a hostile computing environment and exhibit a high degree of fault-tolerance and allow for graceful degradation. It should be adaptive to network topology and configuration changes as computing elements are dynamically added and removed from the network. It should be able to learn from past experiences and improve its detection capabilities over time. It should be able to be easily and frequently updated with attack signatures as new security advisories and security patches become available and new vulnerabilities and attacks are discovered. It will be required not only to detect anomalous events, but also to take automated corrective action. It should be able to perform data fusion and be able to process information from multiple and distributed data sources such as firewalls, routers, and switches. Also it will need to be able to communicate with the hardware-based devices.

Data reduction tools will be necessary to help the IDS process the information gathered from data fusion techniques. Data mining tools will be helpful in running statistical analysis tools on archived data in support of anomaly detection techniques. It should be capable of providing an automated response to suspicious activity. Rapid changes in network conditions and limited network administration expertise make it difficult for system administrators to diagnose problems and take corrective action to minimize the damage that intruders can cause. The ability to detect and react to distributed and coordinated attacks will become necessary. Distributing the computational load and the diagnostic capabilities to agents scattered throughout the network adds a level of fault-tolerance, but it is often necessary for the system administrator to have control over the IDS from a central location.

The IDS should be able to work with other Commercial Off-the-Shelf (COTS) security tools, as no vendor toolset is likely to excel in or to provide complete coverage of the detection, diagnosis, and response responsibilities. The IDS framework should be able to integrate various data reduction, forensic, host-based, and network-based security tools. Interoperability and conformance to standards will further increase the value of the IDS. IDS data often requires additional analysis to assess any damage to the network after an intrusion has been detected. The IDS itself must also be designed with security in mind. It must not place undue burden or interfere with the normal operations for which the systems were bought and deployed to begin with. It must be scalable. As new computing devices are added to the network, the IDS must be able to handle the additional computational and communication load.

Mobile Agent (MA) Technology

A software agent can be defined as a software entity which functions continuously and autonomously in a particular environment able to carry out activities in a flexible and intelligent manner that is responsive to changes in the environment. MAs are a particular type of software agent, having the capability to move from one host to another. Ideally, an agent that functions continuously would be able to learn from its experience. IDSs implemented using MAs is one of the new paradigms for intrusion detection.

Relatively little work has been done on using a mobile agent architecture for the purpose of providing a security capability, such as intrusion detection. If mobile agent architecture is designed for a specific purpose such as system administration or security function maintenance, then strong authentication may be enforced and the residual risk decreases significantly. While MAs are extraordinarily powerful tools, their implementation has been hindered by security considerations. These security considerations are especially critical for intrusion detection systems, with the result that most security research in this field has concentrated upon the architecture necessary to provide security for mobile agents. Such negative results are not fatal to the proposed study since these security issues are likely to be addressed by the research community and there will be few authorized users of the MA-based IDSs within an organization.

Intrusion Detection—Current Scenarios

Intrusion detection by existing systems are less than perfect as there are number of shortcomings of currently deployed IDSs, as there is no generic building methodology, lack of efficiency, lack of portability among monitored environments, limited flexibility that includes tailorability, scalability, and dynamic reconfigurability, limited upgradability of detection techniques, difficult maintenance of rule sets, no performance and coverage benchmarks, and no good way to test effectiveness. Developers continue to solve some of these shortcomings through the refinement of existing techniques, but some shortcomings are inherent in the way IDSs are constructed.

While mobile agents can help improve IDSs in many areas, they offer no help in others. For example, the ability of an IDS to detect attacks from a single vantage point, by looking at information from a single host, a single application, or a single network interface (i.e., single point detection), is the primary problem facing IDS manufacturers. Mobile agent technology cannot enhance the ability of an IDS to perform single point detection of attacks or reduce false positive rates. Moreover, in most cases, mobile agent technology slows down the ability of an IDS to process events thereby actually decreasing its detection ability. This is a severe limitation for single point IDSs attempting to evaluate events in real time. This does not mean that MAs are not useful to IDSs. MAs can solve several major problems with IDSs, but more importantly, as discussed below, they can provide IDSs with performance benefits and heretofore-unseen capabilities. For example, the mobility of agents make them ideal for detection schemes that follow a "cop on the beat," "immune system," or other model.

Intrusion Response—Current Scenarios

As their name implies, IDSs have traditionally focused on detecting attacks. While detection serves a useful purpose, oftentimes a human does not analyze the reports from IDS for some time. This gives an attacker a window of opportunity in which to freely operate before being countered by a systems administrator. During this time, the attacker may steal critical data, install invisible back doors, use the penetrated host to attack other sites, or subtly corrupt information. Ideally, an attacker should not be given any time to extend their grasp on a network. Because of this, many IDSs are beginning to implement automated response capabilities.

The IDS detects an attack and immediately responds in order to kick the attacker out of the network. This sounds simple, but in practice it is very difficult to accomplish. For safety and technical concerns (i.e., the response could be used to an attacker's benefit), IDSs initiate only very weak responses. We present ways in which MAs can help solve this problem, however, first we explore existing automated response mechanisms and the challenges facing them.

Existing Mechanisms

Existing response mechanisms in commercial IDSs are somewhat weak when compared to the goal of automatically ousting an attacker from the network. The automated response mechanisms currently implemented fall into two categories : enhanced notification and attacker filtering.

Enhanced notification mechanisms are designed to inform systems administrators of important attacks as soon as possible. They thus decrease the time window an attacker has before being countered by a human. In the event of an important attack, IDSs e-mail system administrators, pop up notification windows on their monitors, or even page them.

Attack filtering methods actively stop an attacker. One popular technique is to interrupt a TCP connection between an attacker and a target. IDSs do this by sniffing the malicious connection to determine packet sequence numbers and then by inserting reset packets to kill the connection. Another popular attack filtering technique is to dynamically change the routing permissions table in routers and firewalls. Typically, an IDS disallows packets from an attacker's IP address or subnet from traversing the network's routers or firewall. The target can also be cut-off using this technique in order to prevent the attacker from launching attacks from the target host. Using these attack filtering methods, an IDS attempts to disrupt the attacker's access to the target and stop the attacker from sending more malicious packets into the network.

The existing response mechanisms are too weak to stop sophisticated attackers. Currently implemented response mechanisms are not sufficient because they assume that attacks take time to launch and that attackers are limited to using a single IP address or subnet. However, modern computer attacks are usually launched using automated attack programs. These programs break into computers very quickly using only a few packets and can penetrate a host before an IDS detects and responds to the attack. The attack program can quickly install a back door. Then the attacker approaches the compromised machine from a new IP address, uses the back door, and the IDS does not detect the apparent normal entry into the host. Another problem occurs when the attacker is launching denial of service attacks. In this case each packet may be spoofed with a different IP address thus making filtering of the attack packets impossible.

Response Mechanisms Required

Assume an attacker has penetrated a network and corrupted some hosts. The ideal response gathers evidence of the attacker's activity, removes the attacker's access to the network, undoes the damage, and reconfigures the network to resist the attacker's penetration technique. It is impossible in today's environment to automate this ideal response since humans themselves have great difficulty enacting it. We can not automate what we ourselves can not do. However, we can automate an approximation of this ideal response. Our approximation should have the following capabilities not found in current automated response software :

- The ability to dynamically modify or shut down the target. This capability enables the IDS to automatically remove the intruder from the target, protect it from further damage by shutting it down, or perform an enhanced audit of the attacker's actions.
- The ability to dynamically modify or shut down the attacking host. With insider attacks, this enables the IDS to automatically stop the generation of the attack as well as record evidence of the attacker's actions.
- The ability to determine the host which is launching the attack. When attack packets are being spoofed, they can only be traced to an Ethernet wire by querying each router as to the source of the packets. Once the correct Ethernet is found, each host on the Ethernet must be analyzed in order to determine which is responsible for launching the attack. Thus an IDS must provide the capability to trace the path of an attacker.
- The ability to monitor all network traffic to and from the target. It is necessary to record for evidence the packets that the attacker sends to the target. In addition, it is necessary to record packets leaving the target since it may be used as a jump point to penetrate other hosts.
- The ability to modify the routing and firewall permission tables on every firewall and router. We often want to isolate the attacker or target in order to prevent further damage. Such isolation can limit legitimate traffic and so we want to optimally place the filters such that the attacker is constrained the most while allowing the most legitimate traffic.

This list of required capabilities needed to approximate an ideal response implies that security services are installed on every host and network device. This does not mean, however, that every network component needs to have an IDS installed that is aware of the rest of the network. Nor does it imply that these security services need to be proprietary solutions. Each network component could have a security server installed that performs some detect and response functions. The security servers may have a standard API that would allow them to be used by a distributed IDS scheme. Thus, every network device needs detect and respond capability but no single proprietary scheme needs to be installed everywhere.

It is unlikely that all network devices will soon be installed with security servers that can be controlled with a common API. It is also unlikely that companies will want to install a proprietary security solution on every host and network device. The cost of installation and maintenance of such a scheme would be overwhelming. Therefore, it seems unlikely that, without MAs, the security infrastructure that is needed to approximate the ideal response can be cost effectively implemented.

Automated Response Through MA

Mobile agent technology can solve the problem of installing and maintaining the security infrastructure needed to approximate an ideal response. Using MAs, it is not necessary to install a security server on every device as the MAs can automatically travel through the network, install the appropriate software on the appropriate types of network devices and also implement the distributed IDS that detects attacks and issues responses. This way, companies are not locked into using a single proprietary solution and uninstalling one solution and installing another can be almost automatic.

MAs enhance a system's ability to automatically respond because MAs make it possible to make all network components part of the same security scheme. Responses can be initiated at any place in the network, which gives systems the capability to optimize the locations at which they initiate responses. Furthermore, MAs enhance an IDS's ability to trace an attacker through the attacked network, to respond on the target, respond on the attacker, and to collect network/host evidence about the attack.

MAs do not add fundamentally new capabilities to automated response but they may help transition some automated response ideas from an impractical and costly scheme into a solution that can be implemented in a cost-effective manner.

Automated Tracing of Attackers

The IDSs tracing attacker's paths within IDS enabled networks may be possible in near future. This feature is useful for two reasons. First, attackers often log into a chain of many hosts before attacking a target. Thus, to find the attacker one must trace back along the chain. Second, attackers sometimes can spoof their source address. It is necessary to determine the actual source of these packets and the way to do this is to trace the packets from LAN to LAN until the source LAN is found. Finding the actual host launching the packets requires visiting the hosts within a LAN since attackers can spoof MAC addresses as well as IP addresses. Many attacks originate from outside of a network and thus could not ultimately be traced, however insider attacks are a large concern. Whether an attack is from an insider or an outsider, IDSs need to determine this and locate the location of the attacker as best as possible.

Effectively tracing an attacker from LAN to LAN requires the ability to sniff on every Ethernet segment in the network. Finding the host on an Ethernet segment that is lying about its identity requires analyzing each host on an Ethernet segment. Thus, to adequately trace an attacker through a network an IDS needs the capability to sniff on every Ethernet segment and to analyze every host. Ordinarily, the infrastructure required to support this kind of tracing would be prohibitively expensive. However, MAs provide a very cheap way to do this provided that MA platforms are widely installed.

There are several issues that a tracing system should address. If an attacker has compromised a host, then the MA platform may not function. Thus, any tracing system must gather data from many locations and compare the results. In addition, not all hosts may support MAs and thus the system will need to understand the topology of the network and sniff traffic at the optimal locations in order to pick up the attacker's trail.

Finally, what the attacker sends along each link in his attack chain may be completely different data. For example, the attacker could use link encryption. In this scenario, to trace the attacker the system may need to apply sophisticated artificial intelligence techniques or decision-making algorithms. Assuming the existence of MA platforms, the tracing system can automatically deploy across the network with very little installation time needed. The main research problem in building these systems is to anticipate a clever attacker. An automated tracing system needs to Intelligently collect evidence of an attacker's trail, adaptively operate when some hosts are not participating in the tracing scheme (e.g. not running an MA platform), and have the ability to search many paths simultaneously while not overwhelming the network with agents.

Automated Evidence Gathering

Currently, it is impractical to automatically gather evidence for an attack from many different sources. The problem is having the right software running at the right place at the right time. MAs offer the ability to run anything, anywhere, at any time. It is therefore conceivable that evidence may be gathered from different hardware platforms, different operating systems, and even different applications such as web servers. It is very easy to audit so much information on a host that the capacity to store the logs fills up quickly. It is even easier to run up against this barrier when saving the audit logs of every host on the network and trying to record the network traffic on each Ethernet wire. Thus, systems administrators cannot record all evidence in a network.

MAs may determine what types of evidence are most needed for that network, for the type of attack being investigated, and at what locations in the network. This is likely to be different if the evidence is for internal use as compared to legal use. The MAs may then move to the appropriate locations and start up relevant audit services (if they are not already enabled). MAs can thus intelligently audit the network by dynamically reconfiguring the audit capabilities of every host. The MAs can strongly audit suspicious or important network locations while lightly auditing other areas. Thus, MAs can reduce the amount of wasted evidence that must be stored.

Evidence gathering MAs should be in constant contact with IDSs that provide it with suspicious locations in the network. With this collaborative technique, evidence gathering MAs will often be able to fully audit host and network traffic generated by attackers.

MA Operations on an Attacker's Host

In the event of an attack, automated responses normally occur in the network at routers or firewalls. These elements typically try to separate the attacker from the target. However, if possible it would also be beneficial to launch automated responses on the attacker's host. Such a counter-attack may not succeed as the attacker has control of his own host and so this technique would not replace router or firewall-based responses. However, responding on the attacker's host gives an IDS a much greater power to restrict the attacker's actions. Having MA platforms installed throughout a network will enable IDSs to initiate these kinds of responses and thereby necessitate this type of research.

There are not many responses that can be taken by routers and firewalls to stop attacks. The responses consist of filtering out certain types of traffic or killing connections. Alternatively, there are an enormous number of useful responses that could be implemented on an attacker's host. What types of responses are most useful and what types of responses work best against an attacker using particular types of attack tools are to be researched.

MA Operations on a Target Host

When attacked, it is obviously vital to automatically respond on the target host. Such a response can prevent the attacker from using the penetrated host to further compromise one's network and to recover damage done by the attacker.

Much of the research defined for MA operations on the attacking host carry over to this area. However, the attacker will not typically be as firmly entrenched on the target host as he is on the attacking host. The attacker may only have user access, not administrator access to the host, and the attacker probably has not subverted many of the standard host services. Thus, if an IDS acts quickly, the target host will be a correctly functioning system that has an attacker as one of its users.

An MA can be sent by an IDS to the target to engage the attacker. Since the MA is automated it may often move faster than an attacker's manual actions. However, an attacker may use automated tools that can act faster than the MA. Despite the fact that the MA may lose the battle for the target, an IDS should dispatch an MA in the hopes of its success.

The MA needs to determine how the attacker is controlling the system. As the attacker attempts to gain privilege on the system, the MA should counter these attempts and attempt to remove the attacker. The MA will probably need to make use of the attack detected by the IDS in order to figure out how the attacker is controlling the system.

Depending upon the type of host penetrated, the MA may simply take the host down or may try and keep vital services operational while delaying the attacker until a systems administrator can evaluate the situation.

Isolating the Attacker/Isolating the Target

As appealing as they may sound, actions to automatically respond on the target and attacking host may fail. It is vital that uncompromised machines respond at the network level to limit an attacker's actions. Three strategies exist to deter an attacker : isolating the target, isolating the attacker, and creating a cut set between the target and attacker. The fact that MAs can travel to all network elements to implement responses is what enables them to perform these strategies.

Isolating the target involves encircling the target with a barrier such that the target can not launch attacks on the rest of the network. A simple way to erect such a barrier is to cut-off all network traffic along the edge of the circle. More sophisticated filters can be researched that allow "safe" services through the circle. The research problem is that the barrier will probably cut-off some legitimate communication. The network topology must be taken into account and encircle the target should be encircled such that as much vital communication as possible is allowed to continue while still encircling the target. Furthermore, some systems that cannot be allowed to compromise must be placed outside of the circle while other systems that must communicate with the target must be placed inside of the circle. This is an optimization problem that will also require research to properly implement.

Isolating the attacker involves the same logic as isolating the target. One wants to draw a circle around the attacker, as tight as possible, such that the attacker cannot launch attacks through the circle. Again, some hosts may need to communicate with the attacker and thus must reside within the circle.

A third option is to create a cut set between the target and the attacker. This merely separates the two protagonists with an impenetrable boundary. It does not attempt to stop that attacker or the target from attacking other hosts in the network. Creating a cut set is useful when one is primarily concerned about the attacker reaching the target. The cut set technique always can be set-up to eliminate no more legitimate communication than the isolating attacker or isolating target techniques.

MA Operations on Attacker and Target Subnet

MAs can be used to respond on attacker and target hosts because of their flexibility in initiating responses. But, the drawback is that these MAs would sometimes fail in the face of sophisticated attackers. Isolating attackers and targets at routers and firewalls so that the attacker could not thwart the response means that sometimes legitimate traffic can be cut-off. A third response alternative that can be implemented using MAs is for an MA to travel to an uncompromised host on the attacker's or target's subnet. From this position, the MA can launch attacks against the attacking or target host to stop it from functioning. MAs may utilize well-known vulnerabilities or may simply flood the attacker and target hosts with packets. Since MAs can travel to multiple hosts, they can muster sufficient network resources needed to flood any attacked machine. The MAs can then keep the target and attacker from doing further damage until a systems administrator evaluates the situation.

Benefits and Drawbacks

A number of advantages of using mobile code and mobile agent computing paradigms include : overcoming network latency as they can be dispatched from a central controller to carry out operations directly at the remote point of interest, reducing network load as mobile agents along with the computational code travel to the place of data instead of transfer of data itself, executing asynchronously and autonomously as they allow for discontinued operation, structure and composition of mobile agents as they allow for a natural way to structure and design an IDS, adapting dynamically as they can be retracted, dispatched, cloned, or put to sleep as network and host condition changes, operating in heterogeneous environments, and having robust and fault-tolerant behaviour.

The obvious disadvantage of using MAs is the concern that they will introduce vulnerabilities into the network. MA solutions may not perform fast enough to meet the IDS's needs. In addition, the MAs may contain large amounts of code thus prohibiting rapid transfers between hosts. Finally, limited industry experience and modeling tools for formulating MA solutions to applications in general and IDSs in particular are also factors, as is the additional complexity involved in developing agent-based applications when compared with more traditional forms.

The security threats can be classified into four broad categories : agent-to-agent, agent-to-platform, platform-to-agent, and other-to-agent platform.

Not only must IDSs detect attacks quickly, but they must also process system events in real time. This task is becoming ever more difficult as network bandwidth increases. Mobile agent software will generally hinder rather than help an IDS's ability to rapidly process events and detect attacks. MA runtime environments slow down IDS especially if they are implemented in slow interpreted languages.

IDSs are complex pieces of software. Agents that perform IDS services may thus be required to contain a large amount of code. If these agents are supposed to do operating system specific tasks on multiple operating systems then this code base may get extremely large. The size of MA code may limit the functionality of IDS because it will take a long time to transfer an agent between hosts. In addition, such a transfer will require greater computing and network resources. A possible solution to this problem is to have some agents statically locate themselves and have them offer standard Application Programming Interfaces (APIs) to agents that move between machines. Thus, the majority of the code base for the IDS remains stationary while the minority part is mobile.

Large enterprise networks are comprised of several different hardware platforms, running several different operating systems, each having different configurations and running different applications. It is not trivial for the mobile agents to have *a priori* knowledge about how a system is configured, how data is arranged, and still remain lightweight. Static and less transient agents may be more familiar with how data is locally arranged and accessed, and able to act as intermediaries between mobile agents and other platforms. Localized data may be more efficiently manipulated through standard APIs.

The client-server computing paradigm is well understood and quite mature as a technology, but the area of distributed control of mobile agent systems is still the subject of many research efforts. An agent's envisioned autonomous behaviour, involving collaboration with other agents at various network locations, creates a dynamic environment that requires new design methodologies and modeling tools to properly formulate and construct agent-based systems. The lack of mature agent design methodologies and modeling tools makes this task difficult, but the problem is likely to be overcome as commercial demand for these product increases and is eventually satisfied.

MAs that are developed in-house or purchased from trusted vendors are likely to undergo the same software engineering methods as their non-mobile counterparts in order to assure the quality of code. This standard development process historically produces code with many faults. MAs' inherent capabilities, such as moving and cloning, add more complexity to the design and development process. Given this added complexity, IDS will be even more prone to faults than their non-MA counterparts.

Conclusion

At first glance, mobile agent technology offers much to the field of intrusion detection. The idea of mobile and autonomous components intuitively seems useful in intrusion detection and many other applications. However, it is difficult to realize the benefits of mobile agent technology in practice. Despite these difficulties, the technology appears to provide valuable extensions to current capabilities. Although the barriers to creating practical mobile agent systems are high, the ability to move a running program from one hardware platform to another is a useful feature. Ultimately, as the security, performance, emerging technology, and standards barriers that inhibit this technology fall, mobile agents will enter mainstream use. Not only do mobile agents appear to be useful in general, but they appear useful to IDSs. Mobile agents may enhance the performance of IDSs and even offer them new capabilities. However, obtaining these benefits is not easy and will require a substantial commitment of resources to research. There are three main research areas for using MAs to do intrusion detection : performance enhancements, IDS design improvements, and response improvements.

References

1. Anderson, James P., "Computer Security Threat Monitoring and Surveillance," Technical Report, James P. Anderson Co., Fort Washington, PA, April 1980.
2. Amoroso, Edward, Intrusion Detection, Intrusion.net Books, Sparta, New Jersey, 1999.
3. M. Asaka, S. Okazawa, A. Taguchi, and S. Goto, "A Method of Tracing Intruders by Use of Mobile Agents," INET'99, June 1999.
4. Jai Balasubramaniyan, Jose Omar Garcia-Fernandez, David Isacoff, E.H. Spafford, and Diego Zamboni, "An Architecture for Intrusion Detection using Autonomous Agents," Department of Computer Sciences, Purdue University; Coast TR 98-05, 1998. <URL : http ://www.cs.purdue.edu/coast/coast-library.html>
5. Jeffrey, M. Bradshaw, "An Introduction to Software Agents," In Jeffrey M. Bradshaw, editor, Software Agents, chapter 1. AAAI Press/The MIT Press, 1997.
6. Denning, Dorothy E., "An Intrusion Detection Model," IEEE Transactions on Software Engineering, Vol. SE-13, No. 2, pp. 222-32, February 1987.
7. Guy Helmer, Johnny S.K. Wong, Vasant Honavar, and Les Miller, "Intelligent Agents for Intrusion Detection." Proceedings, IEEE Information Technology Conference, Syracuse, NY, pp. 121-24, September 1998.

Network Security Using Virtual Private Networks

S. Ramakrishnan and T. Deiwanayakam

Introduction

Businesses today are faced with supporting a wider variety of communications among a wide range of sites. They want to achieve this challenge with a reduction in the cost of the communications infrastructure. Employees want to access the resources of their corporate intranets as they take to the road, telecommute, or dial in from customer sites. Business partners are joining together in extranet environments to share business information for projects with long-term strategic advantages. Hence, businesses are finding that past solutions to wide-area networking between main corporate network and branch offices, such as dedicated leased lines or frame-relay circuits, do not provide the flexibility required for creating new partner links quickly or for supporting project teams in the field. VPNs using the Internet can solve many of these business-networking problems [IEC01].

Virtual. Virtual means not real or in a different state of being. In a VPN, private communication between two or more devices is achieved through a public network the Internet. Therefore, the communication is virtually but not physically there.

Private. Private means to keep something a secret from the general public. Although those two devices are communicating with each other in a public environment, there is no third party who can interrupt this communication or receive any data that is exchanged between them.

Network. A network consists of two or more devices that can freely and electronically communicate with each other via cables and wire. A VPN is a network. It can transmit information over long distances effectively and efficiently.

The term VPN has been associated in the past with such remote connectivity services as the Public Switched Telephone Network (PSTN), but VPN networks have finally started to be linked with IP-based data networking. Before IP-based networking corporations had spend considerable amounts of time and resources, to set-up complex private networks, now commonly called Intranets. These networks were installed using costly leased line services, Frame Relay, and ATM to incorporate remote users. For the smaller sites and mobile workers on the remote end, companies supplemented their networks with remote access servers or ISDN.

Small to medium-sized companies, who could not afford dedicated leased lines, used lowspeed switched services. As the Internet became more and more accessible and bandwidth capacities grew, companies began to put their Intranets onto the web and create what are now known as Extranets to link internal and external users. However, as cost-effective and quick to-deploy as the Internet is, there is one fundamental problem—security. Today's VPN solutions overcome the security factor using special tunneling protocols and complex encryption procedures, data integrity and privacy is achieved, and the new connection produces what seems to be a dedicated point-to-point connection. And, because these operations occur over a public network, VPNs can cost significantly less to implement than privately owned or leased services. Although early VPNs required extensive expertise to implement, technology has matured to a level where deployment can be a simple and affordable solution for businesses of all sizes. VPNs operate at either layer 2 or layer 3 of the OSI model (Open Systems Interconnection). Layer-2 VPN uses the layer 2 frame such as the Ethernet while layer 3 uses layer 3 packets such as IP. The connection of VPN over a public network is shown in Figure 42.1.

Simply put, a VPN, Virtual Private Network, is defined as a network that uses public network paths but maintains the security and protection of private networks [VPN02].

What is Tunneling?

Tunneling can be defined as a way to transfer data between two similar networks over an intermediate network. Tunneling encloses one type of data packet into the packet of another protocol. Before the encapsulation takes place, the packets are encrypted so that the data is unreadable to anyone monitoring the network. These encapsulated packets travel through the Internet until they reach their intended destination. Once there, the packets are separated and returned to their original format [JOH05]. See Figure 42.2 for the connection of tunnel.

Tunneling generally involves three different protocols :

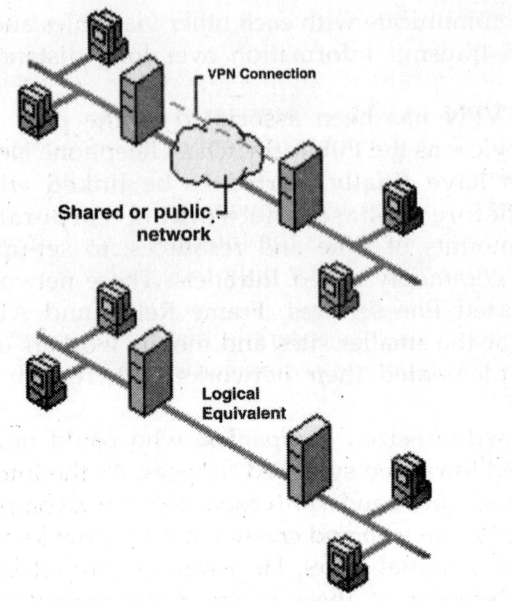

FIG. 42.1
Virtual Private Network

Carrier Protocol : This is the protocol used by the network that the information is traveling over, usually TCP/IP.
Encapsulating Protocol : This is the protocol that the original data is packaged in, like GRE, IPSec, L2F, PPTP, or L2TP.
Passenger Protocol : The original or native data that is being carried from the network where the originating host resides like IPX, AppleTalk, or IP.

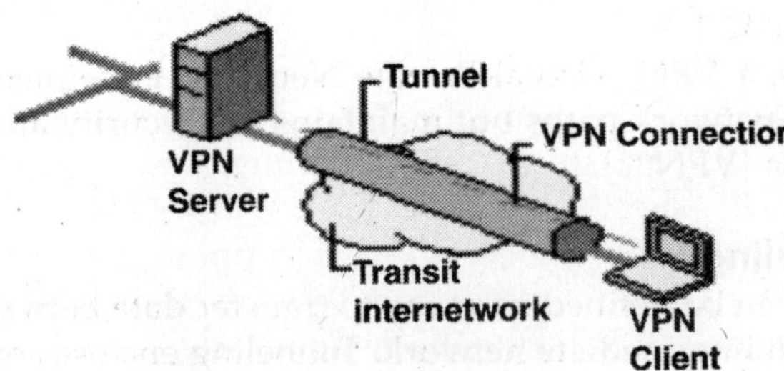

FIG. 42.2
VPN Tunnel [MIC04]

Components of the VPN

VPN consists of hardware and software, but they also require a set of components. These components are simply requirements ensuring the VPN is secure, available and easy to maintain [STE06].

The requirements are :

Authentication : Authentication is the process of verifying the identities of site locations as well as individual users.
Access Control : This ensures that only authorized users are given access to the network.
Confidentiality : This keeps anyone from examining or copying data during transmission across the Internet. *Encryption algorithms* are used to scramble the data so that only those who have the encryption key can read the information.
Data Integrity : This makes certain that no tampering or altering of the data occurs during transmission across the Internet. This is done using *hash algorithms.*

Categories of VPN

(1) *Trusted VPN* : A customer "trusted" the leased circuits of a service provider and used it to communicate without interrupt. Although it is "trusted" it is not secured.
(2) *Secure VPN* : With security becoming more of an issue for users, encryption and decryption was used on both ends to safeguard the information passed to and fro. This ensured the security needed to satisfy corporations, customers, and providers.
(3) *Hybrid VPN* : A mix of a secure and trusted VPN. A customer controls the secure parts of the VPN while the provider, such as an ISP, guarantees the trusted aspect.
(4) *Provider-provisioned VPN* : A VPN that is administered by a service provider.

VPN Architectures

Remote Access VPNs

A remote access VPN connection shown in Figure 42.3 is made by a remote access client, or a single user computer, that connects to a private network [CSUN03].

The user connects to a local ISP that supports VPN using plain old telephone services (POTS), integrated services digital network (ISDN), digital subscriber line (DSL), etc. The remote access client (the VPN client) authenticates itself to the remote access server (the VPN server) and, for mutual authentication; the server authenticates itself to the client. The VPN device at the ISP accepts the user's login, then establishes the tunnel to the VPN device at the organization's office and finally begins forwarding packets over the Internet. Remote access VPN offers advantages such as :

- Reduced capital costs associated with modem and terminal server equipment

- ➢ Greater scalability and easy to add new users.
- ➢ Reduced long-distance telecommunication costs.

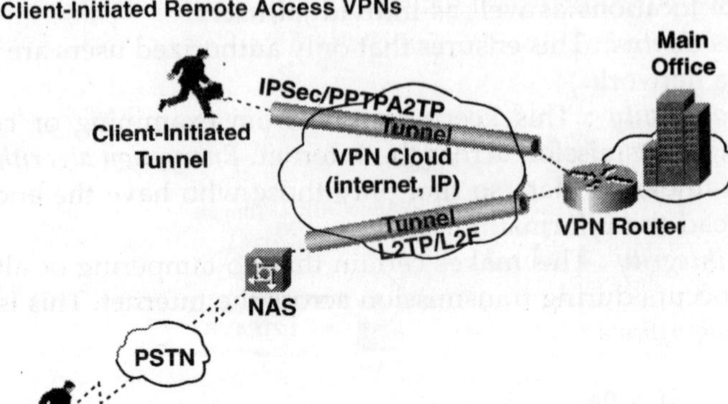

FIG. 42.3
Remote Access VPNIntranet VPNs

It is also known as "router-to-router" or "site-to-site" VPNs. These types of VPNs can be build using the Internet, or even over a part of the ISPs private IP infrastructure. An IP WAN infrastructure uses IPSec or GRE to create secure traffic tunnels across the network which is shown in Figure 42.4.

Benefits of an intranet VPN include the following :

- ➢ Reduced WAN bandwidth costs, efficient use of WAN bandwidth.
- ➢ Flexible topologies.
- ➢ Congestion avoidance with the use of bandwidth management traffic shaping.

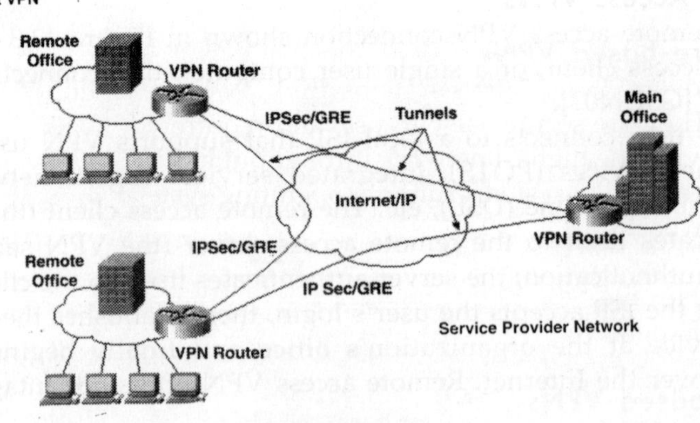

FIG. 42.4
Intranet VPN

Extranet VPNs

Extranet VPNs use many of the same technologies as Intranet VPNs. Extranets differ from intranets in that they allow access by remote users or business partners outside of their company's corporate internal network. The extranet VPN is shown in Figure 42.5.

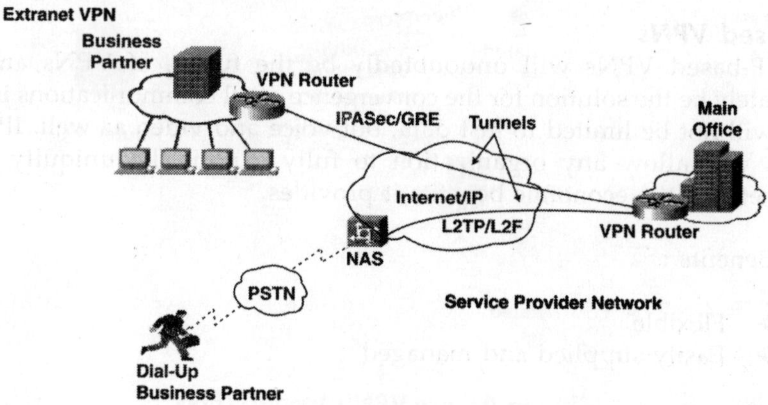

FIG. 42.5
Extranet VPN

Types of VPNs

Software-Based VPNs

Software-based VPNs are ideal in situations where both endpoints of the VPN are not controlled by same organization. It is also best choice where performance requirements are not critical, like remote users connecting over dial-up links.

Drawbacks :

- Performance will degrade progressively as more users are added.

Hardware-based VPNs

Hardware-based VPNs systems are VPN concentrators or VPN-capable routers. They are secure, easy to use, and require very little effort to install. They provide the highest network throughput since they don't need to waste CPU overhead like systems running operating systems or other applications.

Drawbacks :

- Flexible
- Expensive

Firwall-based VPNs

Firwall-based VPNs take advantage of the firewall's security mechanisms, including restricting access to the internal network.

Drawbacks :

- Expensive if no existing firewall is installed.
- Combined firewall/VPN is more complex to maintain and configure.

IP-based VPNs

IP-based VPNs will undoubtedly be the future of VPNs and will ultimately be the solution for the convergence of all communications in total. This will not be limited to just data, but voice and video as well. IP-based VPNs will allow any organization to fully exploit the uniquity of the Internet and the economic benefits it provides.

Benefits :

- Flexible
- Easily supplied and managed

Benefits of VPNs

A well-designed VPN can greatly benefit a company. It can—

- Reduce transmit time and transportation costs for remote users.
- Reduce operational costs versus a traditional WAN.
- Provide flexibility.
- Extend geographic connectivity.
- Reduce demands for technical support services.
- Improve security.
- Provide telecommuter support.
- Improve productivity.
- Provide faster Return On Investment (ROI) than a traditional WAN.
- Provide broadband networking capability.
- Provide global networking opportunities.

Conclusion

VPN is an emerging technology that has come a long way. From an insecure break off of Public Telephone networks to a powerful business aid that uses the Internet as its gateway. As the cost of long-distance telephone calls and leased lines continue to drop, fewer companies may feel the need to switch to VPNs for remote access.

VPN's technology is still developing, and this is a great advantage to businesses, which need to have technology that is able to scale and grow along with them. The success of VPNs also depends on the ability of intranets and extranets to deliver on their promises. VPN will also help to make the possibility of a business expanding its services over long distances and globally, more of a reality.

REFERENCES

1. [IEC01] http ://www.iec.org/online/tutorials/vpn/
2. [VPN02] http ://www.vpnc.org/vpn-technologies.pdf
3. [CSUN03]www.csun.edu/~vcact00f/311/termProjects/700class Virtual% 20 Private%20 Network.doc
4. [MIC04] http ://www.microsoft.com/windows2000/docs/VPNoverview.doc
5. [JOH05] John Maries, "VPNs A Beginner's Guide", Tata McGraw-Hill Edition, 2002.
6. [STE06] Steven Brown, "Implementing Virtual Private Networks", Tata McGraw-Hill Edition, 2000.

Digital Signature in XML

N.R. Wankhade, S.H. Patil and P.D. Patil

Introduction

This paper examines the requirements of signatures, outlines the technologies involved in creating digital signatures, and describes the components of the Digital Signature Standard (DSS). The basic concepts, not the math, are the focus of the technology investigation. Public key encryption algorithms and secure hash algorithms are explained and discussed.

Public key technology is well suited to providing digital signatures. Typically, the signature for an object is created by hashing the object with a one-way hash function and encrypting (signing) the hash value with the private key component of a public/private key pair. The signature is verified by decrypting it with the public key component to expose the hash value and comparing the exposed hash value to a recomputed hash value. If the two hash values match the signature is often considered valid. But is it?

At issue is the identity of the owner of the public/private key pair, i.e., the identity of the user claiming to control access to the private key component that was used to create the signature. In order to validate a signature a recipient must know the identity of the owner and the degree to which the owner protects the private key from disclosure. A signature is of little value when it is not known who created it since the significance of the data object can not be quantified without knowledge of its origin. Also, if an owner does not protect a private key from disclosure, then there is no way of knowing if it was really the owner who created the signature.

Within a small community of users, it is reasonable to assume that all users know the public keys of all other users and that all users know the degree to which all other users protect their private keys from disclosure. Individual users may construct their own quasi-small communities by contacting other users and exchanging public keys and other relevant information via various *ad-hoc* and semi-formal mechanisms. This model has served and continues to serve a growing community of user's concerned about the security of their communications. However, it falls very far short of being a solution for the global internet. The global internet needs a mechanism with which users can acquire the public key of any other user and be able to quantify two things :

➤ The assurance that the identity bound to the public key is correct.
➤ The degree to which the owner protects the private key from disclosure.

We propose to examine the issues and to suggest a criteria with which a user or a user's organization can determine what their requirements are and judge whether existing applications and protocols, and those currently under development, will meet their needs.

Today communicating through email has become a part of our daily lives. More and more official correspondence is also done electronically. There is main concerns regarding internet security when transferring sensitive data (i.e. Tampering).

Tampering : Information that is being transmitted can be changed replaced before the intended party receives the information. An example would be the amount deposited changed or the intended account substituted.

Digital signatures are used to defeat data tampering. When encrypted data is sent, a Digital signature is also sent. The receiving party uses the digital signature to validate the contents of the encrypted data. If data differs in so much as a comma or extra character validation fails.

Concept of Digital Signature

A Digital Signature is an electronic Signature that can be used to authenticate the identity of the sender of a message or the designer of a document, and possibly to ensure that the original content of the message or document that has been sent is unchanged. Digital Signature are easily transportable, cannot be imitated by someone else and can be automatically time stamped. The ability to ensure that the original signed message arrived means that the sender cannot easily repudiate it later.

This is an overview of the securing and desecuring process of files. When using any form of communication, there are a number of security risks.

The main risks are that someone will :

➤ Intercept a message and read its contents.
➤ Send a message under someone else's name and signature.

➢ Change the contents of a message.
➢ Deny sending message.

To reduce these risks, four security services have evolved over time :

➢ Confidentiality—evidence that the contents of the message have not been disclosed to third parties.
➢ Authentication—a guarantee that a message really has come from the person who claims to have sent it.
➢ Integrity—proof that the message contents have not been altered.
➢ Non repudiation—the certainty of knowing that the sender of the message cannot later deny having sent it.

Private and Public Keys

In a public keys system each user has two pairs of keys : two private keys that are kept secret, and two public keys that are made available to all the other users. Private key is used to encrypt information.

Digital signatures deliver critical authentication, tamperproofing and nonrepudiation services for legally enforceable transactions, so it's only a matter of time before they're adopted everywhere in the business-to-business arena. But it's doubtful that many business-to-business trading communities will rush to implement digital signatures without a flexible, general-purpose standards framework for applying and validating signatures on electronic documents. Fortunately, the standards community is well along in defining such a framework : XML Digital Signatures (XML-DSig). XML-DSig is a set of draft specifications that has considerable industry support where it counts : early vendor implementation and ongoing interoperability testing.

What's most important, the XML-DSig framework is application-independent and supports signing of any content type, XML or non-XML, as long as that content can be addressed across the Internet, extranet or intranet via Uniform Resource Identifiers (URI). XML-DSig defines procedures for binding cryptographic signatures to one or more URI-addressable local or network resource and for validating those signatures. XML-DSig also specifies an XML syntax for defining signature blocks that can be embedded in all content types.

Current security technologies in common deployment are insufficient for securing business transactions on the Web. Most existing browser-based security mechanisms, generally adequate for low-value business-to-consumer transactions, do not provide the enhanced security or flexibility required for protecting high-value commercial transactions and the sensitive data exchanges that comprise them.

For instance, Secure Sockets Layer (SSL) provides for the secure interchange of sensitive data between a browser and Web server, but once received, the data is all too frequently left unprotected on the server. In fact, SSL protects the data at a point in its travels when its confidentiality is, relatively speaking, far less likely to be attacked. If you were a hacker, which would you think is a better application of your time : sniffing IP packets in transit in order to obtain a single user's credit card number or breaking into a back-end database containing thousands of credit card numbers? This problem is aggravated in the case where a message is routed from server to server. If the data itself were encrypted, as opposed to just its transport, it would help reduce the incidents of unencrypted data left vulnerable on public servers.

As important as protecting the confidentiality of business messages is ensuring their long-term authenticity (who sent them?), data integrity (have they been modified in transit?), and support for non-repudiation (can the sender deny sending them?); in other words, functionality that ubiquitous, existing Internet security technologies (e.g., SSL and username/password) do not provide alone. The globally-recognized method for satisfying these requirements for secure business transactions is to use digital certificates to enable the encryption and digital signing of the exchanged data. A brief introduction to these concepts is provided below. The term "public key infrastructure" (PKI) is used to describe the processes, policies, and standards that govern the issuance, maintenance, and revocation of the certificates, public, and private keys that the encryption and signing operations require.

The very features that make XML so powerful for business transactions (e.g., semantically rich and structured data, text-based, and Web-ready nature) provide both challenges and opportunities for the application of encryption and digital signature operations to XML-encoded data. For example, in many workflow scenarios where an XML document flows stepwise between participants, and where a digital signature implies some sort of commitment or assertion, each participant may wish to sign only that portion for which they are responsible and assume a concomitant level of liability. Older standards for digital signatures provide neither syntax for capturing this sort of high-granularity signature nor mechanisms for expressing which portion a principal wishes to sign.

Two new security initiatives designed to both account for and take advantage of the special nature of XML data are XML Signature and XML Encryption. Both are currently progressing through the standardization process. XML Signature is a joint effort between the World Wide Web Consortium (W3C) and Internet Engineering Task Force (IETF), and XML Encryption is solely W3C effort. This article presents a brief introduction to the XML Signature specification and the underlying cryptographic concepts.

An Introduction to Public Key Cryptography

Public key cryptography allows users of an insecure network, like the Internet, to exchange data with confidence that it will be neither modified nor inappropriately accessed. This is accomplished through a transformation of the data according to an algorithm parameterized by a pair of numbers —the so-called public and private keys. Each participant in the exchange has such a pair of keys. They make the public key freely available to anyone wishing to communicate with them, and they keep the other key private and protected. Although the keys are mathematically related, if the cryptosystem has been designed and implemented securely, it is computationally infeasible to derive the private key from knowledge of the public key.

The nature of the relation between the public and private keys is such that a cryptographic transformation encoded with one key can only be reversed with the other. This defining feature of public key encryption technology enables confidentiality because a message encrypted with the public key of a specific recipient can only be decrypted by the holder of the matching private key (i.e., the recipient, if they have properly protected access to the private key). Even if intercepted by someone else, without the appropriate private key, this third party will be unable to decrypt the message. It's crucial that confidentiality can be supported without requiring that the sender and recipient exchange any "secret" data in addition to the message itself, as is the case in symmetric cryptography. Indeed it was precisely the requirement of key exchange between sender and recipient, which quickly becomes impractical as the number of participants increases, that motivated the invention of public-key cryptography.

Although confidentiality is typically the first aspect of cryptography that comes to mind, the special relationship between public and private keys also enables functionality that has no parallel in symmetric cryptography; namely, authentication (ensuring that the identity of the sender can be determined by anyone) and integrity (ensuring that any alterations of the message content can be easily spotted by anyone). These new features and, through them, support for non-repudiation (ensuring the origin or delivery of data in order to protect the sender against false denial by the recipient that the data has been received or to protect the recipient against false denial by the sender that the data has been sent) provide electronic messages with a mechanism analogous to signatures in the paper world, that is, a digital signature.

To create a digital signature for a message, the data to be signed is transformed by an algorithm that takes as input the private key of the sender. Because a transformation determined by the sender's private key can only be undone if the reverse transform takes as a parameter the sender's public key, a recipient of the transformed data can be confident of the origin of the data (the identity of the sender). If the data can be verified using the sender's public key, then it must have been signed using the corresponding private key (to which only the sender should have access).

For signature verification to be meaningful, the verifier must have confidence that the public key does actually belong to the sender (otherwise an impostor could claim to be the sender, presenting her own public key in place of the real one). A certificate, issued by a Certification Authority, is an assertion of the validity of the binding between the certificate's subject and her public key such that other users can be confident that the public key does indeed correspond to the subject who claims it as her own.

Largely due to the performance characteristics of public-key algorithms, the entire message data is typically not itself transformed directly with the private key. Instead a small unique thumbprint of the document, called a "hash" or "digest", is transformed. Because the hashing algorithm is very sensitive to any changes in the source document, the hash of the original allows a recipient to verify that the document was not altered (by comparing the hash that was sent to them with the hash they calculate from the document they received). Additionally, by transforming the hash with their private key, the sender also allows the recipient to verify that it was indeed the sender that performed the transformation (because the recipient was able to use the sender's public key to "undo" the transformation). The hash of a document, transformed with the sender's private key, thereby acts as a digital signature for that document and can be transmitted openly along with the document to the recipient. The recipient verifies the signature by taking a hash of the message and inputting it to a verification algorithm along with the signature that accompanied the message and the sender's public key. If the result is successful, the recipient can be confident of both the authenticity and integrity of the message.

Introduction to XML Signatures

XML signatures are digital signatures designed for use in XML transactions. The standard defines a schema for capturing the result of a digital signature operation applied to arbitrary (but often XML) data. Like non-XML-aware digital signatures (e.g., PKCS), XML signatures add authentication, data integrity, and support for non-repudiation to the data that they sign. However, unlike non-XML digital signature standards, XML signature has been designed to both account for and take advantage of the Internet and XML.

A fundamental feature of XML Signature is the ability to sign only specific portions of the XML tree rather than the complete document. This will be relevant when a single XML document may have a long history in which the different components are authored at different times by different parties, each signing only those elements relevant to itself. This flexibility will also be critical in situations where it is important to ensure the integrity of certain portions of an XML document, while leaving open the possibility for other portions of the document to change. Consider, for example, a signed XML form delivered to a user for completion. If the signature were over the full XML form, any change by the user to the default form values would invalidate the original signature.

An XML signature can sign more than one type of resource. For example, a single XML signature might cover character-encoded data (HTML), binary-encoded data (a JPG), XML-encoded data, and a specific section of an XML file.

Signature validation requires that the data object that was signed be accessible. The XML signature itself will generally indicate the location of the original signed object. This reference can :

- be referenced by a URI within the XML signature;
- reside within the same resource as the XML signature (the signature is a sibling);
- be embedded within the XML signature (the signature is the parent); and
- have its XML signature embedded within itself (the signature is the child).

Future Scope

Multiple Signature : This feature will provide the signing of a message by multiple users. The feature might be helpful in real world scenario in which a particular message is needed to be signed and counter by more than one user.

Conclusion

Digital signature provides facility to sign a mail. The client can also verify if the mail sent by the sender is tampered in between the network.

Network Security Using Biometrics

S. ANANDHI AND B. ARUL VENDHAN

Introduction

Network security is a complicated subject, which can be tackled by well-trained and experienced experts. Now-a-days biometrics makes the task more simple by providing prominent security to the users.

Your own personal identity is the best source of security. That is why biometric technology is becoming more common in and across the nation. Biometrics identifies people through their voice patterns, fingerprints, and facial and retina structures. Today medical facilities, airports and local companies are turning to biometrics and doing away with old forms of identification—PIN numbers and passwords.

In a technological world where hackers lurk behind masked doors, there is no price tag for information security. Finding the right technology to save your company from virtual dangers is crucial in today's fast-paced work environment. Protecting your company's information assets is so important. Choosing the right technology becomes tedious. It's easy to see why the demand for reliable network security is high. More than ever, we are using e-mail, and relying on network-based communications. In fact, network-based transactions have grown at a rate that far exceeds our ability to ensure the security of those transactions.

By replacing, or working in concert with current security methods (PIN codes, passwords, smart cards, tokens), biometrics enhance the level of security and convenience available to the user.

There are a variety of biometric technologies relevant to network security. Voice verification and facial scans are currently the two most widely used. Part of the reason is that the necessary hardware infrastructure is already in place to use these technologies. For voice verification, telephones, speakers and microphones are virtually universal and widely accepted. Soon, PC's will be available with image capture devices or digital cameras as standard equipment. Neither method is particularly more expensive.

Why is Internet Insecure?

The Internet is insecure for variety of reasons. Those factors include—

- Lack of education
- Internet's design
- Proprietarism
- Trickling down of technology
- Human nature.

Each of these factors contributes in some degree to the Internet's current lack of security.

Does the Internet Really Need to be Secure?

Yes, the Internet does need to be secure and not simple for reasons of national security. Today it is a matter of personal security. The threat from lax security is more than just a financial one. Banking records are extremely personal and contain reveling information. Until the Internet is secure, this information is available to any one with the technical prowess to crack a bank's online service.

Can the Internet be Secure?

Yes, the Internet can be secure. But in order for that to happen, some serious changes must be made, including the heightening of public awareness to the problem. Most users still regard the Internet as a toy. That needs to change in coming years. Even then we can't say it is cent percent secure. The availability of high-grade technological information both strengthens and weaknesses make security. There is a real need for Internet security.

Types of Network Attacks

A typical attack is not a simple, one-step procedure. It's rare that an attacker can get online or dial up a remote computer and use only one method to gain full access. It's more likely that the attacker will need several techniques in combination to bypass the many layers of protection standing between the attacker and root administrative access.

Physical Attacks

The stereotypical image conjured by most people when they hear the term *hacker* is that imagined feature of a DRAGON. A real hacker need to rely on physical and interpersonal skills such as social engineering and other "wet work" that involves human interaction. Because most people have a false stereotype of hackers, they fail to realize that the person they're chatting with in the office or talking to on the phone may in fact be a hacker in disguise. In fact, this common misunderstanding is one of the hacker's greatest assets.

Social Engineering

Social engineering, or interpersonal manipulation, is not unique to hacking. In fact, many people use this type of trickery every day, both criminally and professionally. You are probably guilty of using social engineering techniques to get something you wanted. Whether it's haggling for a lower price on a lawnmower at a garage sale or convincing your spouse you really need that new toy or outfit, you manipulated the "target." While your motives may have been beginning—if a bit selfish—you're guilty of socially engineering the other party.

Lost Password

One of the most common goals of an attack is to obtain a valid user account and password. In fact, sometimes this is the only way that an attacker can bypass security measures. If a company uses firewalls, intrusion-detection systems, and more, the attacker needs to "borrow" a real account in order to obtain root access and set-up a new account for himself or herself. How can someone get this information? One of the easiest ways is to trick someone else into giving it away.

For example, many organizations use a Virtual Private Network (VPN) that allows remote employees to connect to the network from home—essentially becoming part of the local network. This is a very popular method of allowing people to work from home, but is also a potential weak spot in any security perimeter. Because VPNs are set-up and maintained by the IT department, attackers often impersonate real users, asking one of the IT staff for the password by pretending to have lost the settings. If the IT employee believes the person, he or she willingly and often gladly hands over the keys. Voila! The attacker now can connect from anywhere on the Internet and use an authorized account to work deeper into the network.

Imagine if you were the lowly IT staff person on call and the CEO rang you up at 10 : 30 p.m., irate about a lost password. Would you want to deny her access, with the possibility of losing your job? Probably not. This type of fear is an attacker's best friend.

Social Spying

Social spying is the process of using observation to acquire information. While social engineering can provide an attacker with crucial information, small businesses are more resistant to social engineering because people in small companies all know each other. For example, if one of the IT staff received a call from an attacker pretending to be a distressed CEO, she would probably recognize the voice as not belonging to the real CEO. In this case, social spying becomes more important.

To illustrate one of the non-technical ways in which social spying can be used, consider how many people handle their ATM cards. Do you hide your PIN when you get cash at the ATM? Most people don't; they whip out the card and punch the numbers without noticing who might be watching. If someone else memorizes the PIN, he'll have all the information needed to access the funds in the account—provided that he can get his hands on the ATM card. If he snatches the owner's purse after the ATM transaction, he might get not only the money just withdrawn from the ATM, but the ATM card. Then he could easily go back and withdraw the entire day's limit.

Snooping on people as they actively type their user information isn't the only technique. Most offices have at least a few people who post passwords on or near their computer monitors. This type of blatant disregard for security is every network administrator's worst nightmare.

Dumpster Diving

Have you ever thrown away a credit card statement without shredding it? If so, you're a potential target. While you may consider your trash to be sacred territory, or believe that no one is interested in it because it's dirty, your trash and the trash of your company often constitutes a gold mine. Fishing through garbage to find passwords, also known as *dumpster diving*, can provide an attacker with the crucial information needed to take over your network.

Consider this scenario. You're a network administrator and you receive an anonymous tip that people are posting passwords all around the office. What would you do? Most administrators immediately investigate and send out a memo to everyone in the company stating that this activity is not allowed, and that violations will be dealt with harshly. While this may get everyone to temporarily take down those Post-it passwords, the problem has only been exacerbated; all those passwords are now headed right to the anonymous tipster—who's waiting at the dumpster.

Sniffing

A *sniffer* is a program or device that monitors all information passing through a computer network. It "sniffs" the data passing through the network off the wire and determines where the data is going, where it originated, and what it is. In addition to these basic functions, sniffers can have extra features that allow them to filter one type of data, capture passwords, and more. There are even some sniffers—for example, the FBI's controversial mass-monitoring tool formerly known as *Carnivore*—that can rebuild files sent across a network, such as an email or web page.

A sniffer is one of the most important information-gathering tools in a hacker's arsenal. The sniffer gives the hacker a complete picture of the data sent and received by the computer or network that the sniffer is monitoring. This data includes but is not limited to all email messages, passwords, usernames, and documents. With this information, a hacker can form a complete picture of the data traveling on a network, as well as capture important tidbits of data that can help him gain complete control over the network.

BioPassword Technology

The BioPassword technology was originally developed by SRI International (formerly Stanford Research Institute) between 1979 and 1985 in an effort to create a computer-based security access and identification procedure that would present greater protection than keys, cards, passwords or codes. BioPassword uses our patented keystroke dynamics technology, a proprietary algorithm to make biometric measurements of a keyboard user's individual typing rhythm, when they enter a password. BioPassword adds a transparent layer of authentication during the login process. Currently there is no competition for BioPassword using the keystroke dynamics due to our patent covering the proprietary nature of the algorithm, process and methods.

Through research at RAND Corporation, in 1980, it was identified that the potential of identifying the user typing on a keyboard was feasible. Organizations such as Wells Fargo Bank were involved in gathering and inputting millions of keystrokes during the research and development of the appropriate algorithms. From an R&D standpoint the better part of $6,000,000 US was spent, in the late seventies and into the eighties, to get this into a hardware device that worked in a stand-alone PC environment.

The hardware product was developed and used in the "XT" Personal Computer in the mid-1980's. This hardware device was capable of handling 6 independent users on a stand-alone PC. It was used in organizations such as 3M Corporation. In 1989, NNSII had an option to acquire the technology from International Biometrics Systems Inc, (IBSI) a company located in Minnesota. Prior to 1989, the company's primary business was the acquisition and exploration of mineral properties. Upon the evaluation and recommendation of Gordon Ross, the company raised approx. $2,000,000 CDN to acquire and fund the ongoing development of the technology utilizing hardware that could be used in a network configuration under the Novell operating system. Mr. Ross recommended a software solution but was over-ruled by the existing management at that time. IBSI went bankrupt trying to develop the hardware solution, and as such all rights to the technology, patents, trade secrets, trademarks, and copyrights associated with BioPassword reverted to NNSII in 1993.

Building Credibility in the Security World. In 2000, BioPassword cleared an important hurdle in the authentication of the user after passing the Financial Services Technology Consortium (FSTC)/International Biometric Group (IBG) Comparative Testing program. This program gauged the real-world performance of leading biometric technologies in the two fields of greatest interest to financial services professionals—IT security and e-commerce.

With the participation of the FSTC, comprised of leading banks, financial services providers, research laboratories, universities, technology companies, and government agencies, IBG's testing is the standard for the comparative performance of biometric systems, helping to clarify the often-confusing world of advanced information security. IBG qualified—

BioPassword as a Valid Biometric Solution

Samir Nanavati, a partner with International Biometric Group, said, "Keystroke dynamics is a viable technology because it requires minimal training and no special hardware. It also inhibits employees from sharing passwords—a common way security is breached." "Net Nanny", he said, "is the only company that has brought this technology to a commercial stage. In an industry where new companies quickly come and go, it's considered a real player, as far as the approach that Net Nanny has taken, it's a respectable one," Nanavati said.

"Over the past 12 months all of the biometric technologies have finally come down in price, finally have incorporated standards, finally have adequate accuracy and finally work," says Nanavati, "Specifically for keystroke biometrics, the accuracy was not there, but now it is." Nanavati says the other key for success is tight integration with NT.

Today, the company has re-engineered keystroke dynamics into a software only biometric solution for user authentication in modern computers. BioPassword® is a commercial biometric product specifically designed for the Windows NT and 2000 platforms authenticating client users accessing the network.

Biometric user authentication solves the "Trust" problem since traditional technologies are not sufficient to reduce fraud and protect our computer systems and networks. It is natural to use these technologies in various applications where security is the highest priority, e.g. Law enforcement, physical access control and banking. Securing sensitive data on the Internet is a popular concern. Internet banking and electronic commerce will be sectors where biometric technologies will provide a natural and logical solution.

BioPassword presents a unique approach to improving the security of passwords and User Authentication. Password typing is the most widely used identity verification method in Web-based electronic commerce. Due to its simplicity, however, it is vulnerable to imposter attacks. Keystroke dynamics and password checking can be combined to result in a more secure verification system. In a "one to many" environment of the internet and electronic commerce, BioPassword enhanced verification, whether a digital signature or an authenticated transaction, can provide a simple biometric layer that can bind the user to a digital signature or transaction in such a manner that no other biometric technology can offer.

Tools

Biometric verification is used to confirm the identity of a person by digitally measuring physical characteristics, such as voice, face, fingerprint and comparing those measurements with previously filed information. This biometric information, called "bioprints," is stored in a reference database, or written on smart card carried by the person. Keyware developed the LBV Security Server which seamlessly combines multiple biometric technologies into one solution, providing a high level of security.

By replacing, or working in concert with current security methods (PIN codes, passwords, smart cards, tokens), biometrics enhance the level of security and convenience available to the user. During the log-on process, for example, you now use a four-digit pincode or password. Through the use of LBV, your voice and face are verified by the system. By doing so, you eliminate the possibility of someone else gaining access to your computer, someone who might have stolen your pincode or password. In other words, no one can sign on as you—except you. Biometrics involves a one-to-one matching procedure (verification), rather than a one-to-many (identification). A person's live biometric data is being matched against a bioprint in a database, such as on a smart card. If it matches, it means that the person is who he or she claims to be, and access is granted. Using a password in a one-to-many system, the system is checking against a full database of passwords. The system only cares if the password is a valid one, not if the person using the passcode is authorized to use it.

There are a variety of biometric technologies relevant to network security. Voice verification and facial scans are currently the two most widely used. Part of the reason is that the necessary hardware infrastructure is already in place to use these technologies. For voice verification, telephones, speakers and microphones are virtually universal and widely accepted. Soon, PCs will be available with image capture devices or digital cameras as standard equipment. Neither method is particularly capital-intensive.

Any company exploring the use of biometrics in its transactions should consider a vendor whose product offers the flexibility to incorporate additional biometric methods down the road. While network security may be a company's only current biometric application, there may be a future need to utilize the technology for additional applications, such as physical access control. Consequently, the need for other methods, such as facial scans and fingerprint imaging, will come to the forefront.

Example Tools

BioLink Mouse

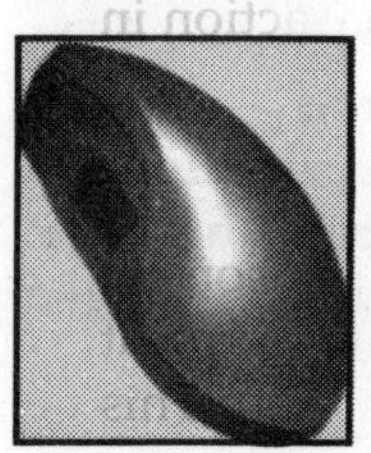

A patented fingerprint scanning methodology that is tightly integrated into a standard two-button mouse. Advanced optics and scanning methodology allow the U-Match mouse to generate a superior image. Unlike other commercially available mouse-based input devises, the U-Match Mouse does not capture the fingerprint image. Rather, it scrambles the algorithm at the point of scan. This methodology offers a superior level of security and an un-matched level of privacy.

BioLink Software Development Kit (SDK)

BioLink Technologies International, Inc is looking forward to working with technology partners that are interested in creating a broader awareness of biometrics and more importantly of authentication security. SDK provides support to design custom applications that incorporate our authentication capabilities quickly and easily. It is not necessary to have an understanding of biometrics in order to develop applications using our SDK. Because of this, your development team can fully focus on security into your application and not biometric issues.

BioLink Authentication Center

A highly secure client-based desktop security protocol that provides desktop access security and NT logon support. Co porations and institutions can reduce password-related help desk calls and greatly increase network security with the BioLink Authentication System. Additionally, all files and applications can be protected with a biometric protocol. BioLink is the only solutions available offering DOS and Safe Mode protection, making BioLink the industry's most robust biometric security solution.

BioLink Authenteon Server

BioLink has introduced a revolutionary line of biometric authentication servers for medium to large networks that perform high-speed authentication against a large database of users. Few solutions exist today that can support a "pure biometric search" against a large database of biometric I.Ds. BioLink has pioneered unique technologies that enable corporations to manage their networks through advanced biometric identification. The Authenteon servers are stand-alone devices that are easily integrated into existing networks and with limited conflicts with existing S/W topologies.

BioLink On-Line

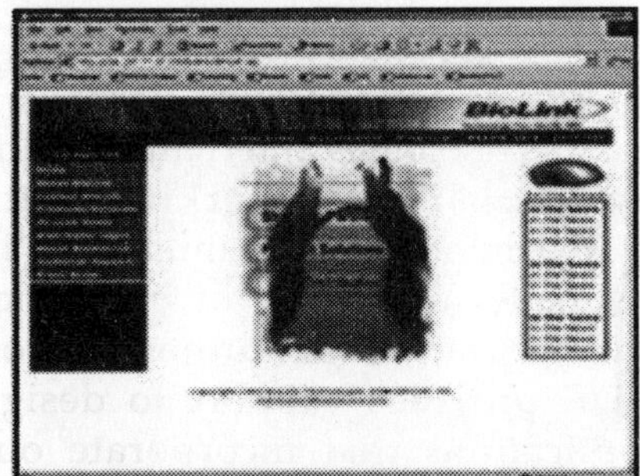

Based on BioLink's patented Authenteon server technology, BioLink will offer large-scale authentication servers for critical or secure transactions and access over the Internet. Until now, high-speed and ultra-secure biometric identification technology has not been available for commercial Internet applications supporting a large user database. BioLink On-line supports a "pure biometric search" capability supporting applications such as on-line banking, securities trading, personal documents access, on-line medical applications and general access protocols. In addition to reducing unauthorized access, identity fraud and e-Commerce fraud . . . BioLink On-Line is a powerful tool for Internet business striving to maintain repeats customers.

BioLink U-Match Mouse

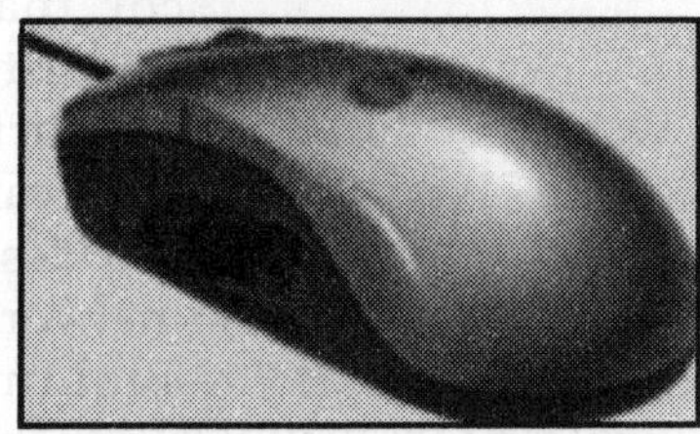

The BioLink U-Match Mouse® is a standard two-button computer mouse with a small fingerprint scanning device embedded in it that functions as a lock on a computer or a network that can only be accessed by authorized persons.

Conclusion

Biometrics is the greatest boon to the mankind and network security can be achieved through this successfully. In near future we are going to work with biometrics tools. As such we need have our written signature anywhere. Bio-key International's biometric finger identification products are designed to accommodate a variety of business and government uses and technologies.

References

1. *Maximum Security*, Anonymous work, Techmedia Publication, 1999.
2. *Strategies for Securing Web Services*, M.S.V. Janakiram, Information Technology, Vol. 13, No. 2; December 2003, pp. 22-24.
3. *User Identification through Keystroke Biometrics*, Sudeep Gaurkar, Chellappan L., Electronics for you, Vol. 36, No. 1; Jan. 2004., pp. 132-34.
4. www.biometrics.org, www.isl-biometrics.com, www.nist.gov/biometrics.html

Security in WEP Algorithm

K. GOMATHI, S. PUNITHADEVI AND S. VIDYA

Introduction to WEP

Wireless technology uses Wired Equivalent Privacy (WEP) as a method of encrypting and decrypting wireless communications typically between a client and an access point connected to a wired LAN. Wireless LAN communications introduced the Wired Equivalent Privacy (WEP) protocol to bring the security level of wireless systems closer to that of wired ones. WEP is part of an international standard; it has been integrated by manufacturers into their 802.11 hardware and is currently in widespread use. WEP depends on the use of a secret key to encrypt and decrypt packets traveling between the wireless network card and access point.

Security Goals of WEP Protocol

The primary goal of WEP is to protect the confidentiality of user data from eavesdropping.

- *Access Control* : Ensure that your wireless infrastructure is not used.
- *Data Integrity* : Ensure that your data packets are not modified in transit.
- *Confidentiality* : Ensure that the content of your wireless traffic is not learned.

Why WEP?

- Wireless connections have important security issues to keep the intruders from accessing, reading and modifying the network traffic.

- But mobile systems need to be.
- Connected. We need an algorithm, which provides the same level of security that physical wire does.

WEP Algorithm is used to

- Protect wireless communication from eavesdropping.
- Prevent unauthorized access to wireless network.

Description of WEP Protocol

WEP incorporates two main types of protection are *secret key and encryption.*

WEP relies on a secret key, which is shared between the sender and the receiver.

SENDER : Mobile station (e.g. Laptop with a wireless Ethernet card).
RECEIVER : Access Point (e.g. base station).

Secret Key

Secret key is used to encrypt packets before they are transmitted. The secret key is a simple 5- or 13-character password that is shared between the access point and all wireless network users. This key is all-important to WEP in that it is also used in the encryption process to uniquely scramble each packet of information with a unique password. This ensures that if a hacker cracks one packets key, he won't be able to view every packet's information. To do this, WEP defines a method to create a unique secret key for each packet using the 5- or 13-characters of the pre-shared key and three more Psuedo-randomly selected characters picked by the wireless hardware. *For example,* let's assume that our pre-shared key was "games". This word would then be merged with "abc" to create a secret key of "abcgames", which would be used to encrypt the packet. The next packet would still use "games", but concatenate it this time with "xyz" to create a new secret key of "xyzgames". This process would randomly continue during the transmission of data.

Initialization Vector (IV)

This changing part of the secret key is called the Initialization Vector because it initializes the encryption process for each packet of data sent.

Integrity Check Value (ICV)

Integrity Check Value (ICV) is used to ensure packets are not modified in transit.

RC4 Encryption

WEP uses RC4 encryption algorithm known as *"stream cipher"* to protect the confidentiality of its data. The process of encrypting a WEP frame is essentially a *3-step process.*

For the purpose of this discussion, we will assume the use of a 40-bit key. In the first step, WEP computes a 32-bit *cyclical redundancy check (ICV)* on the payload of the frame and appends it to the end of the frame.

Next, one of potentially up to four keys, which are all shared between Wireless LAN (WLAN) members, is selected and appended to a 24-bit initialization vector (IV). One of the problems with WEP is the use (or misuse) of the IV. Typically, the IV starts at some pre-determined number (such as 0) and incremented by one for each packet that is transmitted. Using the data frame+ICV, and the secret key+IV, the message gets encrypted using the RC4 algorithm. This is accomplished by creating a key stream using the secret key+IV and XORing the key stream with the data payload.

The frame that is sent is the resulting cipher text and the IV. It should be noted for clarity that the IV, in addition to the header and key number, is sent in the unencrypted portion of the frame.

The receiving station uses the sent IV and the shared secret key to decrypt the cipher text, again using RC4 to accomplish this.

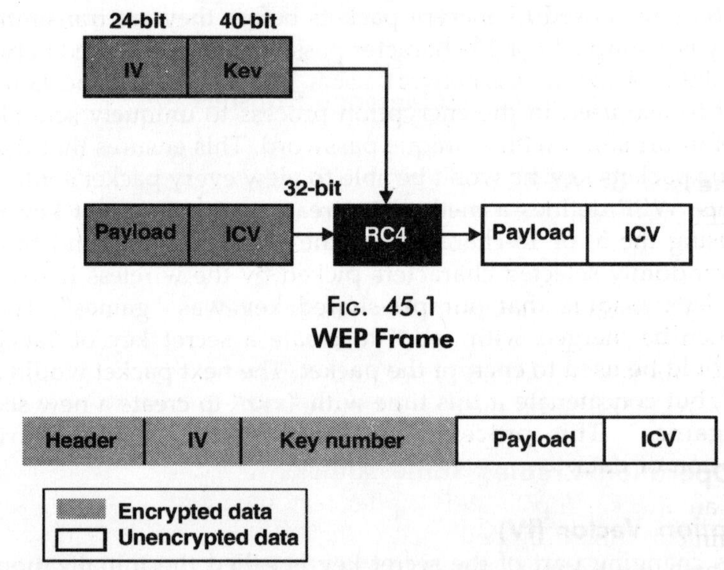

FIG. 45.1
WEP Frame

FIG. 45.2
Example of WEP Encryption and Format of WEP Frame [NEW]

Message Transmission

To send a message M :

- Compute a checksum c(M).
- Pick an IV v and generate a key stream RC4(v, k).
- XOR <M, c(M)> with the key stream to get the cipher text.

➤ Transmit v and cipher text over a radio link.
➤ When received a message M use transmitted v and the shared key k to generate the key stream RC4(v, k)
➤ XOR the cipher text with RC4(v, k) to get <M′, c′> Check is c′=c(M′), If it is, accept M′ as the message transmitted.

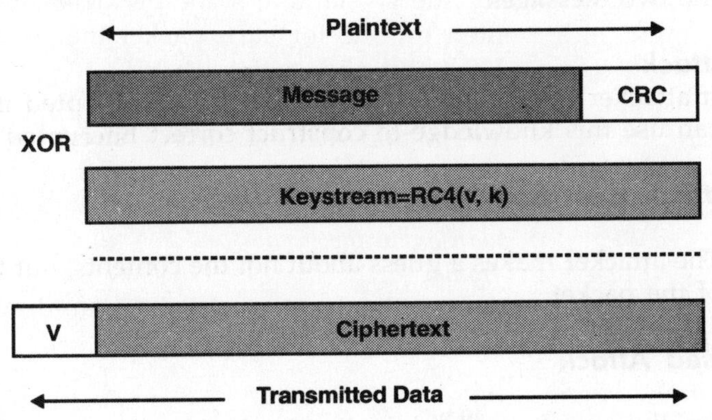

FIG. 45.3
Picture of Message Transmission

Weaknesses of WEP

WEP has been widely criticized for a number of weaknesses :

➤ WEP's use of RC4 is weak
➤ Key management and key size is poor
➤ The IV is too small
➤ The ICV algorithm is not appropriate
➤ Authentication messages can be easily forged

This Operation Creates Some Attacks

If an attacker flips a bit in cipher text, then after decryption, that bit in the plaintext will be flipped.

If an eavesdropper intercepts two cipher texts encrypted with the same key stream, it is possible to obtain the XOR of the two plaintexts.

Knowledge of this XOR can enable the Statistical attacks to recover the plaintexts.

Attack Types

➤ Passive attacks
➤ Active attacks
➤ Table base attacks

Passive Attack

- A passive eavesdropper can intercept all Wireless traffic.
- By XORing two packets, attacker obtains the XOR of two-plaintext messages.
- The resulting XOR can be used to infer data about the content of the two messages.

Active Attack

- If attacker knows the exact plaintext from Encrypted message, he can use this knowledge to construct correct Encrypted packets.

Active Attack from both ends

- The attacker makes a guess about not the contents, but the headers of the packet.

Table-based Attack

- Small space of possible initialization Vector allows attacker to build a decryption table. Once he learns the plaintext for some packet, he can compute the RC4 key stream.

Defenses of WEP to these Attacks

- Integrity Check (IC) field.
- Used to ensure that packet has not been modified in transit.
- Initialization Vector (IV).
- Used to avoid encrypting two cipher texts with the same key stream.
- Used to argument the shared key and produce a different RC4 key for each packet.

Additional Defenses

Combine Several Methods to overcome Weakness of WEP

VPN's and Secure LAN (SLAN)

The idea behind using a VPN over a wireless link is that packets going to and from an access point will be secure using a much stronger level of encryption, such as IPSEC. In addition, access to the wired network can be controlled with a more robust method of authentication with a VPN server.

In addition, specialized "VPN" open source software is currently being developed to allow Authorization, Authentication and Accountability for insecure networks.

SLAN's are "similar to a VPN and provides server authentication, client authentication, data privacy, and integrity using per session and per user short life keys."

Remote Access Dial-in User Service (RADIUS)

RADIUS authentication, where clients gain access to the network by supplying a username and password to a separate server. This information is securely sent over the network eliminating the possibility of passive snooping.

Dynamic Keys

To reduce the possibility of key compromise, eliminate the use of static keys, and instead are implementing per-user/per-session keys combined with RADIUS authentication. Clients must authenticate with a RADIUS server-using network credentials, and WEP keys are dynamically distributed securely to the client.

There are several *advantages* to this method of key distribution. Dynamic keys offer less administrative overhead, since keys are automatically changed with each user logon. In addition, dynamic keys eliminate the vulnerabilities described earlier with using WEP and static keys.

Conclusion

The paper demonstrates WEP protocol and describes several practical attacks. Consequently, the study recommends that WEP should not be counted on to provide strong link level security, and that additional precautions be taken to protect network traffic. It will motivate a redesign of the WEP protocol to address the vulnerabilities that found. Further hope is that this paper will expose important security principles and design practices to a wide audience, and that the lessons identified will benefit future designers of both WEP and other mobile communications security protocols.

References

1. Steven M. Bellovin, "Problem areas for the IP security protocols" In *6th USENIX Security Symposium*, San Jose, California, July 1996. USENIX.
2. Borisov, N., Goldberg I., and Wagner D. "Intercepting mobile communications", *MOBICOM 2001.*
3. Goldberg I., "An analysis of the Wired Equivalent Privacy protocol", Black Hat Briefings, July 11, 2001.
4. Fluhrer S, Mantin I., and Shamir A. "Weaknesses in the key scheduling algorithm of RC4".
5. Kent S., and Atkinson R., "Security architecture for the Internet protocol".
6. L.M.S.C. of The IEEE Computer Society, "Wireless LAN Medium Access Control (MAC) and Physical Layer (PHY) specifications".
6. Postel J., and Reynolds J.K., "Standard for the transmission of IP datagrams over IEEE 802 networks".

Websites

1. http ://www.isaac.cs.berkeley.edu/isaac/wep-faq.html
2. http ://www.cisco.com/warp/public/cc/pd/witc/ao350ap/prodlit/1281_pp.htm
3. http ://www.sans.org/infosecFAQ/wireless/war.htm
4. http ://www.sans.org/infosecFAQ/wireless/equiv.htm

SAN Security

ANTONY SELVADOSS THANAMANI
D. SARAVANA PRAKASH AND P. JAYA KUMAR

Introduction

At the edge of the enterprise, growing populations of geographically dispersed servers challenge IT administrators to reactively respond to each server's individual storage demands. Studies by IDC conclude that a storage administrator can manage seven times more SAN storage than distributed storage. In addition, Forrester Research studies indicate that the capital costs for a given amount of storage can be reduced by 30% by implementing storage networks and pooling disk and tape storage resources.

Fragmented resource management efforts perpetuate inefficiency and waste. When expanding storage of an individual server the tendency is to increase capacity well beyond the immediate requirement, attempting to delay the server's next storage crisis. This aggressive method of expanding storage one server at a time leads to inefficient storage utilization levels, wasting valuable resources. Gartner estimates that storage utilization levels in many companies are less than 50%.

Distributed backups, commonly managed independently on each server, necessitate the duplication of tape hardware and administration efforts, further complicating IT management. Central IT management is accountable for the protection of all enterprise data, yet is fully dependent on distributed personnel for ensuring backup execution. Best practice standards, such as frequent testing of backup integrity and off-site replication, become goals that are impossible to achieve.

Storage at the edge of the enterprise—typically at a departmental or remote office level—is often an organization's fastest growing segment. Edge storage presents significant challenges in management and data protection.

Storage Research Corporation estimates that 89% of all distributed storage is currently backed-up over the LAN, indicating sufficient bandwidth exists to support storage traffic in most organizations. Two goals are to ensure that the storage traffic does not interfere with the existing LAN traffic and to ensure that both types of traffic will have sufficient bandwidth. Often standard Ethernet technologies such as Virtual LANs (VLANs) may be implemented to segment the existing network for both performance and security purposes.

When one thinks of the word security in association with information storage subsystems within Storage Area Networks (SANs), the first thought that comes to mind is of computer hackers infiltrating those information storage subsystems and wreaking havoc. Unauthorized human access to stored information in a SAN infrastructure is a big concern, but there is yet another concern that needs addressing and that is technology containment. For example, in a SAN infrastructure where various technologies *(such as Windows NT and UNIX)* are not contained, Windows NT server(s) would see every available Logical Unit Number (LUN) storage resource and try to take ownership of them all. In brief, technology containment keeps servers from gaining unauthorized or accidental access to certain storage resources within the SAN.

SAN Designs Must Include Security Plans

SANs are open systems infrastructures offering many different file systems, software, volume and disk management formats. This calls for a security plan, which must be worked out during the SAN design and development phase for these reasons :

1. Maximum data access and integrity.
2. Effective fabric management.
3. Highest level of protection against outside threats.

This paper concerns SAN data access and security, and SAN fabric management and security by presenting technologies and methodologies.

SAN Data Access and Security Concerns

SAN Data Access Requires Security Measures

The first concern when implementing a SAN is to provide a higher level of data access and integrity than Direct-Attached Storage (DAS) subsystems provide. This requires new technologies and methodologies over those typically available for DAS subsystems.

Generally, any single SAN implementation would require multiple security methodologies to maximize data access. For example, a shared

Random Array of Independent Disks (RAID) array is a storage subsystem that presents logical disks or LUNs to hosts on the SAN for use. Without security measures, any host on the SAN fabric would be able to see those LUNs and potentially write data to them. In a scenario where data would be stored on those LUNs, data corruption or data loss could occur.

Issues on Data Access and Security

- Segregate operating systems at the port level on the SAN fabric.
- Segregate different application types on the SAN fabric.
- Isolate any single LUN on an array, permitting only a certain host(s) access to that LUN and no others.
- Ensure that hosts see their storage ports and storage, from host side.

SAN Fabric Management and Security Concerns

SAN Fabric Management Requires Security Measures

Implementing SAN infrastructures require a fundamental level of SAN fabric security, especially when adding switches to the SAN fabric, and managing SAN fabric configuration changes. This level of security more closely resembles the common security concerns in traditional Transmission Control Protocol/Internet Protocol (TCP/IP) networks. This same level of security is also very important in collocation environments where multiple SAN fabrics are in use, and owned by multiple organizations, in close roximity with each other.

Issues on Fabric Level Security

- To manage switch-to-switch security on the SAN fabric; also, how can we enforce security policies that prohibit unauthorized switches or hosts from attaching to the SAN fabric.
- To centrally manage security and configuration changes on a SAN fabric.
- To ensure that only authorized hosts connect to the SAN fabric and to a specific port designated by an administrator.
- How can we ensure that the tools used to manage the SAN fabric, and SAN management requests are coming from an authorized source?
- How can we ensure that configuration changes on the SAN fabric are valid when there are multiple points of configuration management?

SAN Security Technologies and Methodologies

Multiple technologies and methodologies are used to provide the highest level of security for a SAN.

SAN Data Access and Security

- Fabric zoning
- LUN masking
- Persistent binding

SAN Fabric Management and Security

- Fabric-to-fabric security
- Host-to-fabric security
- Management-to-fabric security
- Configuration integrity security

The next discussion is about the technologies and methodologies that ensure data access security, and fabric management security for SANs.

SAN Data Access and Security

Fabric Zoning

SAN implementations make data highly accessible; as a result, there is a need for data-transfer optimization and finely tuned network security. Fabric zoning sets-up the way devices in the SAN interact, establishing a certain level of management and security.

Zoning

Zoning is a fabric-centric enforced way of creating barriers on the SAN fabric to prevent set groups of devices from interacting with other devices. SAN architectures provide port-to-port connections between servers and storage subsystems through bridges, switches, and hubs. Zoning sets-up efficient methods of managing, partitioning, and controlling pathways to and from storage subsystems on the SAN fabric, which improves storage subsystem utilization, data access, and security on the SAN. In addition, zoning enables heterogeneous devices to be grouped by operating system, and further demarcation based on application, function, or department.

Types of Zoning

There are two types of zoning : soft zoning and hard zoning.

Soft zoning uses software to enforce zoning. The zoning process uses the name server database located in the FC switch where the port numbers and World Wide Names (WWNs) are stored that are used to identify devices during the zoning process

Hard zoning uses only WWNs to specify each device for a specific zone. Hard zoning requires each device to pass through the switch's route table so that the switch can regulate data transfers by verified zone.

Zoning Components

Zone configurations are based on either the physical port that devices plug into, or the WWN of the device. There are three zoning components :

- Zones
- Zone members
- Zone sets

Zone

A zone is composed of servers and storage subsystems on a SAN that access each other through managed port-to-port connections. Devices in the same zone recognize and communicate with each other, but not necessarily with devices in other zones unless a device, in that zone, is configured for multiple zones. Figure 46.1 shows a three-zone SAN with zones 1 and 3 sharing the tape library in zone 2.

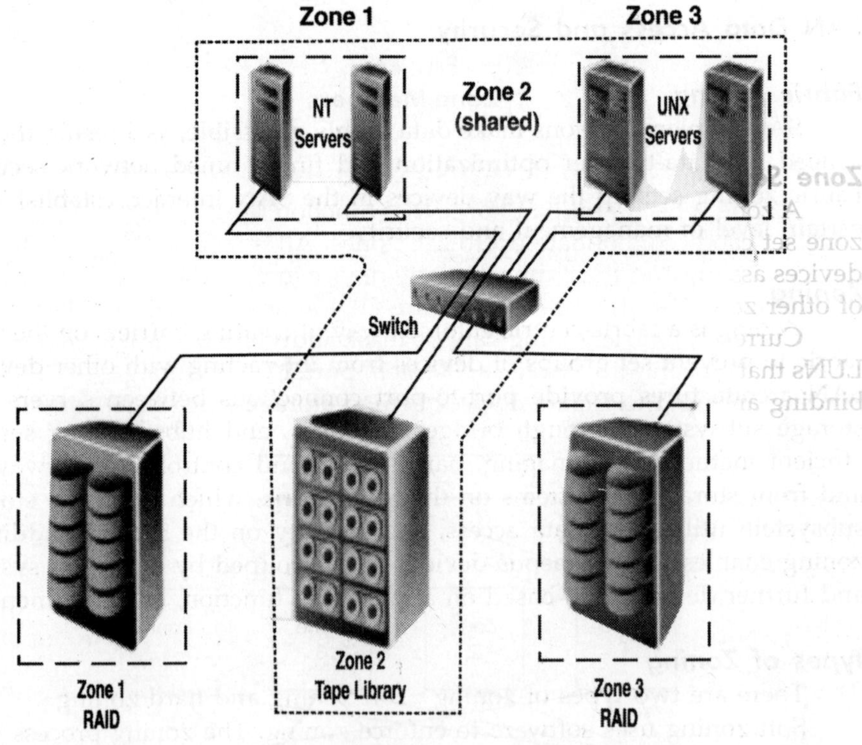

Fig. 46.1
Three-Zone SAN Fabric

Zone Member

Zone members are the devices within the same assigned zone. Zone member devices can only interact with members within their assigned zone and to have the access over outside its assigned zone it should be configured in other zones. Each zone member is identified by a WWN or port number, each device has a unique WWN.

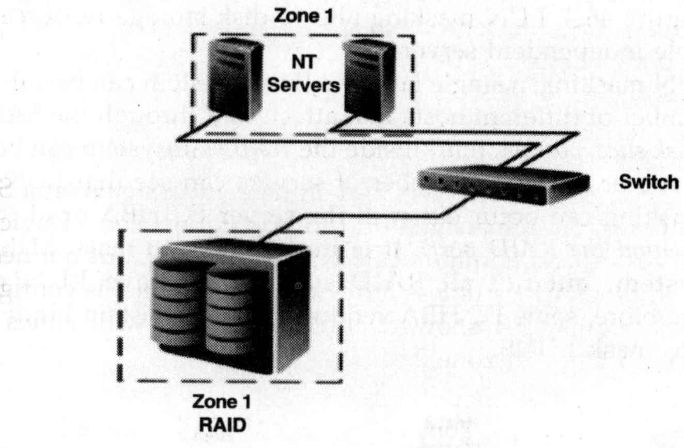

FIG. 46.2
Zone Members

Zone Set

A zone set is a group of zones that function together on the SAN. Each zone set can accommodate up to 256 zones. All devices in a zone see only devices assigned to their zone, but any device in that zone can be a member of other zones. In the following figure all 4 zones see Member A.

Currently, fabric zoning cannot mask individual tape or disk storage LUNs that sit behind a storage-subsystem port. LUN masking and persistent binding are used to isolate devices behind storage-subsystem ports.

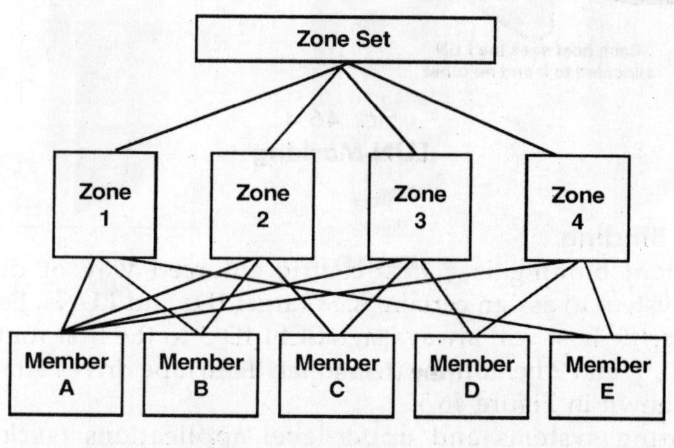

FIG. 46.3
Zone Set

LUN Masking

LUN masking is a RAID system-centric enforced method of masking multiple LUNs behind a single port. LUN masking configuration occurs at the RAID-array level, using World Wide Port Names (WWNs) of server FC HBAs. See Figure 46.4. LUN masking allows disk storage resource sharing across multiple independent servers.

With LUN masking, a single large RAID subsystem can be sub-divided to serve a number of different hosts that attach to it through the SAN fabric. Each LUN *(disk slice, portion, unit)* inside the RAID subsystem can be limited so that only one or a limited number of servers can see that LUN.

LUN masking can occur either at the server FC HBA or at the RAID subsystem *(behind the RAID port)*. It is more secure to mask LUNs at the RAID subsystem, but not all RAID subsystems have LUN masking capability; therefore, some FC HBA vendors allow persistent binding at the driver level to mask LUNS.

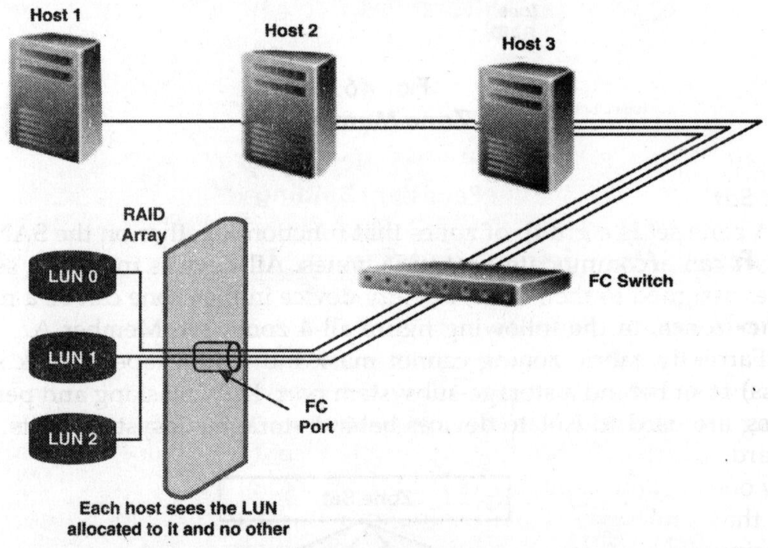

FIG. 46.4
LUN Masking

Persistent Binding

Persistent binding is a host-centric enforced way of directing an operating system to assign certain SCSI-target IDs and LUNs. For example, where a specific host will always sign SCSI ID 3 to the first router it finds, and LUNs 0, 1, and 2 behind the port to the three tape drives attached to the router, as shown in Figure 46.5.

Operating systems and upper-level applications *(such as backup software)* typically require a static or predictable SCSI target ID for their storage reliability persistent binding makes that possible.

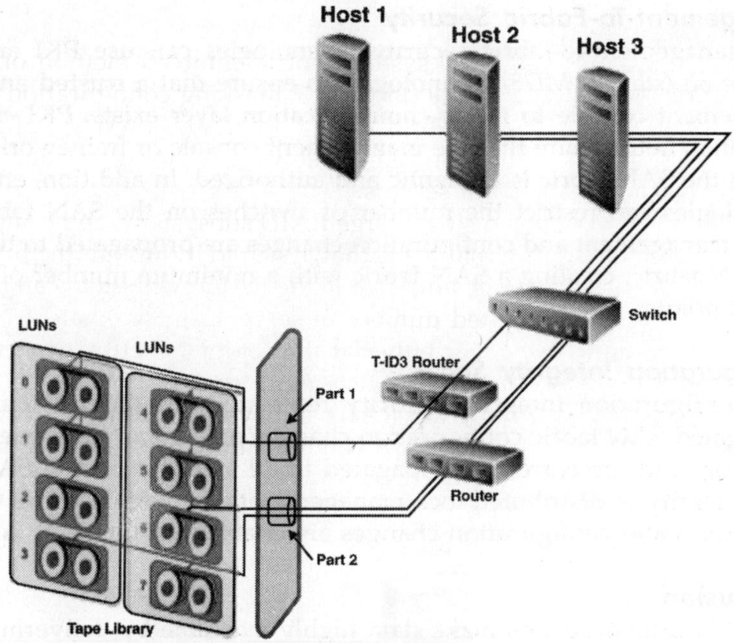

FIG. 46.5
Persistent Binding

SAN Fabric Management and Security Technologies

Fabric-To-Fabric Security

Fabric-to-fabric security technologies permit Access Control Lists (ACLs) to allow or deny the addition of a new switch to the SAN fabric. Access lists filter SAN traffic by controlling whether routed packets are forwarded or blocked at the router interface. For example, access lists can allow one host the right to access a certain part of the SAN and deny another host that same access. ACLs can provide a basic level of security for accessing the SAN fabric. Public Key Infrastructures (PKIs) technology can be applied as a mechanism for authenticating the identity of a new switch. In addition, fabric-wide security databases help to ensure that all new authorized switches added to the SAN fabric inherit fabric-wide security policies, so that a new, out-of-the-box switch does not become a non-secured access point.

Host-To-Fabric Security

Host-to-fabric security technologies can apply ACLs at the port-level on the SAN fabric to allow or deny a particular host's FC HBA the right to access a specific port. This would prevent an unauthorized intruder host from attaching to the fabric via any port. The host's ability to log into the fabric is explicitly defined and is allowed with this model.

Management-To-Fabric Security

Management-to-fabric security technologies can use PKI and other encryption *(such as MD5)* technologies to ensure that a trusted and secure management console to fabric communication layer exists. PKI and other encryption help ensure that the management console or framework used to control the SAN fabric is authentic and authorized. In addition, encryption technologies can restrict the number of switches on the SAN fabric from which management and configuration changes are propagated to the rest of the SAN fabric, creating a SAN fabric with a minimum number of security control points.

Configuration Integrity Security

Configuration integrity security refers to technologies that ensure propagated SAN fabric configuration changes only come from one location at a time, and are correctly propagated to all switches on the SAN fabric with integrity. A distributed lock manager is one way of ensuring that only serial and valid configuration changes are enabled on the SAN fabric.

Conclusion

SAN infrastructures make data highly available by delivering shared storage subsystems in open, non-proprietary environments via any-to-any connectivity. The advantage of any-to-any connectivity can be a liability unless well thought out security practices are in place to manage how servers and storage subsystems interact within the SAN. Shared storage subsystems within a SAN infrastructure require safeguards to ensure that data is protected, and to prevent unwanted access by unauthorized systems and users.

This discussion briefly explored some of the technologies and methodologies used to ensure that only authorized systems and users can access storage subsystems within the SAN. Each technology and methodology has advantages and disadvantages; therefore, consideration must be given to each based on a SAN security strategy developed during the SAN design and development phase. Moreover, to expect that the required level of security for a SAN can be achieved from any one of the previously discussed technologies or methodologies, independent of all others, is unwise. The astute information storage architect clearly understands, in heterogeneous SAN environments with diverse operating systems and storage subsystems, that a combination or some measure of all the aforementioned technologies and methodologies could be required to ensure that the SAN is secure from unauthorized systems and users.

Finally, it is essential to re-examine the SAN security strategy as the SAN infrastructure evolves, and as new technologies and methodologies emerge. This will ensure that the proper level of security is in place within the SAN at all times.

REFERENCES

1. An Overview of WORM Technology : Storing Fixed Content Non-Erasable Data; Search—www.datalink.com.
2. Extending the Reach of Fibre Channel SANs ; Search—www.stonefly.com
3. Storage Area Network Security : Data Access & Fabric Management ; Search—www.datalink.com.
4. "Cisco Storage Networking Solution—The Strategic and Financial Justification of SANs White Paper"; Search-www.cisco.com for "justification of SAN".
5. Storage Networking over a Metro Network; Search—www.cisco.com.

Part VIII

Network Applications

Growth of Networks from Basic Network to High Speed Networks

S. Sumathy and N. Narayana Moorthy

Introduction to Computers

A computer is a digital Electronics machine which performs all mathematical operations and it produces the results in user defined form. Single computer is called as stand alone machine.

Networks

Networks are defined as the group of computers connected together for sharing of informations. Generally the networks are classified as LAN (Local Area Networks), MAN (Metropolitan Networks) and WAN (Wide Area Networks) based on the distance and media for connections.

Server : The computer machine which provides services for others is called as server.

Client : The computer machine which request services from others is called as client.

Need/Advantages/Goals of Networks

The following are the advantages of networking the computer together :

1. Easy to communicate from one place to other place.
2. Sharing of resources (Both hardware and software).
3. Saving of Cost.
4. More Reliable.

Network Topology

The physical way of connecting the computer together is generally called as the network topology.

The various network topologies are :

- BUS Topology
- RING Topology
- STAR Topology
- MESH Topology
- CELLULAR Topology

Considering the various factors as follows can make the selection of these topologies :

- Cost
- Ease of Installation
- Future Growth
- Trouble shooting aspects

The Bus Topology consist of one lengthy cable called as main cable and as many as drop cables or short cables which connects the computers to the main cable through T-Connectors. The ends of the main cables are terminated with devices called as Terminators for avoiding the signal reflections. Here one machine can act as server and others can act as client. Here we need to work on the collisions, i.e., Congestion or Network Traffic because of which we lose the informations. We work with CSMA\CD (Carrier Sense Multiple Access with Collision Detection) and CSMA\CA (Carrier Sense Multiple Access with Collision Avoidance). Protocol for overcoming the Network Collisions. In case of Star network we have one Hubs or Switches through which we connect the computers with individual cables. This topology is more cable fault tolerant. In Ring Topology we configure all the computers in the form of Ring or Cellular form. Here we make use of Token Passing.

Physical Topologies

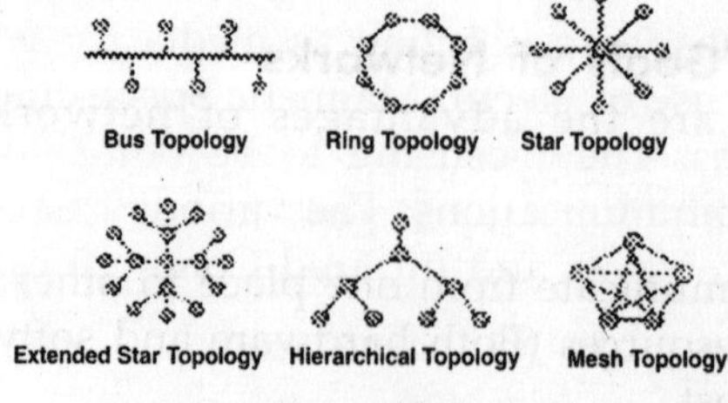

FIG. 47.1
Physical Topologies

1. Transmission Media

The pathway for contacting each other is called as the Transmission Media. They are Cable Media or Cable Less or Wireless Medias.

The general Characteristics or Factors to be considered before choosing any media are as follows :

- Cost
- Ease of Installation
- Bandwidth (Capacity)
- Attenuation
- Immunity from EMI (Electro Magnetic Interdernces's)

Cable Medias

The copper conductor is used for carrying the signals in cable medias. The general cable and TWISTED PAIR Cables and FIBRE OPTIC Cables. These are further classified as Thick NET and Thin NET Co-Axial cables and unshielded and shielded Twisted Pair and Single Mode and Multimedia Fiber Optic Cables.

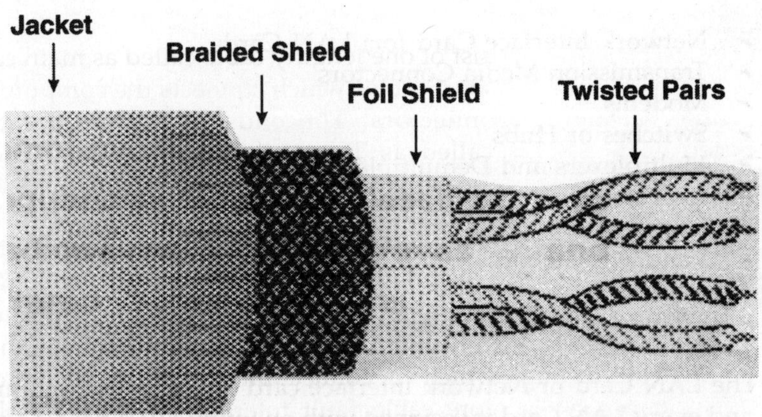

FIG. 47.2
Twisted Pair Cable

Cable Less Medias

The Earth's Atmosphere is acting as media for wireless or cable less communications. The use of Electro Magnetic Spectrum is used for selection of various frequencies. The Licensing to be obtained from Government Bodies for wireless communications. The various frequencies are classified as Radio waves, Microwaves and Infrared Communications.

2. Protocol

The rules and regulation followed between two and more computer entities are called as Protocols.

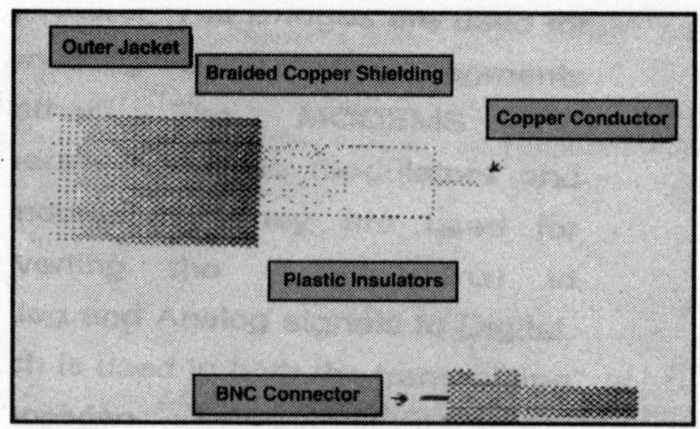

FIG. 47.3
Cable Less Medias

Network Connectivity Devices

The following are the various Network and Internetwork connectivity devices. By configuring these devices we can achieve the High Speed Computer Network communications. They are :

- Network Interface Card (or) LAN Cards
- Transmission Media Connectors
- Modems
- Switches or Hubs
- Multiplexers and Demultiplexers
- Repeaters
- Bridges
- Remote Switches
- Routers
- Channel service units and digital Service Units, etc.

The LAN Card or Network interface card is acting as the Transceiver. Each and every LAN Card is assigned with an unique IP Address and HOST NAME. This IP ADDRESS is used for identifying the computers available in the network. Each LAN Card will be combined with Transmission Media with Media connectors. The examples for Media connectors are T-Connectors, RJ-45, 8-PIN Connectors and Media couplers, etc. The Repeaters are used as Amplifiers. Because when the signal is transmitted for longer distances it gets weakened. So in order to boost the signal strength we make use of Repeaters. The bridges are used for connecting the various segments together. The MODEMS are generally called as modulators and Demodulators. They are used for converting the digital signal to Analog anf Analog signals to Digital, which is used in both the transmitting and Receiving end. The remote Switches are also used for connecting to Remote Locations.

The routers are mainly used for selecting path from multiple paths. They are mainly used for sending the informations from one network to another network. The Channel service units and Digital service units are used for avoiding the electrical interferences on the actual datas.

The 7 Layers of the OSI Model

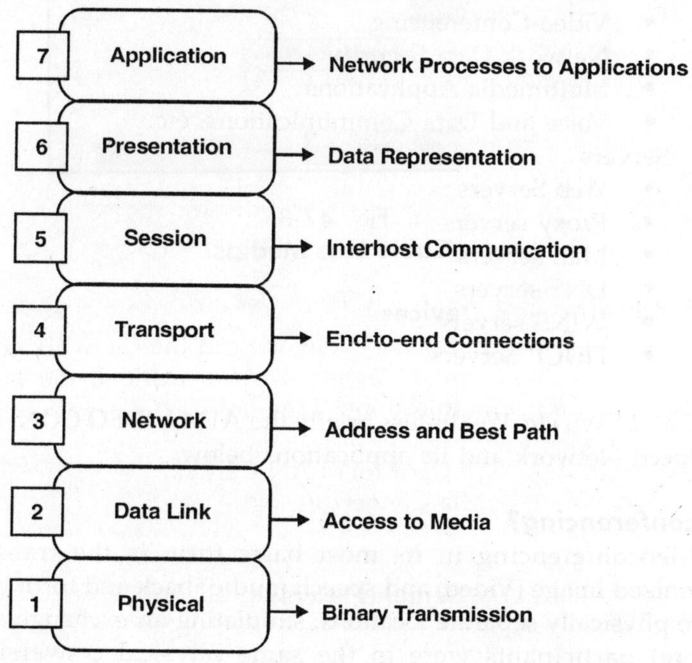

FIG. 47.4
The 7 Layers of the OSI Model

TCP/IP Address

Each machine available on the network has to be identified by means of IP Address and Machine Name. The IP Address is the 32 bit where it is separated by group of 8 bits. Each 8 bits can be used for identifying the class of network and Host Name. There are Various classes of TCP/IP Addresses available. They are Class A, B, C, D, E Based on the bit positions.

Application of High Speed Networks

The High Speed Networks are useful in the following Areas :

1. Communication
2. Distributed Processing
3. Distributed Database Systems
4. Sharing of Data and Resources
5. Internet

- E-Mail
- E-Learning
- Digital Library
- E-Shopping
- Education
- Video-Conferencing
- Network Data Security
- Multimedia Applications
- Voice and Data Communications, etc.

6. Servers
   - Web Servers
   - Proxy servers
   - Mail servers
   - DNS servers
   - WINS servers
   - DHCP Servers

IIS and PWS etc. We discuss briefly the ATM VIDEO CONFERENCING High Speed Network and its applications below.

Videoconferencing?

Videoconferencing in its most basic form is the transmission of synchronized image (Video) and speech (audio) back and forth between two or more physically separate locations, simulating an exchange as if the two (or more) participants were in the same physical conversion. This is accomplished through the use of cameras (to capture and send video from your local endpoint), Video displays (to display video received from remote endpoints), microphone (to capture and send audio from your local endpoint), and speakers (to play audio received from remote endpoints).

Why are Standards, Openness, and Interoperability Important?

H.323 is an International Telecommunications Union (ITU) standard for videoconferencing over IP. It is an umbrella standard that specifies mandatory and optional requirements in several areas to enable a complete "call" or communication sequence. The standard also defines four major components that may be part of the call-terminals, gateways, gatekeepers, and multipoint control units. The reason for the standard is to enable interoperability between different vendor's implementation of these components. As is the case with all standards, there is a danger of either over-specification or under-specification. If the standard is over-specified, it may become difficult to implement in the form of a cost-effective product. If the standard is under-specified, there may be room for different interpretations that lead to equally compliant yet non-interoperable implementations.

What are the Basic Ingredients?

Like all good recipes, developing a videoconferencing environment requires a combination of good ingredients, careful preparation, and practice. Attention to detail will only enhance the experience.

The network transport is the actual network layer your sites. This can be IP (Internet Protocol), ISDN, ATM.Frame Relay, DSL, Carrier pigeons, dog sleds, whatever. It is a link typically provided across long distance by commercial providers. Each of these network types has its own peculiarities which lend themselves, or not, to videoconferencing.

The network services are special features provided by the transport layer. These include concepts such as quality-of-service where some kinds of traffic are given preferential treatment to other traffic, and multipoint or multicast services, where traffic from one site can be delivered to more than one destination. This last concept allows you to run videoconferencing between multiple sites, potentially allowing everyone to see everyone else. It may also provide varying levels of security for your videoconferencing.

The "connecting"candle provides the mechanisms by which two or more sites can call each other. This requires special features such as directory services, which are like dialing instructions, authentication and authorization services, which allow you to control who can use your videoconferencing systems and how, and accounting services, so you can bill people afterwards. This candle is usually always on, since it needs to be available all the time. Some products though make do without it, which may or may not be important in your environment.

The "Conferencing" candle is of course the whole point of this cake. It contains the audio and video signal, usually compressed and encapsulated in some fashion, and also supports data or application sharing which allows you for example to view presentation material at full quality or a remote computer desktop, or share files around amongst the participants.

Uses of Videoconferencing

One of the most frequent questions we get is "how would I use videoconferencing? In this section we have taken several approaches to an answer. First we'll give some general idea of how videoconferencing can contribute to higher education. Next we'll zero in on a few areas that are using videoconferencing to improve or broaden their reach and service. Finally, we will describe explicit case studies including those with direct ViDe member involvement.

General Uses

In considering the use of videoconferencing for meetings, it helps to think broadly about what a "meeting" really is. In the following illustration, meeting that include videoconferencing are shown as instances of one-to-one, one-to-many, and many-to-many communication.

In each of the above cases, the quality of the audio and video are critical to the success of the remote participation.

What participants see may be

- Voice Activated-where the incoming video from the current speaker's location is displayed to all other sites.
- Continuous Presence (Sometimes called "Hollywood Squares")—where each location can see all other locations (or a selected subset of all locations) at the same time.

What participants hear may be

- Half Duplex audio (sometimes likened to "Walkie-talkies")—where participants can only hear one speaker at a time (audio from the dominant speaker's site suppresses audio from all others) and must indicate somehow when speaker control should be passed.
- Full duplex audio—where audio is "natural" in the sense that everyone can hear everyone else at all times.

Meeting control may be

- No Control—where full-duplex audio is continuously available from all sites and people can "talk over each other". In this case, the lead speaker is determined by general consensus of those present, just as in a physically proximate meeting. (The view of participant sites would still be either continuous presence or voice-activated).
- Chair Control—where a feature is included in the videoconferencing technology (either at the terminal endpoints or in the MCU) to pass chair control via some designated mechanism (electronic hand raising"). The site possessing chair control is seen and heard by others until chair control is passed.

Specific Applications

Telemedicine/TeleHealth

Telemedicine is a growing field made possible by improved and more widely available and affordable telecommunication services.

Telecommuting

Telecommuting is a fast growing trend in many geographical areas—both rural and urabn—as companies and employees realize many benefits that might be gained by this.

Tele-Education

There are many opportunities for enhancing education with videoconferencing. These include remote-teacher/remote-specialist applications, as well as classsroom-to-classroom interaction. It can also be scaled to more than 2 sites, allowing virtual education "teams" to be created.

In the remote-teacher approach, a simple H.323 system, attached to a TV or a projector allows a class to interact with a remote instructor. Depending on the situation, the remote instructor may use a fixed or a mobile system (e.g a zookeeper, or museum staffer), or include a mixture of live and recorded video (e.g. for medical training). Most H.323 (and other video conference) systems allow for flexible encoding arrangements, where a camera can be managed separately to the encoding device.

Judicial Applications

The judicial system has found videoconferencing to be a cost-effective and productive technology for its needs. A number of counties have begun to install videoconferencing's system in jails and courthouses. These systems are used most commonly for "video arraignments", where a prisoner will go to a videoconferencing room in jail. Another system in the courtroom has dedicated cameras to show the judge, prosecutor and defense attorney. The prisoner can see all of the members in the court, and the information is simultaneously recorded with a split screen 4 ways, so a complete record of the preceding is made. This provides several benefits of the court system, as reduce the number of defendants who need to be transport from jails to courthouses, reduce the overcrowding of courthouses holding facilities, reduces the security risks associated with transporting and handling defendants, saves time and saves money.

Remote Laboratories

Two combined forces are helping to make remote laboratories a reality. First, there is ever expanding technology, both on the end point side and in networking infrastructure. Second, there is the tightening of budgets along with the increasing cost of large laboratory instrument and equipment. Another area where videoconferencing is expending is to provide a way for researches to share, for example, a scanning tunneling electron microscope using existing (and ever chapter) network infrastructure. The names for these extensions to videoconferencing are often referred to as "Remote laboratories" or "Co-laboratories".

Remote laboratory allow scientists to actually "do science together" across great distance. Videoconferencing allows scientists to discuss their science, teach and learn from one another, and even give suggestions about things like further research ideas. But remote lab laboratories actually bring videoconferencing, data collaboration and remote instrument control into lab settings providing a way for scientists to plan together, work together, and excrement together, both (or all) parties having access to the data, the instruments, the documentation that is generated by any scientific endeavor.

- Administration, including general accounting, travel, and purchasing : The web has been used very successfully as the basis for many administrative operations including general accounting, purchasing and instructional aspects. intranets often handling this function, but some times they are part of group messaging software.

- Presentations such as lectures, seminars, and courses : With higher band with networks, lectures and seminars would be delivered to participating researchers lab, lab users, etc. through videoconferencing. This is "just" videoconferencing.
- Meetings, conferences, and informal instructions among researches : The mechanisms of travel and conventional telephony would be augmented with an advanced videoconferencing functionality that borders on "virtual presence." Here's where it starts to get really interesting.
- Laboratory interactions involving excremental facilities as well as one or more people : A "virtual laboratory" environment would be created by conferencing all laboratories instrumentation to be compatible with automated control, and by augmenting network videoconferencing capabilities with currently available, network-windows-based lab instrument control software.
- Publications : Reports, journal papers, conference presentations : standard-based representation for electronic imaging, textual information and graphical information, and a methodology for efficient co-authorship would further the electronic exchange of data and facility the preparation and dissemination of reports and publications. Videoconferencing could be used for joint preparation.
- Public relations and requirement; Increase the ease with which interviews, both for press and for potential hires can be occur.

Surveillance and Security

We usually thing of videoconferencing as being two-way and interactive, with both parties equally participating in the exchange. However, videoconferencing can also be used as a one-way monitoring technology simply by selectively muting audio and/or video on one side.

For instance, many campus and corporate environments have extensive LAN/WAN infrastructures that include both internet and internal connectivity, and in parallel providing a closed circuit TV/security system. An H.323 surveillance solution would allow video from these is a LAN connection and allow video from this source to their viewed, recorded and easily integrated with other organizational data systems.

MPEG

MPEG-2 videoconferencing is one of the higher quality forms of videoconferencing.

Motion JPEG (MJPEG)

MJPEG, for 'motion-JPEG', is an encoding technique that simply jpeg-compresses each video frame before transmission. There are several advantages to this approach, and some disadvantages. The biggest drawbacks are that there are very few products that support it, and it has been seen as a failed technology of the past. Both of these are changing again, and MJPEG is making a string comeback.

The main advantages of MJPEG are that JPEG-compression is very cheap to do in hardware, is extremely fast, quite robust, and it supports almost any size video frame you want to transmit.

Simple Internet Protocol (SIP)

SIP stands for Session Initiation Protocol, and is a part of the IETF standardization process. SIP is a signaling protocol for establishing calls and conferences over IP networks. The session set-up, change or tear down is independent of the type of media that will be used in the call; a session may include different types of data, including audio, video, and many other format. SIP originated in the mid-90's (about the time H.323 was becoming finalized as a standard) so that it would be easy to invite people to view an IP multicast session like a shuttle launch on the M-bone. Those who are most excited about SIP believe this development is as significant as the HTTP protocol, the technology behind web pages, that allows a single page with clickable links to connect you to text, audio, video, and other web pages. This possibility is behind SIP's rapid adoption as a Voice Over IP standard.

SIP is modeled after other Internet text-based protocols such as SMTP and HTTP, and was designed to establish, change, and tear down calls between one or more users in an IP network in a manner totally independent of the media content of the call. Like HTTP, SIP moves control over the application to the endpoint, eliminating the need for a central switching function.

Wireless and Satellite Video

Wireless local area networks are now becoming common, and so the question arises as to whether videoconferencing can be done over such networks. The answer is a qualified yes. Video and audio are more demanding of network quality than are simpler things like email and web browsing. Dropped packets and network traffic competition cause video and audio to fail long before email and web browsing. The net result is that the wireless distance that can be achieved for video is significantly less than that for other applications.

Another factor that works against wireless video is that wireless networks are completely shared by all users, as if dumb hubs were being used on a wired network. Most wired networks today use switches, which isolate the traffic from one station to another. Thus if there are many users on wireless network, then video will degrade faster than other applications.

Another factor that works against wireless video is that wireless networks are completely shared by all users, as if dumb hubs were being used on a wired network. Most wired networks today use switches, which isolate the traffic from one station to another. Thus if there are many users on wireless network, then video will degrade faster that other applications.

Teleportation Technologies

Several companies have developed systems which "teleport"a 3-D, full-sized holographic image of a person into a room. The virtual image of a real person can be placed behind a lectern or desk, in front of a wall, curtain, or other background. This virtual person can see the person or audience in front of him or her and can make eye contact with them. They can hold a normal dialogue. This form of virtual presence makes it seem as if the whole person is right there in the room.

Future of Networks

The future of communication Networks looks as follows. The Internet will keep on growing with more users and faster communication links and routers. Internet Engineers will keep on improving the router technology and the protocols to offer better quality of service especially for distribution of video and also for videoconferences. The cable TV and telephone companies will deploy video-on-demand networks using a hybrid fiber-coaxial cable technology and using High-Speed transmission over telephone lines. ATM Networks may replace other LANs first as interconnection backbones and then as institutions will start using Video Conference from the desktop.

Some difficult Questions about the Future Evolution are the following.

- What are the future roles of ATM and of the INTERNET? Will the internet Protocols and technology progress enough to make migration to ATM Unnecessary (or) Will there be co-existence of ATM and Internet Networks used by different Applications?
- Will the Telecommunication Companies set-up a commercial Wide Area Network that will complement the internet and provide a better alternative for videoconferencing (or) other Real-Time (or) Interactive Services?
- What is the future role of SATELLITE Distribution Systems for Video (or) Information-on-demand Networks?
- Will the long-Anticipated demand for cellular data Networks and devices materialize?

Killer Apps—Mobile Banking Thro' SMS—A Cost Reduction Approach

R. Manoharan, V. Ashok and S. Sivanandam

Introduction

According to research firm Ovum, mobile commerce is currently pegged at a little over $ 5 billion world wide and is expected to grow to over $ 35 billion by 2007. Other like Forrest Research estimates the same at @ 22 billion by 2005. And Banking is going to be major benefactor of the same. According to studies by some global firms one of the most used banking with the service for Mobile Commerce would be Mobile Banking with the service like transfers, balance and trading, bringing the revenue for mobile bankers.

SMS is emerging as the hottest app of the new millennium, and banks have also latched on to it, perking up their value-adds.

With the increased penetration and acceptance of mobile phone usage and particularly of Short Messaging Service (SMS), banks are now viewing this application and SMS as a delivery channel and as an integral part of anytime anywhere banking

The SMS facility can today be used by the customer of a bank to receive alerts and allow him to do banking transactions (called pull transactions).

As in any IT investment what is essential here also, is to keep under check the total cost of ownership, to reap the benefit of competitive differentiation in the form of increased customer retention, and to go beyond and attract and acquire the profitable tech savvy young customers.

Before we go in for m-banking thro' SMS let us look some of the options available today for our Networking.

RAS

Leading ISP's continue to drive the RAS market in India. The market took a hit last year with a several ISP's exiting the business. However, that will change the incumbents like BSNL and MTNL now bullish about internet service. RAS market in India will be worth $ 75.69 million by 2006. It stood at $43.83 million at 2001. The research agency opines that further growth in the segment will be slow, and find it will be some time before access prices start rising again.

"Many ISP's have lately realized that it is better to focus on investing in products or platforms which will enable them to quickly deploy a host of value added services over dial-up. These operates will be going in for RAS, says Rajnajoy Punja, vice-president, marketing, India and SAARC, Cisco.

Wireless

Wireless is one segment that looks really promising, Gartner predicts that there will be 70 million users of public hotspots by 2007. Even in India, wireless networks are on the rise moving beyond enterprise LANs into public hotspots and (very soon) into homes. "Nearly 20% of CTOs in India have already initiated wireless in their enterprises, and another 30% are going to do so in the coming year," says Prabhod Vyas, Director, Sales, D-Link.

Although wireless technology has gained substantial mind share, it has yet to gain proportionate market share. This is because organizations are still waiting for wireless technology to mature and stabilize. However steps like the delicensing of the WLAN spectrum will help the market to grow. "Reforms may not always mean an open delicensed environment. Delicensing of appropriated frequency bands is necessary since much of it is to deregulate other bands for licensed usage. The healthy proliferation of wireless will depend on business plans that may follow an unregulated or regulated usage of spectrum or both," says Joydeep Bose, Director, Strategy, Co-operate Technology Group, Intel India.

Cabling

It's going to be a big fight between structured cabling standards such as the existing CAT5/CAT5e and the emerging CAT6/7 on one side, and fiber on the other. With the prices of fiber coming down and functionally going up, this wars seems to be heating up by the day. "CAT6 will be the prevalent standard in 2005, but till then CAT5e will rule the market," says Mehta.

However D.S. Nagendra, Country Sales Manager for Krone, feels that in terms of cabling technology there is a fair amount of growth happening in CAT6. "CAT6 is fast becoming a commodity product. More than 70% of shipments in high ends markets are on CAT6, UTP," adds K.K. Shetty, Country Manager, AMP Netconnect, Tyco Electronics.

Growth in the cabling market is primarily coming from B & C class cities, while the verticals that are driving growth are BPO (including call centre), software and BFSI. Also, the high-end market is moving from CAT6 to intelligent cabling.

Managed Network Service

Managed Network Service (MNS) offers a total networking solution that reduces operational costs and frees enterprises to focus on their core business. According to Gartner, 32% of a company's IT budget is spent on internal resources to service IT. Research has provide that a company with about 5000 employees can benefit in the range of $ 9 million to $ 18 million every year by outsourcing its IT infrastructure management. This can be achieved through MNS. Although globally organization have recognized the great opportunity in outsourcing, in India, apart corporate houses, not many companies are going in far MNS.

Network Integration

The development in technology, the concept of Network Integration has also changed. Today, apart from LAN/WAN, Network integrators are also focusing on areas like network security implementation/audits and checks, bandwidth provisioning, development of new technologies such as WLAN and IP telephony, defined quality of service for certain applications, etc. "The network is no longer limited to leased lines and VSATs but is now shifting towards wireless-based WLAN," says Col H.S. Bedi, Managing Director, Tulip IT services.

Voice-over-IP

VoIP's growth is being driven by multiple factors on three fronts : applications necessitating voice convergence, the spread of broad band, the cost benefit. "VoIP" witnessed significant growth both in the carrier and enterprise segment. While the major driver for VoIP deployment and the carrier font was network utilization since carreets wanted to optimized usage of their network capacities, on the enterprise VoIP from the driver are manifold", says Ganjoo of Nortal.

Corporate started running their internal networks on IP. The first wave saw different housed developing station gateways across various branches to lower communication costs. Note IP phones came in and now basic IP-BPX solutions are being installed. But the issue of VoIP being restricted to closed user groups is still a problem that deters widespread acceptance.

In spite of that, VoIP is expected to grow substantially and BPO units, service companies and enterprises will drive.

Mobile Devices

Mobile devices have become necessary for improving the productivity of mobile workers. Other reasons given for the purchase of handheld devices include improvements in wireless network and the need provide mobile access to enterprise application (Bank). The decrease in the price of these devices has also contributed to the mobile revolution. However security is a top concern.

How Does Basis SMS Work?

The user first types a message and then sends it to the mobile number of the person concerned though the messaging centre number. All messages sent will be received at the Short Messaging Service Centre (SMSC) of service provider which will then be sent to the recipient's number. In a typical banking application, the end user will enter the banking service name (say BAL for account balance) followed by the parameters (service number like 777) required for service as required by the bank. Subsequently, he will receive an SMS message as the response for the response for the request he had placed. Let us now evaluate different Process Models of deployment for SMS Banking.

Process Model A

In this approach, the bank will tie up with all mobile service providers who are interested in offering the service to and the above mentioned infrastructure will allow it to offer SMS banking to its customers. The customer will send a message to a designated number as published by the mobile service provider with the service name and parameters in the order as specified by the bank.

Process Model B

As outlined, one of the problems with the Model A is that bank will need a tie up with all the mobile service providers and have an arrangement that is similar to the one described for Model A with all the service providers. In the light of these complications and cost implications, there is yet another approach that the bank could take that does not require tie-ups with each of the mobile service providers and still provides SMS banking to its customers.

The customer will send the SMS Message to the particular number published by the bank instead of the number published by the mobile service provider. At the bank will be a GSM mobile modem that is embedded with a mini SMS gateways that will have capability similar to that of the SMSC of the mobile service provider. This service will receive the SMS message from the end customer. It will process the message, connect to the SMS service of the bank using the parameters that the customer has sent and send response the end customer after the response is received from the SMS service of the bank.

Process Model C

Let us have a look at the approach of a different nature wherein the bank ties up with a third party service provider (BPO) for the purpose of networking. The role of third party service provider is to ensure that he maintains connectivity with all the mobile service providers. Once again in this model, there is the convenience to the customer of having a single number that the third party service provider blocks with every mobile service provider on behalf of the bank. The customer will as earlier send the

SMS message with necessary reaches the mobile service provider, the SMSC of the mobile service provider will redirect the message to this third party service provider. On reaching the third party service provider, based on the keyword that the end user has keyed, the third party service provider will make a secure URL connection to the SMS service of the bank.

Often one is faced with multiple options and there is one universally preferred or recommended option. For starters I would say that the choice really comes down to Process Model B and C, as in Model A, the issues of having tie up with multiple vendors are cumbersome. Moreover in Process Model B and C the customer convenience is given precedence with his not having to grapple with multiple numbers. The choice finally narrows down to Process Model B wherein the bank needs to invest in hardware and will also need to invest in people to manage the infrastructure. Also, if the bank does not have comfort in shouldering this responsibility then makes ample sense for the bank to bring in a third party networking service provider as Process Model C. So IT decision-makers and CIO of banks should have single thought that with projected 25 million base of mobile users in India by 2004. SMS is, without any second thought, emerging as the killer application for connecting people and remote banking in particular. In offering anytime, anywhere banking this application's potential needs to be fully exploited whichever is the model best suited to the bank in case.

Conclusion

M-Banking is cheaper than ATM Banking and more likely to happen than Networking.

A bank source reports these costs per transaction Rs. 150 at a branch, Rs. 30 at an ATM, Rs. 15 with phone and Rs. 10 for internet and m-banking. Clearly banks should try to shift common transactions to on line modes (where, further, cost drops and usage goes up). Especially when banks in India don't share ATMs they pass on cost of dedicated branded ATMs. In low-density areas with 20 foot balls a day to the customer.

Will banks go the m-way? Of course they will. The appreciate 'Costs' and "Savings" better than most. But those who learn the m-lesson early will gain the edge and customer.

References

1. Express Computer, Vol. 14, No. 43.
2. Express Computer, Vol. 14, No. 40.
3. Dataquest, Vol. XXI No. 2.
4. Dataquest Supplement.
5. Web Site www.dqindia.com.

Bibliography

A. Alwan *et.al.*, Adaptive Mobile Multimedia Networks, *IEEE Communications Magazine* 34(4), April 1996.

Adre Giraro, Redouance Ziadance, "Revenue Optimization of B-ISDN Networks," IEEE Transaction on Communications, Vol. 43, Mar. 1995.

Alberto Leon-Garcia, Indra Widjaja; *"Communication Networks,"* Tata McGraw-Hill Publishing Company Limited, New Delhi.

Anderson, James P., "Computer Security Threat Monitoring and Surveillance," Technical Report, James P. Anderson Co., Fort Washington, PA, April 1980.

Andrew S. Tennanbaum, "Computer Networks", Tata McGraw-Hill Publishing Company Limited, New Delhi.

Baxer "Networking Security", Tata McGraw Hill, 1996.

Borisov, N., Goldberg, I., and Wagner, D., "Intercepting Mobile Communications", MOBICOM, 2001.

Bruce Schenier, "Applied Cryptography", John Wiley & Sons Inc., 2001.

Budde, P., "Information Technology Management," Paul Budde Communication, Vol. 7, 1996.

Charles Perkins and Pravin Bhagwat, "DSDV Routing over a Multishop Wireless Network of Mobile Computers," from Mobile Computing, Norwood (MA) : Kluwer, 1996.

China-jin Wang, Paul N. Weissler, "The Use of Artificial Neural Network for Optimal Message Routing," IEEE Network, Mar./Apr.

D. Johnson and D. Maltz, "Dynamic Source Routing in *Ad-Hoc* Wireless Networks," from Mobile Computing, Norwood (MA) : Kluwer, 1996.

D.P. Bertsekas, "Dynamic Models of Shortest Path Routing Algorithms for Communication Networks with Multiple Destinations," in Proc. 1979 IEEE Conf. Decision Contr., Dec. 1979.

Daniel Camara and Antonio Alfredo F. Loureiro, "A GPS/Ant-Like Routing Algorithm for *Ad-hoc* Networks," In IEEE Wireless Communications and Networking Conference (WCNC'00), Chicago, IL, September 2000.

Davie, B., Doolan, P. and Rekhter, Y., "Switching in IP Networks : IP Switching, Tag Switching and Related Technologies," Morgan Kaufmann, 1998, ISBN 1-55860-505-3.

Denning, Dorothy E., "An Intrusion Detection Model," IEEE Transactions on Software Engineering, Vol. SE-13, No. 2, pp. 222-32, February 1987.

Derek Atkins "Internet Security", Echmedia, 1998.

Dr. M. Jain, Satish Jain, "Data Communication and Networking", BPB Publications, New Delhi.

Emmanouel, A. Varvarigos and Dimitri P. Bertekas, "Performance of Hypercube Routing Schemes without Buffering", IEEE/ACM Transaction on Networking, Vol. 2, No. 3, June 1994.

Eric Bonabeau, Marco Dorigo and Guy Theraulaz, "Swarm Intelligence—From Natural to Artificial Systems," Oxford University Press, New York, 1999.

F. Effenberger, H. Ichibangase and H. Yamashita, "Advances in Broadband Passive Optical Networking Technologies," *IEEE Communications Magazine,* Dec. 2001.

G. Di Caro and M. Dorigo, "AntNet : Distributed Stigmergetic Control for Communications Networks," *Journal of Artificial Intelligence Research,* Vol. 9, 1998.

G. Varaprasad, R.S.D. Wahida Banu, "Flexible Routing in a Mesh Network", SIS 2004, IITM, Chennai.

———, "Routing In Communication Network Using Neural Network", National Conference On Intelligent Systems, Automation Signal Processing NCISASP'03, March 1, 2003.

———, "Shortest Path between Source to Destination in a Mesh Network" ICET 2004, Bhuwaneswar.

George Apostolopoulos, Roch Guerin, Sanay Kamat and S.K. Tripathi, "Intradomain QOS Routing in the IP Networks, Feasibility and Cost/Benefit Analysis", IEEE Networks, Sept./Oct. 1999.

Gianni Di Caro and Marco Dorigo. "AntNet : A Mobile Agents Approach to Adaptive Routing," Technical Report IRIDIA/97-12, Universite Libre de Bruxelles, Belgium.

Guy Helmer, Johnny, S.K. Wong, Vasant Honavar and Les Miller, "Intelligent Agents for Intrusion Detection," Proceedings, IEEE Information Technology Conference, Syracuse, NY, pp. 121-24, September 1998.

Holger Christein, Peter Schulthess, "A General Purpose Model for Presence Awareness," Distributed Systems Department, University of Ulm, Germany.

Ioannis N. Kassabalidis, *et. al.,* "Adaptive-SDR : Adaptive Swarm-based Distributed Routing," In IEEE WCCI 2002, Signal Processing for Wireless Communications, Honolulu, Hawaii, May 2002.

James D. Solomon, "Mobile IP : The Internet Unplugged", Prentice Hall, 1998.

Jeffrey, M. Bradshaw, "An Introduction to Software Agents," in Jeffrey M. Bradshaw, editor, Software Agents, Chapter 1. AAAI Press/The MIT Press, 1997.

John Maries, "VPNs A Beginner's Guide", Tata McGraw-Hill Edition, 2002.

Joseph Bannister, Flaminio Borgonovo, Luigi Fratta and Mario Gerla, "A Performance Model Deflection Routing in Multi Buffer Networks with Non-Uniform Traffic", IEEE Transactions Networking, Vol. 3, No. 5, Oct. 1995.

K. Oida and M. Sekido, "An Agent-based Routing System for QoS Guarantees", Proc. IEEE International Conference on Systems, Man, and Cybernetics, Oct. 12-15, pp. 833-38, 1999, September 28-29, 1998.

Kapoor, K.V., "Problem and Solution in Operations Research", New Delhi, Sultan Chand & Sons Educational Pub., 1998.

Krishana Bala, Thomas, E. Stern, David Simchi-Levi, Kavitha Bala, "Routing in a Linear Lightware Network", IEEE/ACM Transactions on Networking, Vol. 3, No. 4, Aug. 1995.

Levesque, A. and Pahlavan, K., Wireless Data, "The Mobile Communications Handbook", IEEE Press, 1996.

Liscano, R., Ghavam, A., Barbeau, M., Graym, T. and Georganas, N., "Enabling Secure *ad-hoc* Communications in the Enterprise", Proceedings of the 1st International Conference on *Ad-hoc* Networks and Wireless, Toronto, Ontario, Sept. 2002.

M. Asaka, S. Okazawa, A. Taguchi and S. Goto, "A Method of Tracing Intruders by use of Mobile Agents," INET '99, June 1999.

M. Heissenbttel and T. Braun, "Ants-Based Routing in Large Scale Mobile *Ad-Hoc* Networks", Technical Report, University of Bern, 2003.

M. Naghshineh and M. Schwarz, Distributed Aall Admission Control in Mobile/Wireless Networks, in: IEEE PIMRC '95, 1995.

M. Azizoglu and A. Mokhtar, "Adaptive Wavelength Routing in All-Optical Networks," *IEE/ACM Transactions Networking*, Vol. 6, No. 2, April 1998.

M.J. Moyer, J.R. Rao, P. Rohatgi, A Survey of Security Issues in Multicast Communications, *IEEE Network*, Dec. 1999.

M.S.V. Janakiram, Strategies for Securing Web Services, Information Technology, Vol. 13, No. 2, December 2003.

Mcgladdery, W. and Clifford, R., "Survey of Current and Emerging Wireless Data Networks", Proceedings of Canadian Conference on Electrical and Computer Engineering, IEEE Canada, 1993.

Mesut Gunes, Udo Sorges, and Imed Bouazizi, "ARA : The Ant-colony Based Routing Algorithm for MANETs." In International Conference on Parallel Processing Workshops (ICPPW'02), Vancouver, B.C., Canada, August 2001.

Metz, Christopher, "IP Switching : Protocols and Architectures", McGraw-Hill, New York, 1999, ISBN 0-07-041953-1.

N. Frigo, "Local Access Optical Networks," IEEE Network, Nov./Dec. 1996.

Nareshchandra Laisharam, "Inflection Point", Voice & Data, July 2003.

Neil F. Johnson, Zoran Duric, Sushil Jajodia, Information Hiding : Steganography and Watermarking—Attacks and Countermeasures.

Newman, P., Edwards, W., Hinden, R., Hoffman, E., Ching Liaw, F., Lyon, T. and Minshall, G., "Transmission of Flow Labelled IPv4 on ATM Data Links Ipsilon Version", May 1996.

Newman, P., Edwards, W., Hinden, R., Hoffman, E., Ching Liaw, F., Lyon, T. and Minshall, G., "Flow Management Protocol Specification for IPv4 Version 1.0", May 1996.

Newman, P., Edwards, W., R. Hinden, R., E. Hoffman, F. Ching Liaw, T. Lyon, and G. Minshall, "Ipsilon's General Switch Management Protocol Specification Version 2.0", March 1998.

Perkins, C.E., "Mobile IP : Design Principles and Practices", Addison Wesley, 1997.

Perkins, C.E., IP Mobility Support (RFC 2002) October 1996.

Perkins, C.E., IP Mobility Support (RFC 3220) January 2002.

Preuss, S. and Clemens, H., "Spontaneous Networking," Workshop on Future Services for Networked Devices (FuSeNetD 1999), In Conjunction with Eurescom 1999, Heidelberg, Gernamy, Nov. 8-9, 1999.

R. Howard, Dynamic Probabilistic Systems, Vol. 1, Markov Models , Wiley, 1971.

Rekhter, Y., Davie, B., Katz, D., Rosen, E. and Swallow, G., "Cisco Systems Tag Switching Architecture Overview", February 1997.

Reuven Cohen, Yoram Ofek and Adrrian Segall, "A New Label—Based Source Routing for Multi-Ring Networks", IEEE Transactions Vol. 3, June 1995.

Roger Chen, C.V., Georges A. Makhoul and Dikran S. Meilisetain, "A Queuing Analysis of the Performance of DQDBS," IEEE/ACM Transactions on Networking, Vol. 3, No. 6, Dec. 1995.

S. Banerjee, B. Bhattacharjee, Scalable Secure Group Communication over IP Multicast, *IEEE Journal on Selected Areas in Communication*, Vol. 20. October 2002.

S. Dixit and P. Lin, "Advances in Packet Switching/Routing in Optical Networks," *IEEE Communications Magazine*, Feb. 2001.

S. Lipperts and B. Kreller, "Mobile Agents in Telecommunications Networks—a Simulative Approach to Load Balancing", Proc. 5th Intl. Conf. Information Systems, Analysis and Synthesis, ISAS'99, 1999.

S. Rafaeli, D. Hutchison, A Survey of Key Management for Secure Group Communication, ACM Computing Surveys, September 2003.

S. Rajagopalan and B.R. Badrinath, "An Adaptive Location Management Strategy for Mobile IP", 1995.

S. Sen *et. al.*, Quality of Service Degradation Strategies in Multimedia Wireless Networks, in: IEEE VTC'98, Ottawa, 1998.

S.K. Das and S.K. Sen, Quality-of-Service Degradation Strategies in Multimedia Wireless Networks, in : *IEEE Vehicular Technology Conference* (VTC'98), Ottawa, Canada , May 1998.

Shyamanuja Das "High Growth, Low Margin", Voice & Data, July 2003.

Simonds, "Network Security", McGraw Hill, 1998.

Steven Brown "Implementing Virtual Private Networks", Tata McGraw-Hill Edition 2000.

Steven, M. Bellovin, "Problem Areas for the IP Security Protocols" in 6th USENIX Security Symposium, San Jose, California, July 1996, USENIX.

Sudeep, Gaurkar, Chellappan L., User Identification through Keystroke Biometrics, Electronics for you, Vol. 36, No. 1, Jan. 2004.

T. Hardjono, B. Cain, Secure and Scalable Inter Domain Group Key Management for N-to-N Multicast, *Bay Networks*, 1999.

Toh, C., *Ad-hoc* Mobile Wireless Networks : Protocols and Systems. Prentice Hall, 2002.

Ulyess Black, "Voice over IP", 1999, Prentice Hall, New Delhi.

W. Goralski, M. Kolon, "IP Telephony", 1999, Tata McGraw Hill, New Delhi.

W. Trappe, J. Song, R. Poovendran, K.J.R. Liu, Key Management and Distribution for Secure Multimedia Multicast. *IEEE Transactions on Multimedia*, Dec. 2003.

Whay C. Lee, Michael G. Hluchy and Pierre A. Humblet, "Routing Subject to Query of Service Constraints in Integrated Communication Networks", IEEE Network July/April 1995.

William Stallings "Cryptography and Network Security", Pearson Education (Singapore) Pte. Ltd., 2003.

Index